CRISIS OF THE EUROPEAN MIND

A STUDY OF ANDRÉ MALRAUX
AND DRIEU LA ROCHELLE

CRISIS OF THE EUROPEAN MIND

A STUDY OF ANDRÉ MALRAUX
AND DRIEU LA ROCHELLE

Barrie Cadwallader

CARDIFF
UNIVERSITY OF WALES PRESS
1981

© UNIVERSITY OF WALES PRESS, 1981

British Library Cataloguing in Publication Data

Cadwallader, Barrie
   Crisis of the European mind.
   1. Europe—Civilization
   2. France—Intellectual life
   3. European War, 1914–1918—Influence and results
   I. Title
   940′.01   CB203

   ISBN 0–7083–0759–0

Text set in 11/12pt Linotron 202 Times, printed and
bound in Great Britain at The Pitman Press, Bath

Contents

		Page
Introduction		vii

PART 1

CHAPTER	I	The Battle of Ideas	1
CHAPTER	II	The Awakening of Asia	22
CHAPTER	III	The Decline of the West	28
CHAPTER	IV	Crisis of the European Mind	58

PART 2

CHAPTER	V	Drieu and the Dream of Europe	147
CHAPTER	VI	Malraux and the 'Death of Europe'	177
CHAPTER	VII	Drieu: The Decadent	206
CHAPTER	VIII	Malraux: The New Man	225

Conclusion	255
Index	265

Introduction

The work is a political study of the *crise de l'esprit* suffered by André Malraux, Pierre Drieu La Rochelle and a number of other French intellectuals in the aftermath of World War I; a crisis born of the devastation of war and exacerbated by fears that the European age of world history was nearing its end. Many, including Drieu and Henri Massis, felt that if Europe remained in the state of division with which she had been satisfied, not only would her role in the world continue to shrink but the day would soon come when she would lose control over her own destiny. Europe thus became, for both men, a task at once magnificent and necessary. It was to the past, and specifically to the 'calm and full harmonies of the Middle Ages',[1] that they and many others now turned for a judgement on the present and an inspiration for the future.

Europe, Massis believed, constituted a reality—not so much geographical or ethnological as historical. As the heir to a double legacy, that of philosophy and law inherited from Greece and Rome and that of religion inherited from Israel, Europe was a unity whose binding force, developed in this tradition, was a cultural one. During the Middle Ages, under the Holy Roman Empire, Europe did enjoy a certain degree of political unity, but this disappeared as the Renaissance—despite its recovery of the 'treasures of antiquity'—'sacrificed' the *coordinatio ad unum* of life through the temporal and spiritual unities of Law, Knowledge and Faith to individual initiatives, political pluralisms and juridical particularisms. However, despite the breakdown of the *Respublica Christiana* and the subsequent upheavals of wars, revolutions and involutions, Europe as the heir to a 'sovereign synthesis' remained a historical and cultural reality still capable, Massis felt, of restoring that lost integrity from which Europe's present crisis derived.

The task of recovery was, however, as Massis recognized, a difficult one. Quite apart from her own material and moral weakness, Europe suddenly found herself pitted against an adversary championing 'an antithetical view of life' and intent on destroying, by physical as well as spiritual arms, all that she held most dear. Asia, it seemed, had awakened from a millenarian lethargy to launch a Marxist and mystic crusade against the West. In this perilous condition Europe's first task, Massis insisted, was to denounce the propaganda of the 'Asiaticists' who, on the pretence of opening the West to the ideas of the East, were betraying Civilization and their own vocation. To which André Malraux responded that such a charge was inadmissible as the concept of Western civilization defended by Massis and his supporters was no longer viable.[2]

Prominent among the 'Asiaticists' denounced by Massis was Romain Rolland, who defined his task—in August 1919—as the reconciliation of the spiritual traditions of East and West. Many, inspired by Rolland's vision of a new age of synthesis, now turned to the East in the hope of discovering a new viaticum for exhausted Europe—a presumption which Paul Nizan dismissed as a reactionary diversion:

> L'on nous avait accoutumés à penser à l'Orient comme au contraire de l'Occident: alors du moment que la chute et la pourriture de l'Europe étaient des faits absolument simples et clairs et distincts, la renaissance et la floraison de l'Orient n'appartenaient pas moins à l'ordre des évidences. Il renfermait le salut et la nouvelle vie des Européens, il avait des remèdes et de l'amour du reste. On usait un peu partout avec imprudence des analogies antiques et de l'histoire officielle des religions: on ornait l'Asie de toutes les vertus humaines que l'Occident achevait de perdre depuis tantôt trois cents ans et ne réclamait plus que dans la colonne d'agonie des quotidiens anglais. L'esprit de la civilisation planait sur l'Inde, la Chine nous semblait plus merveilleuse qu' à Marco Polo. Qui donc nous aurait révélé de bonnes raisons humaines de nous intéresser à l'Asie: les grèves à Bombay, les révolutions et les massacres en Chine, les emprisonnements au Tonkin. Et non Bouddha.[3]

Equally contemptuous of the flight into Oriental mysticism were the Leninists of *Clarté*, led by Henri Barbusse. If the term *ex Oriente lux* had any meaning for this dedicated group of 'Asiaticists' it lay in the example of the Soviet Union and of colonial peoples struggling for national liberation. *Clarté*'s critique of the 'heavenly abstraction' of French and European interest in the mystic East did nothing, however, to calm Massis's fears, since Leninism, he judged, was just as deadly an opponent of Graeco-Latin and Christian principles as was the 'land of eternal thought'. In fact they constituted an allied force whose single-minded ambition, Massis believed, was the obliteration of Western civilization.

Where Massis and his colleagues stood in horror of the 'Asian monolith', Surrealists danced in heady expectation. In a dream of dragging Civilization into the abyss, these 'révoltés' responded to 'Western fears' by combining, in a 'total anti-West', both contemplative and revolutionary elements of the Oriental movement.

Our aim in examining this complex movement, its aforementioned supporters and dedicated opponent, is to shed light on that 'crisis of European consciousness' which the writings of André Malraux and Drieu La Rochelle constantly acknowledge and for which both men, no less than Massis, Rolland, Barbusse and the Surrealists, sought a remedy. It is intended to show that the 'Oriental question' disputed by these intellectuals—like other questions relating to Europe's crisis and survival—was, for all its philosophical depth and cultural range, an ideological crucible in which political attitudes were being fired. In this respect it marked the prelude to a conflict, no less verbal though far more violent, that was to embroil the whole of Europe in the late 'thirties and early 'forties.

It is within this context of intellectual crisis and political ferment that we shall attempt to situate the diagnoses and literary responses of two important writers, each apparently belonging to opposite ends of the political spectrum: Malraux, the 'Asian adventurer' and 'Communist', and Drieu La Rochelle, the 'European witness' and Fascist. An important reason for choosing Drieu and Malraux is that each imposes himself within the problematic concerns of the subject in so far as each, from his own stand point, analysed the crisis of European civilization. Drieu's position was explicitly political and his early essays are a constant appeal for European unity; Malraux's 'idea of Europe', on the other hand, harbours no illusions as to the efficacy of a federated 'patch-up' of European civilization. His more metaphysically-felt estrangement led him to talk of the 'death of Europe' and the 'death of Man'. Yet the writings of both men, despite their very different emphases, point to the same storm-centre: a keen sense of the fragility and hollowness of European civilization—Drieu's *Le Jeune Européen* to some extent mirroring and answering Malraux's 'D'une jeunesse européenne', both projections of the European *crise de l'esprit*.

As Nietzschean activists Drieu and Malraux assigned to freedom a primordial role and accepted the 'affirmation of existence' as a fundamental value preceding and conditioning essence. Both emphasized the need to steep their lives in action—the 'great action'—and this concern explains their apparent commitment as much as does political conviction itself. But, of course, both were primarily writers and intellectuals, not men of action in the narrowest sense. From action, and they knew the limitations placed upon them as writers, they hoped for the lived experience that would 'authenticate' their art, not justify them as political animals. Drieu made such an observation in his essay of 1930, 'Malraux, l'homme nouveau':

> Si l'on prend un écrivain au pied de la lettre dans ses ébauches d'action on trouvera matière à moquerie et à mépris, mais on le méconnaîtra. Les amorces que lance dans l'action un écrivain ne s'épanouissent jamais en exploits admirables mais ce sont les garanties de son humanité.[4]

For Drieu, Malraux reflected the happy proportion of literary transposition and faithfulness to a lived experience. It was this view of the literary act—'written in blood'—that united both men, Drieu believed, in a sense of fraternity, a telling and pathetic indication of which we find in Drieu's funeral instructions:

> Naturellement enterrement non religieux, strict minimum, mais des fleurs . . . pas de prêtres, pas de buis à côté du cadavre. Seulement dans la voiture: Mme Sienkiewicz, Mme Edouard Laffon. Mme Suzanne Tézenas. Pas d'hommes. Sauf Malraux, s'il est là.[5]

The parallel between these apparently very different writers may be taken even further. The heavy insistence which both placed upon the value of the lived experience might be traced back to their unhappy and sedentary childhoods, in which many critics have sought to locate the source of their mythic self-projection. The frustrated desire to make contact with the 'real world' led both, as adolescents, into an imaginary universe, dominated by heroic fantasies. Both finally escaped. Drieu's first confrontation with the 'real' came—as he joyfully informs us in *Interrogation* (1917)—through active participation in the Great War, and for Malraux it might be argued that one of the major incentives behind his decision to travel to Asia was the desire to 'agir au lieu de rêver'.[6] Both, in their very different enterprises, discovered 'Europe' and were brought to a deeper understanding of the crisis afflicting their generation. Of this alienated and 'violent' generation it fell to Malraux and Drieu to give, if not the most profound expression of the *crisis of civilization*, certainly a highly representative and disquieting one. Yet if they echo pre-war voices, notably Nietzsche's, and reflect the tendencies of their day, their writings also prefigure some of the attitudes today associated with the existentialist movement. Certain features of Sartre's *L'Être et le néant* are already contained in germ in Malraux's *La Voie royale,* and Albert Camus's *L'Étranger* might well owe something to the trial in *Les Conquérants.* Drieu's *Le Feu follet* might also be said to prepare the climate of sensibility for the existentialist hero.

If each can be said to participate in a kind of representative originality, Malraux, in his preoccupation within the European crisis with the possibilities of a 'New Man', might justifiably lay claim to a profound originality. The necessity for an alternative to the bankrupt ideals of a 'dead Europe' led him to project a new kind of man to explore the boundless realm of possibility opened up by 'God's death', and by the failure of traditional humanism, in a death-dominated search for new values:

> Que faire du cadavre des idées qui dominaient la conduite des hommes lorsqu'ils croyaient leur existence *utile* à quelque salut, que faire des paroles de ceux qui veulent soumettre leur vie à un modèle, ces autres cadavres? L'absence de finalité donnée à la vie était devenue une condition de l'action. A d'autres de confondre l'abandon au hasard et cette harcelante préméditation de l'inconnu. Arracher ses propres images au monde stagnant qui les possède . . . 'Ce qu'ils appellent l'aventure, pensait-il, n'est pas une fuite, c'est une chasse: l'ordre du monde ne se détruit pas au bénéfice du hasard, mais de la volonté d'en profiter' . . . (D'où montait, sinon de la mort, cette exigence de choses éternelles, si

lourdement imprégnée de son odeur de chair?). Qu'était ce besoin d'inconnu, cette destruction provisoire des rapports de prisonnier à maître, que ceux qui ne la connaissent pas nomment aventure, sinon sa défense contre elle? Défense d'aveugle, qui voulait la conquérir pour en faire un enjeu.[7]

Malraux's attempt to establish new co-ordinates of life to replace those which Europe had lost did indeed lead him to portray a new kind of man who, in retrospect, seems uninvitingly Fascist. Malraux's portrayal of a 'New Man' thereby throws up an extraordinary irony, given the subsequent careers of Malraux and Drieu. For it was not the 'Fascist' Drieu who established a kind of ideal image of Fascist man in this disturbing prototype of the 'New Man', but the 'Communist' Malraux. This irony, and the factors which produced it, are examined in this study. The study will reveal that, for Malraux as for Drieu, the central 'temptation' in the crisis-ridden period between the wars was a political one. It was to this 'Temptation of the West' that many, fleeing the 'Asian menace', fell victim.

NOTES

[1] Drieu La Rochelle, *Drôle de voyage* (Gallimard, 1933), p. 20.
[2] André Malraux, 'Défense de l'Occident', *N.R.F.* (June 1927), pp. 817–18.
[3] Paul Nizan, *Aden-Arabie* (Maspéro, 1976), p. 67. Édition originale: Rieder, 1931.
[4] Drieu La Rochelle, 'Malraux, l'homme nouveau', *N.R.F.* (December 1930), p. 882.
[5] Quoted in F. Grover, *Drieu La Rochelle* (Gallimard, 1962), p. 61.
[6] André Malraux, *La Voie royale* (Livre de poche, 1973), p. 27.
[7] André Malraux, *op. cit.*, pp. 37–8.

PART 1

CHAPTER I

The Battle of Ideas

On entretient la vieille loi du sang . . .
Devant l'idole Civilisation, tous se prosternent.
(P. J. Jouve)

For many 1914 signalled the beginning of the struggle between the powers of light and darkness. Germany, eternal beast of prey, descended upon God's earth. Justice, Right, Civilization were all in danger. Pre-war differences were now overtaken as a ground-swell of patriotic fervour carried the nation into a united thrust—*L'Union Sacrée*—to repel the invader: 'quelle belle mort pour les bons gosses qui, au seuil de la vie, se sont offerts joyeux en holocauste pour le salut de tous'.[1] In this death grapple of the flesh and spirit France was assigned a role comparable to that of Christ when he died to expiate the sins of the fallen human race. To this simple faith were added far less noble elements.

Newspapers like *Le Temps, Les Débats, Le Figaro, L'Echo de Paris, Le Journal, Le Matin, L'Homme libre*, and periodicals such as *La Revue des deux mondes, La Revue de Paris, L'Illustration, La Revue hebdomadaire, La Revue* and *Les Annales* called upon the legions of France to crush the infidel. Roland and Charlemagne were spirited up to despatch 'la brute sanglante à face humaine' to perdition.[2] None who had brought offerings to her black altar could be spared, neither Goethe who had 'magnifié l'antique instinct destructeur de sa race', nor Beethoven, nor even Bach.[3] The entire German race was to blame, the living and the dead. It is no surprise, therefore, that 'German' science should be reviled,[4] that writers should speak of 'la faillite de la littérature et de l'art allemands', that one, claiming to speak for many, should venture to say: 'je crois très sincèrement et sans aucun parti pris qu'il n'est point possible de

1

tenir l'Allemagne pour l'une des grandes nations intellectuelles de l'Europe'.[5]

Action Française spared Germany no insult, in the art of which Maurras and Léon Daudet were the masters. Barrès, with almost daily articles in *L'Écho de Paris,* brought his contribution to the polemic. In his estimation the Germanic soul had found no better symbolic form than in 'la botte remplie de crottin'.[6] This apostle of nationalism would admit of no scepticism, of no neutralism where a suffering divinity was threatened with extinction. There were, quite simply, those who believed and served and those who worshipped other idols. Among the damned stood the pacifists—'les pionniers du germanisme'[7]—ranged behind the Judas of them all, Romain Rolland.

The generation that went to war in 1914 was, broadly speaking, deeply imbued with the heroic virtues preached by Barrès. This romantic response to war comprises inevitably the flood of patriotic literature, journalistic and other, produced for home consumption. The escalation of Teutonic violence is, in these works, matched only by the boundless devotion of French martyrs to the cause of Justice:

> Qu'est-ce que la France?—C'est la Grâce.
> —Le monde, n'ayant pas la France, aurait-il eu la possibilité de faire son salut?
> —Non! Puisqu'elle est la Grâce, il ne peut rien sans elle.
> —La douce France est-elle encore douce?—elle est dure chaque fois qu'il le faut pour que sa douceur dure.
> —Et jamais son épée injustement n'a lui?
> —Non.[8]

Out of the 'Divine Tragedy'[9] a 'French Miracle'[10] is being wrought. Heroes positively abound. It would appear that their deaths are due less to the excesses of men than to a surfeit of Grace:

> Une impatience empoigne le bataillon qui tend les bras de désir vers la butte aimée . . . Dans un élan fou de vaillance et d'amour, on le vit s'élancer, ses chefs en tête sur les flancs de la colline . . . En vain les balles sifflaient. Hypnotisés, extatiques, les yeux levés vers le ciel . . . les hommes couraient délivrer la divine prisonnière. Ascension sublime! La terre jaillie des explosions entre dans leur bouche grande ouverte, ils en avalent, communion vivifiante.[11]

2

Even when one writer, Eugène Lemercier, can admit to having boots 'greasy with human brains', he will not be shaken from that national and Christian mysticism which has summoned him to war.[12] He feels that in the very midst of death he is still in life: 'ô mon pays si beau! cœur du monde où repose ce qu'il y a de divin'.[13] After weeping tears of revolt he is again able to say that since it is not the will of God that the cup be taken away, then, His will be done.[14] Like Lemercier, André Fribourg in *Croire* never doubts that some divine hand is at work to illumine and sanctify a life to its last moment.[15] He had hoped for epic contests but realizes that he will probably die at the bottom of a ditch, torn apart by a missile thrown by an invisible hand.[16] And yet he continues to believe, for a noble impulse must have a noble source. And to sustain him he has been granted resignation, the gift which comes to those who know the worth of sacrifice:

> Guerre, tu impliques un acte de foi et de renoncement. Nous avons subi, pour obéir à tes règles, l'humiliation, la mortification, la souffrance . . . Tu es une épreuve brûlante qui tue ou régénère. Des hommes nouveaux sortiront de ton creuset . . . Ils rachètent leurs frères qui ne se battent pas.[17]

Fribourg's message is simple; it is the very title of his work. We must *believe,* like the martyr of all causes.

Another work of this type is Henry Malherbe's *La Flamme au poing* which received the Prix Goncourt for 1917. In the very midst of war Malherbe lives in the company of abstract beings like Love and Death, which are themselves but pale reflections of some metaphysical reality:

> Nous accomplissons une besogne mystérieuse et qui doit être grandiose, formidable. Si le but vers lequel nous allons n'était pas noble, vaste, nous n'agirons pas ainsi . . . Quand serons-nous assez perspicaces, assez dignes, pour entrevoir les mobiles secrets de tant de violences imposées par le destin?[18]

The creatures who inhabit Malberbe's universe are not so much physical beings as images meant to evoke the torment of his soul. Even inanimate objects participate in this moral suffering: devastated villages, battered ploughs, carts and wagons bewail their sorrows and beg for pity or revenge.[19] All things are uplifted by this suffering willed by Providence, and all act with a single purpose: 'vous agissez en communion avec la terre que vous défendez'.[20]

Despite some writers' undying devotion to the Just Fight, whether the driving force was felt to be 'Patrie', 'Civilisation', or 'Gloire'—or all Three in One—the tone of war literature as a whole changed after 1915. Moreover, as more and more information became available, despite press censorship and 'official' optimism, it gradually dawned on many at home that fine words and noble principles could not easily be reconciled with the emerging picture of brutality. By 1917 the voices which were carrying furthest were those which expressed the confusion, brutality and suffering of war. There was revolt in the air, too, as poets and novelists now cursed those ideals which had sent out millions to die. No-one, perhaps, has expressed this mood better than Wilfred Owen:

> If in some smothering dreams you too could pace
> Behind the wagon that we flung him in,
> And watch the white eyes writhing in his face,
> His hanging face, like a devil's sick of sin;
> If you could hear, at every jolt, the blood
> Come gargling from the froth-corrupted lungs,
> Obscene as cancer, bitter as the cud
> Of vile, incurable sores on innocent tongues,—
> My friend, you would not tell with such high zest
> To children ardent for some desperate glory,
> The old Lie: Dulce et decorum est
> Pro patria mori.[21]

Many now took up their pens in order to 'communiquer l'horreur à ceux qui ne sauront pas'.[22] One such writer was Georges Bonnet whose L'Âme du soldat appeared in 1917. Bonnet's business is to destroy legends. He informs us that the heroic and devoutly patriotic soldier portrayed in the press does not exist. Neither does the conventional 'Boche', that cruel and unintelligent beast always ready to run away from danger. Only the naive or the bigoted can speak of French martyrs and German murderers, of French heroes and German cowards. Bonnet is not so self-assured. He can see only men living and suffering; their nationalities count for nothing. They are corporate, a living cell of humanity being battered by an infernal machine. They have no illusions about bravery, waste no words on patriotism and civilization, and their religious zeal, so dear to the imagination of civilians, is non-existent. War might evoke grandeur in the minds of non-combatants, Bonnet suggests, but there will never be enough glory in heaven or on earth to cover all the blood and shame.

Henry Dispan de Floran, killed in action in 1918, has the following to say of the courage and invention of men of letters fighting the good fight from the rear:

> Nous les soldats, nous ne sommes que les instruments des civils et des gouvernants. On nous impose le plus effroyable des supplices et l'on nous paie en hypocrites paroles d'affection, en larmes de crocodiles . . . La France de l'avant agonise, râle dans la boue et dans le sang. De tout ce supplice de tous ces charniers, l'inepte, la moutonnière la féroce France de l'arrière fait de la littérature et quelle littérature! Jamais il n'y eut un style plus écœurant, plus émasculé! Faut-il s'en étonner? Ce sont les eunuques de l'Institut qui tiennent aujourd'hui le marché littéraire. Comme ils sont heureux les ignobles vieillards que le talent agonise au fond de quelque tranchée et comme avec profit ils hurlent à la mort du fond de leurs fauteuils![23]

Bonnet and Henry Dispan de Floran are not alone in attacking those at home who mistake their own desires for reality—those interminable 'rhéteurs qui prêchent l'amour avec colère'.[24] How can they, asks one combatant, be made to understand that war defies representation in human form. It has nothing to do with human estimates of courage and devotion. It is a non-human zone where human concepts no longer have any relevance. Time itself has fallen apart: 'nous sommes là, voilà tout. Nous sommes tout court, sans heure et sans lieu humains'.[25] Another asks: 'à quoi nous sert notre courage? Un homme se défend-il contre le tremblement de terre qui va l'engloutir? Tire-t-on des coups de fusil sur un volcan?'[26] And yet another wonders: 'pourquoi crier si fort à l'héroïsme quand il n'y a que misère et nécessité? Pourquoi faire de nous des héros et des saints quand nous ne sommes que des bêtes de somme qui marchent sous le fouet du bouvier?'[27] Courage is a useless passion, and 'Gloire', says one writer mockingly, was never intended to mean cowering in a trench waiting to be blown to bits by screaming metal, 'elle est bien bête et bien trop fière, la Gloire! Elle ne se laisse pas courtiser par les boueux que nous sommes'.[28] If soldiers have in the past been only too honoured to lay down their lives for their country, today, Paul Cazin informs us, they can imagine a greater honour still, 'c'est de vivre longtemps et d'être heureux.'[29]

A young lieutenant of 21, Paul Lintier, expresses this sentiment with poignancy. He tells us that if he survives the hecatomb he will know how to live. He had never thought that there was joy in the mere facts of breathing, of opening his eyes to the morning light, of feeling warm or cold, or even of suffering. He had believed that only certain hours in life were worth living and that he could let the others pass him by. He now senses the importance of every passing minute. If he lives he will make a point of getting out of each second of life every sensation that it can yield. He will be quite capable of interrupting a sentence or of staying a gesture just to repeat to himself that he is alive and that life surrounds him.[30] Lintier did not live to realize this simple ambition; neither did millions of his countrymen, allies and enemies who surely felt as he did although they had not his powers of expression. It was for such victims that Georges Duhamel wrote his *Vie des martyrs* (1916).

Vie des martyrs is intended as a hymn of compassion for the 'humble soldiers' whose wounds Duhamel tended as a wartime surgeon. He feels that whatever he does for the wounded is inadequate, unworthy and mediocre, for he realizes that around their beds a sinister comedy is going on in which men wear grinning masks. Neither the corpses which he buries every morning, nor the daily sufferings of the wounded are sufficient to disarm those appetites, stop that scheming and brand those ambitions which even their martyrdom serves to foster. At such moments Duhamel doubts of everything: of man, of the world, of the fate reserved for the just cause, of everything except the suffering of men. In 1918, as a kind of sequel to his *Vie des martyrs,* he published *Civilisation,* to which the Prix Goncourt was awarded. Once again, this time in his interpretation of civilization, Duhamel strikes the same note of pity and humanism. Civilization, he informs us, has appeared to him as a chorus of tuneful voices singing in perfect harmony; or as a marble statue on the summit of a parched hill; or it is as a man saying 'Love one another!' or 'Render good for evil'. And yet, he notes, for nearly two thousand years men have been repeating these words over and over again, and the high-priests have been too concerned

6

with secular matters to conceive any other thought of like greatness or beauty. He himself, he goes on, has studied with care that monstrous Moloch in its lofty position and writes to tell men that civilization is not in that thing any more than it is in the shiny instruments of the surgeon. 'La civilisation', writes Duhamel, 'si elle n'est pas dans le cœur de l'homme, eh bien! elle n'est nulle part'.[31]

Such a declaration, like so many of its kind, is less significant for the humanitarian ideal it sought to inspire than for the profound sense of disillusion which was its source. Nowhere is the nature and scope of this disillusion more apparent than towards the end of *Civilisation*, when a group of African stretcher-bearers are shown gazing in silent disbelief at the mangled victims of centuries of European civilization.

What foundered in the trenches of 1914–18 were those jealous virtues of patriotic devotion and 'civilized intelligence' which had given the war its purpose and meaning. The response to the ensuing mood of numbed bewilderment, which Benda has characterized as *la fin de l'Éternel*, Valéry as *la crise de l'esprit* and Marcel Arland as *le nouveau mal du siècle*, was by no means uniform. If a common feature of wounded idealism was a keen sense of the fragility of previously unshakeable faith, this new conviction was not always prompted by the conscious hope of building afresh according to sounder principles. In other words the impulse, although frequently masked by the aspiration to a kind of humanitarian religiosity, was basically negative. As such it strengthened the conviction, expressed by Valéry in his famous essay of 1919, that European civilization had suddenly been drained of all life and inspiration:

Il y a des milliers de jeunes écrivains et de jeunes artistes qui sont morts. Il y a l'illusion perdue d'une culture européenne et la démonstration de l'impuissance de la connaissance à sauver quoi que ce soit; il y a la science, atteinte mortellement dans ses ambitions morales, et comme déshonorée par la cruauté de ses applications; il y a l'idéalisme difficilement vainqueur, profondément meurtri . . . le réalisme déçu, battu, accablé de crimes et de fautes; la convoitise et le renoncement également bafoués; les croyances confondues dans les camps, croix contre croix, croissant contre croissant; il y a les sceptiques eux-mêmes désarçonnés par des événements si soudains, si violents, si émouvants, et qui jouent avec nos pensées comme le chat avec la souris,—les sceptiques perdent leurs doutes, les retrouvent, les reperdent et ne savent plus se servir des mouvements de leur esprit.[32]

The most extreme and indeed defiant expression of this crisis of values was Dada, which, for all its bellicose pronouncements, was less an engine of war dedicated to the annihilation of cultural certainties than a post-mortem confirming that they had already expired. To Dadaïsts none of Civilization's 'fallen idols' seemed capable or, for that matter, deserving of restitution; neither Religion, which (like art and literature) had become the servant of *patrie*, nor Science which had furnished the instruments of war; neither Reason which at best was irrelevant in a world struck with hopeless insanity, nor Progress whose true meaning was scientific warfare consecrated by Church and State. Nothing, Dadaïsts bellowed, could be salvaged from the wreckage of governing ideals. Civilization was 'dead':

> Plus de peintres, plus de littérateurs, plus de musiciens, plus de sculpteurs, plus de religions, plus de républicains, plus de royalistes, plus d'impérialistes, plus d'anarchistes, plus de socialistes, plus de bolcheviques, plus de politiques, plus de prolétaires, plus de démocrates, plus de bourgeois, plus d'aristocrates, plus d'armées, plus de police, plus de patries, enfin assez de toutes ces imbécillités, plus rien, plus rien, rien, RIEN, RIEN, RIEN.[33]

This cynicism, born of the war in its senselessness and horror and generalized to include society, history and the world, was but one, if the most extreme, expression of intellectual despondency in the immediate post-war period. Other writers, like Cocteau and Giraudoux, were to seek refuge in the creation of an autonomous world of fantasy, and others still, like Malraux, were to seek in *dépaysement* another avenue of escape from the ruins of a 'dead civilization'.

The shock of war which drove Dada along the path to deliberate absurdity and launched Malraux on his Asian adventure, led others, even as the war in Europe raged, to undertake the hopeful enterprise of cultural renewal. Prominent among these were Romain Rolland and Henri Barbusse whose assertive faith in radical alternatives sparked off a heated and lasting controversy with the 'defenders of civilization'.

Not only was Germany considered by the defenders of civilization to be the national enemy of France but, on a cultural and philosophical level, she was her very antithesis. Chaos and the Irrational played the same part in her make-up as did Order and Reason in France. It was on this basis, and before the war, that Rolland first came under attack. His alleged preference for Kultur—detected in his novel sequence *Jean-Christophe*—was diagnosed as a rejection of Civilization. From this initial premise it was but a short step to the conclusion that Rolland's anti-war stand was in essence pro-German. Such a conclusion was reached by a host of critics led, in the main, by Henri Massis.

The model for part of Christophe's life and personality is Beethoven. Not only is music as it were the central protagonist of the novel sequence, but it dominates the structure, composition and style of the work:

> Comment juger de mon œuvre et de mon esprit, si l'on n'est musicien? La musique n'est pas seulement le sujet de quelques chapitres de mon roman, ou de quelques volumes de critique: elle est la forme même de mon esprit, elle pénètre l'essence de ma pensée et de mon art, elle est la clef de ma composition littéraire.[34]

Of equal symbolic significance is the hero's name. 'Jean' is, as Rolland tells us elsewhere, the Precursor (John the Baptist), 'Christophe' is the Christ-(or God-)bearing giant, and 'Krafft' is Force or Primal Energy.[35] In volume 10, entitled *La Nouvelle Journée*, the hero justifies his second name. The Precursor has fulfilled his function of denouncing the generation of vipers and makes way for Christophe who, emerging from the river, is now ready to preach the gospel of the New Day: Primal Energy, or 'Krafft'.

Another symbol, suggested rather than defined, is the river. A passage in Rolland's *La Vie de Ramakrishna* (1929) clarifies his intentions in *Jean–Christophe*. It informs us that of all rivers the most sacred is the one which springs constantly from the depths of the soul and which is drawn irresistibly toward the conscious, dominated ocean of Being. And just as water rises again as vapour to the clouds which refill the reservoir of rivers, so the cycles of creation form a continuous chain. From the source to the sea, and from the sea to the source, it is all the same Energy-Being, without beginning or end.[36] The unending flow of the river in *Jean–*

Christophe has something of the flow of music, and its great power suggests the life force.

In these themes we see why the work made such an impact upon Rolland's contemporaries. Gide noted in his *Journal* (30 January 1917) that despite the 'artless' nature of the work Rolland had succeeded in capturing the ideas and feelings of his generation. For those who rejected Catholicism, but found Positivism unacceptable, Rolland provided, in his worship of the life force, an attractive alternative. For those again who, on a political level, rejected the nationalist dogma of Barrès, here was a symbolic bridge across the Rhine whereby the humanist traditions of France and Germany could meet and mingle. Rolland thus gave powerful support to the notion of there being two Germanies—the Prussian Germany and the humane Germany of Goethe—in opposition to the widely held belief, dear to the Massis school, of Germany as a single entity whose hereditary enemy was France. It was to combat this latter belief that Rolland wrote *Au-dessus de la mêlée,* which was published in September 1914.[37] Three months later, in an article entitled 'Les Idoles', he moved on to the offensive. He accused the cultural establishment, directly and forcefully, of having sacrificed the loftiest moral values to the false god of *raison d'État.*

Henri Massis opened the case against Rolland in August 1913 with an article entitled 'Romain Rolland ou le dilettantisme de la foi'.[38] In Massis's estimation *Jean–Christophe* was the natural product of an ideology and an aesthetic which had always distilled and diffused the most venomous poisons. Its origin was essentially Germanic. The classical virtues of Reason and Order, clarity and measure were denied by Rolland who had to be regarded as a Romantic.[39] Rolland's universe was 'inorganique', 'imprécis', 'ténébreux', his vision of the world 'chaotique', his conception of life 'anarchique', and his 'soumission à l'instinct' evidence of 'animalité indécente'. He recognized the primacy of 'la déraison qu'il nomme sensibilité, inconscient ou instinct'.[40] His greatest passion, and the surest indication of his chaotic sensibility, was music:

> Le génie de la musique, en effet, est indépendant de toute réflexion, de toute intention consciente: il ne s'arrête ni aux formes de l'espace, du temps ou de la causalité; il croit saisir

10

directement en lui le rythme continu de la vie. Aussi bien ne nécessite-t-il nullement l'intervention des concepts et chasse la raison. Du même coup, *il dérationalise et dénationalise*: il parle une langue primitive et universelle qui fait appel à l'instinct et aux puissances sourdes et végétatives de l'âme.[41]

Herein lay the essence of the attack on Rolland; he was accused of having sacrificed rational and national values to a universalist ideal in which personality was dissolved and a return to nothingness advocated. In the 'twenties Rolland's interest in the East involved him in this very same political as well as cultural criticism.

Another writer of the 'twenties to pose as defender of what Massis was to describe as the 'idées-mères de l'Occident' was René Johannet, who added his contribution to the anti-Rolland campaign in June 1914. He entitled his article 'Ainsi parlait Romain Rolland', intended quite obviously to show that Rolland was nothing less than the mouthpiece of so many German Zarathustras.[42] Johannet provided the following biographical information on Rolland:

> Monsieur Romain Rolland (de son vrai nom Zebedäus Moser) est né le 14 Juillet 1848, à Gotha. Orphelin de père et de mère dès l'âge de quatre ans, il fut recueilli par un vieux révolutionnaire français, échappé aux journées de Juin, qui, s'étant réfugié dans la petite ville, s'éprit d'amitié pour l'enfant, l'éleva, lui enseignant le français et la clarinette.[43]

The case against Rolland would appear to be that he was in fact a German Jew with a musical and revolutionary background. The eccentricity of this argument was matched only by its incredible factual inaccuracy. Even Rolland's date of birth was incorrectly stated. Johannet's remarks were, however, highly significant. In the 'twenties, *La Revue universelle*, for which he wrote, denounced in no uncertain manner Germans, Jews and revolutionaries as enemies of Civilization. In evidence it pointed to Bolshevism—a 'Judeo–Germano–Asiatic' putsch against the West. And Johannet, as if to underline the political, rather than purely philosophical or cultural nature of his defence of Civilization, not only wrote an *Éloge du bourgeois* (1927) in which his debt to Maurras was clearly discernible, but defended the Fascist dictatorship in Italy.

11

When, at the outbreak of war, Rolland took up a position 'above the struggle', a torrent of criticism, not to say abuse, was unleashed against him. Massis was one of the first to react with an article entitled 'Romain Rolland parle'.[44] Apart from repeating his former criticisms, Massis also accused Rolland of deserting 'moralement, pratiquement même sa patrie'.[45] Rolland posed as a neutral, wrote Massis, when it should have been clear to any man of good will that France was:

> Terre de l'Humanité et terre de l'Esprit, terre du Sacrifice et de la Charité, celle qui en dépit de ses erreurs, de ses blasphèmes, est l'élue, la choisie par Dieu, lorsqu'il veut que quelque chose de grand s'accomplisse ici-bas.[46]

However, these truths (which Massis, like other supporters of the 'Holy War', held to be of divine inspiration) were lost to Rolland for it was 'l'Allemagne qui l'a formé'.

Other critics following the lead given by Massis were not slow to stress Rolland's debt to Germany. He was accused of being 'aux trois-quarts de cerveau germanique',[47] an 'apologiste de la Kultur germanique',[48] 'un philosophe de couche prusso-germanique'.[49] Mention was made of his 'goût pour l'Allemagne, son peu de goût pour la France',[50] his 'sensibilité de métèque',[51] 'sa formation germanique'.[52] His work was described as 'un panégyrique rentré de l'Allemagne',[53] 'un solennel braiement en l'honneur de la Kultur',[54] and he was compared to 'Pierre qui ne connaît plus son maître au Jardin des Oliviers'.[55] Others, in less philosophical mood, simply accused him of being a German agent.[56]

Rolland's left-wing affiliations, notably with the Zimmerwald and Kienthal groups,[57] led to further accusations being levelled against him. He was now regarded as a defeatist.[58] When, in 1917, he hailed the Russian Revolution as an attempt to create a more just and sane social order he again came under attack. The culmination of such attacks came in 1920 when Jean Maxe, another contributor in the 'twenties to Massis's *La Revue universelle*, published his *De Zimmerwald au bolchevisme, ou le triomphe du marxisme pangermaniste*.[59]

The 'peace offensive' launched by Rolland in 1914 was by 1916 bringing to public attention men, books and movements which had peace for their aim. It was at this time that Barbusse's *Le Feu* appeared. For Barbusse the war was the most important political experience of his life. It marked his break with social-democracy and his first move towards acceptance of the principles of revolutionary socialism. In 1919 he was to publish *Clarté*, a novel which led to the formation of the *Clarté* group and the founding of an international review of the same name, which he edited for some years. This review was sympathetic to the Soviet Union and to national liberation movements throughout the world and hostile to imperialism and the 'defenders of civilization'. At the same time, it firmly rejected the 'idealistic Orientalism' of Rolland in favour of a Marxist interpretation of the East. Rolland was thus to find himself in the unenviable position of being attacked not only by the Right but also by the revolutionary Left (which included Barbusse, who joined the Communist Party in 1923). We can appreciate the nature of the opposition between Barbusse (and his comrades) and Rolland on the question of the East in the 'twenties only if we recognize the decisive role which the war played in the ideological formation of Barbusse. His interpretation of the war and his analysis of events in the East are linked. Both reflect the political consciousness of a revolutionary socialist.

Prior to the war Barbusse had been known as a 'humanitarian' and 'pacifist'. He was also a socialist and, as such, duty-bound to support the resolutions adopted at the International Socialist Congresses of Stuttgart (1907), Copenhagen (1910), and Basle (1912). The war manifesto unanimously adopted in 1912 in Basle had in mind the kind of war between Britain and Germany (and their allies) which actually broke out in 1914. The manifesto declares unequivocally that such a war 'cannot be justified by even the slightest pretext of being in the interest of the people', it being conducted 'for the profits of the capitalists' and 'the ambitions of dynasties', as an outgrowth of the imperialist predatory policy of the great nations. The manifesto states that governments must remember that with the prevailing conditions of Europe and 'the mood of the working class' they cannot unleash a war without danger to themselves. It refers to the example of the Commune of 1871 and of October–December 1905 in Russia to warn governments that they can expect similar treatment should they declare war. The Basle manifesto thus establishes the tactics of workers' revolutionary struggle on an international scale against their governments in the event of war, and stresses this warning by repeating the words of the Stuttgart resolution to the effect that in case of war socialists must take advantage of the 'economic and political crisis created by the war to arouse the people and thereby to hasten the downfall of capitalist class rule'.[60]

However, with the outbreak of war these same socialists (with the exception of the Bolsheviks and the odd individual like Liebknecht) quickly forgot their declarations on international solidarity and socialist revolution and, participating in their home cabinets, voted for war appropriations and press censorship. They did more. They justified the war from the (bourgeois) standpoint of national liberty and 'defence of the fatherland'. The French socialists, for example, like their own bourgeoisie claimed that the cause of France could not be separated from that of 'Humanity' and 'Civilization'.[61] Objectively, therefore, they supported the *Union Sacrée* as unequivocally as did the nationalists, and with the same assurance as they had supported their own internationalism only two years previously. Many socialists in France (as elsewhere) did, however, attempt to justify their defence of *patrie* (indefensible, naturally, for 'foreign' socialists) as 'une guerre contre la guerre' or as a struggle against 'l'oppression étouffante de l'impérialisme'.[62]

One socialist leader in France claimed that by taking up arms French workers were in fact fighting for the creation of socialism (not in France but in Germany).[63] This attitude was all the more dishonest for being pronounced at the funeral of Jean Jaurès who had called for a general strike against the war at the National Congress of the Socialist Party on 16 July 1914. If socialists could use Jaurès's unequivocal opposition to the war to justify their own support of it they were capable of any distortion. It came as no surprise, therefore, that some should interpret the war as 'une lutte de *tous* les peuples contre le militarisme allemand', that even Jean–Richard Bloch should parody Marxism by claiming that:

> La guerre de la révolution contre le féodalisme se rouvre. Les armées de la République vont-elles assurer le triomphe de la démocratie en Europe et parfaire l'œuvre de 93? Ce sera plus que la guerre inexpiable au foyer, ce sera le réveil de la liberté.[64]

Barbusse also supported this view. Convinced that German

imperialism was 'le seul impérialisme', he enlisted, believing that through and beyond war against Germany lay for humanity the hope of social, indeed socialist progress: 'une guerre *sociale* qui fera faire un grand pas, peut-être le pas définitif à notre cause'.[65] And so, at the outset of war, Barbusse was convinced that 'Justice' and 'Right' were on the side of Republican France against imperialist Germany, and that Germany's defeat would assist the struggle for socialism. His justification of the war as a progressive war, as 'une guerre de libération sociale comme celle de 1792'[66] would, by his own admission, prove to be mistaken. What he discovered little by little, and noted in letters to his wife, was that the war, far from serving the interests of socialism, was in fact being fought to establish the supremacy of one finance-capital group over another. A purely economic process—the concentration of production and capital—had led to the terrible social calamity of war in which the people and the socialist cause were the losers and the capitalists alone the victors.[67]

In the early days of the war the feeble attempts of frightened, homesick soldiers to retain a modest humanity inspired Barbusse with pity and admiration. A generous humanitarian indignation was aroused in him. However, what transformed this indignation into an understanding of the real meaning and significance of the war and convinced him of the necessity of revolutionary action against capitalist governments was the realization that, as Lenin stated: 'even in war times, in the war itself the same class antagonisms that rend the people will continue to exist'.[68]

The first indication we have from Barbusse of the existence of class divisions at the front comes in his letters of 13 and 14 January 1915, where he complains of inadequate provisions and of their unequal distribution. His anger is apparent as he writes of 'arrivistes' and 'incapables', of 'trench tourists' and of 'journalistes conduits par des officiers d'État-major'.[69] Whilst he is further appalled by the privileges accruing to the 'officer caste' he has nothing but the greatest admiration for those, 'qui, depuis le début de la campagne, ont accompli sans manquement l'énorme, écrasant et terrible labeur du simple soldat'.[70] And for the first time confusion creeps into his thought. He feels as if a part of his being has escaped him and is acting not only contrary to his own interests and moral principles but, more importantly, for *some force* which as yet he cannot define. Everywhere he sees an 'interminable dépense d'héroïsme [qui] s'accomplit pour des causes que je persiste à trouver vagues, sans attaches avec le profond de nous-mêmes et en réalité contraires à notre destinée humaine'.[71] His sense of alienation deepens as he remarks indignantly that whereas 'officiers d'administration' are decorated for their company's bravery and live in relative comfort, the 'pauvres types de la ligne qui auront tout fait et tout risqué', are given no credit and have to survive in conditions better suited to sewer-rats.[72] After every battle, while the staff officers perorate amongst themselves on the virtues of patriotism and bravery, the 'pauvres types' return silently to their trench positions with heads bowed in memory of their fallen comrades.

From such observations Barbusse is led to express his anxieties over the future. He feels obliged to admit the inevitability of future conflicts in which the same people will bear the brunt unless something is done to change 'la conception actuelle des nationalités'.[73] He sees it as his duty to contribute to such a change. Previously he had seen German imperialism as the sole offender and Republican France as one of her victims. His letters of 23 March and 14 April demonstrate how his opinion has altered. *All* nations are to blame.[74] He now recognizes (what Lenin had stated at the outbreak of hostilities) that the war is an imperialist armed conflict of the bourgeoisie of all nations. Mankind is faced with the alternative of adopting socialism or of experiencing years and even decades of armed struggle between the great powers for the artificial preservation of capitalism by means of colonies, monopolies, privileges and national oppression of every kind.[75]

Barbusse had for some time been engaged on a literary venture which he hoped would contribute to a change in the prevailing attitudes to war.[76] On 3 August 1916 *L'Œuvre* began publishing *Le Feu* in serial form. Barbusse was, however, unhappy about its presentation. His letters of 6 and 7 August and of 6 September complain of the editor's attempt to make the text 'plus Acadoumic' by cutting out entire passages. He was further frustrated by government censorship.[77] Despite the mutilation of his text Barbusse's message clearly began to get through. He was inundated with readers' letters congratulating him for having revealed 'la vérité sur les poilus'.[78] Heartened by this response and further encouraged by the support of his fellow soldiers,[79] Barbusse decided that the decisive moment had come to wage a battle of ideas.[80] He felt that *La Revue hebdomadaire* and *L'Écho de Paris* had, with the full backing of the State-machine, been spreading their lies for too long.[81] He now understood why—their fear and hatred of socialism:

> Comme tous ces gens ont une haine féroce, obstinée, invincible, du socialisme et de la libération des exploités! Que de sophismes où l'influence de Barrès et des écrivains catholiques se révèle dans le style philosophico-religieux, et dans la pensée . . . sur le besoin de la discipline et la nécessité de s'asservir à des idées et à des hommes. C'est une predication constante, plus ou moins cachée, vers l'imitation du passé d'ancien régime, d'esclavage et d'abus.[82]

Although *Le Feu* was received favourably in many quarters,[83] it also inspired the deepest antagonisms. In the forefront of the attack was *Action Française:*

> Ignoble livre . . . Tison qu'un promeneur idiot jette dans une boutique pour épater le monde. Un livre où il n'y a que de la boue . . . Livre las et dissolvant . . . Tentative de la démoralisation de la France . . . *Le Feu* ne pouvait servir que les desseins de l'ennemi. *Le Feu* est inspiré de la négation du devoir, du dévouement et du sacrifice . . . Pas un beau sentiment, un geste pour la France. Œuvre immorale et fausse . . . Barbusse dégoûtant et criminel . . . Barbusse est coupable d'intelligence avec l'ennemi . . . Barbusse par ses bouquins est un agent de l'ennemi, voilà tout.[84]

Despite the nationalists' claim to have uncovered another enemy agent—'confirmed' by the French military authorities[85] —German and Austrian government officials were not in the least convinced. Finding Barbusse's work just as distasteful and dangerous as did their French enemies they forbade its publication. In the meanwhile the storm of criticism continued in France. A Church spokesman, clearly conscious of the duty of citizens to render unto Caesar the things that are Caesar's, proffered his opinion of Barbusse: 'si les conseils de Guerre collent au mur un pauvre soldat qui refuse à sa patrie le sacrifice de son sang, quel châtiment méritez-vous, Monsieur Barbusse?'[86] The Chambre des Députés obviously shared this opinion for the statement it published repeated almost word for word that issued by the Church.[87]

Far from discouraging Barbusse such attacks simply strengthened him in his resolve to see reason take an active form. He was convinced that if the scourge of war was to be finally eliminated, the forces of the proletariat would have to seize State power and themselves lay the foundations of a new social order, classless and world-wide.

In the foregoing pages it has been seen that cultural and philosophical convictions were not simply matters of pure spirit. If Massis, for example, found Rolland's aesthetic and 'anti-rationalist' predilections distasteful, he did not omit to judge them according to political criteria. This was because Massis, like Johannet, considered the cultural heritage of France, and indeed the cause of humanity, to be inseparable from the absolute justice of the French national cause. Rolland's 'eclecticism' (especially his interest in German culture) was seen therefore not simply as a rejection of the fruits of French civilization but as a betrayal of *patrie*: a thesis which, in Massis's estimation, was wholly confirmed by Rolland's war-time declarations. In condemning France, along with the other belligerent nations, for sacrificing true human values to imperialist greed, Rolland suggested that France was capable of acting other than according to the noblest intentions. For Massis the suggestion was literally blasphemous, for it supposed that an antagonism existed between two spheres: that of God and that of France. Since, according to Massis, France was God's temporal instrument, luminous with His radiance, Rolland's 'neutralism' was an infringement of divine and national law.

Romain Rolland and Henri Barbusse, the former from the standpoint of humanitarian idealism, the latter from that of revolutionary socialism, both condemned the war as an inhuman form of sacrifice. Both were branded traitors because their conception of civilization differed from that of the nationalists. When, in the 'twenties, Rolland turned to India and Barbusse to the Soviet Union for fresh inspiration, the banner of civilization—borne once more by Massis—was again raised against them and their cause. While Rolland and Barbusse continued to be divided by ideological differences—often giving rise to bitter words—they remained united nonetheless in their contempt for those who had justified the World War in philosophico-religious terms and now invoked similar principles to defend European

18

imperialism in the East. In this respect the intellectual and ideological conflict arising out of the war was carried into the 'twenties, where the same protagonists—Rolland, Barbusse, Massis and the Dadaïsts/Surrealists—continued the debate on the meaning of civilization.

Whatever the political and philosophical preferences of these intellectuals and their supporters, whether like Rolland and Barbusse they sought their inspiration in the East or, like Massis, remained jealously attached to the West, all were driven by a common ambition: to awaken European man to the possibilities of renewal. In this ambition they were joined by André Malraux and Pierre Drieu La Rochelle.

NOTES

1 Gustave Hervé, *La Guerre sociale* (13 October, 1914).
2 Léon Daudet, *Action Française* (22 August, 1914).
3 Louis Bertrand, *Revue des deux mondes* (15 April, 1915), p. 751.
4 Émile Picard, *Revue de Paris* (1 April, 1915).
5 M. T. de Wyzewa, *Revue des deux mondes* (15 August, 1915), p. 935.
6 Maurice Barrès, *L'Écho de Paris* (30 August, 1914).
7 Maurice Barrès, *L'Écho de Paris* (18 December, 1914).
8 Edmond Rostand, *Le Vol de la Marseillaise* (Charpentier, 1919), pp. 300–1.
9 Henry Bataille, *La Divine Tragédie* (Charpentier, 1916).
10 Georges Champenois, *Le Miracle français* (Jouve, 1916).
11 Jean des Vignes–Rouges, *Bourru, Soldat de Vauquois* (Perrin, 1917), pp. 11–12.
12 Eugène Lemercier, *Lettres d'un soldat* (Chapelot, 1917), p. 135.
13 Eugène Lemercier, *op. cit.*, p. 12.
14 Eugène Lemercier, *op. cit.*, pp. 127–39.
15 André Fribourg, *Croire* (Payot, 1917).
16 André Fribourg, *op. cit.*, pp. 135–6.
17 André Fribourg, *op. cit.*, p. 149.
18 Henry Malherbe, *La Flamme au poing* (Albin Michel, 1917), p. 85.
19 Henry Malherbe, *op. cit.*, p. 62.
20 Henry Malherbe, *op. cit.*, p. 21.
21 Wilfred Owen, 'Dulce et decorum est', *The Collected poems of Wilfred Owen*, edited by C. Day Lewis (Chatto, 1963), p. 55. Quoted by permission of The Owen Estate and Chatto & Windus Ltd.
22 Max Buteau, *Tenir* (Plon, 1918), p. x.
23 Quoted in 'Les Intellectuels aux côtés de la patrie', *Clarté* (15 July, 1925).
24 Paul Cazin, *L'Humaniste à la guerre* (Plon, 1920), p. 166.
25 André Pézard, *Nous Autres à Vauquois* (Renaissance du livre, 1918), p. 230.
26 Jean Galtier–Boissière, *En rase campagne* (Berger–Levrault, 1917), pp. 288–9.
27 Léon Cathlin, *Les Treize paroles du pauvre Job* (Perrin, 1920), p. 52.

[28] André Maillet, *Sous le fouet du destin* (Perrin, 1920), pp. 98–9.

[29] Paul Cazin, *op. cit.*, p. 168.

[30] Paul Lintier, *Ma Pièce* (Plon–Nourrit, 1916), p. 166.

[31] Georges Duhamel, *Civilisation* (Mercure, 1918), p. 272.

[32] Paul Valéry, 'La Crise de l'esprit', *Variété* (Gallimard, 1967), pp. 15–16.

[33] Quoted by Maurice Nadeau, *Histoire du surréalisme* (2nd edn, Seuil, 1964), p. 33.

[34] See W. T. Starr, *Romain Rolland. One against all* (The Hague: Mouton, 1971), pp. 133–4.

[35] Romain Rolland, *Le Voyage intérieur* (Albin Michel, 1959), p. 259.

[36] Romain Rolland, *Essai sur la mystique et l'action de l'Inde vivante* (Stock, 1929–30). 3 Vols. I *La Vie de Ramakrishna*, p. 16.

[37] 'Au-dessus de la mêlée' first appeared in the *Journal de Genève* (22–23 September, 1914) and was later published, under the same title in a small volume containing some of his other war articles, by Ollendorff, 1915.

[38] Henri Massis, 'Romain Rolland ou le dilettantisme de la foi', *L'Opinion* (30 August, 1913). The same article is published in *Romain Rolland contre la France* (Floury, 1915), pp. 17–27. It is from this text that we quote.

[39] Henri Massis, *op. cit.*, p. 24: 'ce mysticisme m'apparaît bien plutôt comme une névrose de l'intelligence: c'est proprement le mal romantique. Même dialectique puérile, même révolte, même insubordination, même individualisme qui fausse tout.'

[40] Henri Massis, *op. cit.*, p. 21.

[41] Henri Massis, *op. cit.*, p. 26.

[42] René Johannet, 'Ainsi parlait Romain Rolland', *Les Lettres* (15 June, 1914), pp. 457–508.

[43] René Johannet, pp. 458–9.

[44] Henri Massis 'Romain Rolland parle', *L'Opinion* (24 April, 1915). Later published in *Romain Rolland contre la France* (Floury, 1915). It is from this text that we quote.

[45] Henri Massis, *op. cit.*, p. 9.

[46] Henri Massis, *op. cit.*, pp. 11–12.

[47] A. Guinon, *Le Gaulois* (7 August, 1915).

[48] *La Liberté* (19 November, 1914).

[49] William Vogt, *A propos du moins Romain des Rollands furieux* (Chez l'auteur, 1916), p. 25.

[50] *Le Gaulois* (18 August, 1915).

[51] *Action Française* (29 April, 1915).

[52] *La Dépêche* (17 October, 1914).

[53] *Le Bonnet rouge* (21 September, 1915).

[54] *L'Action* (28 October, 1914).

[55] André Maurel, 'Un écrivain de la guerre; Monsieur Romain Rolland', *Mercure de France* (1 September, 1917), pp. 5–19. For similar criticisms see *Le Matin* (23 October, 1914); *La Liberté* (23 October, 1914); *Le Figaro* (22 December, 1915).

[56] See Camille Mauclair, *Le Progrès de Lyon* (25 October, 1914) and Aulard, *L'Information* (6 March, 1915).

[57] See René Cheval, *Romain Rolland: L'Allemagne et la guerre* (Presses

Universitaires de France, 1963), pp. 590–5.

[58] Isabel Debran, *Monsieur Romain Rolland, initiateur du défaitisme* (Geneva: Henri Jarrys, 1918).

[59] Jean Maxe, *De Zimmerwald au bolchevisme, ou le triomphe du marxisme pangermaniste* (Bossard, 1920). See also, by the same author, 'L'Idole "L'Européén" Romain Rolland', *Les Cahiers de l'Anti-France*, Vol. I (Bossard, 1922).

[60] "Manifesto of the International Socialist Congress at Basle", *The Collected Works of V. I. Lenin*, Vol XVIII (Lawrence and Wishart, 1930), pp. 468–72.

[61] See Jean Fréville, *La Nuit finit à Tours* (Éditions sociales, 1951). pp. 37–8.

[62] See Jean Fréville, *op. cit.*, p. 38.

[63] See Raymond Lefebvre, 'Notes sur la guerre de 1914', *Clarté* (21 December, 1921), pp. 67–9.

[64] See Raymond Lefebvre, pp. 68–9.

[65] Henri Barbusse, *Paroles d'un combattant* (Flammarion, 1921), pp. 7–8.

[66] *Lettres d'Henri Barbusse à sa femme* (Flammarion, 1937), p. 99.

[67] See Annette Vidal, *Henri Barbusse, soldat de la paix* (Les Éditions françaises réunies, 1953), p. 60.

[68] *The Collected Works of V. I. Lenin*, p. 88.

[69] *Lettres d'Henri Barbusse à sa femme*, p. 136 (Letter dated 30 May, 1915). Hereafter referred to as *Lettres*.

[70] *Lettres*, p. 147 (Letter dated 20 June, 1915).

[71] *Lettres*, p. 147 (Letter dated 20 June, 1915).

[72] *Lettres*, pp. 161–2 (Letter dated 27 July, 1915).

[73] *Lettres*, p. 199 (Letter dated 23 March, 1916).

[74] *Lettres*, pp. 201–2, 'la crise actuelle est l'aboutissant logique et fatal des vanités nationales, et que chacun en prenne sa responsabilité' (Letter dated 14 April, 1916).

[75] See *Lettres*, p. 202.

[76] See Barbusse's letters dated 9 February and 19 March, 1916.

[77] Barbusse's letters of 15 September and 20 October, 1916, tell of his letters of protest to the relevant authorities. In his letter of 8 September, 1916, he urges friends to try and lift the ban on certain key passages of his work.

[78] *Lettres*, p. 216 (Letter dated 6 September, 1916). See also A. Vidal, *op. cit.*, pp. 64–5.

[79] *Lettres*, p. 277 (Letter dated 13 October, 1916).

[80] *Lettres*, p. 234 (Letter dated 26 October, 1916).

[81] *Lettres*, p. 226: 'comme il va y avoir à lutter contre toute cette littérature falsifiée qu'un gouvernement de rénégats et de réactionnaires laisse s'étaler impudemment, et qui a en ce moment l'estampille officielle' (Letter dated 13 October, 1916).

[82] *Lettres*, p. 226 (Letter dated 13 October, 1916).

[83] See A. Vidal, *op. cit.*, pp. 63–5. See also Romain Rolland, *Journal des années de guerre* (Albin Michel, 1952), p. 1086.

[84] Quoted in A. Vidal, *op. cit.*, p. 66.

[85] See A. Vidal, *op. cit.*, p. 68.

[86] *Lettres*, p. 256.

[87] See A. Vidal, *op. cit.*, p. 67.

CHAPTER II

The Awakening of Asia

The world war has shown as nothing else has the satanic nature that dominates Europe today. Every canon of public morality has been broken by the victors in the name of virtue. But the cause of all these crimes is the crass materialism.

(Mahatma Gandhi)

Four years of war helped to deprive Europe of the world leadership which it had taken centuries to build up. The war left Europe physically broken, and the U.S.A., whose intervention had ensured the complete defeat of Germany, now emerged as the richest and most powerful nation on earth. On the other side of the world another giant of the future, the U.S.S.R., was just emerging. Japan and the British dominions also found their positions considerably strengthened. At the same time Europe's hold on the rest of the world seemed to be slipping as nationalist movements, stimulated by the experience of war, by Europe's decline and by the 'Wilsonian principle' of self-determination, sprang up all the way from North Africa to Asia. An era of military and cultural conquests dating back to the Renaissance seemed to be coming to an end.

We find the following declaration of 1852 in the introduction to Golownin's edition of *A Captivity in Japan*:

> Heretofore the Japanese people have known no wants beyond those which their strict laws and customs have enabled them to gratify; but a freer intercourse with foreigners must necessarily have the effect of expanding their intelligence and improving their taste. The products of European ingenuity and industry will excite their interest, and to obtain the necessaries of life will no longer be the boundary of all earthly wishes among the mass of the people. These changes will open new and lucrative markets for mercantile transactions in a part of the world heretofore closed against British enterprise.[1]

It did not occur to this generous spirit that the opening up of Japan to the rest of the world might do more than simply foster 'new and lucrative markets for mercantile transactions'. In 1860 Japan was feudal, unprogressive and cut off from the outside world; by 1900 she was modern in government, army, navy and industry, and ready to prove her worth in a contest with one of the Great Powers. She fought the war of 1904 to prevent the mainland of the North China coast from falling into Russian hands, and her victory cleared the way for her ensuing expansionist policies. Her economy became dependent upon the acquisition of foreign markets and raw materials, and her participation in World War II was, in major part, dictated by this economic need. Japan's victory over Russia in 1905 sent a wave of anticipation and unrest throughout Asia and inspired the deepest concern within Europe itself.[2] For Japan had defeated one of the mightiest powers in Europe not by an uncompromising resistance to Western influence, but by boldly adopting Westernization. The constitution of her new State was based on the Imperial German model, and her military power—the foundation of the new structure—drew strength from the same source.

Japan's willingness to adopt Western methods in industry as in State organization, to say nothing of the profound social, political and cultural changes which these encouraged, was somewhat exceptional. Further south, the solid foundations of religious belief, law and custom—Islamic, Hindu and Confucian—had stood reasonably firm against Western penetration despite the superiority of Western armed power, far-reaching administrative and economic reforms and the growth of educational institutions fashioned on Western lines. In the main the Moslem ulama, the Chinese scholar and the Indian Brahman had retained their time-honoured position as temporal and spiritual guides to the peoples of Asia. However, by the beginning of the twentieth century, events began changing all this and led many to speak of the 'rising tide of colour', the 'Yellow peril' and the 'revolt against Civilization'.[3] The dawn of the twentieth century found the great imperial movement which Europe had taken centuries to build up being threatened.

Some 600 years before, Europe awoke from the Middle Ages under a new impulse. The rich humanity of Greece and Rome was restored to life, and with this Renaissance the intellectual life of Europe celebrated a careless independence that ecclesiastical

23

rule had never allowed. This dawn released in Europe new energies, and of all its results none was of greater moment than the launching of enterprise overseas. In the fifteenth and sixteenth centuries the Portuguese, English, French and Dutch set out on voyages of exploration to the East, and by the middle of the nineteenth century Britain had secured India, Holland the East Indies, while France and Portugal were only less successful because war in Europe had robbed them of territories which once seemed within their grasp. Meanwhile, Russia had travelled the same easterly course by land until, by the middle of the nineteenth century, she reached the Pacific Ocean. Whatever the original impulse which drove European man to explore the 'mysterious East', by the nineteenth century commerce had become its permanent justification.

The European settlements which sprang up on the coasts of Asia as transit points for incoming and outgoing goods provoked political difficulties with existing rulers. The European Powers' response to such controversies, which threatened their commercial interests, usually took the form of an armed intervention followed by tighter administrative centralism. Throughout the East, from Aden to Singapore, the process was carried through relentlessly and led to profound changes not only in the political and economic life of the East but in customs, ethics and thought. For as traditional autocracies were dethroned and the economic revolution—embodied in factories, railways and telegraphs—spread, the foundations of religious belief, law and custom from which such autocracies derived their support were seriously undermined:

> Whatever the tyrannies and caprices of nature or man, the Moslem who prayed with his face toward Mecca, the Hindu who fulfilled his caste dharma or the Chinese who did ritual honour to his parents and ancestors felt sure of his place in the universe because he was in accord with eternal and divine law.[4]

All these old certainties were now shaken and the systems of social organization based upon them thrown into question. The peoples of the East had begun to think those 'dangerous thoughts' which had inspired the British, French and American revolutions. The belief in divine right of rule was collapsing and an alternative being sought in some form of popular government

24

based upon the representative principle. In China this popular upsurge affected every aspect of social relations. By the turn of the century the traditional and basically conservative doctrines of Feng Shui and Confucianism were for the first time encountering the formidable obstacle of popular disbelief. In 1911 the Manchu dynasty fell and Sun Yat-Sen hoisted the Republican flag. In India the Western assault had also made breaches in ancient custom and thought. Political ferment was growing as liberal and secularist ideas inherited from the West gained ground. Every new railway opened by the British, every factory built, every educational or administrative reform increased the area and speed of change. By the turn of the century a united and independent India had for the first time become an accessible ideal.

Lenin who, in 1917, would lead the peasant-supported proletariat of Russia to victory over the Tsarist régime, wrote of Asia in 1913 (in an article entitled 'Backward Europe and Advanced Asia'):

> The 'European' spirit has already awakened in Asia, the peoples of Asia have become democratic minded . . . Following the 1905 movement in Russia, the democratic revolution spread to the whole of Asia—to Turkey, Persia, China. Ferment is growing in British India . . . Hundreds of millions of the downtrodden and benighted have awakened from medieval stagnation to a new life and are rising to fight for elementary human rights and democracy.[5]

Viewing the urge for revolution and socialism as the most progressive feature of modern civilization Lenin described the West, enmeshed in imperialism and conservatism, as 'backward' and the East, stirring with social change, as 'advanced'. But Lenin, of course, remained a 'Westerner' in several senses. Progress to him meant the acceptance by the East of Marxism, the product of German philosophy, English political economy, and French socialism. He believed, moreover, that the West, because of its industrial base and higher organization, was, after it had 'buried' imperialist capitalism, predestined to lead the East. According to circumstances, the one or the other strand in Lenin's thought came to the fore. When the dawn of revolution seemed to rise over Europe, the 'Western' element in Leninism

25

assumed the greater weight. In the 1920's, with the revolutionary tide in the West seemingly on the ebb, *Clarté* stressed the 'Eastern' element in Leninism: the struggle of colonial peoples against imperialism. If the words *ex Oriente lux* had any meaning for the *Clarté* group it was in this Leninist sense, and had nothing to do with light shining from a mystic, religious East.

With the dawning of the twentieth century the unchanging, 'inscrutable' East had become the scene of seething political activity and of a democratic upsurge. The Russian Revolution of October 1917 added another dimension to the movement in Asia, and many now turned to the Communist exemplar for guidance. It was at this time that some writers in France, Massis among them, began to suggest that this huge and diversified continent could, under the leadership of the Soviet Union, march united against the West. Others, like Drieu La Rochelle, clearly conscious of the possibility of a confrontation between East and West, hoped that the League of Nations might head off such a movement by carrying the benefit of its spirit and method to Asia. The League of Nations was, however, no substitute, Drieu felt, for a strong and purposeful united Europe.[6] The fears expressed by Drieu, Massis and many others were as much a product of events in Europe as in Asia, for in each of the defeated nations the four years of war were succeeded by some four years of revolutionary activity.[7]

Challenged by world events, by the 'intellectual Bolshevism' of *Clarté* and by Rolland's 'Orientalism', Henri Massis and *La Revue universelle* rose to defend the West, or—to be more precise—the political and cultural treasures of the national past as preserved by the Catholic Church. For Massis, hope lay in the reconquest of a lost integrity, the recovery of a harmony of spiritual and social observances most grandly celebrated in the institutions and devotions of medieval Christian civilization. As the defender of European cultural values and the instrument of the divine purpose, France, Massis believed, was entrusted with a mission towards the rest of the world—a 'mission civilisatrice' which first Germany, then the Asian masses led by the Soviet Union, threatened to destroy.

NOTES

[1] Quoted in G. F. Hudson, *Questions of East and West* (Odhams Press, 1953), p. 105.

[2] For alarmist reactions in France, see *Dépêche coloniale*; e.g. 'La guerre russo-japonaise, causes et conséquences', *Dépêche coloniale* (27 January, 1906).

[3] 'Le Péril jaune, un document sensationnel', *Écho de Paris* (10, 11, 12 January, 1905). See also Henri Lorin, 'A Propos de péril jaune', *Dépêche coloniale* (1 February, 1905); 'La Défense de l'Indo-Chine, rapport Deloncle', *Dépêche coloniale* (10 May, 1905).

[4] G. F. Hudson, *op. cit.*, pp. 110–11.

[5] V. I. Lenin, *The Awakening of Asia* (Moscow: Progress Publishers, 1965), pp. 21–3.

[6] See Pierre Drieu La Rochelle, *Genève ou Moscou* (Gallimard, 1928).

[7] The post-war revolts in Europe were presaged by the Easter uprising in 1916 in Dublin, and like it they contained nationalism and from the Bolshevik Revolution they drew their socialist content. The collapse of Tsarist Russia was followed by the collapse of the Ottoman Empire. The German Empire and the Austro-Hungarian Empire collapsed shortly before the Armistice, and it was only considerable allied pressure in Berlin, Vienna and Budapest that prevented revolutionary organizations from securing these cities. The Czech lands had their socialist militancy headed off by nationalist fervour through the adherence of the Masaryk-Wilson plan to set up an independent State. Revolts in Finland, Estonia and Lithuania were crushed by the German army, with the collusion of the Allied Forces. The early post-war years also saw the establishment of the British, French and Italian Communist Parties.

CHAPTER III

The Decline of the West

*Nous autres, civilisations, nous savons maintenant que
nous sommes mortelles. Nous voyons maintenant que
l'abîme de l'histoire est assez grand pour tout le monde.
Nous sentons qu'une civilisation a la même fragilité
qu'une vie.*

(Paul Valéry, 'La Crise de l'esprit')

If Asia's old certainties were now undermined, so too were
Europe's. How could a war which was waged for 'Patrie' and
'Civilisation', and whose cost in human life was unprecedented,
fail to have damaged those very ideals which gave it purpose and
meaning? In *Bouddha Vivant* Paul Morand writes:

> Aujourd'hui les Français [savent] que tout ce massacre a été vain,
> que, huit ans après, il ne reste rien des principes au nom de quoi
> l'on se battait, mots usés pour avoir été trop portés au cimier des
> casques.[1]

However, while the social, cultural and psychological shock of
four years of war disturbed established patterns of thought and
expression—so allowing Dada to flourish—it also prepared the
way for new methods of investigation and articulation. And yet it
has to be said that the World War was not alone responsible for
the loss of faith in established values, for the search for new
idioms of expression or for the growth of the (sometimes bewil-
dering) notions which burgeoned in its aftermath. Science and
experimental psychology had already contributed, and would
continue to contribute, to create the impression that every notion
we entertain and every concrete object perceived is but a fragile
assemblage ready to disintegrate at the impact of some fresh
discovery. Human intelligence—the measure of all things—came
to be regarded not only with suspicion but even with scorn. The
human psyche and the material universe were filled with un-

fathomable prodigies which Reason seemed powerless to grasp let alone resolve. The subliminal world of the Surrealists and Malraux's universe of mysterious signs and symbols have this much in common: both turn away from rationally recognizable evidence in an attempt to penetrate the threshold of the unknown forces enveloping human life. It was to the East, the very antithesis of an excessively rational West, that such men turned for a 'new object of love'. Science and Reason were held to have led Western man into an impasse.

The revolution in science began at the turn of the century with Hertz's discovery of the photo-electric effect. In 1895 Röntgen discovered X-rays. A year later Henri Becquerel prepared the way for Pierre and Marie Curie's discovery of the radioactive properties of radium. The following year J. J. Thompson identified the electron. These and others discoveries, far from reinforcing the current ideas concerning the function and value of scientific knowledge, seemed to challenge their very foundation. For where science had formerly conveyed the reassuring impression of conquering progress and had appeared to make steady inroads into the field of the unknown, it now very rapidly came up against a plethora of perplexing phenomena which accepted hypotheses and general explanations could do nothing to resolve. A universe of baffling complexity, which man had not even begun to understand, let alone reduce to an indivisible unity, was suddenly revealed. This general uncertainty was reflected in the field of philosophical expression. In an article entitled 'Les Bases de la croyance' published on 15 October 1896 in the *Revue des deux mondes,* Brunetière articulated post-Schopenhauer discontent with science by proclaiming 'la faillite de la science'. 'Plus la science progresse', he wrote, 'plus elle s'éloigne de la réalité pour s'enfoncer dans l'abstraction'. Schopenhauer had already claimed that external reality was an illusion. Science, he asserted, is concerned with matter, its investigation, analysis and dissection; its constituent elements are probed and broken down until the whole is explained by the sum of its parts. Life in the meantime slips through the fingers of the analyst without yielding up its secret; nor does science produce moral values or create an ideal to which man might commit himself.

In this state of general uncertainty a thinker appeared whose theories seemed to offer an escape route from the impasse to which Reason and the scientific spirit had led. The essential ideas of Henri Bergson's philosophy are to be found in *Essai sur les données immédiates de la conscience* (1889), in *Matière et Mémoire—Essai sur la relation du corps à l'esprit* (1896), *Introduction à la métaphysique* (1903) and *L'Évolution créatrice* (1906). According to Bergson the underlying reality of things is beyond the grasp of reason whose function is to furnish concepts. Concepts, like that of time for example, are arbitrary, static and finite, whereas the true and vital nature of life is continuous movement. Reason, therefore, is divisive for it isolates man's sentient being from the totality of a universe in flux. If man is to achieve a satisfactory apprehension of the nature of existence he must abandon reason, whose access to metaphysical knowledge is barred, and rely on intuition. Only by intuition can he break through to a higher reality and unite the mysterious rhythms of life with his own consciousness. Bergson's description of the triumphant upward thrust of the *élan vital* against the downward pull of matter is an attempt both to escape the trappings of materialism and biological determinism and to seek out deeper channels of thought. As such it provided a ready-made justification for those who wished to go in pursuit of the unknown along the path of irrational mysticism. It could be argued that Proust, Apollinaire, the post-impressionists, Fauvists and Surrealists would all have existed without Bergson, but Bergsonism encouraged their view that art and literature were to be repositories of spiritual experience and not dull reflections of reality.

If the scientific discoveries of the last years of the nineteenth century provoked a grave spiritual crisis, exemplified in Bergsonism, those of the first quarter of the twentieth century gave every reason to believe that the crisis would deepen. Of this period one scientist has noted: 'classical physics was shaken to the very foot of the cellar stairs'.[2]

The theories of Planck, Rutherford, Geiger, Bohr, de Broglie, Heisenberg and Schrödinger were, of course, mystifying for the average man of culture even in simplified form. However, the theories of one scientist in particular seemed to eclipse all others in complexity and mystery even when illustrated in communicable terms. Between 1908 and 1918 Einstein's relativity theory became known to physicists and mathematicians (mainly in Germany) although it was claimed at this time that only three men in the world understood it.[3] In 1916, however, Einstein wrote a small, non-technical book about special and general relativity theory for those interested in the general philosophical point of view.[4] Later, around 1920, hundreds of books, pamphlets, articles in journals and newspapers were published about Einstein and his theories. Popular lectures on relativity theory were delivered all over the world drawing vast audiences who listened in bewilderment to the arguments pro and con. An American magazine announced a prize for anyone able to explain relativity theory in 3,000 words or less.[5] Einstein was claiming that space was somehow curved and though long considered infinite was in reality both finite and, paradoxically, boundless. His theory of time was just as perplexing. Two clocks travelling concurrently through space at different velocities would, if simultaneously observed, indicate different times and, Einstein claimed, nevertheless both be correct. Such theories gave the average intellectual the impression that logical reasoning was at best a hindrance to an understanding of the world, at worst irrelevant. New forms of investigation and expression were required to penetrate and translate the new realities of life. The return to traditional religion and the growing interest in Eastern religions were not unrelated to the discovery of a universe of infinite complexity and uncertainty. Man was being driven inwards, and the leap of psychology and psychoanalysis into the centre of public attention seemed to confirm this tendency.

The ground had already been prepared in the social writings of the decade and a half leading into war. The importance of unconscious mental processes was stressed as was the dubious nature of 'knowledge' about society. The shift towards subjectivity and self-doubt was stimulated by the experience of war. Freud's theory of psychoanalysis most clearly emphasized this new trend. In the five years or so before war psychoanalysis had become an international movement, and after 1918 its growth was resumed and developed on a still larger scale. Major centres sprang up in Vienna, London, New York, Budapest and Berlin. Freud himself now devoted his energies to the social and historical implications of his earlier formulations and, in 1930, published the most famous of these: *Civilization and its discontents*. Meanwhile Carl Jung was pursuing his own line of enquiry which led him to affirm the existence of a vast collective unconscious in which, he claimed, the same myth-symbols of different climes and times kept recurring.[6] Unlike Freud, Jung, who had studied Oriental philosophy and

31

religion, stressed the therapeutic value of faith, and so lent prestige to those who, by mystic transport or religious experience, sought knowledge of a superior, transcendental kind. The 'irrational' also found vigorous support at the popular level of philosophical expression. Certain pre-war forces now asserted themselves and post-war ones, symptomatic of an already growing sense of malaise, came into their own.

The particular contribution made by such eminent figures as Tolstoy, Anatole France, Barrès, Maurras and Péguy to the assault upon the traditional notion of man as predominantly rational was, as Crémieux, analysing youth's malaise, put it: 'une interprétation héroïque de la vie. Le monde paraissait plat, l'existence monotone et mesquine, l'homme moyen éprouvait le besoin de se dépasser, de se trouver des motifs de l'action'.[7] If one adds here the influence of Gide and Dostoyevsky (for whom self-will, spontaneous and gratuitous action, the coexistence of conflicting emotions were the true properties of what was fundamentally an irrational and chaotic personality), one can scarcely wonder that the harrowing question of the day was 'comment agir?'[8]

In the search for a course of action none had greater influence than Nietzsche, whose ideas provided the moral stimulus for those who found in science no incentive for living but who were not, on that account, prepared to accept faith.[9] For Christian morality born, he believed, of weakness and pity, Nietzsche substituted the morality of the Superman. Men, he demanded, must become what they already were—men without God. They must 'think dangerously', for without God as their ethics they depend on their own physical and moral courage to make life mean something to which, with their whole being, they can say 'Yes'.[10] The new prominence of Nietzsche in the 'twenties is, if we believe Malraux, a symptomatic expression of the post-war pressures to which many intellectuals were subject: the questioning of established values, of the traditional image of man, the search for the deepest sources of energy and power in human nature.

The *crise de l'esprit* inspired by the challenge to traditional literary canons, moral, social, scientific and political values appeared to have an even more sombre determinant. There was talk of the approaching 'death' of Civilization. For a generation

32

that revelled in calling itself lost Oswald Spengler's *The Decline of the West* (whose impact was felt in France in the 'twenties)[11] was the answer to all its fears. Spengler was more than a historian; he was the darker mood of the day, and his fatalistic formulae simply confirmed for many what they had already experienced in war: European civilization had entered a period of decline. Malraux was one of many to share this view. Spengler wrote:

> I see the drama of a number of mighty cultures, each springing with primitive strength from the soil of a mother-region, to which it remains firmly bound throughout its whole life cycle; each stamping its material, its mankind, in *its own image*; each having *its own idea*, *its own* passions, *its own* life, will and feelings, *its own* death . . . Each culture has its own new possibilities of self-expression which arise, ripen, decay and never return.[12]

Such fears did not arise or spread in a vacuum. They were fanned, if not inspired, by the devastation of war, the triumph of revolution in Russia, the rise of the European proletariat and political events in Asia. Once again the cry 'la civilisation en danger' rang out, only this time it referred to a conflict far greater than that between France and Germany. The protagonists were now seen to be Europe and Asia. When, in 1922, Romain Rolland penned the following words, he might have been speaking for all those who, for one reason or another, were turning away from a 'dying' Europe and seeking a sign farther East:

> Nous sommes un certain nombre en Europe, à qui ne suffit plus la civilisation d'Europe. Des fils insatisfaits de l'esprit d'Occident, qui se trouvent à l'étroit dans la vieille maison . . . Nous sommes quelques-uns qui regardons vers l'Asie.[13]

The East's penetration of Europe at this time was, however, not the only evidence of decline. The whole world seemed to be 'invading' the emptiness of Europe. Thus Malraux wrote:

> Ce n'est plus l'Europe qui envahit la France en ce début de siècle, c'est le monde qui envahit l'Europe, le monde avec tout son présent et tout son passé, ses offrandes amoncelées de formes vivantes ou mortes et de méditations.[14]

In this commotion of images invading and soliciting European consciousness there were, as Paul Morand pointed out, many disarming fascinations. Black art forms was one.

The fashion for Negro art forms began at the turn of the century with an exhibition in Paris of wooden statuettes brought from the Ivory Coast and the Congo. The artists of the Rue Ravignan were impressed by the bold, geometrical shapes of these carvings which despite (or perhaps because of) their elementary form exuded an inexplicable power of appeal which the studied technique of Western art forms had failed to capture. The name of 'Cubists' was soon attached to the young painters who became exponents of the new tendencies of 'dissociation', 'recombination', sharp angles and geometrical simplification. In all of this was expressed the desire to recapture that pre-intellectual state wherein man's sentient being was in harmony with his surroundings and not, as in the West, alienated from them by dint of an organizing intelligence. This rich and pungent 'primitivism' was also associated with 'black music'—jazz.

Morand responds to this summons from the darkness and goes out to see what lies beneath the appeal of graphic art and the overwhelming melancholy that calls from the saxophones of Parisian night-clubs. His impressions of the 'Black world' are to be found mainly in three works, *Magie Noire* (1927), *A.O.F. Paris-Tombouctou* (1928) and *L'Hiver caraïbe* (1929). In these works the Negro is portrayed as a destructive and superstitious creature whose blood, however much diluted by 'adulterated unions',[15] still races with the savage excitement of ancient rites and primitive instinct. The obscure compulsions of the 'primitive psyche' which Morand from an aesthetic point of view found so fascinating, convinced him that Europe was playing a dangerous game. In her 'negromania' she was undermining her own intellectual supports and collapsing into a dark underworld of blind, irrational impulse.[16] The spectacle of 'white' social degeneration, evoked in *Ouvert la nuit* (1922), *Fermé la nuit* (1923) and *L'Europe galante* (1925) reinforced these fears. Europe was weak, vulnerable, 'dying'; her apparent life consisted of the last spasm of her agony and this agitation was self-destructive. Like Drieu whose torment he shared, Morand would doubtless have supported Malraux's assertion, also made in the context of a European temptation—the East—that 'en vérité, une culture ne meurt que de sa propre faiblesse'.[17]

34

In *Bouddha Vivant* (1927), Morand effectively dramatizes the French preoccupation with the East in the 'twenties. Not only does he attempt, like Malraux, to reveal the deep and disturbing reasons for this attraction but, like so many others of the period, including Massis and his supporters, he also betrays many of the fears which it inspired. Of these fears none had greater substance than the spectre of Communism.

Bouddha Vivant opens with a biographical account of Renaud, a Frenchman of noble birth. This account is designed to establish Renaud less as a personage in his own right than as the incarnation of a certain climate of sensibility peculiar to the 'twenties.[18] Parisian café-life and its feeble and disembodied search for 'definitions' quickly sickens him.[19] He drifts for a time in left-wing circles until, more from lethargy than genuine concern, he becomes interested in the East and its growing influence in Europe.[20] His earlier infatuation with Spengler, Keyserling and other 'German pessimists' strengthens this awakened interest to such an extent that he decides to abandon the West. Stifling all literary ambition he sets out for Shanghai where, in the summer of 1925, he founds a newspaper, *Jeune-Chine*. If he had hoped to find something worthwhile in China he is quickly disappointed: 'à son mépris pour l'Occident vint s'ajouter, en moins d'un an, l'horreur de l'Orient nouveau'.[21] When his newspaper is seized by the authorities he leaves China for the Kingdom of Karastra where he enters the employ of Prince Jâli. For the first time in his life Renaud knows tranquillity. It is, however, short-lived. His master is curious about the West and after some deliberation decides to see it for himself.

Jâli's first encounter with European civilization takes place in London, in the damp and dingy appartment of Angèle Ventre. For the first time in his life he is brought face to face with a form of poverty unknown in the East, a poverty lacking in dignity.[22] The whole of London seems infected.[23] 'Pourquoi, en Occident', he asks, 'où chacun ne pense qu'à l'argent, n'y en a-t-il pas au moins assez pour tous?'[24] His thoughts turn to Buddha in whom, he believes, Europe might find the answer to its suffering. Renaud disagrees: 'le bouddhisme c'est: ne pas désirer, ne pas agir. Or, si l'Occident n'agit pas il meurt'.[25] Shortly afterwards Renaud dies of an intestinal disorder. Up until the very last moment he clings to life with a passion which dismays the

Oriental: 'Jâli n'avait pas compris qu'un Blanc, même supérieur, n'est jamais supérieur à la vie, puisqu'il croit en elle'.[26] Jâli nonetheless undertakes to save the West. Materialism, he believes, has failed it. Religion will deliver it.[27]

Jâli's efforts to preach Buddhism to the white race begin in London. At a public meeting he is approached by Primus Kayser, the editor of a German Buddhist review, who informs him of the tremendous popularity of Buddhism in Germany:

> Frère, -commence-t-il, -Schopenhauer espérait qu'un jour les puissances asiatiques réclameraient à leur tour, dans les traités, le droit d'inonder l'Europe de missionnaires bouddhistes . . . Venez en Allemagne. Venez à notre magnifique renaissance bouddhiste assister! Trois revues florissantes! En une seule année deux mille cinq cents livres édités à Leipzig, tous sur le bouddhisme! Venez voir notre pagode, près de Berlin. Des zélateurs en masse! . . . Nous seuls, qui avons inventé le subconscient, pouvons comprendre l'Orient, 'ce subconscient du monde.'[28]

Despite this heartening news Jâli realizes the enormity of the task before him. Social and racial prejudices, eroticism, scepticism, utilitarianism, the bankruptcy of religion and the unequal distribution of wealth all make recovery in the West difficult. The situation is further aggravated by the growing influence of Bolshevism, which has fired the 'racially inferior' with an all-consuming hatred of Western civilization.[29] After centuries of white domination the coloured masses are at last rising against their masters, at the very moment when the latter are weak, divided and least able to face the challenge. So appalled is Jâli by the senseless anger of 'ces affranchis, ces bâtards'[30] that he decides to leave England for France. Purification of the body and soul will enable him, he believes, to overcome all obstacles and save the French.

All his effort is for nothing for he quickly discovers that the French are beyond redemption despite their affinity with the East through acceptance of the teachings of Bergson and Einstein:[31] 'personne ici ne tient à être sauvé. On répète: "toute sagesse vient de l'Orient"; mais nul n'y croit'.[32] Indeed the contemplative East no longer has anything to offer France. If France still retains a choice it is one between Americanization and Bolshevization.[33]

Jâli falls in love with an American girl whom he follows to New

York. His whole enterprise is now bankrupt for he has been infected by a Western malady: desire.[34] A final adventure in a New York restaurant where he is made to understand that the 'monsieur d'Asie' is not a very welcome guest disgusts him with the West altogether, and he starts for his native country rich in destroyed illusions and angry dreams:

> Jâli se consolait par des visions troubles, celles d'une apocalypse sans consistance, dont le monde occidental était la nécessaire et quotidienne victime. Ce crépuscule des Dieux pâles, avec écroulement de banques en carton, dont il se donnait à soi-même l'imaginaire spectacle, était la chose qui le soulageait le mieux.[35]

Morand's presentation of the opposition between East and West contains many of the elements associated with this hotly-debated subject in the 'twenties, notably the (usual) antithesis between a religious and contemplative East (represented by Jâli) and a materialistic and active West. In so far as this novel is concerned with Jâli's attempts to save a bankrupt and foundering West, Morand's conclusion, like Malraux's and Drieu's, is that the East, itself experiencing Westernization, is unable to help. However, just as Malraux's *La Tentation de l'Occident* is in essence the diagnosis of the European crisis (despite its formal comparison of the civilizations of East and West), Morand's *Bouddha Vivant* is less an elucidation of 'Oriental wisdom' than the dramatization of European disintegration, aided and abetted by Bolshevism.

Morand's conclusion thus goes far beyond that of the basic incompatibility of Oriental mysticism and Western materialism. He prophesies a global confrontation of cataclysmic proportions inspired by the failure of racial and social hierarchies to contain the inferior orders: 'les continents vont être écrasés sous les masses.'[36] In a passage fraught with Drieu-like sentiments, he imagines a devastated earth probing the cosmic darkness with a last flickering beam:

> Aujourd'hui que l'Occident arrive à l'avant-dernier degré de la surproduction, de la vitesse, de l'anémie et de la névrose, entrevoit, comme remède unique à une prochaine catastrophe, la nécessité de ralentir le rythme de la vie, de refréner ses besoins et de ne pas céder à toutes les exigences de la matière, il se retournerait volontiers vers l'Asie, lui demandant ses secrets

d'antique sagesse. Mais l'Asie renonçante et apaisée a disparu: le monde entier vit désormais sous le signe de la machine. De cette lutte qui relève de l'Apocalypse, qui dira l'issue? Un jour viendra peut-être où il n'y aura même plus d'Orient et d'Occident, mais une seule misérable nation terrestre interrogeant l'espace interplanétaire à coups de signaux lumineux.[37]

Whatever the excesses in Morand's work the anxieties which produced them were, for someone of his political outlook, well-founded. After the tragedy of World War I Europe's hold on the coloured world did indeed appear to be slipping. Nearer home, in Russia, the 'lower orders' had achieved State power and their victory seemed certain to stimulate and inspire revolutionary changes throughout the world. Such a prospect horrified Morand for its being not altogether impossible. Indeed, he took it seriously enough to advise the French worker against any truck with Communism: 'dangereux véhicule des populations misérables'.[38] Elsewhere, and inverting Marx, he has declared that Communism is 'la religion des foules, c'est l'opium du peuple'.[39] In *Bouddha Vivant* a Communist agent explains his mission as follows:

> Nous fabriquons la haine en série . . . il ne s'agit pas de mettre sur pied quelque chose de construit, de cimenté, comme un empire colonial, il s'agit de fabriquer, sans chercher à comprendre des explosifs, de façon à desceller complètement la cellule initiale, l'élément aryen.[40]

For Morand, therefore, both Communism and the 'rising tide of colour' threaten Aryan supremacy. Both are born of hatred and both propelled by a will to destruction. Morand's fears that Western civilization would be engulfed by such forces hardened him in his racialism and anti-Communism and made him a Nazi sympathizer.

Morand was of course not alone in articulating fears of the 'Red peril'. Henri Massis and his colleagues, for example, expressed similar trepidation. In this both they and Morand shared one of the major concerns of those men who, in the supposed conflict between East and West, took it upon themselves to defend *homo occidentalis*.

Believing that the Western concept of Man was no longer viable, Drieu and Malraux saw no reason to rush to its defence.

And a return to Christian principles, such as Massis recommended, was not only impracticable but seemed altogether insufficient to fill that inner void, the 'absence de principe' which Malraux and Drieu identified as the heritage of modern man. For Malraux and Drieu, therefore, the issue was not, as it was for Massis, Rolland and Barbusse, one of a choice between rival spiritual worlds or political doctrines—all of which, they felt, had lost their original force and relevance—but of a desperate search behind the chaos of wrecked ideals for new principles of coherence. To this extent both men were, at the outset at least, far closer to the naked pessimism of the Dadaïsts/Surrealists than to the assertive faith of Massis, Rolland and Barbusse in ready-made solutions to Europe's *crise de l'esprit*.

If Morand's work expressed concern at the state of a civilization dedicated to self-destruction, Dadaïsts (and Surrealists) rejoiced in the fact. Their frenzied efforts to render the universal destruction complete expressed a desire to have done, once and for all, with a civilization whose corruption and meaninglessness had been dramatized in the mindless slaughter of war. Cultural certainties had put themselves at the service of the carnage and in so doing demonstrated their hypocrisy and futility. Language itself—the war-time vehicle of hysterical propaganda—did not escape the débâcle. By virtue of its inner consistency and coherence it had dared give human form to unspeakable bestiality. When Dadaïsts shrieked incoherent poems as they danced crazily about the stage, they were at least, they believed, establishing a semantic code reconciled with its object—a pathologically insane society. Any 'mindless' impulse, whether poem, gesture or mass riot, therefore assumed absolute validity. Picabia proclaimed himself a 'genius' when he entitled an ink-blot 'Sainte Vierge'.

However, behind the movement's systematic and provocative nonsense lay a serious intent to apprehend an absolute psychological reality free from the tyranny of reason, morality and literary convention and innocent of their 'crimes'.[41] Breton first came to suspect the existence of this strange realm on an evening in 1919 when, dozing, he became aware of a mental substance, relayed to him through a weird image, which seemed just as real if not more real than the conscious rational mind.[42] In this sibylline world of pulsating shapes Breton believed he had discovered the source of poetic inspiration and the magic realm of the authentic self. By verbal automatism this 'superior reality' could be released, and 'l'innocence première',[43] forfeited through the sin of reason, recovered.

In his belief in the unconscious as the primordial psychic reality, his emphasis on the stuff of dreams and hypnotic trances, his acceptance of the mind's free associations and his recognition of the importance of all mental experience, however trivial or immoral, Breton claimed to be exploring not only the source of true poetic inspiration first tapped by Nerval, Rimbaud and Lautréamont, but conducting a scientific investigation of the mind inspired by Freud's psycho-analytic method.[44] The results of this method, published in 1921 as *Les Champs magnétiques*, were offered, therefore, as those of an experiment in the scientific sense of the term and not for scrutiny as mere 'literature'.

Aragon's 'Une Vague de rêves', published in 1924, summarized the Surrealist activity of the early years as expressed in *Littérature*, the ironically-named organ of the movement until June 1924. *Littérature* was presented as a laboratory for verbal transcriptions of a transcendent Surreality whose sublime radiance, it was claimed, would eventually illumine and regenerate the soul of a harried humanity. In it, automatic texts swimming in a sea of images were complemented by accounts of dreams, hallucinatory states and hypnotic trances. The path to phenomenological realities, lying behind the façade of accepted reality, was at last open, promising all who would follow it the fulfilment of desire.

1924 also saw the official foundation of the Surrealist group headed by Breton who gave it its charter: *Le Manifeste du surréalisme*. Here Breton denounced European culture for having renounced mental freedom in the name of logic and common sense.[45] Language, he complained, has been reduced to the sterility of utilitarianism, nowhere more evident than in the attitude of realism, 'faite de médiocrité, de haine et de plate suffisance'.[46] Realism, he insisted, has engendered a profusion of uninspired novels, each with its own pointlessly specialized observations, inane analyses, vacuous descriptions and dull characters.[47] Thus has the imagination been reduced to slavery, and language and literature have become recreations scarcely superior to a game of chess.[48] And yet an antidote, to which

40

everyone has access, exists in the wondrous expanses and vertiginous depths which come to light in dreams.[49] This inspirational source can be tapped and its obscure wonders brought to the surface to augment and transform the rational through the conquest of the irrational.[50] By wedding two states that are contradictory only in appearance man can achieve Surreality, which is neither dream nor reality but the fusion of both: 'je crois à la résolution future de ces deux états, en apparence si contradictoires que sont le rêve et la réalité, en une sorte de réalité absolue, de surréalité . . . C'est à sa conquête que je vais'.[51]

This 'primordial coherence', anterior to the development of the notion of contradiction, is that same mental wonderland which the child creates by the simple exercise of imagination.[52] Formal education exorcizes this state of grace and for it substitutes reality. Henceforth only in dreams will the adult relive that priceless enchantment which, as a child, was at his daily command unless Surrealism teaches him the way back.[53]

Surrealism's affinity with the child's capacity to reorganize the world according to desire explains its insistence on the legitimacy of another private world equally indifferent to the criticisms of the rational: the world of the insane. In this twilight zone 'imagination' is once again the grand-master, bidding its guardian fashion the world according to his innermost compulsions. If Breton finds much to admire in the mentally disturbed—to the point of attempting by simulated madness to resolve poetically the false opposition of reason and insanity[54]—he is nonetheless fully aware that society is not similarly impressed.[55] Its attitude, dictated by rational propriety's aversion for anti-social behaviour, is one of repressive cruelty. Claiming that all acts of individuals are to some extent anti-social, Breton demands the immediate release of 'ces forçats de la sensibilité'.[56]

Surrealism's refusal to be bound by the rational controls imposed upon human existence, and its desire to transcend these limitations, are reflected in its interest in the 'mysterious Orient', an Orient suitable for confounding the West and its logical values. In a 'Lettre aux recteurs des universités européennes'[57] the Surrealists, while denouncing the moral and rational foundations of Western education, at the same time indicate an authority which they are prepared to recognize and uphold: 'les lois cosmiques de l'être'. Their concern to break through to this higher form of reality is emphasized in their 'Lettre aux écoles du Bouddha'[58] and 'Adresse au Dalaï-Lama'[59] where they call upon the sages of the East to orient their minds away from 'la pourriture de la raison' toward 'ces cimes parfaites où l'Esprit de l'Homme ne souffre plus'. The same issue of *La Révolution surréaliste* (15 April 1925) contains an article by Théodore Lessing entitled 'L'Europe et l'Asie'.[60] European man is portrayed as being rooted and active in the world, seeking through science the *fait accompli*, 'the real causes' of things, whereas the Oriental seeks only to live in contemplation 'sans conduite dans l'existence, sans actions'. The European in wanting to bring the universe to man, loses it to his own rational constructions whilst the sage, by offering himself up to the universe, transcends consciousness of it and so succeeds in living in communion with the essence of things, at one with the 'Tout'.

Surrealist discontent with the façade of accepted reality, mummified in the shrouds of logic and mechanistic knowledge, is further emphasized in an article by Philippe Soupault entitled 'La Vanité de l'Europe' published in March 1925 as part of a (non-Surrealist) enquiry into Oriental interest in France.[61] Soupault sees Henry Ford as the archetypal representative of a crassly utilitarian West, 'un génie et un exemple', a mentor whom every poor demented Westerner aspires to emulate. Ford stands as the supreme embodiment of the Western ideal of the 'homme réussi', its most shining product. A reading of his *My Life and work* reveals, writes Soupault, that 'l'esprit d'un "grand homme" d'Occident n'est occupé que de trouver des solutions d'ordre pratique'.[62] This sterile pursuit—the *sine qua non* of Western life—is the source of incomparable and incomprehensible self-esteem. However, states Soupault, in its suffering, Europe is turning eastward:

> Comme un grand corps malade, l'Europe s'est tournée et retournée sur sa couche sanglante et elle appelle au secours, elle réclame pour son esprit, affaibli, *démoralisé*, une lumière. Cette souffrance presque mortelle l'a obligée à réfléchir, à chercher un appui et la vanité a cédé devant l'ombre de la mort.[63]

Soupault wonders, not entirely hopefully, whether even a humbled Europe can profit from contact with the East, whether its spiritual flame has not been extinguished for ever. What is certain is that if it does not attempt a renaissance it will become what it is geographically—an insignificant peninsula of the great Asian continent. André Breton, noting in the same enquiry the bankruptcy of Western values, welcomes the growing influence and inevitable triumph of the Orient: 'je n'attends pas que "l'Est" nous enrichisse ou nous renouvelle en quoi que ce soit, mais bien qu'il nous conquière'.[64]

At the same time as Surrealism was a defence of 'la vie intérieure' and its manifestations, it was also a crusade against any principle or institution which inhibited its free expression. No authority was to be unchallenged, no convention spared in the determination of Surrealists to bring to the surface that immanent reality to which they aspired and on which, they believed, the recovery of Western man depended. Their aggressively anti-social revolt—'ouvrez les prisons, licenciez l'armée, il n'y a pas de crimes de droit commun'—endorsed any refusal to accept the rational and moral demands of a civilization whose 'war record' made criminal excesses, even murder, look like innocent games:

> On conçoit que le surréalisme n'ait pas craint de se faire un dogme de la *révolte absolue*, de l'insoumission totale, du sabotage en règle, et qu'il n'attende encore rien que de la violence. L'acte surréaliste le plus simple consiste, revolvers aux poings, à descendre dans la rue et à tirer au hasard, tant qu'on peut, dans la foule.[65]

Surrealism's declaration, on 1 December 1924, of a 'new set of human rights', which presumably extended to madmen and murderers, must be seen less as a statement of constructive intent than as a reactive expression of irreducible opposition to society's disciplinary formulae. All forms of social and cultural conservation were to be destroyed especially the 'Holy Trinity' of 'Patrie', 'Religion' and 'Famille'. However, the Surrealists denunciation of France as a nation of 'pigs and dogs',[66] their condemnation of the 'masochistic sin-consciousness' of the Church, its 'Pape chien' and his 'prêtres branlants'[67] and their vituperation against the *caserne* of family honour and propriety were too virulent to be purely ideological. The early Surrealists, like the Dadaïsts before them, were not demanding 'Justice', but the *tabula rasa*, not the revolutionary transformation of society but its obliteration:

> Nous souhaitons, de toutes nos forces, que les révolutions, les

guerres et les insurrections coloniales viennent anéantir cette
civilisation occidentale . . . et nous appelons cette destruction
comme l'état de choses le moins inacceptable pour l'esprit.[68]

Their general disgust with politics and its systems of certainties
precluded hope of any positive revolutionary solution—'le salut
pour nous n'est nulle part.'[69] As with Drieu, revolution was prized
as a means of pure destruction and nothing more. For the early
Surrealists there was no revolutionary order, only disorder—
Oriental hordes armed with flaming torches leaving destruction
and death in their path: 'c'est au tour des Mongols de camper sur
nos places'.[70]

Not content with calling criminals, madmen and historical forces
to the service of their hatred of a civilization whose justification
had gone up in smoke, the Surrealists mobilized all the legions of
the apocalypse which their frenzied imaginations could seize:

> Nous aurons raison de tout. Et d'abord nous ruinerons cette
> civilisation qui vous est chère, où vous êtes moulés comme des
> fossiles dans le schiste. Monde occidental, tu es condamné à mort.
> Nous sommes les défaitistes de l'Europe. Que l'Orient, *votre
> terreur*, enfin à notre voix réponde. Nous réveillerons partout les
> germes de la confusion et du malaise. Nous sommes les agitateurs
> de l'esprit. Toutes les barricades sont bonnes, toutes les entraves à
> nos bonheurs maudits. Juifs, sortez des ghettos. Qu'on affame le
> peuple, afin qu'il connaisse enfin le goût du pain de colère! Bouge,
> Inde aux mille bras, grand Brahma légendaire. A toi Égypte! Et
> que les trafiquants de drogue se jettent sur nos pays terrifiés. Que
> l'Amérique au loin croule de ses buildings blancs au milieu des
> prohibitions absurdes. Soulève-toi, monde! Voyez comme cette
> terre est sèche et bonne pour tous les incendies. On dirait de la
> paille. Riez bien. Nous sommes ceux-la qui donneront toujours la
> main à l'ennemi.[71]

To wish starvation on populations in order that they might the
better punish the 'criminal' values of 'Civilization' is hardly
indicative of revolutionary consciousness, still less of simple
human compassion. The early Surrealists expressed no solidarity
with the proletarian masses, the 'fellateurs de l'utile, les branleurs
de la nécessité' as they disdainfully called them.[72] Never having
been compelled by desire—nor indeed, one may say, by necessity—
to work, they proclaimed their hands to be pure.[73]

The essentially non-materialistic nature of the Surrealist revolution was brought out in the pamphlet entitled 'Un Cadavre', published on the occasion of Anatole France's death. For the Surrealists, Anatole France was civilized intelligence itself, the perfect embodiment of 'l'esprit français', 'le traditionnalisme', 'le réalisme', 'le bons sens'. He was art personified, 'le *maître* éternel', the French language incarnate, 'le mainteneur de la langue française'.[74] In a word, he was everything they despised. The fact that he was acclaimed by Right and Left made him all the more despicable in Surrealist eyes, and led one of the Surrealists, Louis Aragon, to wish for an eraser to rub out this 'human filth' hailed simultaneously by 'le tapir Maurras et Moscou la gâteuse'.[75] This reference to the Soviet Union was heavily criticized by Jean Bernier, the editor of *Clarté*, to whom Aragon replied on 25 November 1924:

> Il vous a plu de relever comme une incartade une phrase qui témoignait du peu de goût que j'ai du gouvernement bolchevique, et avec lui de tout le communisme . . . Si vous me trouvez fermé à l'esprit politique, et mieux: violemment hostile à cette déshonorante attitude pragmatique . . . c'est, vous n'en pouvez douter, que j'ai toujours placé, que je place *l'esprit de révolte* bien au delà de toute politique. La révolution russe, vous ne m'empêcherez pas de hausser les épaules. *A l'échelle des idées, c'est au plus une vague crise ministérielle. Il siérait, vraiment, que vous traitiez avec un peu moins de désinvolture ceux qui ont sacrifié leur existence aux choses de l'esprit.* Je tiens a répéter . . . que les problèmes posés par l'existence humaine ne relèvent pas de *la misérable petite activité révolutionnaire qui s'est produite à notre orient au cours de ces dernières années.* J'ajoute que *c'est par un véritable abus de langage qu'elle peut être qualifiée de révolutionnaire.*[76]

It is evident that material activity was not merely shunned but positively scorned. The Revolution, for Surrealists, was clearly not concrete but spiritual: *'un cri de l'esprit qui retourne vers lui-même* et est bien décidé à broyer désespérément ses entraves'.[77] Its goal was—as stated in the Manifesto—complete mental freedom, for the moment strait-jacketed by the law of Reason, embodied, in the final analysis, in the State. The Surrealists' vituperations against the State—'Patrie', 'Devoir', 'Raison' etc.—were a demand that the State be the State of 'human nature' which they revealed in their writings. This injunction was addressed to the State itself: if it would recognize its necessary essence it would become 'Surrealism', the true freedom of man, through its own reform of itself. Convinced of the omnipotence of thought the Surrealists presumably believed that their enemies had only to hear their words or read their texts to capitulate. They were, however, soon to realize that the power of social and economic determinism under 'Western skies' was too great to permit the spiritual revolution to which they aspired. It was necessary to 'concretize' the revolutionary ideal.

Disputes within the movement frequently occurred, promising to carry the Surrealists towards political action, hitherto dismissed by them with Dadaïst contempt. On 2 April 1925 members of the group met to discuss which of the two principles, Surrealist or revolutionary, was the more likely to direct their course of action.[78] Without reaching an agreement on the subject they nonetheless declared that, before any Surrealist or revolutionary preoccupation, what predominated in their minds was 'un certain état de fureur' with as yet no strategic application points.[79] If the signatories of this declaration were unable to make a clear choice between the two principles discussed, they were at least united in 'fury'—a sentiment somewhat removed, one would imagine, from the preoccupation of some of their fellow members with the search, in Oriental wisdom, for 'un mysticisme d'un nouveau genre'.[80] In the following months both tendencies continued—'fury' in the shape of a 'Lettre ouverte à M. Paul Claudel', and mystic transport in the 'Lettre aux écoles du Bouddha' and 'Adresse au Dalaï-Lama'. In July 1925 Breton assumed the editorship of *La Révolution surréaliste* with the intention of ensuring the continued integrity of the Surrealist movement. While declaring his opposition to those for whom Surrealism was merely a literary and artistic movement, he also insisted on the necessity to avoid the repetition of 'acts of sabotage' from within the organization threatening the group's autonomy.[81] And yet the fundamental ambivalence remained, expressed by Breton himself. Declaring Surrealism's refusal to contribute to 'l'abominable confort terrestre' and stressing its obedience only to the 'merveilleux' and its promise of the 'au-delà', Breton nonetheless stated the intention of proceeding to the concrete: 'nous demeurons acquis au principe de toute action révolutionnaire, quand bien même elle prendrait pour point de départ *une lutte de classes*'.[82] This declaration scarcely needs comment. *Political* revolution was clearly no longer regarded as a 'shamefully pragmatic attitude' unworthy of those who, only a few months previously, were claiming to have sacrificed 'their existence to things of the mind'.

Certain events were responsible for the shift in emphasis. With the revolutionary government of Canton extending its influence in China, and the U.S.S.R. winning the support of a substantial section of the international working-class a new revolutionary crisis among the Asian and European masses seemed a possibility. At home a monetary crisis was looming and in Morocco the French were engaged in a war against the Riffs led by Abd-el-Krim. Such events, especially the last named—probably because of its immediacy—were viewed with horror by conservative French intellectuals, who quickly rallied to the side of 'La Patrie menacée'. In a statement headed 'Les Intellectuels aux côtés de la Patrie',[83] they declared their support for the French government's 'heroic defence' of 'Civilization' in face of a colonial uprising which was less important for what it was than for what it presaged: 'Asiaticism' was threatening to engulf the West. Nothing could have been better calculated to inspire Surrealist interest in the affair than the trepidation of those who were, once again, calling for the establishment of an *Union Sacrée* against the 'Barbarian'. Determined to show their enemies that Surrealism was a threat not only to their intellectual and cultural positions but to their social and political ones as well, the Surrealists rallied to the Riff cause and formed a 'united front' of their own with the *Clarté* group: 'les événements de la Guerre du Riff vinrent nous jeter littéralement les uns sur les autres'.[84] There followed shortly a *rapprochement* between the Surrealists, the *Clarté* and *Philosophies* groups and *Correspondance* (a Belgian Surrealist periodical) which culminated in the publication of 'La Révolution d'abord et toujours' where, despite the occasional characteristically Surrealist phrase, the doctrine of socio-economic revolution was clearly stated. The Surrealists appeared to have recognized that no revolution on the level of ideas was possible without first carrying through a revolution in social realities. They even suggested that given the power of social and economic determinism under the existing régime the latter had become the more urgent task: 'nous ne sommes pas des utopistes: cette Révolution nous ne la concevons que sous sa forme sociale'.[85]

This step towards social and political action was viewed with dismay by Drieu La Rochelle, a close friend of Louis Aragon and collaborator with the Surrealists in the pamphlet directed against Anatole France. Drieu felt that his friends were abandoning their quest for an Absolute, the sense of which was so lacking in Europe,[86] in favour of the fiction of a redemptive Orient:

> Quelles sont ces superstitions? Comment peut-on préférer l'est à l'ouest? Pour moi je ne crois pas plus aux sociologues russes qu'aux économes américains. Quant aux bacheliers chinois ou indous, je vous en prie . . . je ne puis pardonner une image aussi faible: la lumière vient de l'orient . . . Alors, les Russes et les Chinois et les Palotins, au commandement d'Ubu, vont se ranger en colonne de compagnie et, avec les Riffains, marcher sur Paris et sur New-York et démolir la *Revue des Deux Mondes* et la Maison Blanche?[87]

Obsessed as he was with universal decadence, Drieu felt unable to join his friends in their new found optimism.

Confirmation of Surrealism's move towards political alignment was expressed on 30 November 1925 in the form of a joint issue of *Clarté*. Earlier in the month the Surrealists had given a clear indication of their desire for political expression by issuing a statement to *L'Humanité* to the effect that Surrealism had never had any revolutionary theory.[88] The significance of this declaration, stressed *L'Humanité*, lay in its accompanying acceptance of the necessity for a revolutionary theory based on the realities of class-divided society.

In *Clarté*'s editorial of 30 November Jean Bernier substantiated the claim in *L'Humanité* by stating that the union of Surrealists and *Clarté* was cemented by the acceptance of the Marxist conception of revolution,[89] and, in the same issue of *Clarté*, the Surrealist Robert Desnos emphasized his group's commitment to the alliance in the most unequivocal terms:

> Dès leur réunion avec *Clarté* les surréalistes ont reconnu que la révolution était possible seulement sur le plan économique et social, que toute révolution dite de l'esprit n'était en réalité qu'une manifestation bourgeoise. De même ils ont souscrit au principe de la dictature du prolétariat comme seul capable de

réaliser le bouleversement et de supprimer les distinctions de classes.[90]

The December issue of *Clarté* announced the disappearance of *Clarté* and its supersession by *La Guerre civile*. The Surrealists made the same announcement in *La Révolution surréaliste* for March 1926 without, however, declaring the suspension of their own enterprise. This volte-face—or at least unwillingness to surrender Surrealist autonomy to a joint endeavour—had already been hinted at by Breton in an article appositely entitled 'La Force d'attendre', published in *Clarté* in December of the previous year. Here, while acknowledging that no work of the mind could be valid unless conditioned by the desire for *real* improvement of the living standards of an entire world, Breton nonetheless claimed that there was as yet no reason to oppose the cause of pure spirit to that of the Revolution.[91] Breton was still clearly convinced—despite previous declarations to the contrary—that Surrealism was not simply compatible with political activity but even transcended it in its scope. Indeed, for Breton, Surrealism included the social revolution as merely one aspect of total revolt. The newly formed alliance collapsed and *La Guerre civile* never appeared. And so, for all his revolutionary ardour, Breton remained intransigent on the question of Surrealism's autonomy—an attitude severely criticized by a former Surrealist, Pierre Naville, who returned after two years of military service a dedicated Marxist.

In a tract written in 1926 Naville defined the Surrealists' dilemma in the sharpest possible terms by raising the crucial question of priority: was it necessary to believe in a liberation of the mind anterior to the abolition of the bourgeois conditions of material life or, on the contrary, was the abolition of the bourgeois conditions of material life a necessary condition of the mind's liberation?[92] Depending upon its answer, wrote Naville, Surrealism had the choice between: either persevering in a negative attitude of an anarchist order, an attitude dictated by a refusal to compromise its own existence and the sacred character of the individual in a struggle that would lead to the disciplined action of the class-struggle; or committing itself unreservedly to Marxist revolution and thereby to the realization that spiritual force, a substance which derives from the individual, is intimately linked to a social reality which, in fact, it supposes.[93] According to Naville the second course was the only

49

one possible. Hence it was time to assert the primacy of matter over mind, and abandon diversionary concerns such as 'l'usage abusif du mythe Orient', which, like the 'mythe Occident', had no valid basis:

> Le salariat est une nécessité matérielle à laquelle les trois quarts de la population mondiale sont contraints, indépendante des conceptions philosophiques des soi-disant Orientaux ou Occidentaux. Sous la férule du capital les uns et les autres sont des exploités . . . Les querelles de l'intelligence sont absolument vaines devant cette unité de condition.[94]

In September 1926 Breton answered Naville in his 'Légitime Défense'. Whilst reaffirming his faith in Marxist revolution, he nonetheless claimed the right to pursue his love affair with the East, if only because the object of his affections struck terror in the hearts of the 'defenders of civilization'.[95] The mere fact that Henri Massis, for example, lost no opportunity to denounce 'Asiaticism' was in itself, Breton insisted, a powerful argument for seeking inspiration there:

> Trop de signes [écrit Massis] nous font craindre que les doctrines pseudo-orientales, enrôlées au service des puissances de désordre, ne servent en fin de compte qu'à ranimer les dissensions qui, depuis la Réforme, se sont abattues sur l'esprit de l'Europe, et que l'*asiatisme*, comme le germanisme de naguère, ne soit que le premier message des Barbares.

Breton was happy to report that Valéry, too, was confounded by the 'monsters of Asia', whilst Maurras, also alluding to the murky powers of the Orient, had insinuated that:

> Toutes les grandes catastrophes de notre histoire, tous les grands malaises s'interprètent par les chaleurs du même miasme juif et syrien, par l'âpre folie de l'Orient et sa religion sensitive, et le goût de l'orage proposé de la sorte aux esprits fatigués.

Breton asked why, under such conditions, should Surrealists not continue to claim their inspiration from the Orient. What was intolerable, he asserted, was that the 'equilibrium of man', broken in the West for the sake of its material nature, should hope to recover itself by consenting to new sacrifices to its material nature. Yet this was precisely what Barbusse and his 'cretinizing' newspaper, *L'Humanité*, were seeking.[96] Breton's attack on Barbusse and the Communist Party, which was designed to discredit Naville's question in advance by challenging the Communist monopoly on revolution, culminated in the claim that 'la flamme révolutionnaire brûle où elle veut'.[97] And so while endorsing Marxist revolution—even to the point of conceding that there was no viable alternative—Breton still asserted the validity of the Surrealist experiment:

> Dans le domaine des faits, de notre part aucune équivoque n'est possible: il n'est personne de nous qui ne *souhaite* le passage du pouvoir des mains de la bourgeoisie à celle du prolétariat. *En attendant*, il n'en est pas moins nécessaire, selon nous, que les expériences de la vie intérieure se poursuive et cela bien entendu, sans contrôle extérieur, même marxiste.[98]

If anything, this declaration marked a retreat even from the position established as a result of the break with *Clarté*. The shift of power was no longer to be pursued but merely *desired*; meanwhile the Surrealists chose to conduct their experiments in freedom. The simple truth was that Breton refused to regard the social revolution as the fundamental answer to human problems since it sacrificed, he believed, human desires and non-materialistic aspirations to wholly economic considerations. The solution envisaged by Breton was one beyond, and even independent of, the social revolution, one essentially psychological and *individual* in character, whose importance he urged Marxists to recognize. Mental exploration, therefore, despite formal recognition of the necessity for social action, still remained Surrealism's fundamental and abiding vocation.

In spite of Breton's defence of the Surrealist position, Naville's pointed remarks were not lost on the Surrealists, five of whom joined the Communist Party in 1927.[99] The gesture—essentially symbolic since there was no question of their abandoning Surrealism to become militant Communists—did very little to disarm the hostility of the party rank and file. Breton hoped that this hostility would abate with time, but the reluctance of Surrealists to devote themselves to political action and their continued emphasis on the speculative side of the movement[100]—betrayed all too clearly in the *Second Manifeste du surréalisme* (1930)—made reconciliation impossible. The Aragon Affair of 1932 dramatized once and for all the fundamental incompatibility

51

of Communism's concept of class-struggle and Surrealism's instinctive tendency towards transcendence. While in the Soviet Union attending the Second International Congress of Revolutionary Writers at Kharkov, Aragon, in addition to signing a declaration condemning Freudianism and Breton's Second Manifesto, also wrote a poem entitled 'Front Rouge' whose violently revolutionary language exposed him to government prosecution. The Surrealists, led by Breton, immediately sprang to Aragon's defence. They did so, however, in a manner which exploded their revolutionary credibility. Breton argued in effect on behalf of political immunity for the poet on that basis—established in the *Premier Manifeste*—that poetry could not be considered the vehicle of rational thought, the poet being no more responsible for his poetry than the dreamer for his dreams. The contradiction in all this was self-evident. Here were self-proclaimed revolutionaries, dedicated by the fact to the overthrow of capitalist class-rule and conscious, presumably, of the terrible risks which such commitment involved, protesting, at the very moment when the government took them at their word, that they were, after all, merely poets, and 'irresponsible' ones at that. Those Communists who published an anonymous letter in *L'Humanité* on 9 February 1932 did not fail to bring this demonstration of bad faith to the attention of the Surrealists. It was largely to answer this attack that Breton wrote 'Misère de la poésie', only to be promptly denounced as counter-revolutionary by Aragon who had now turned away from the 'hallucinatory enterprise' to embrace practical politics and its artistic counterpart, socialist realism.[101] In 1935 the Surrealists finally broke with the Communist Party, so ending a decade of futile effort to reconcile Marxist and Surrealist activity.

Born as a reaction to the 'treason of intelligence' during the war and drawing its inspiration from the 'irrational', Surrealism first led to a thorough-going idealism, the outer world being denied for the sake of an inner one which each *subject* was to explore systematically. Whence the superior reality of the unconscious, whose exploration would contribute to the emancipation of European man, all of whose troubles were attributed to the dissociation of his mental faculties. This revolutionary subjectivism the Surrealists hoped would, by contagion, transform other men's thought and change their very lives, despite the fact

52

that a 'European citadel' organized on the basis of subliminal phenomena defying every law of concrete experience and seemingly undergoing a continual process of metamorphosis was a reality hard to imagine. In any event, these hopes went unrealized, for the patterns of thought and modes of behaviour Surrealists wanted to reach could be influenced only through the forms of that material world which they refused to recognize. In order to escape this impasse they were obliged to attach, in a collective effort of revolution, the interests of the mind to those of the working class. Only thus, they felt, could they seriously hope to challenge the 'civilized might' of the capitalist West. The Surrealists did not, however, participate in the struggle as political revolutionaries, and each crisis betrayed, in a clash between the Surrealist and Communist forces, the ambivalence, if not the antinomy, of their position.

What divided the movement and eventually split it were those same issues which divided Rolland and Barbusse: the nature of freedom, the value of individualism and of personal transformations, the social and political role of the intellectual, the significance of the Russian Revolution and the attraction of the East. By merging its Freudian venture—Oriental metaphysics and barbarian daydreams included—with Marxist revolution, Surrealism had hoped to resolve these inner tensions and, at the same time, to convince its enemies that it was not simply a revolt against traditional modes of thinking and expression but an attack on a whole social order and its system of values. The attempted synthesis proved to be unacceptable to the political revolutionaries and unsatisfactory to the Surrealist devotees of 'révolte de l'esprit'. Ultimately the Surrealist forces returned to the *subject* which had constituted the movement's very being at its origin and from which they had been unable, in fact, to free themselves. In the final analysis, Surrealism's failure to cross the great divide between spiritual revolt and political revolution rescued it for bourgeois respectability and signalled the end of its efforts to raise European consciousness to the level of men's dreams. The task of refurbishing the corroded powers of European consciousness would be left to others less reluctant to temper spiritual ambition with political necessity.

NOTES

[1] Paul Morand, *Bouddha Vivant* (Grasset, 1927), p. 13.

[2] Gilbert W. Castellan, *Physical Chemistry* (Massachusetts: Addison-Wesley, 1964), p. 385.

[3] Leopold Infeld, *Albert Einstein* (New York: Charles Scribner's Sons, 1950), p. 3: '[Around 1917] a physicist remarked to Professor Eddington; "You are one of three men who understand relativity theory". When a pained expression appeared on Eddington's face, the physicist said, "Professor Eddington, you shouldn't be embarrassed; you are too modest." [The professor] replied, "No, I am not embarrassed; I am only wondering who is the third"'.

[4] Albert Einstein, *Relativity: the special and general theory* (New York: Holt, 1920).

[5] See Leopold Infeld, *Albert Einstein*, pp. 120–1. See also Maurice Nadeau, *Histoire du surréalisme* (Éditions du Seuil, 1945), p. 29 and p. 71, and Paul Morand, *Bouddha Vivant*, p. 174.

[6] The new study of anthropology reinforced to some extent the emphasis Freud and Jung placed upon unconscious motivation: e.g. Malinowski's study of the New Guinean Islanders.

[7] Benjamin Crémieux, *Inquiétude et reconstruction: essai sur la littérature d'après-guerre* (Corrêa, 1931), p. 20.

[8] See Marcel Arland, 'Sur un nouveau mal du siècle', *N.R.F.*, (February 1924), p. 158: 'l'actualité de Dostoïevsky est un signe fort net, jamais l'on ne s'était en France senti plus près de certains des héros des *Possédés* ou des *Karamazov*.'

[9] See André Malraux, 'D'une jeunesse européenne', p. 139: 'si Nietzsche trouve tant d'échos dans des cœurs désespérés, c'est qu'il n'est lui-même que l'expression de leur désespoir'.

[10] For Nietzsche's influence in France at this time see Geneviève Bianquis, *Nietzsche en France* (Alcan, 1929).

[11] See André Fauconnet, *Un Philosophe allemand contemporain: Oswald Spengler, le prophète du déclin de l'Occident* (Alcan, 1925).

[12] Oswald Spengler, *The Decline of the West*, translated by C. F. Atkinson (Allen and Unwin, 1926), Vol. I, p. 21.

[13] Preface to Ananda Coomaraswamy, *La Danse de Çiva* (Paillart, 1922), p. 7.

[14] André Malraux, *La Tentation de l'Occident* (Grasset, 1951), p. 143. Édition originale, 1926.

[15] Paul Morand, *Magie Noire* (Grasset, 1928), pp. 167–8.

[16] Paul Morand, *A.O.F. Paris-Tombouctou* (Flammarion, 1929), pp. 127–8.

[17] André Malraux, *La Tentation de l'Occident*, p. 144.

[18] Paul Morand, *Bouddha Vivant*, p. 18: 'à toute autre époque, on eût dit de Renaud qu'il avait mal tourné: mais comme, aujourd'hui, c'est le monde, qui tourne mal, on se contenta de reconnaître qu'il marchait avec son temps.'

[19] Paul Morand, *op. cit.*, p. 15: 'il laissa donc les autres au café occupés à "se définir", ayant rapidement vu que c'est la vie qui définit et le temps qui classe'.

[20] Paul Morand, *op. cit.*, p. 16: 'Renaud condamna, pour faire comme tout le monde, l'Occident et, d'enthousiasme, sans beaucoup réfléchir, reporta sa mise sur l'Orient. Il s'y montra acharné. Partout où, à travers l'Europe, l'Asie apparaît, il se lançait sur ses traces.'

[21] Paul Morand, *op. cit.*, p. 18.

[22] Paul Morand, *op. cit.*, p. 77: 'ce mélange de misère, de mauvaise odeur et de tristesse n'existe pas en Extrême-Orient; les indigents ont l'air d'y avoir choisi leur état, comme un métier; leur vue n'offusque pas les riches.'

[23] Paul Morand, *op. cit.*, pp. 82–4.

[24] Paul Morand, *op. cit.*, p. 77.

[25] Paul Morand, *op. cit.*, p. 97.

[26] Paul Morand, *op. cit.*, p. 106.

[27] Paul Morand, *op. cit.*, p. 138.

[28] Paul Morand, *op. cit.*, p. 140.

[29] Paul Morand, *op. cit.*, pp. 141–5, p. 150, p. 151.

[30] Paul Morand, *op. cit.*, p. 152.

[31] Paul Morand, *op. cit.*, p. 174.

[32] Paul Morand, *op. cit.*, p. 187.

[33] Paul Morand, *op. cit.*, p. 185.

[34] Paul Morand, *op. cit.*, p. 205: 'Jâli n'est qu'un homme qui va essayer de retrouver une femme, au delà des mers.'

[35] Paul Morand, *op. cit.*, p. 227.

[36] Paul Morand, *op. cit.*, p. 229.

[37] Paul Morand, 'Orient contre Occident', *Papiers d'identité* (Grasset, 1931), p. 206.

[38] Paul Morand, *L'Hiver caraïbe* (Flammarion, 1929), p. 148.

[39] Quoted in Stéphane Sarkany, *Paul Morand et le cosmopolitisme littéraire* (Klincksieck, 1969), p. 221.

[40] Paul Morand, *Bouddha Vivant*, pp. 142–3.

[41] See Jacques Rivière, 'Reconnaissance à Dada', *N.R.F.* (1 August, 1920), pp. 216–37.

[42] André Breton, *Les Manifestes du surréalisme*, (Le Sagittaire, 1955), pp. 22–3.

[43] André Breton, 'Pourquoi je prends la direction de la révolution surréaliste', in Maurice Nadeau, *Documents Surréalistes* (Éditions du Seuil, 1948), p. 48.

[44] André Breton, *Les Manifestes du surréalisme*, pp. 12–13.

[45] André Breton, *op. cit.*, p. 12: 'nous vivons encore sous le règne de la logique'.

[46] André Breton, *op. cit.*, p. 9.

[47] André Breton, *op. cit.*, pp. 9–10.

[48] André Breton, *op. cit.*, p. 11.

[49] André Breton, *op. cit.*, pp. 13–15.

[50] André Breton, *op. cit.*, p. 13: 'si les profondeurs de notre esprit recèlent d'étranges forces capables d'augmenter celles de la surface, ou de lutter victorieusement contre elles, il y a tout intérêt à les capter d'abord, pour les soumettre ensuite, s'il y a lieu, au contrôle de notre raison'.

[51] André Breton, *op. cit.*, p. 15.

[52] André Breton, *op. cit.*, pp. 36–7: 'l'esprit qui plonge dans le surréalisme

revit avec exaltation la meilleure part de son enfance . . . C'est peut-être l'enfance qui approche le plus à la "Vraie Vie" . . . l'enfance où tout concourait cependant à la possession efficace, et sans aléas, de soi-même.'

53 André Breton, *op. cit.*, p. 37.
54 See André Breton and Paul Eluard, *L'Immaculée conception* (Éditions Surréalistes, 1930).
55 André Breton, *Les Manifestes du surréalisme*, p. 8.
56 *Documents Surréalistes*, p. 35.
57 'Lettre aux recteurs des universités', *Documents Surréalistes*, pp. 30–1.
58 *Documents Surréalistes*, pp. 33–4.
59 *Documents Surréalistes*, pp. 31–2.
60 Theódore Lessing, 'L'Europe et l'Asie', *La Révolution surréaliste*, (15 April, 1925), pp. 20–1.
61 'Les Appels de l'Orient', *Les Cahiers du mois*, (February/March, 1925).
62 Philippe Soupault, 'La Vanité de l'Europe', *Les Cahiers du mois*, pp. 64–5.
63 Philippe Soupault, p. 67.
64 André Breton, *Les Cahiers du mois*, p. 251.
65 André Breton, *Les Manifestes du surréalisme*, p. 53.
66 'Lettre ouverte à Paul Claudel', *Documents Surréalistes*, pp. 36–7.
67 'Adresse au Pape', *Documents Surréalistes*, pp. 32–3.
68 *Documents Surréalistes*, p. 36.
69 *Documents Surréalistes*, p. 37. See also 'Deux Documents intérieurs', *Documents Surréalistes*, p. 44: 'la réalité immédiate de la révolution surréaliste n'est pas de changer quoi que ce soit à l'ordre physique . . . L'adhésion à un mouvement révolutionnaire quel qu'il soit, suppose une foi dans les possibilités qu'il peut avoir de devenir une réalité'.
70 *Documents Surréalistes*, p. 39.
71 Maurice Nadeau, *Histoire du surréalisme* (Éditions du Seuil, 1964), p. 80.
72 Maurice Nadeau, *op. cit.*, p. 79.
73 Maurice Nadeau, *op. cit.*, p. 80.
74 'Un Cadavre', *Documents Surréalistes*, pp. 11–15.
75 *Documents Surréalistes*, p. 14.
76 *Documents Surréalistes*, pp. 25–6 (Our italics).
77 *Documents Surréalistes*, p. 43 (Our italics).
78 *Documents Surréalistes*, p. 43.
79 *Documents Surréalistes*, pp. 43–4.
80 *Documents Surréalistes*, p. 44.
81 *Documents Surréalistes*, p. 51.
82 *Documents Surréalistes*, pp. 50–1.
83 Reproduced by *Clarté* (15 July, 1925).
84 *Clarté* (30 November, 1925), p. 1.
85 'La Révolution d'abord et toujours', *Clarté* (15 October, 1925), p. 6.
86 Drieu La Rochelle, 'La Véritable erreur des surréalistes', *N.R.F.* (1 August, 1925), p. 167: 'il est vrai qu'on a entièrement perdu en Europe le sens de l'absolu, et j'espérais que votre petite bande, par des voies d'ailleurs bien souvent futiles, n'avait faussé compagnie à la masse perdue que pour remonter vers cette source seule féconde.'
87 Drieu La Rochelle, 'La Véritable erreur des surréalistes', p. 168.

88 See Jean Bernier, 'Où nous en sommes', *Clarté* (30 November, 1925), p. 3.

89 Jean Bernier, 'Où nous en sommes', p. 5: 'ce qui fonde notre union, c'est cette acceptation de la conception marxiste de la révolution'.

90 Robert Desnos, 'Le Sens révolutionnaire du surréalisme', *Clarté* (30 November, 1925), p. 10.

91 André Breton, 'La Force d'attendre', *Clarté* (15 December, 1925), pp. 12–14.

92 Pierre Naville, 'Que peuvent faire les surréalistes', *La Révolution et les intellectuels* (Gallimard, 1927), pp. 121–2.

93 Pierre Naville, *La Révolution et les intellectuels*, p. 105.

94 Quoted by André Breton, 'Légitime Défense', *Documents Surréalistes*, p. 69.

95 André Breton, 'Légitime Défense', pp. 68–9.

96 André Breton, 'Légitime Défense', p. 57.

97 André Breton, 'Légitime Défense', p. 59.

98 André Breton, 'Légitime Défense', p. 67 (Our italics).

99 The five were Aragon, Breton, Eluard, Péret and Pierre Unik.

100 e.g. André Breton, *Nadja* (N.R.F., 1928). See also, André Breton and Paul Eluard, *L'Immaculée conception* (Éditions Surréalistes, 1930).

101 See Louis Aragon, *Pour un réalisme socialiste* (Denoël et Steele, 1935).

CHAPTER IV

Crisis of the European Mind

'Orient'. Ce mot doit correspondre à une inquiétude particulière de ce temps, à son plus secret espoir, à une prévision inconsciente; il ne doit pas revenir avec cette insistance absolument en vain.

(André Breton)

From December 1921 to the following April, Henri Barbusse and Romain Rolland engaged in a heated debate over the political and social role of the intellectual. The controversy attracted considerable attention in France and to a lesser extent in Germany,[1] and even aroused official Soviet interest, as Leon Trotsky expressed his opinions on some of the major issues raised in the dispute.[2] The French Right preferred to blur the antagonisms between Barbusse and Rolland. For them, Barbusse's Leninism and Rolland's international pacifism and 'Orientalism' were identical in their harmful effect on French culture and society.[3] When, in the course of the debate, Rolland praised Gandhi's political doctrine and tactics, he was not only reiterating his faith in the spiritual and moral resources of the individual and justifying his long-standing commitment to Indian philosophy as a whole, but elaborating a strategy that would free him of the charge, made by Barbusse, that he was an ivory-tower humanitarian whose high-minded individualism could not successfully mediate between the oppressive present and the 'liberating future'. In other words, Gandhism enabled Rolland both to reaffirm his philosophical orientation and, at the same time, to offer a tactic for action, non-violent and 'non-Marxist', which would allow France and Europe to proceed to the liberating future. The 'Oriental question', therefore, in the controversy between Rolland and Barbusse, pertained not only to modes of thinking and perception but to the 'correct' choice of method for achieving social change. For the 'anti-Orientalists', led by Henri

58

Massis, the burning issue was how to revive the order, 'protective substance' and 'intimate cohesions' of Graeco-Latin and Christian civilization,[4] how to prevent the 'Orientalists', whether Leninist, Buddhist or Gandhist, from establishing a new faith and a new human order. Believing that the 'chaotic spirituality' and 'revolutionary nihilism' of the East reflected the misery of a world that ignored God, Massis pointed the way to the Christian City wherein lay the solution to all human problems.

To prescribe a return to faith and, more specifically, to Roman Catholic orthodoxy as a reasoned method of combating the European crisis seemed to André Malraux an altogether futile exhortation: 'M. Massis sait fort bien que nul ne va à la foi par raison'.[5] If Malraux regarded religion and reason as mutually exclusive (and 'outmoded') devotions, Massis was altogether unperturbed by their combination. This was because, as his anti-Rollandism clearly demonstrated, religion, like rationalism, and indeed nationalism, was a form of classicism. Uncompromising in its opposition to Romantic excess, to revolutionary change, to Germanism and to 'Asiaticism', it stood in every sphere as the very incarnation of French continuity. This continuity had been guaranteed by the victory of 1918, of which Massis wrote: 'c'est en notre langue qu'a été pensée la victoire, c'est l'esprit français, la controverse française qui en sont sortis légitimes, intacts'.[6] Henri Ghéon, in his 'Réflexions sur le rôle actuel de l'intelligence française', published in November 1919, claimed that 1918 represented more than the victory of democracy over autocracy; it was above all the triumph of 'la vraie sur la fausse culture', of 'l'Occident sur l'Orient'.[7] Jacques Rivière went even further and, in his 'Le Parti de l'intelligence française', wrote:

> L'intelligence française est la seule qu'il y ait au monde. Nous seuls avons su conserver une tradition intellectuelle . . . nous seuls avons continué de croire au principe d'identité. Il n'y a que nous dans le monde, je le dis froidement, qui sachions encore penser.[8]

Adrien Mithouard, speaking in 1918 as mayor of Paris, ventured to describe his city as the capital of Western civilization[9] and Massis, in more philosophical though no less ambitious mood, saluted 'French intelligence' as the 'gardienne légitime de la vocation occidentale'.[10]

This view of 'French intelligence' was not calculated to curry favour with Romain Rolland whose preferences were brought to the attention of the French public by a defiant 'Déclaration d'Indépendance de l'Esprit', published in *L'Humanité* on 26 June 1919. Here Rolland called upon the 'travailleurs de l'esprit' to dissociate themselves from the tyranny of an 'intelligence' which, during the war, put Science at the service of governments, Art at that of hysterical propaganda, and Reason at that of sophistry. Claiming that man's patrimony—'La Pensée'—had been vilified by those who regarded themselves as its representatives, Rolland made the following appeal:

> Debout! Dégageons l'Esprit de ces compromissions, de ces alliances humiliantes, de ces servitudes cachées! L'Esprit n'est le serviteur de rien. C'est nous qui sommes les serviteurs de l'Esprit. Nous n'avons pas d'autre maître. Nous sommes faits pour porter, pour défendre sa lumière, pour rallier autour d'elle tous les hommes égarés . . . Nous ne connaissons pas les peuples. Nous connaissons le Peuple—unique, universel . . . le Peuple de tous les hommes tous également nos frères. Et c'est afin qu'ils prennent, comme nous, conscience de cette fraternité, que nous élevons au-dessus de leurs aveugles batailles l'Arche de l'Alliance,—l'Esprit libre, un et multiple, éternel.

While Rolland was pleading the cause of the 'Esprit Indépendant' and Massis extolling the virtues of 'Intelligence Française', Barbusse was seeking an alliance of all those interested in establishing an 'Internationale de la Pensée'. Following his appeal in *Le Populaire de Paris* on 17 January 1919, a committee (which included Barbusse, Anatole France, Duhamel, Paul Vaillant-Couturier, Victor Cyril and Magdelaine Marx) was formed and issued a declaration of intent.[11] Undaunted by accusations of being Bolsheviks in the pay of Germany[12] and true to that spirit of internationalism which constituted the movement's very being at its origin, the signatories of this declaration widened their appeal and successfully recruited to the international committee of the 'groupe Clarté' (as it had come to be known) Blasco Ibañez, Upton Sinclair, H. G. Wells and Stefan Zweig.[13]

So broadly based a movement, though richly humanist in spirit, lacked ideological cohesion and political purpose. These weaknesses were apparent to Raymond Lefebvre who, in March 1919, urged the foundation of a literary review free of political nuance and committed unreservedly to the principles of the Third International.[14] A process of ideological clarification was begun and *Clarté* emerged in January 1921 as an 'organe d'éducation révolutionnaire' seeking, through its aim of promoting a 'révolution dans les esprits', to assist the revolutionary organization of the working class—the Communist Party—in its struggle for 'le communisme libérateur':[15]

> 'Clarté' se définit ainsi: 'Centre d'éducation révolutionnaire internationale'! 'Clarté' n'est pas un parti; le parti qui répond à ces conceptions existe déjà: c'est le P.C. International. 'Clarté' reste à côté et en dehors des organisations et des organes polémiques, politiques ou doctrinaires. Elle se trouve par là même en mesure d'apporter à la tâche du Parti Socialiste Communiste une contribution plus spécialement intellectuelle. Impuissante en soi à précipiter l'évolution historique cette action intellectuelle à laquelle les révolutionnaires russes apportent tous leurs soins s'avère de jour en jour comme étant un des facteurs même du succès.[16]

Declarations of this kind were not viewed sympathetically by the government of the day (the 'Bloc National') whose election victory of November 1919 was due in no small part to fears of revolutionary violence, forcefully expressed in a pre-election poster portraying 'l'homme au couteau entre les dents'. *Clarté*'s regional offices in Nancy and Bordeaux were raided by the police early in 1921 and several of the staff arrested on conspiracy charges.[17] Protests from Henri Barbusse, Anatole France and Romain Rolland[18] were answered with increased police activity, this time directed against Barbusse.[19] Despite intimidation of this kind the *Clarté* team persevered in its internationalist aspirations and laid plans for expansion in the political, economic and artistic spheres by the introduction of foreign correspondents.[20]

One of the abiding principles of *Clarté*, and one particularly in evidence during Barbusse's editorship, was its defence of that revolutionary nation 'qui, jeune, courageuse et libératrice, dresse son geste de lumière à l'Orient'.[21] Readers were informed not only of the political and economic practices of the Soviet Union and of the systematic attempts made by internal and foreign enemies to sabotage them but, through articles by Lunacharsky (the Soviet Union's 'Commissar for Enlightenment') were kept in touch with the literary and cultural life of the new régime.[22] And in all that *Clarté* published on the subject of the Soviet Union was expressed the determination of Barbusse and his associates to convince the French public of the need to 'défendre par tous les moyens la Russie socialiste'.[23] When the fifth anniversary of the October Revolution came around, *Clarté* celebrated the event in a special issue[24] (containing a letter from Lenin) and Barbusse proudly and solemnly declared: 'que tous les exploités de l'univers aient le culte de cette date dont l'anniversaire est déjà revenu cinq fois. C'est celle du début laborieux et martyrisé, mais éclatant et invincible de l'Ère du Prolétariat'.[25]

Barbusse's sympathy for the Soviet Union's rupture with an 'historically outmoded' apparatus of national and international oppression was shared by Romain Rolland who, announcing the death of the old ideal of the national fatherland, called upon France as early as May 1917 to 'remettre sa montre à l'heure . . . l'Europe travaille à des organisations nouvelles, comme ces "Soviets" de Russie, noyau d'une Internationale des peuples'.[26] Whilst condemning revolutionary violence,[27] Rolland nonetheless saw it as his duty from the very outset to defend the Russian Revolution, and its 'great architect' Lenin, against their detractors.[28] If opposition to revolutionary violence made for a certain ambivalence in Rolland's attitude to the Soviet Union, he was clear and uncompromising in his denunciation of 'le blocus affameur, l'écrasement de la Révolution russe par la coalition des bourgeoisies de l'Europe, alliées, germaniques et neutres'.[29] The hatred directed against him by the reactionary press he considered his honour, merit and pride and the measure of the services that he rendered to the Soviet Union.[30] That the Soviet authorities shared this view was demonstrated by their endorsement of his election in June 1918 to the Academy of Social Sciences in Moscow.[31]

Rolland's sympathy for the Soviet Union, like Barbusse's, went hand in hand with his support for the revolutionary wing of the socialist movement[32] and with his open hostility to the 'socialistes nationaux', guilty in his eyes of sacrificing 'la foi internationale et le sang des millions d'hommes, prenant avec impudence la direction de la guerre, et se faisant payer chèrement un tel concours par les conservateurs'.[33] Rolland's critique

62

of social-democracy—'le socialisme national'—was, like his denunciation of all 'national ideologies', international in scope.
When, for example, German social-democracy participated in
the suppression of the revolutionary uprising in Germany early in
1919, Rolland denounced its treachery, and the treachery of
social-democracy in general, whilst at the same time paying
tribute to those internationalists, like Luxemburg and
Liebknecht, who had perished.[34] His outspoken defence of the
international revolutionary movement earned him the respect of
those most deeply involved in its promotion.[35]

The fact that Rolland was considered by revolutionary socialists (Bolsheviks included) to be the enemy of capitalism and the
ally of the proletariat made him an obvious candidate for
inclusion in Barbusse's *Clarté* group. A *rapprochement*, actively
pursued by Barbusse, proved however to be abortive,[36] largely
through Rolland's continued insistence on remaining an 'esprit
indépendant'. This attitude which, during the war, was the
hallmark of Rolland's defence of the rights of 'Reason' and
'Justice', and to which tribute was paid at the time by revolutionary socialists[37] was, after the armistice, to frustrate Barbusse in
his efforts to secure Rolland's participation in collective activity
both with *Clarté* and with the left-opposition in the Socialist
Party. Indeed, while Barbusse, Vaillant-Couturier and Lefebvre
were, in collaboration with the left-opposition, speaking about
'real man', 'concrete man' and in the concreteness of these words
referring to the image of man whose realization they called for in
socialism, Rolland continued, in his worship of the 'esprit
indépendant', to deify 'L'Homme abstrait'. Describing this period in *Quinze ans de combat* (1935) Rolland wrote of himself:

> Il apprenait, à ses dépens, que la liberté de l'esprit n'existait pas
> plus en fait que les autres libertés abstraites, dont lui avait fait don
> la Déclaration des Droits de l'Homme abstrait, patenté par la
> Révolution bourgeoise . . . Il s'obstina, pendant des années, à
> défendre cette *liberté abstraite de l'esprit*, sans prendre garde que,
> pour que ce fantôme prît substance, il fallait d'abord lui conquérir,
> lui labourer le terrain où l'idée-plante s'enracinât . . . Il persistait
> à revendiquer par l'arbre-liberté, le droit de ne pas dépendre de ce
> champ de labour—autant dire: de demeurer les racines en l'air
> . . . *Dans son entêtement à garder* [*ses idées*], *il ne s'aperçoit pas
> que ce qu'il serre contre sa poitrine, ce sont beaucoup moins des*

idées que des mots: la noix est vide, il ne tient plus que la coque. Où donc l'amande a-t-elle passé?[38]

The pursuit of an abstract object ('la coque') as opposed to the real object ('l'amande') whose content was to be found in *reality* —in society—was also, at this time, characteristic of Rolland's attitude towards the Soviet Union. For example, although he defended the Soviet Union against its imperialist aggressors and reactionary detractors he appears to have judged the Russian Revolution only from the moral point of view. In his article 'Devant la Révolution Russe' (1918)[39] he conveys the impression that he attached little or no importance to the revolutionary theory and practice of the Bolsheviks or to the economic necessity to be achieved. In this sense (and in marked contrast to the *Clarté* group) his support for the Bolsheviks, like his denunciation of imperialism, derived from a generous but abstract and speculative humanism. And so, oblivious to Lenin's confrontation with imperialism in the *concrete* of the Russian situation, that 'current situation' which political action (itself defined by the current situation) was to transform between February and October 1917, Rolland, with an eye on 'Eternity',[40] could only express his regret that revolutionary violence should have tarnished noble intentions. Rolland was himself, some years later, to reflect upon his somewhat heady detachment in the crucial period following the Russian Revolution. He wrote: 'en ces années critiques où la Révolution livrait en URSS sa lutte à mort . . . [je me fis] l'apôtre et le martyr du refus de l'esprit à la fatalité de la violence'.[41] Rolland's sympathy for the Soviet Union in its early years was, therefore, not strictly political in nature, despite his obvious hostility to capitalism and imperialism. If he welcomed the October Revolution it was because he saw it as a salutary brake on a civilization burning itself up and because he glimpsed, in the heroic dedication and vitality of the Russian people, the promise of a restoration of those 'valeurs éternelles'—'Humanité', 'Liberté'—which the war had done so much to dethrone.[42] It was this idealism,[43] suppressing in its scope the concept of class-struggle, which distinguished Rolland's attitude towards the Soviet Union and the East from that of revolutionary socialists, and which, between 1921 and 1923, was to involve him in a dispute with Barbusse and *Clarté*.

On 26 November 1921, in an article published in *L'Humanité* and entitled 'Clarté', Barbusse—with Rolland doubtless in mind—attempted to demonstrate how *Clarté*'s attitude towards society differed fundamentally from that of 'pacifists', 'anarchists' and 'reformists'. Unlike 'pacifists' who supported and advocated peace as an absolute and eternal principle in isolation from social and historical formations, 'anarchists' who knew what they did not want without being able to articulate what they wanted, and 'reformists' whose theory of gradualism was the ointment for capitalism's every sore, Barbusse and his associates expressed their solidarity with the revolutionary proletariat, alone capable of ending wars (by abolishing classes) and of building a new and just society in which social ownership of the means of production would replace private ownership. In this fundamental economic and political task *Clarté*, Barbusse emphasized, had no intention, nor indeed did it have the pretention, to replace or even to speak for the organization of the working class. It intended only to lend practical support to the revolutionary Party by attempting to develop consciousness of the need for new social relations in an area of the 'superstructure' dominated by the 'ruling class', which the Party could not for the moment hope to penetrate. Here, through the propagation of an idea, wrote Barbusse, *Clarté* could play its part in the downfall of the existing system: 'c'est par la vulgarisation de la notion intelligente des réalités que la révolution universelle deviendra possible'.

It was specifically to combat the 'intellectual Bolshevism' of *Clarté* and of all doctrines which spurned the classic, reasoned, nationalist sentiment that the Manifesto 'Pour un parti de l'Intelligence' (published on 19 July 1919) proposed the organization of an intellectual federation of Europe under the aegis of victorious France, the guardian of all civilization.[44] The document, drawn up by Henri Massis, held the Catholic Church to be the only legitimate moral power and, whilst stressing the need to reform man's spiritual being, made no secret of its political contempt for plutocracy which it dismissed as the party of ignorance. It concluded with a statement of its *raison d'être*: 'le parti de l'intelligence, c'est celui que nous prétendons servir pour l'opposer [au] bolchevisme'.

The enthusiasm with which the Manifesto was greeted by an impressive cross-section of the conservative intelligentsia encou-

65

raged Massis to seek out new recruits beyond the ranks of acknowledged Royalists. When his enterprise was given financial backing by Charles Maurras and Jacques Maritain he founded *La Revue universelle* with himself as editor and Jacques Bainville as publisher. The first number appeared on 1 April 1920 and, celebrating the eternal supremacy of French thought, proposed to gather all who took sides against destruction, all opposed to the international of revolution.

Most of *La Revue universelle*'s opposition to revolution was concentrated in articles on the Soviet Union. In Russia, 'royaume de l'Antéchrist',[45] human flesh, one learns, is sold in the market place when victims have not previously been plunged into sacks of vermin or had their vital parts removed by the Petersburg Institute of experimental medicine.[46] In Russia the sacred altar of property and capital has been desecrated[47] and the civilized works of Peter the Great reduced to the rubble of a prison yard.[48] Against this backdrop of desolation stands the unholy figure of Lenin, 'une âme béante sur le néant',[49] a coward, a liar and an agent of Germany[50]—when not accused of being its paymaster.[51] If unable to decide on whether the Soviet Union was master or servant of Germany, *La Revue universelle* was at least in no doubt that it was a product of Jewish ingenuity.[52] It provided evidence for this claim in the form of 'La Confession d'un bolchevik', published in May 1922,[53] and purported to have come to *La Revue universelle* from 'un membre de l'extrême gauche nationaliste du parti des Soviets'[54] by way of a Western Communist.

Never a periodical to conceal from its readers the awesome dimensions of the anti-European conspiracy, *La Revue universelle*, in articles like 'La Menace de l'Asie',[55] 'Le mouvement asiatique et l'Europe',[56] 'Le Nationalisme asiatique',[57] 'Les Révolutions contre l'Europe',[58] and 'Les Soviets et l'Orient',[59] examined Bolshevism's Asian connection.

If *La Revue universelle* was always ready to publicize the horrors of 'Judeo-Soviet' rule, to expose its proletarian enthusiasts[60] and denounce its Asian neophytes, it was no less prepared to identify and applaud those institutions and associations whose activities and ideals it held to be compatible with its own. One such institution, in whose ideal Bainville claimed to have glimpsed the divine—and whose praises René Johannet never tired of singing—was capitalism.[61] Another was Fascism whose bourgeois militancy *La Revue universelle* hoped France might be persuaded to adopt. Salvation offered no other course and the sword and the crucifix, Johannet imagined, recognized no greater cause.[62] Mussolini had shown what courage and a revolution of deeds could achieve. The current of history was turning and the future, wrote Johannet, belonged to the bourgeoisie, for it had proved that it was even better able than the proletariat to impose a dictatorship:

> Le retournement bulgare, le coup fasciste, l'aventure espagnole mettent de plus en plus en lumière les immenses possibilités bourgeoises du monde contemporain . . . Le point capital de l'affaire réside dans l'expropriation du champ démocratique et parlementaire par des bourgeois, qui en ont assez de voir leur pays saccagé par les fourriers de l'anarchie[63] . . . Mussolini élève la voix, fait régner la terreur dans les quartiers communistes; Mussolini bafoue la Chambre, le parlementarisme et la liberté; bref Mussolini dit: Je veux. Obéissez. Que répond l'électeur? Il répond: Présent![64] . . . Le fascisme qui a renouvelé l'Italie renouvellera-t-il le monde?[65]

Johannet greeted Fascism not, as would Brasillach, as an emotional surge with only the vaguest hint of direction and purpose,[66] but as a consciously-directed movement of counter-revolution. *L'Humanité* did not, of course, share Johannet's sympathies but it had no quarrel with his definition of Fascism. On 31 October 1922 Paul Louis wrote in *L'Humanité*:

> Quelles sont les caractéristiques de cette dictature fasciste? Il faut fixer ce moment d'histoire. Elle est bourgeoise: les grands industriels, les grands agrariens sont derrière elle et l'envisagent comme leur suprême recours. Elle est l'arme de la classe possédante contre le prolétariat, et cette classe possédante, qui a vécu tant de mois dans la crainte d'une révolution ouvrière, retrouve aujourd'hui sa sérénité dans la contre-révolution préventive . . . Cette dictature est militaire . . . Enfin, cette dictature sera pénétrée d'esprit nationaliste, chauvin, impérialiste.

And on 1 November 1922 in *L'Humanité*, Marcel Cachin defined Fascists as:

> Les hommes du capitalisme impérialiste, parfaitement conscients des nécessités historiques imposées par sa conservation. Pour

tenter d'empêcher le développement des idées de la révolution sociale, ils ont réalisé leur révolution blanche.

For all his professed devotion to the cause of French and European Intelligence—'la vérité existe, la vérité est représentée dans le monde par l'Europe, c'est-à-dire la culture gréco-latine [et] la religion chrétienne'[67]—Johannet knew the type of society he wanted as surely as did Cachin and Louis. So did the other members of Massis's *La Revue universelle*. Their defence of the Graeco-Latin and Christian West was more than a spiritual barrier against the dark dissatisfactions of a hostile world; it was an authoritarian political philosophy rooted in a social and economic system whose disappearance they desperately feared.

Romain Rolland's plea on behalf of the 'esprit indépendant' which refused to submit to the tyranny of forces—whether of Right or Left—was reiterated in 1920 in the form of a novel entitled *Clérambault*, the chronicle of one man's struggle with his conscience during the war. Clérambault is a successful writer and gentle humanitarian who, in the hysteria of war, uses his pen to cement the union of the national spirit with the cause of humanity. Following his son's death at the front he begins to question the justice of the cause which he has espoused. His conclusion is that the professed intentions of the participants to save a civilization in which love, and not violence, is triumphant, is a cynical lie. His efforts to mitigate the abuses and evils of the conflict quickly earn him the reputation of being a pacifist, a defeatist and a traitor. The hostility aroused by his denunciation of the sanctification of suffering culminates in his not-unexpected assassination on Good Friday. The symbolic significance of his martyrdom is clear: it is the sacrifice freely made for the good of all and in the certain knowledge of the resurrection and ultimate triumph of 'Justice' and 'Truth'.

Clérambault was hailed as 'une ontologie de l'individualisme pur'[68] and quickly became, as Rolland himself later wrote, 'un Évangile, un point de rassemblement pour les Objecteurs de conscience français'.[69] It was, however, for the very same reasons vigorously criticized by Jean Bernier of *Clarté*.[70] Bernier contended that life for Rolland was a cruel and meaningless phenomenon stricken with insane violence: 'la violence triomphe sous le régime capitaliste, elle triomphera sous le régime communiste . . . aucun idéal formulé ne se propose à lui. L'idéal révolutionnaire est souillé de violence'.[71] Since Rolland, Bernier wrote, had no faith in an after-life he was unable to embrace religion. And yet, like a redundant mystic still craving an Absolute, he was driven to seek it in man (despite his incurably pessimistic view of him), and found it not in present man but in necessity's *fait accompli*: future man. So it was with his followers who, alienated from the present and from faith in life everlasting, trusted in the future. They hoped and would continue to hope, for this hope in so far as it existed was their sacred ideal, presaging in the realization of its own future the miraculous transformation of the world:

> En attendant il faut donc être bon, être juste, rayonner doucement, chacun dans sa sphère étroite, travailler ainsi, puisque leur Dieu sera les hommes (les hommes transformés) à hâter l'ineffable règne. Ils seront les fourriers de leur Dieu, ils lui prépareront le cantonnement 'Terre' ou 'Espèce humaine'. Le cantonnement fait, le Dieu viendra et ce sera l'âge d'or.[72]

If man was to be restored his nature, alienated in the forms of finance, imperialism and gods, it was not enough, suggested Bernier, to speak of him—as did the 'Rollandists'—in the future anterior with his essence somehow already mystically reappropriated. Only by the politics of *practical* reappropriation, by revolution, could man hope to negate his own negation and recover his essence. Revolution was, therefore, the very practice of the logic immanent in alienation, a logic, Bernier asserted, lost on Rolland who sat 'dans son cabinet de travail, abstrait dans son fauteuil'.[73]

The issues raised by Bernier were brought up again, though less abrasively, by Henri Barbusse in an article in *Clarté* entitled 'L'autre moitié du devoir. A propos du Rollandisme'.[74] Barbusse addressed himself to those left-wing intellectuals who prided themselves on being disciples of Rolland, but who effectively, Barbusse claimed, 'usent et abusent de l'autorité et de l'exemple de Romain Rolland'. Rolland's merit was to have risen above the passions that produced and intensified the war to proclaim with great dignity 'l'indépendance de l'esprit et les droits de la pensée'. His courageous example was, however, not sufficient in itself to prevent future conflicts for, as Barbusse stressed, 'les causes sociales de la guerre subsistent intactes'. Words alone were powerless to halt those forces which used the people as instruments of their greed. In this respect the role of 'pure moralists' was, Barbusse asserted, negative. They arrived, and could only arrive, after the event, after wars had broken out, become entrenched and begun devouring their children:

> Les entrepreneurs des affaires universelles se rient de cette cérémonie morale, et ne se dérangent pas de leurs occupations; les profiteurs continuent à s'enrichir sur la surface de la terre vivante; la diplomatie et les parlements—police secrète et police ouverte des capitalistes— continuent à rattacher solidement entre eux, par des traités et des lois, les intérêts de la Richesse à travers la chair humaine.

Moral outrage, therefore, however nobly formulated, remained unarmed unless allied to the principle of constructive intent. This principle Barbusse defined as the attempt to 'édifier contre l'ordre social qui est la vérité de fait, un ordre idéal qui n'est tout d'abord que vérité théorique, œuvre spirituelle, comme une science'. To find the content of this new order one had to *turn to society* and undertake an analysis of the ensemble of the social relations. This positive effort to get down to the concrete problems themselves, that is, to their knowledge and to use that knowledge to produce society's transformation was, Barbusse insisted, shunned by the Rollandists be it through aversion to politics, fear of violence or the hope of discovering another path to humanity's restoration. All such reservations were dismissed by Barbusse as puerile. Politics, he claimed, was a method of 'realization' in a domain in which all things awaited realization and where 'pure spirit' evaporated unless concretized. In this connection he defended socialism's constructive action based on 'cette géométrie sociale révolutionnaire' whose fundamental laws, like those of the applied sciences, were error-free. *Collective* and disciplined, this action alone could produce, out of the economic roots from which it sprang, that *realized* ideal to which humanity aspired. It was the only solution; there could be no other. The 'miraculous' solution of the Rolland- ists whereby, after centuries of *individual* moral perfectibility, humanity would perhaps have recovered itself, was nothing short of a capitulation towards illusion.

As for (revolutionary) violence Barbusse considered it a much distorted concept. Violent action was not a *sine qua non* of socialist

70

advance but, he stressed, it had to be recognized that social justice—realized reason[75]—could be achieved only if those who demanded it were prepared to implement and enforce it by assuming and exercising political power. The type of violence necessary to the assumption of power could not be determined in advance. What was certain was that 'violence' ('constraint') was in itself a neutral element which could be qualified as 'good' or 'evil' only according to the use to which it was put. For example, even the gentlest humanitarians admitted of the need to 'constrain' common-law criminals. And yet these same gentlemen, when confronted by the criminal activities of a military, imperialist régime, retreated into their 'ivory towers' with nothing to offer in the way of 'constraint' but their own moral outrage. Failing to recognize that institutionalized barbarity would not yield to the imprecation of pure spirit they denounced all—oppressor and oppressed—who courted 'violence' in pursuit of their aims. As far as the 'violence' of revolutionaries was concerned Barbusse replied as follows:

> La violence n'a ici pour but que de désarmer. Son intervention n'est, à tous égards dans l'ensemble de la conception sociale révolutionnaire . . . qu'un détail et qu'un détail provisoire.

Since for Barbusse an ideal had meaning only in so far as it contained the promise of its own practical realization, the servants of pure spirit—the Rollandists—remained 'réformateurs négatifs', indistinguishable, whatever they said or wished, from conservatives. Victims of the disillusionment created by the failure of socialists to prevent the war, they remained rooted in the past, impervious to the exigencies of the present, unable to realize the future, and 'independent'. Barbusse concluded by reminding the Rollandists of their duty: 'la pensée humaine doit se rendre indépendante pour fructifier en actes, et non pas pour être indépendante. Les "rollandistes" n'ont accompli que la première moitié de leur devoir d'hommes de pensée'.

Rolland's reply on 14 December, after registering preliminary courtesies, established its author's clear intention to speak not for the Rollandists but for himself and himself alone.[76] He was distressed that his unwillingness to join the *Clarté* project should have been interpreted as confirmation of his tendency towards 'detachment'. His writings, wrought of a world's suffering, were,

71

he claimed, living testimony to the contrary. If he had not joined *Clarté* it was because he disagreed with the excessive rationalization of men who claimed to be able to reduce 'l'énigme de l'évolution humaine à un problème de géométrie Euclidienne'. As for Barbusse's contention that socialism's 'géométrie sociale' was as immune from error as the fundamental laws of science, Rolland replied that the comparison was unfortunate given scientists' reluctance to affirm any such immunity. In any event Rolland did not share Barbusse's faith in the 'doctrine of neo-Marxist Communism' which he regarded as 'peu conforme au véritable progrès humain' and 'entachée d'erreurs funestes et cruelles'. Although he held the bourgeois coalition of American and European governments largely responsible for the errors committed by the Soviet régime he nonetheless accused the Soviet leadership of having sacrificed the loftiest moral values, 'Humanity', 'Liberty' and 'Truth', upon the altar of *raison d'État*. He had no intention, he stressed, of sanctifying militarism, police terror and bloody force because they were the instruments of a Communist dictatorship instead of those of a plutocracy. Violence was not, as Barbusse claimed, merely a 'detail'—a formula no doubt just as acceptable to any bourgeois Minister of Defence—it was a conditioner[77] whose human object responded to its every impulse. In this respect, wrote Rolland, the argument that the end justified the means was fundamentally false:

> Car la fin (si rarement atteinte et toujours incomplètement) ne modifie que les rapports extérieurs entre les hommes. Mais les moyens modèlent l'esprit de l'homme, ou selon le rythme de justice, ou selon le rythme de violence. Et si c'est selon ce dernier, aucune forme de gouvernement n'empêchera jamais l'oppression des faibles par les forts.

It was for this reason that Rolland considered it essential to defend 'moral values' (especially since the human spirit was most susceptible to change during periods of radical social transformation). The article closed with Rolland's reiteration that he would not serve any instrumentalities which, though bursting the chains of past oppressions, threatened to impose new fetters. His final words, borrowed from Schiller, were 'contre *tous* les tyrans'.

Barbusse replied to Rolland in *Clarté* on 1 February 1922.[78] On this occasion Barbusse addressed his comments directly to

Rolland whom he chided for having defended certain Rollandist notions which Barbusse had attacked in his previous letter as distortions of Rolland's outlook. By espousing 'Rollandism' Rolland had made himself the instrument, claimed Barbusse, of a system of (bourgeois) thought which would use any stick to beat its real enemy. Apart from this important consideration Rolland had not, continued Barbusse, answered the fundamental criticism, namely that Rollandism offered no real, practical, viable solution to human misfortune. Indeed, by claiming that Communism would be the substitution of one form of 'tyranny' for another, Rollandism was effectively seeking to deliver itself, through fear of an unrealized future, from today's necessity to think the *practical* termination of *present* tyranny.[79]

Barbusse restated his belief in the 'soundness' of the laws of applied science. What was fragile and problematical, he contended, were not the steadfast links which experimental science forged between phenomena, but the metaphysical hypotheses which it was prepared to entertain for want of closer examination. So it was in the field of social forms. While conceding that the theory and practice of Communism had not yet been perfected he nonetheless felt that Rolland's superficial analysis obscured the latent strength of the doctrine, particularly its systematic, international, and dynamic character—something which the directionless and defensive Rollandists could not offer. As for the errors of 'certains communistes maladroits', Barbusse claimed that they were either local or momentary and did not in themselves invalidate the doctrine. Barbusse concluded his defence by attacking Rolland for his failure to extend his discussion of violence to those Western imperialist countries who were actively sabotaging Soviet efforts. The fact was that the Soviet Union was battling for survival, abandoned of the support of those whose indifference and disenchantment could only retard the gigantic experiment in social reconstruction:

> Vous avez beau consentir à charger d'une certaine part de responsabilité la scélératesse des gouvernements bourgeois, l'arrachement sanglant d'un pays hors de la vieille oppression où sont encore incrustés les autres ne vous inspire que des variations sur le mot de 'violence' et, en définitive, que des critiques, sœurs de celles des anarchistes et des bourgeois.

Rolland's reply (2 February 1922) was just as forceful and frank as had been Barbusse's.[80] Whilst claiming the right to 'rester dans la

Révolution' Rolland refused to subscribe to the doctrine of class-struggle which he defined as 'chauvinisme prolétarien' and dismissed as no less invidious than 'national chauvinism'. He would not, he wrote, abandon his independence as an 'homme de pensée' to Communist dogmatism, to 'pensée de parti' which he compared in its narrowness to 'pensée d'Église', 'pensée de caste'.[81] Neither could he share Barbusse's optimism in a proletarian future. He regarded the masses as essentially selfish and apathetic with a potential only for destruction.[82] The West, bled white through war, could not afford to suffer further injury through revolution and could not, even if it desired, summon up the tremendous human vitality necessary to ensure revolutionary success. Returning to the theme of violence Rolland accused Barbusse of opposing force with force, a method whose only outcome would be the destruction of both sides. He proposed another method, that of Mahatma Gandhi's 'non-acceptation', which he defined as the refusal of the *individual* to comply with the dictates of 'l'État criminel'. To Barbusse's call for mass political action Rolland thus replied with an appeal to a unique force in which no-one was allied except to himself: 'la conscience individuelle, seule, religieusement seule et nue,—conscience, levier du monde'.[83] Rolland reiterated his determination to serve no cause save that of 'Truth' and 'Freedom'—even at the expense of the Revolution itself[84]—in whose name he once again defended the free individual conscience and its 'sens quasi-mystique du divin'.

(In a postscript Rolland returned to Barbusse's 'géométrie sociale' and, referring to Einstein's theories and their impact upon reality, declared that 'il n'y a pas de lois dans la nature . . . la loi vient de nous, de nous seuls'.[85])

Rolland's appeal to men of free individual conscience was to receive an immediate response, in the main favourable, from a score of intellectuals whose statements were published in *L'Art libre* in March and April of 1922.[86] The views of the pro-Rolland intellectuals revealed an almost unanimous opposition to violence, commitment to individualism and pluralism, a belief in personal transformations, acceptance of solitude as the proper sphere for the intellectual, and above all a concept of internationalism which transcended class interests. The most severely critical response to Rolland's appeal came from Marcel Martinet who published an article entitled 'Les Intellectuels et la révolution' in *L'Humanité* on 25 March. Here Martinet dismissed Rolland's concept of independence as 'vaniteuse retraite' and 'de la bouillie pour les chats'. Defenders of 'Independence of the Mind' had been repetitious and far too generous towards the 'imbecile and cruel social régime', while at the same time brimming with complaints about proletarian demagoguery. That such spirits should have fled the proletarian cause was, according to Martinet, neither a surprise nor a tragic loss. Their like would return and grudgingly limp along in the train of the Revolution just as today they whined and moaned in the service of bourgeois tyranny. Martinet did not attempt in any systematic manner to dispute the moral objections of the intellectual; he spat on them: 'tant pis pour nos scrupules! Depuis que tant d'hommes agonisent et meurent pour nous [en URSS] nous pouvons jeter, dans la solidarité du bloc révolutionnaire, jusqu'aux scrupules de notre honneur!'

Martinet's tirade was answered by Rolland in his 'Lettres aux amis communistes',[87] in which, after restating his position *vis-à-vis* revolutionary violence and 'Independence of the Mind', he broached the subject of the French Revolution and evaluated its impact upon intellectuals like Wordsworth, Coleridge and Schiller. Rolland's conclusion was that the lesson which history taught was that a revolutionary movement which scorned the 'forces of the heart' was destined to alienate the best of liberal thinkers and so deprive itself of those 'grandes forces morales dont le rayonnement sur la masse des esprits est immense'.[88] Rolland's claim that European intellectuals such as Coleridge and Wordsworth had deserted the French Revolution because of its excesses was challenged by the famous historian of the French Revolution, Albert Mathiez, in an article entitled 'L'Élite européenne et la Terreur' published in *Clarté* on 1 June 1922.

An ideological debate in which History was now called upon to judge the present and plot the future, and in which passions were clearly inflamed, seemed a far cry indeed from the measured tone and relative specificity of the original exchange between Rolland and Barbusse. One writer had already attempted to narrow the area of disagreement by reducing the dispute to its essentials. In an article entitled 'A propos du Manifeste Communiste',[89] Amédée Dunois claimed that a Marxist instructed in the thought of the Communist Manifesto would have little difficulty in discovering the solution to the dispute. Barbusse's slogan, wrote Dunois, was Revolution; Rolland's was Freedom and Martinet's was Freedom through Revolution. A Marxist's, continued Dunois, would be Proletariat: solidarity with the proletariat in its historic mission to realize the Revolution and Freedom. The choice was clear: intellectual and heart-felt solidarity with the proletariat or *de facto* solidarity with the bourgeoisie. He asked Rolland to declare what lay beneath his use of the equivocal term 'Freedom': Freedom with the proletariat or Freedom with the bourgeoisie, Freedom with the great Russian Revolution or Freedom with the dishonourable victors of Versailles? Some years later Rolland was to acknowledge that

> Dunois touchait la note juste. Il eût pu ajouter—ce que l'expérience m'a, depuis, fait reconnaître,—qu'en dehors de la cause pour laquelle combat le prolétariat, toute 'liberté' est un leurre. Mais je lui répondais: *Avec le prolétariat, toutes les fois qu'il respectera la vérité et l'humanité! Contre le prolétariat, toutes les fois qu'il les violera!* [90]

If Rolland could, with hindsight, confess to having defended 'Freedom' in the abstract, at the time of his controversy with Barbusse he showed no signs of abandoning that position for a materialist one. Indeed, he had not spent the war years defending his concept of freedom against the pressures of State violence in order to surrender it immediately afterwards to the devotees of revolutionary violence. He continued, after the armistice, to tread the path of pacifism illuminated now by 'l'étoile lointaine de Gandhi, dont [il allait] être le réflecteur de la lumière sur l'Occident'.[91]

Rolland's interest in Gandhi was part of a wider interest in the Orient going back to his days at the École Normale. It was also closely related to his belief that Europe, consumed by flames of violence and driven by materialism, was rushing headlong towards the abyss. In the early months of the war he expressed the opinion that Europe was committing suicide and that Asia was ready to snatch from her her living heritage.[92] The prospect of Asian domination seemed to him all the more possible because of the threatening attitude of Japan, whose insatiable militarism prompted him to dub it the Prussia of the Far East.[93] Within fifty years, he wrote in May 1918, mysterious and ancient Asia will have clasped us in a spiritual and physical embrace.[94] Rolland's feelings about this possibility were mixed. If at times dismayed by the prospect he found it no more alarming—indeed probably less—than the *de facto* domination of Asia by European imperialism. When the Hindu luminary, Rabindranath Tagore, launched a swingeing attack on the 'cannibalistic tendencies' of Western civilization in a lecture to the Imperial University of Tokyo in 1916, Rolland was quick to record his approval.[95] At this time Rolland believed that the West was certain to pay a heavy toll for its predatory policies.

The outbreak of the Moroccan war convinced him that the confrontation between Europe and Asia was imminent. In a reply to Barbusse in 1925, Rolland described the Moroccan war as ruinous for France and a blunder even from a narrowly national point of view. If he had in the past expressed concern for Europe's survival, it was, he wrote, because he had dared to articulate what was there for all eyes to see. The brutal and greedy imperialism of European nations, which had long threatened to provoke a massive reaction from African and Asian peoples, was at last reaping the whirlwind. In his warning Rolland included the Communists, who, he claimed, saw only the destruction of imperialism in the awakening of the East, but the forces thus aroused would not distinguish between European imperialism and European Communism; the Asian steamroller would one day flatten Moscow's Bolshevism: 'la guerre du Maroc achève d'unifier ces masses tourbillonnantes et dérive vers l'Occident la fureur du guêpier'.[96]

In addition to recording approval of Tagore's denunciation of European civilization, Rolland was also pleased to note that the Hindu philosopher had, in the same lecture, expressed ideas about the unity of mankind which were not unlike his own: the war was merely the negative side of a great movement of action and reaction, the darkling dawn from which would spring unity, peace and light. From the crisis in a materialistic civilization would emerge an era of unprecedented moral and spiritual development.[97] Rolland's admiration for Tagore—first expressed in a letter to Sofia Bertolini in December 1913[98]—was reciprocated by Tagore who, in May 1922, wrote to Kalidas Nag that men like Romain Rolland had accepted voluntarily the career of penance and purification (Tapasyâ) for the welfare of Humanity as a whole. For such men, wrote Tagore, there was no distinction between their country and the Universe. That was why they were being hounded by the champions of patriotism and nationalism. Expressing his deepest sympathy for Rolland and his small band of colleagues Tagore concluded that the ultimate victory would be theirs for they were on the side of Truth wherein was real Liberty and true Emancipation.[99]

Rolland viewed contact with Tagore as not only enriching for himself but as a means of contributing to the union of the two halves of humanity.[100] As Tagore tended the spirit of Asia so did Rolland hope to lead the thinking of his own race on to plateaux as yet unglimpsed by his countrymen.[101] Rolland believed that he had been entrusted with a mission whose end would be the union of Europe and Asia.[102] In a letter to Tagore dated August 1919 he wrote:

> Après la catastrophe de cette honteuse guerre mondiale, qui a marqué la faillite de l'Europe, il est devenu évident que l'Europe ne suffit plus à se sauver soi-même. Sa pensée a besoin de la pensée d'Asie, comme celle-ci a profit à s'appuyer sur la pensée d'Europe. Ce sont les deux hémisphères du cerveau de l'humanité. Si l'un est paralysé, le corps dégénère.[103]

Considering the harmonization of the two halves of humanity to be the most noble task of mankind in the coming centuries, Rolland undertook to acquaint European readers with the best of Asiatic thought. To this end he urged Tagore to assist him in the founding of an international review, free of political bias, which would devote generous space to the thought of Asia.[104] Although the review failed to materialize, the fraternal spirit which was the inspiration for the project continued and found partial satisfaction with the founding of the monthly review *Europe*, whose first number appeared in February 1923. Its spiritual leader was Rolland and the ideal to which it aspired may be gathered from the following statement made in its first issue:

> Si l'Europe ne se ressaisit pas, elle périra. Déjà, de grandes voix prophétiques annoncent sa déchéance irrémédiable. La civilisation occidentale sent le cadavre, clame la voix la plus écoutée de l'Asie.[105]

What attracted Rolland to Tagore in particular and to Indian philosophy in general was—in marked contrast to the West's preoccupation with material progress—a conception of human progress in the spiritual sense. His interest in this aspect of human progress is brought out in his preface to Ananda Coomaraswamy's *La Danse de Çiva*.[106] Here Rolland insists that whereas India has, through the domination of a supreme and sovereign synthesis, realized the perfection of a vast collective soul, the West, dominated by cold, hard logic, has been unable to blend all the varieties and dissonances of experience into a comprehensive world-view. Total unity in its greatest perfection is what attracts Rolland to India and to Brahmin thought in particular. Not only does Brahminism contain all the other schools of Asiatic thought but it is even capable, unlike Christianity, of adjusting itself to the vast new hypotheses of modern science. Not even the cosmogony of Einstein, of stellar space, nebular spirals, boundless creations in space-time, is beyond the compass of Brahmin thought. It is with the promise of ultimate harmony that Rolland addresses the European reader:

> Je ne propose pas à des Européens d'épouser une foi de l'Asie. Je les engage seulement à goûter le bienfait de ce rythme magique, le souffle large et lent. Ils y apprendront ce dont l'âme d'Europe a le plus besoin aujourd'hui: le calme, la patience, la virile espérance, la joie sereine.[107]

Far from admitting her need of Asia, Europe has for centuries trampled it underfoot, plundered it in the name of Christ and Civilization, without once a suspicion that she was playing the part of Alaric on the ruins of Rome. But, continues Rolland, just as Rome vanquished the conquering barbarians and Greece vanquished Rome, so will India and China finally vanquish Europe: a victory for the soul. Rolland finds nothing to fear from such a victory and is pleased to note that some dedicated Europeans, mainly Germans, are already trying to open the floodgates. He singles out Herman Hesse and Count Keyserling as two of the very finest minds to have begun the spiritual crusade. More generally he praises the Germans for being the first, amongst Europeans, to have turned to Asia for 'l'aliment que leur esprit affamé ne trouvait plus à son gré en Europe'.[108]

79

Rolland's admiration for German attempts to awaken European interest in Oriental philosophy was expressed elsewhere in his writings.[109] In a letter to Tagore in April 1921 he referred the Hindu scholar to Karl Neumann's translations of Buddhist texts, and an entry in his diary in April 1923 described Hermann Hesse's *Siddharta* as one of the most profound of European works devoted to Hindu thought.[110] If dissatisfaction with the 'spirit of the West' prompted Rolland to seek new ideals in Oriental thought, the same principle, it is partly true to say, obtained in Germany. Thomas Mann has described the mood of post-war Germany in the following terms:

> The German people suffered a collapse, physical and mental, which they are a long way from having completely surmounted, such a collapse as history doubtless has never known before our time. For it is without precedent that a great civilized nation, conscious of having rendered eminent and original services to humanity should find itself one fine day in the character and position of an outcast, an *inimicus humanae naturae*, stigmatized, outlawed and abandoned by all, and to be fought to the death by a league of all civilized nations ... What followed was an unparalleled fall, a complete and unconditional capitulation, the surrender of a moral fortress that had long defended itself with clenched teeth, but that, finally, was left without the slightest power of resistance. The demoralization had no limits, it could be seen in the deep and almost fatal anxiety of a whole nation that despaired of itself, of its history, of its finest treasures, all of which, from its first origins seemed refuted and reduced to absurdity by such a result.[111]

It was in this atmosphere of demoralization and doubt that interest in the East was rekindled more strongly than ever. The discourses and parables of Chuang-Tse (translated by Martin Buber) had been favourably received in Germany, and to Chinese wisdom was added the message of ancient India—texts of Vedic and Buddhist mysticism—and Hindu influence was strengthened by the powerful impression made by Tagore's writings and visits. The effect of this movement towards the East was to raise doubts about the pre-eminence of European culture. The vogue of the subject was enhanced by the spirit of Versailles and the set-back to the Wilson programme, and Russia 'the Orient of the West' now tempted many with the example of a new human order. If we are to believe E. R. Curtius, a broad section of the educated youth in Germany, in a somewhat anarchical enthusiasm often mingled with religious aspiration, invoked the Bolshevik ideal.[112]

German interest in the East did not go unnoticed in France, as may be gathered from the attention given the subject, in the person of Primus Kayser, by Paul Morand in *Bouddha Vivant*. And Henri Massis (and *La Revue universelle*) regarded German (and French) preoccupation with the East—both metaphysical and political—as part and parcel of 'l'œuvre destructive que les intellectuels d'outre Rhin ont entreprise—depuis la fin de la guerre—pour nous *désoccidentaliser*'.[113]

There were those on the Catholic Right who whilst sharing Massis's profound sympathy for the 'esprit gréco-latin' disputed both his alarmist diagnosis of the German condition and its implications for Western culture. Jacques Benoist-Méchin, for example, in a reply to Massis's 'L'Offensive germano-asiatique contre la culture occidentale', attributes the crisis in Germany not to any frustrated ambition for spiritual conquest but to the monetary crisis. Now that the crisis has eased, the philosophical gloom has begun to lift. Spengler, writes Benoist-Méchin, has given way to Max Scheler, whose philosophy is rooted in Augustinian Platonism, and to Fritz von Unruh, whose spiritual quest is in the best traditions of *homo occidentalis*.[114]

Maurice Betz, in another reply to Massis, raises further objections to the latter's assessment of cultural tendencies in Germany.[115] Massis's claim that the doctrines of Spengler and Keyserling were born of the despair and bitterness of defeat is, writes Betz, demonstrably false: *The Decline of the West* and Keyserling's *Diary of a philosopher* are pre-war works. So too, adds Betz, are the majority of the translations of Oriental literature and philosophy. After expressing dismay at Massis's suggestion that Thomas Mann is an apostle of Spengler, Betz concludes, with evidence borrowed from a German source, that increasing numbers of German youth are turning to Catholicism for inspiration and to French Catholic writers for guidance.

If Betz hoped to disqualify Massis's case on its chronological inaccuracies he was, unfortunately, missing the point. Massis's thesis was not based upon the dating of German 'doctrinal deviations' but rather upon their existence. To this extent Betz's findings might actually be said to support Massis's interpretation: profound pessimism and 'Asiaticism' were already powerful movements in Germany before the war defeat. Massis would merely have added, not unreasonably, that such tendencies could not but have been strengthened by the physical and spiritual collapse of 1918.

Massis was not alone in interpreting Germany's movement toward the East as the expression of a destructive impulse. This 'fatal malady', though not restricted to Germany, did, some writers claimed, have its origins there, a fact which Jean Caves attempted to demonstrate in an article published in March and April of 1924 and entitled 'Le Nihilisme européen et les appels de l'Orient'.[116] Caves identified two symptoms of the will to destruction: the celebration of a philosophical honeymoon with India and a political *rapprochement* with Russia.

The first part of Caves's article concentrates on Germany's efforts in the philosophical field to purge itself of Graeco-Latin influence. Caves claims that Goethe, Schlegel, Schopenhauer and, more recently, Herman Keyserling all belong in that category of German thinkers who, whether outwardly aggressive or essentially passive, 'repoussent avec horreur ces limitations qui font les délices de la pensée grecque et de sa fille, la pensée française, de Platon et de Descartes, d'Aristote et de S. Thomas'.[117] Turning from the general to the particular, Caves examines those doctrines which have made Keyserling—and his 'School of Wisdom' in Darmstadt—the focus of an almost religious veneration. For Keyserling, writes Caves, the Westerner is a 'Gewaltmensch', an 'homme de puissance' whose unruly passions threaten his very survival. Unlike the Chinese, who believes in a pre-established harmony between man and the world, and unlike the Hindu, who sets himself apart from the world, the Westerner is involved in a determined struggle for existence. It is from this sense of struggle that the West has developed its thirst for power and conquest as well as for social change and scientific progress. The Westerner is a 'warrior' who will suffer neither authority nor compromise. He must conquer or die—a state of mind which was to be powerfully expressed in Malraux's Garine. The 'Gewaltmensch' has no inner life since all his time is taken up in struggle: with nature, other men, or in the form of international competition. If Europe, brought to her knees by the idol of 'puissance', is to rise once more she must learn, Keyserling insists, that salvation is not the inevitable product of material progress but the gift of spiritual elevation. However, writes Caves, if Keyserling is convinced of the bankruptcy of Western values he does not on that account urge the West to pursue the Orient's 'rêve stérile de l'Infini'. What is required is a healthy fusion of the best elements of both civilizations, an ideal to which Keyserling has dedicated his 'School of Wisdom'.

What Caves, like Massis, finds disturbing about the ideals of the 'Asiaticists' is the suggestion that the spiritual life of Europe, nourished for so long by Graeco-Latin roots, requires the fresh inspiration of a new source. However, if Caves (like Massis) is ostensibly concerned with the philosophical or cultural aspects of the 'Asiatic' threat, he does not fail to record his political interest. This, effectively, is what he does when, in the second part of his article, he considers the case of Russia.

Supporting his thesis with examples drawn from Tolstoy and Dostoyevsky, Caves—like Massis—claims that the term nihilism is not only the governing characteristic of the Russian soul but the dominant feature of Soviet politics. He sees Lenin as the product of that compulsive will to destruction embodied in Dostoyevsky's Stepanovitch. However, adds Caves, responsibility for the modern Russian phenomenon lies with Europe: it is her materialism which sowed the seeds of death and perversion harvested by Russia, it is from her that Lenin inherited his willingness, like Stepanovitch's before him, to sacrifice a hundred million souls in the name of an ideal. Russia has merely hatched and brought to maturity those evils, spawned by the West, of which Tolstoy had warned his countrymen: the entombment of intelligence, the worship of finance, the consecration of the machine and the celebration of class-struggle. Similar warnings are today being issued by Tagore, Gandhi and, in China, the Confucian Kou Houng-Ming who has declared that if Europeans burst the 'reservoir of peace' that is China 'leur entreprise se retournera contre eux, car ils auront déchaîné du même coup 400 millions d'hommes jusqu'ici retenus par leurs coutumes, leur religion et qui, sous la conduite du Japon, pourraient devenir redoutables pour le reste du monde'.[118]

If Caves, like Massis, reveals a certain antipathy for Western materialism, he carefully avoids any endorsement of 'Asiaticism'

83

since, in his estimation, it is, like Bolshevism, allied to German metaphysics. He finds evidence of this disturbing phenomenon in E. R. Curtius's assessment, in the *Neue Deutsche Rundschau* (1921), of the new cultural orientation of Germany:

> La France se sentait le porte-flambeau de l'Europe. Quand aujourd'hui elle continue à vouloir jouer ce rôle, elle ne trouve plus chez nous d'auditoire. La jeune Allemagne regarde l'Est, tournant le dos à l'Occident. Ceci indique un revirement décisif. Les esprits se tournent vers la Russie, et au-delà vers les Indes et la Chine. Les sympathies que le bolchevisme rencontre auprès de notre jeunesse ne sont que l'indice extérieur de ce revirement. L'attitude qu'on a vis-à-vis du bolchevisme n'est pas ce qui importe. Ce qui importe c'est qu'elle est l'expression d'un changement de direction de l'intelligence occidentale.[119]

With its hopes of spiritual hegemony dashed and spurning the cultural leadership of France, Germany has joined Russia in 'la danse Macabre' whose 'Sirens of death' are today summoning Europe to destruction.[120] Traditional values are disintegrating and Europe's Graeco-Latin pedestal is turning to dust. Europe's only hope, writes Caves, would appear to lie, as some of the most perceptive minds of the day have shown, 'dans l'approfondissement intérieur de l'âme ... dans un retour immédiat sur soi-même, dans une conversion'.[121] There is, however, every indication, as Drieu La Rochelle has suggested, that the state of affairs may well worsen. Meanwhile, Caves concludes, Europe's fate hangs in the balance.

German interest in the East did not go unnoticed by *Clarté*, whose analysis of the movement bears a certain resemblance to that of Massis. Both situate Germany's post-war fascination with the East in the despair of defeat; both detect a profound pessimism verging on the self-destructive, and both agree that German intellectuals have concluded that with them the whole fabric of civilization and of Western culture has failed. However, where Massis excludes his own 'triumphant' culture from the 'fatal anxieties' of German thought (of necessity excluding, in the process, those intellectuals, like Rolland, who have already 'betrayed' it to the East) *Clarté* includes it; and where Massis discovers in the 'Germanic soul' a natural affinity with 'Asiaticism' *Clarté* perceives the necessary flight into obscurantism of moribund ideology. Typical of *Clarté*'s approach to the subject of German interest in the East is N. I. Bukharin's article, 'La Crise de la culture bourgeoise'.[122]

In his survey of German intellectual trends, Bukharin makes the following assertions:

'La culture s'est écroulée'. 'La foi que nous avions en une humanité civilisée est ébranlée'. Ces mots caractérisent parfaitement l'état d'esprit des classes qui périssent, leur pessimisme, leur angoisse, leurs alarmes devant l'inévitable . . . On fuit tout ce qui est 'extérieur'; on s'enfonce en soi-même; on contemple; on se simplifie l'âme, Dieu, les sages de la Chine, les fakirs, l'enseignement des yogas, le spiritisme . . . On se dresse sur la pointe des pieds et l'on prétend sauter dans 'le monde de la superconscience!' 'Les chercheurs du mystère', les mages, les devins, voilà ceux qui donnent le ton. C'est pourquoi l'on goûte particulièrement l'art nègre, les primitifs etc. On attribue à ces pauvres 'sauvages' une psychologie de désillusion, un état d'âme d'impérialiste raffiné, mais meurtri dans la bataille: et pour imiter ces nobles modèles, on zozote comme des gosses, on fait joujou, on est des dadaïstes et des Naturmenschen . . . Le chaos de tous côtés. Le 'grand style' n'existe plus. L'unité de l'idéologie est détruite. La civilisation bourgeoise n'a plus sur elle que des lambeaux . . . elle tremble pour l'avenir.

If the Leninists expressed little sympathy for Germany's *crise de l'esprit* and still less for her flight into Oriental mysticism, believing both to be symptomatic of the decline and disintegration of bourgeois society and culture, their critique failed to impress those equally vociferous opponents of German cultural trends: Henri Massis and *La Revue universelle*. This was because Massis and his colleagues saw Oriental mysticism and Leninism as related maladies: the former being the incubation stage of the latter. One of the clearest formulations of this diagnosis is to be found in Maurice Muret's article 'La Pensée allemande et l'Orient' published in *La Revue universelle* in August 1921.[123]

Muret's investigation of the eastward orientation of German intelligence is in essence a political critique. Indeed he impresses upon the reader that thought, far from being the condition of its own evolution, is subject to, indeed conditioned by, external political stimuli and pressures. Thus can be explained, he suggests, the miraculous conversion of Germany's intellectual élite from pre-war anti-Asiaticism, inspired by fears of Pan-Slavism and 'le péril jaune', to post-war pro-Asiaticism, which reveals itself as a fascination with Oriental philosophy and culture:

> L'origine et l'essence politiques de ce mouvement des esprits est indéniable. Le fond de leur pensée est celui-ci: 'Nos vainqueurs n'ont rien à nous apprendre. Nous renions l'Occident, mais nous regardons avec curiosité et sympathie vers l'Orient, berceau de toutes les civilisations humaines. Retrempons-nous dans le bain de jouvence des idées asiatiques, de toutes les idées asiatiques. N'écartons même pas sans recours ce bolchevisme qui, honni et redouté par nos vainqueurs, doit nous être de ce fait sympathique.'[124]

Bolshevism, which Muret—like Massis—defines as a return to Russia's Asiatic origins and destiny,[125] has won German intelligence to the cause of 'Asiaticizing' Europe. After assessing the importance of Spenglerian doctrine to the transformation of German intelligence, examining the 'dubious' part played by German writers, translators and newspaper proprietors of Jewish extraction, identifying the leading figures, German and Asian, in the Oriental movement and specifying the nature of their appeal, Muret concludes with a general observation and an appeal of his own:

> L'asiatisme ne se présente pas seulement aux regards des Européens sous forme de philosophies hindoues, chinoises et japonaises. L'asiatisme peut se présenter—et il se présente dès maintenant—*sous un visage moins séduisant: le visage bolcheviste.* Le jour où ce danger deviendrait menaçant, l'instinct de la solidarité européenne ne l'emportera-t-il pas sur toutes ces amitiés asiatiques, fondées sur la colère et le dépit? Après la guerre comme avant, l'humanisme gréco-latin et la tradition chrétienne restent pour l'Occident la source de toute rénovation, et de toute restauration intellectuelle, la garantie de tout progrès moral. Hors de là, point de salut pour l'Europe.[126]

If 'German intelligence', out of despair, was, as Muret claimed, guilty of collaboration with Bolshevism, it was no more or less desperate an alliance than that which was to be established twenty years later between 'French intelligence' and Nazism in the face of the 'Red menace'. Whence the prophetic and ironic quality of Muret's appeal. Pre-war 'anti-Germanism', of which

La Revue universelle was a leading propagator, was to become a luxury which, in the 'forties, many defenders of 'French intelligence' were prepared to forgo in defence of a 'Graeco-Latin and Christian world' threatened by Bolshevism.

Although it was in Germany, where the shock of war had been greatest, that conditions proved most favourable to the growth of interest in the East, France was herself, at this time, not unreceptive to 'séductions orientales': a development whose importance Fernand Baldensperger attempted to assess in an article published early in 1922.[127] At the beginning of the eighteenth century, writes Baldensperger, 'Orientalism' found expression in the writings of Voltaire, Addison, Parnell and Montesquieu, while at the turn of the nineteenth century, though the subject was this time treated in greater depth, the East again found favour with European writers (notably Schlegel and Schopenhauer). All in all, continues Baldensperger, Europe has, through its various national literatures, displayed no great difficulty in assimilating such values as the East appeared to offer. Today, however, things are very different. The startling discovery made by twentieth-century man in the philosophies of the East is of an entirely new concept of personality and, indeed, of reality. Whereas the West represents to the highest degree the 'extrême détermination de l'individu'[128]—a concept, writes Baldensperger, which Tagore contemptuously dismisses as another facet of Western 'mécanisation'—the essential characteristics of the new wave of Oriental thought sweeping the European continent might be defined as 'un certain abandon de la personnalité consciente, une moindre affirmation des possibilités extérieures de la connaissance'.[129] For the Oriental, continues Baldensperger, reality as we perceive it is mere illusion. To erect systems in terms of this mistaken view of reality is to be the dupe of illusion. Our particular world-view has its origin in the 'esprit grec', where time and space were for the first time subjected to the measure of the intelligence.[130] Henceforward, truths were demonstrable by experimentation, observation and logical deduction. On these bases alone could general laws be established.

Baldensperger finds Western, and especially German, apologists for Oriental philosophy a little too hasty in proclaiming the bankruptcy of European civilization. Europe has not abdicated her spirituality, nor is she likely to do so. A general act of contrition on the part of the West is unnecessary. We need only redefine our fundamental values. Then will the cloud of materialism now hanging over the West be dispersed. Here Asia can be of help by making Europeans aware of the limitations of dry logic and systematization. This can be Europe's first step to a deeper perception of the world. If Europe is to profit from contact with the East, she must, insists Baldensperger, surrender nothing of that eternal spirit which beneath a surface of change and uncertainty has been her deepest inspiration: the 'miracle grec' and the 'fait français'.[131] The life of the spirit as defined by these fundamentals has, up to the present day, remained essentially unaltered as indeed has the notion of the well-defined personality. Abjuring nothing of these principles which have been her honour and strength, the West, concludes Baldensperger, welcomes still closer ties with the East.

It was, as previously stated, to the establishment and the consolidation of such ties that Rolland wished to contribute. Part of his contribution lay, as he indicated in his letter to Barbusse on 2 February 1922, in convincing Europe of the need to avoid violence: 'je sentais venir (he later wrote) la "Tempête sur l'Europe" . . . Je la flairais dans l'air, de mes naiseaux fiévreux. Et je cherchais . . . pour notre Occident, quel refuge, quel rempart lui opposer'.[132] Rolland found such a refuge in Gandhi. In the Mahatma's thought he found ideas and ideals which were present to some extent in his own thinking—especially as expressed in *Clérambault*—even before he had heard of Gandhi. At the basis of Gandhi's faith in non-violent but active resistance Rolland discovered a specific and active love by which, he felt, an industrial and self-devouring West could still be saved.[133] It was this message that Rolland conveyed to Barbusse in his letter of 2 February 1922.

Rolland's interest in Gandhi was shared by *Clarté*. However, where Rolland saw in Gandhism a universally applicable strategy of (non-violent) change, *Clarté* was at pains to stress the historical and political specificity of the movement. An example of this approach is Ram-Prassad-Dubé's article, 'Les aspects sociaux du mouvement Gandhi dans l'Inde', which appeared in *Clarté* on 1 March 1922.[134] Ram-Prassad-Dubé views Britain's relationship with India as one of political and economic domination. Whilst the 'mother country' has prospered and its empire grown, the

Indian population has been reduced to slave-status. Humiliated and starved but not defeated, the people have arisen to demand their freedom. A European people in similar straits would, claims Dubé, *resort to armed force*. India, however, because of its social and religious traditions, its vast terrain and linguistic diversity, has chosen another path. Gandhi leads the way. Although Gandhi does not fully appreciate that the ultimately determining element in society is the economic one, Dubé nonetheless pays tribute to his programme of social regeneration, the aims of which are to eliminate caste distinctions and religious intolerance, to secure the principles of non-violent resistance and of personal sacrifice, and to promote the use of the spinning wheel as an economic weapon against foreign capitalists. After examining each of these elements in turn, Dubé observes that Gandhi as a leader incorporates two tendencies: on the one hand the constitutional approach which leads to concessions and compromise and, on the other, the individualist approach to social and political problems. The former is already undermining Gandhi's position as a political leader but the latter, based upon the implementation of Hindu philosophical principles, has penetrated the masses and carried them to new heights in the anti-imperialist struggle. If Gandhi is doomed to failure as a politician, his teachings, concludes Dubé, mark an important step forward in the development of a social revolution which is certain to go far beyond him.

In his reply to Rolland's letter of 2 February 1922, Barbusse again insists on the utopian facets of Rollandism.[135] Despite its flair for justice and truth, its generous hopes, goodwill and faith, Rollandism is a negative force in so far as it offers nothing concrete, nothing amounting to even the simplest of imperatives like 'voilà ce qu'il faut'. Similarly, Barbusse considers intellectual criticism and protest to be admirable but limited; besides lacking the courage, practical sense, and the capacity to implement their humanitarian dreams, Rollandists lend prestige to reformist illusions and gains which, far from weakening the State apparatus, actually strengthen it. Whilst Barbusse regards Communism as 'la simple contre partie réfléchie du capitalisme international', incorporating in a vast and stable structure the theory and practice of a society born of human aspiration and nourished by the efforts of each and all, Rolland sees in it the negation of freedom. That Rolland chooses 'freedom' is perfectly consistent with his position, argues Barbusse, for freedom (unlike equality,—a scientifically exact and attainable ideal) is a vague and tentative notion which can easily be made to suit any circumstance.

As for Rolland's reflections on violence, Barbusse interprets them to be confused, arbitrary, lost in verbalism. Against Rolland's 'sophistic' and 'scholastic' repudiation of all forms of violence, he holds that 'constraint' is not only an essential element of social struggle, but it is also part of the cohesion and discipline of a functioning society. It is inherent, he insists, even in Gandhi's tactic of non-cooperation, which he compares to the weapon of the political strike. Claiming that strikes depend for their effectiveness upon unanimity or near unanimity of consent, Barbusse argues that even this consent involves an element of constraint. For without massive participation, which in turn presupposes firm leadership and a collective organization capable of ensuring that *everyone* strikes after strike action has been decided by the majority, the inevitable result will be defeat.

When, in his previous letter, Barbusse had characterized Rolland's thought as anarchist and bourgeois, Rolland had taken offence. Barbusse insists that the charge is justified by the unreal and non-applicable nature of Rolland's theories—his ethical, sentimental approach to social problems. Moreover, his approbation of individualist solutions coupled with his indictment of all collective efforts as thinly-veiled tyrannies are not only the stock-in-trade of directionless anarchism, but also common-place formulations of the ruling class. As a result of his ambiguous stand Rolland can expect to have the support not only of 'les esprits nobles' but of conservatives, 'half-liberals', 'half-pacifists' and even enemies; in a word, of all those whose real aim it is to 'déconsidérer l'expérience révolutionnaire russe'. If the rapacity of 'the metallurgical and militarist oligarchy' is one day tamed it will not be because of wishful-thinking but through the organized efforts of those who, inspired by the example of the Russian people, are today dedicated to the struggle for socialism.

Despite the attempts of Barbusse and *Clarté* to convince Rolland of the specificity of the Gandhi doctrine of non-violence to the Indian situation, Rolland continued, with the publication of his essay on Gandhi[136] and his preface to *La Jeune Inde*,[137] to present it as the only method capable of saving European, indeed world, civilization from total destruction.[138]

Rolland's enthusiastic defence of Gandhi, notably in the essay published in *Europe*, prompted Barbusse to attempt an analysis of the Indian leader's ideology. This he did in an article published in *Clarté* in July 1923 and entitled 'Révolutionnaires d'Orient et d'Occident—A propos de Gandhi'.[139] Here Barbusse's clear intention is to destroy the legend of Gandhi as 'le symbole de la non-violence, en opposition formelle, fondamentale, et tranchée avec les révolutionnaires d'Europe'. Indeed Barbusse goes so far as to claim that there is greater similarity between the doctrines of Gandhi and Western revolutionaries than there is difference—a point with which Rolland will to some extent agree in his preface to *La Jeune Inde*.[140] Praising Gandhi's efforts in the practical field, Barbusse describes the Mahatma as a 'vrai révolutionnaire'—an error which Gandhi will himself rectify by stressing that he has nothing in common with Bolshevism.[141] Gandhi, the incarnation of the revolutionary virtue of 'pensée-action', has found his antithesis ('pensée-rêve') in the person of Rabindranath Tagore, Romain Rolland's spiritual brother. 'Moral perfection', Barbusse emphasizes, lies, as Gandhi has shown, in achieving concrete results and not, as Rolland and Tagore appear to suggest, in wishful-thinking. Barbusse concludes with an appeal to all, whether European or Asian, to link arms in an effort to '[mettre] de la chair et du sang dans le mot pratique'.

Rolland's essay on Gandhi and Barbusse's reply were answered by the Indian Marxist Evelyn Roy in an article entitled 'Mahatma Gandhi, révolutionnaire ou contre-révolutionnaire'.[142] Roy begins by providing a brief summary of the contrasting positions of Barbusse and Rolland. Rolland, he writes, presents Gandhi's programme of non-cooperation in a manner calculated to strengthen his own theory that non-violence, based on suffering, self-sacrifice and brotherly love, is Europe's only guarantee against self-destruction. Barbusse, on the other hand, who belongs to the ranks of those who oppose force with force and dictatorship with dictatorship has attempted to argue that Gandhi is not a sacrificial lamb whose martyrdom will be the redemption of humanity but, on the contrary, a revolutionary for whom non-violence is quite simply the most appropriate and effective tactic in the circumstances. Indeed, continues Roy, Barbusse

91

believes that if Lenin himself had been in Gandhi's place, he would have acted no differently. In this way, writes Roy, Barbusse has sought to deprive Rolland of an important weapon in his battle against the methods and aims of Bolshevism.

Roy now turns to a closer examination of Gandhism in order to show that Rolland has overestimated the success of the programme of non-cooperation especially in the educational field and legal profession. The boycott of foreign fabrics and of alcohol was more successful because it challenged the government on a crucial issue, a financial one. Indeed, far from being, as Rolland claims, an example of 'saine discipline' and 'hygiène nécessaire' the liquor boycott represents (in *real* terms) an attempt to deprive the government of the enormous profits which monopoly control of the market assured it. Although Roy regards Gandhi's opposition to the caste-system as just, he nonetheless insists that such a system, already in the process of disintegration, will disappear not as a result of Gandhi's appeals for justice and humanity but through the growth of industry and its impact upon existing social relations.

The boycott of foreign fabrics formed the most important part of the programme of non-cooperation, not only because it coincided with the reactionary social philosophy of Gandhi, who, spurning the trappings of modern civilization, prescribed the use of the spinning-wheel, but also because the keystone of the movement was the native spinner, whose ability to compete with Lancashire manufacturers was given a tremendous boost by the boycott. It should come as no surprise that the programme of non-cooperation was financed by the manufacturers of Bombay, Calcutta and Madras; in other words by those who (together with the propertied class) represent India's rising bourgeoisie. As for the proposed establishment of a 'trésor de guerre' in 1921–2, that, too, Roy insists, must be seen as the handywork of the nascent capitalist class, whose interests had not been served sufficiently by the Montagu and Chelmsford reforms. This 'fund' was the determining factor in Gandhi's tactics: it can be glimpsed in his 'appel aux miséreux de Bombay et de Madras'; it is evident in his recommendation not to use the textile workers to political effect; it is the very reason for his opposition to the call for all-out civil disobedience and for his insistence on passive resistance, respect for law and order and for private property.

Roy makes these observations not simply to dispel Rolland's illusions on 'le rôle spirituel de son nouveau Messie' but, he insists, in order to provide the basis of a correct analysis of historical events. And these events reveal Gandhi for what he really is: 'un timide réformateur social, terrifié par la grandeur du mouvement qu'on lui demandait de diriger, cherchant vainement à le comprimer dans les limites de sa propre philosophie réactionnaire'. As a result of his treachery at Chauri-Chaura and his shameful capitulation at Bardoli—which Rolland describes as 'un acte d'exceptionnelle valeur morale'—228 peasants were sentenced to death by hanging and the entire movement of non-cooperation suffered a reversal. Gandhi's arrest followed shortly afterwards to be followed in turn by increased police brutality and widespread repression. To Rolland's claim that Gandhi was arrested because 'sa non-violence était plus révolutionnaire que violence' Roy replies that it was precisely because Gandhi posed no revolutionary threat that he was arrested. He had become so far removed from the mass movement that the government was able to deal with him with impunity. The silence which fell upon India after his arrest was neither the glorious vindication of the philosophy of 'Âme-Force' nor the disciplined response of the masses to their leader's appeals for calm, but acquiescence in the incarceration of a leader who had refused to lead, whose betrayal of the aspirations of the insurgents had already debarred him from effective control of the movement.

For Rolland, continues Roy, events on the Indian continent are the materialization of a 'moral' struggle between the forces of Good and Evil, between the Legions of Heaven and those of Hell. Gandhi is the new Messiah whose spiritual crusade is waged not only for the salvation of India but for that of the whole world. India's triumph will be therefore the triumph on earth of the forces of light over those of darkness, of spirit over matter, of God over Satan. For the Marxist, who understands that the world is governed by economic forces subject to material laws, such a conception of the world is not mere metaphysical gibberish but an ideological formulation whose inner purpose is to assist the forces of counter-revolution:

Romain Rolland et toute l'école des impérialistes spirituels qui croient que le monde doit être racheté par la force d'âme, le sacrifice de soi et la souffrance acceptée, essayent d'utiliser M. Gandhi comme une preuve de leur thèse que l'Europe a hâté sa propre fin par l'usage de la violence, dont le bolchevisme n'est que la forme finale concentrée.

India, say Rolland and his friends, has been saved by spiritual arms; if Europe followed India's example she too would be saved. But, insists Roy, the simple fact is that India has not been saved; it is still struggling to free itself from social and economic backwardness and political subservience. Its present struggle is not dictated by spiritual concerns but by concrete needs like bread and land. It is for this reason that the peasants of India gave their blood. It is for this reason that the workers and peasants followed Gandhi and abandoned him when he betrayed them.

In the political struggle, during which class divisions in Indian society have become more pronounced, Gandhi has sided with the bourgeoisie. And so despite his very real contribution to the development of the national struggle in the fields of agitation and organization, Gandhi will go down in history not as a revolutionary but as a counter-revolutionary. His 'moral philosophy' could not but be defeated by the armed might of the British Empire. But he would not have failed so miserably if he had recognized, and acted in the knowledge, that economic forces and material laws will not yield to the feeble powers of the individual and if he had only trusted in the Indian people's irresistible drive for freedom. Gandhi (whose place has now been taken by others more likely to respond to the exigencies of the situation) can consider himself fortunate to have been canonized by the sterile intellectualism of crisis-ridden Europeans in search of new illusions. Such Europeans are also fortunate to have found a new Messiah to arm them against the embrace of reality.

Clarté's defence of the 'New East' and its opposition to the 'moral ceremony' of the 'Old', defended by Tagore, Gandhi and by Rolland himself, recognized violence not only as the motor of social change—as 'the reality of justice'—but as an ineluctable feature of the modern world. Rolland's refusal to accept this view sprang from the conviction that whilst violence most certainly existed it was not only morally indefensible but also, because of its cumulative effect on man's psyche, incapable of ensuring the necessary harmonization of the exigencies of the socio-economic revolution and the eternal needs of the spirit.

If the clash between 'Will' and 'Idea', exemplified in the Rolland/Barbusse debate, was an active ingredient of the French *crise de l'esprit*, the same situation, Malraux would have us believe, obtained in Asia. In fact it was this very clash between 'moral force' and a philosophy of violence, between 'eternal thought' and the 'modern imperative' that Malraux identified as the dramatic reality of life on the Asian continent—a reality powerfully depicted in the persons of Tcheng-Daï and Hong.

The attraction of the East, which Baldensperger monitored in 1922 and over which Barbusse and Rolland had clashed, was by mid-decade considered to be so important an issue as to be the subject of a special double number of the *Cahiers du Mois* for February and March 1925.[143] This publication, inspired by the enquiry of François and André Berge and Maurice Betz into the 'wave of Orientalism' sweeping France and Europe, carries the title 'Les Appels de l'Orient'. François Berge stresses that the enquiry can in no wise be considered an idle excursion into exoticism. It arises out of the deep sense of urgency felt by a public which has recognized that the very destiny of the West is imperilled: 'toutes nos valeurs intellectuelles, morales, sociales, ont été jetées dans la guerre et toutes y ont été blessées'.[144]

Berge informs the reader that the war has left Western civilization in a state of spiritual exhaustion and that many minds are now turning to the East in the hope of discovering a new Messiah and the inspiration for a spiritual renaissance. Others, led by Henri Massis, are maintaining that the Orient has little to offer that is not pernicious in nature, and that what is needed is a return to those traditions whence we once derived unity and strength—to which, again, others reply that we cannot resuscitate that which is dead. And so the debate has gone on. What is certain is that we Europeans are no longer alone in the world. We have to contend with an awakening Asia which we ourselves have stirred to life:

> Les peuples orientaux s'européanisent et même s'américanisent en prenant notre machinisme, notre nationalisme, notre imbécile folie de politique, notre dualisme philosophique et moral, nos méthodes scientifiques.[145]

Berge asks whether the West can assimilate those values which,

95

prior to European intervention, had for centuries ensured religious and moral unity in Asia, whilst at the same time maintaining those qualities which have contributed to its superiority in other domains and have constituted its most positive and glorious achievements.

Not all contributors to 'Les Appels' betray that sense of crisis alluded to by Berge. Some simply ignore it, others deny its existence, and there are those who use it merely as a platform for the presentation of geographical or climatic observations. Alice Louis-Barthou, for example, in her enthusiasm for stark contrast gives a rather exotic not to say bookish picture of life in the East:

> J'ai l'Occident en abomination. Cela représente pour moi la brume, le froid, le gris, la mécanique, la science meurtrière, les usines avec tous les vices, le triomphe du bruit, de la bousculade, de la laideur. C'est le matérialisme, l'utilitarisme, l'agitation stérile etc. j'en passe . . . et des meilleurs. L'Orient, c'est le calme, la paix, la beauté, la couleur, le mystère, le charme, le soleil, la joie, la vie douce et le rêve; enfin tout le contraire de la civilisation haïssable et grotesque.[146]

André Siegfried, in another short article in 'Les Appels', also points an accusing finger at Western materialism. He describes the Westerner as the slave of production, the victim of those very forces which he has unleashed and, in a paragraph reminiscent of a famous biblical quotation, he accuses the West of having forgotten that production was made for man and not man for production. He denounces as heresy that 'religion de l'activité, de l'énergie, de la force' which is practised in the West and of which the modern American is the high priest.[147]

Abel Bonnard sees the problem in much the same light. He is not surprised, he writes, to see Europeans turning away from a civilization which offers only the most degrading reasons for existence and seeking refuge, further east, in a system of thought which has always regarded material progress as the basest of pursuits. If he expresses alarm at the rapidity with which Western ideas—particularly that of action—are penetrating the East he nonetheless feels that Asia still retains sufficient spiritual resources to free the West from the stranglehold of materialism and return it to the path of true principles: 'elle peut restaurer en nous le sens d'une vie noble, délicate et souveraine'.[148]

Bonnard's enthusiasm for man's spiritual life would appear to have waned as the years wore on. When, in 1938, a number of 'Cagoulards' were brought to trial for armed conspiracy, Bonnard was amongst the very first to lament the 'martyrdom of heroes' and to demand the punishment of the real 'agents provocateurs': Communists and Jews.[149] By May 1941, when he published two articles in the collaborationist *Je suis partout*, that spiritual flame to which he had laid proud claim in 'Les Appels' seems finally to have been extinguished. He invited 'fellow reactionaries' to abandon their petulant isolationism in order to assist Germany in its historic mission of ridding Europe of the Jew.[150]

The articles of 'Les Appels' so far mentioned might tentatively be described as narcissistic in tone since the overriding concern lies in the suffering which Europe has inflicted upon itself. Indeed, most of the comment will remain restricted essentially to a consideration of the situation in Europe. Time and again one finds the same attack upon the spiritual blindness of the West, upon its insane cultivation of 'le progrès mécanique' as 'une machine de guerre',[151] and the same basic opposition between East and West: 'l'Orient est esprit. L'Occident est matière';[152] 'la vertu de l'Europe est action, celle de l'Asie contemplation'.[153] However, not all comment is restricted to specifically European problems, and here we signal an important departure if we remember that Malraux was himself, between 1926 and 1928, to deal not only with the crisis affecting Europe but with the impact of Western values upon a once contemplative East.

Sylvain Lévi, a specialist in Oriental studies, expresses his inability to understand the point of view of those who claim that the West is in danger from the East. The very reverse is the case, writes Lévi: 'l'orgueil dément de l'Europe surexcité par un siècle d'admirables inventions prétend faire la loi au reste du monde'. The East is being undermined in its beliefs, arts and customs; its institutions, its political, economic and social life, and its deepest aspirations are being contaminated by a materialistic West.[154] In hatefilled desperation nationalist Asia is turning to Moscow and Tokyo for inspiration: in short, to those peoples who have adopted Western methods in order the better to combat the West.[155] As another contributor puts it:

[L'Oriental] s'est, sans presque réagir, laissé dépouiller de ses biens et souvent asservir et réduire en esclavage. Mais voici qu'il nous observe, car nous avons abusé de notre force: il étudie à notre école. Les jeunes générations de l'Asie nous imitent. Avec l'excès du néophite elles prêchent la brutalité et quelquefois le culte de la matière.[156]

The ancient wisdom of the East is giving way to Western modes of thought characterized, as Paul Masson-Oursel suggests, by 'l'idolâtrie de la force et l'oubli des valeurs spirituelles'[157]—an observation which André Malraux was to make in June 1927 in terms very similar to those so far expressed in 'Les Appels':

Que certains peuples de l'Asie aient hérité de l'Europe le nationalisme en même temps que la façon de l'utiliser, cela n'est pas très étonnant, mais les conséquences d'un tel héritage sont inéluctables, et c'est nous qui les avons déterminées. La grande imprudence européenne est dans l'aide que nous n'avons cessé de prêter à la destruction de l'autorité traditionnelle qui, dans toutes les contrées d'Asie était liée à la culture. La substitution des valeurs d'énergie persévérante aux valeurs spirituelles est la marque même des temps modernes. En détruisant ces valeurs spirituelles, nous avons préparé, chez nous et au loin, le règne de la force, et en particulier, de la plus grande, celle qui dure.[158]

If Malraux, here, as in *La Tentation de l'Occident*, is concerned to reveal the origins of violence in Asia, Valéry and Gide, in 'Les Appels', are more concerned about the possibility of this violence being used against the West.[159]

While Jean Bacot, in 'Les Appels', also examines the question of violence, though to focus exclusively on its Western face (imperialism and hungry materialism) he also discusses another peculiarly European phenomenon: action. Whereas the Oriental, he writes, 'réfléchit longuement pour agir peu, l'Européen impulsif agit beaucoup et réfléchit peu'. And in a witty, not least of all ironic remark, he describes the 'homme d'état' as having time only to 'passer à une autre action et il abandonne la réflexion, désormais idéale, à la sagacité des historiens'. He summarizes the European's peculiar thirst for action as follows: 'faire n'importe quoi plutôt que n'agir point' (a formula that would not be inapplicable to the hero of Malraux's *Les Conquérants*). The consequences of such an attitude are, Bacot continues, a refusal to accept responsibility for one's actions and an avoidance of any form of true commitment. Thought is considered the enemy of action, at least of that useless action, that sterile agitation to which the European is so partial and of which revolution, Asian only by adoption, is one of the most fiery products.[160] Azouaou Mammeri makes a similar observation. Speaking of the Oriental he assures the reader that 'les actes de violence en général lui répugnent . . . les dernières révolutions orientales ne sont que les conséquences de l'influence occidentale sur les peuples qui en sont touchés'.[161]

Lévi, Bacot and Mammeri, like Malraux (and Drieu), are not the only thinkers to view the new Orient as a European product. Jean Schlumberger, while making the same observation, introduces another idea which will play an important part in Malraux's work, the European creation of the autonomous individual: 'l'Europe a inventé l'individu autonome aux idées coordonnées, insatiable dans la conquête du monde réel'.[162] These words could have been spoken by Ling of *La Tentation de l'Occident* and define the attitude of which Garine (*Les Conquérants*) is the powerful expression.

At this point one might turn briefly to the writings of a specialist in Oriental thought, René Guénon, whose *Orient et Occident* (1924) and *La Crise du monde moderne* (1927) examine many of the issues raised in 'Les Appels', and later, in more dramatic form, in the writings of André Malraux.

The European's tendency to approach the contemplative East with an assurance of superiority derives, suggests Guénon, from his inability to consider thought other than as the lever of material progress.[163] His is a universe of reality, his home that of visible being,[164] and Reason and Science the obedient servants of his hungry materialism.[165] Feverish, aimless activity is his substitute for the loss of a governing ideal, and restless enterprise the necessary product of a purposeless, spirit-starved life:

> Engagé dans l'action au point de nier tout ce qui la dépasse, il n'aperçoit pas que cette action même dégénère ainsi, par défaut de principe, en une agitation aussi vaine que stérile.[166]

Guénon, like so many other intellectuals of the period— including Malraux and Drieu—locates the origin of Europe's disorder in the Renaissance, where integral unity was broken and

99

transcendent value—the unifying Principle—was reduced to values: humanist ones.[167] It was out of this arrogant assertion of individual worth, claims Guénon, that a new civilization was born: 'une civilisation édifiée tout entière sur quelque chose de purement négatif, sur ce qu'on pourrait appeler une absence de principe'.[168]

Despite the fact that the discovery and exploitation of the East have long since grown to the proportions of a great imperial movement, Europe's domination, writes Guénon, has until quite recently been restricted to the economic and political spheres; ancient custom, the binding force of religious feeling, and sacred principles remaining essentially unaffected.[169] Today, however, the European malady is spreading through every stratum of Oriental life, and the area and speed of infection is growing as successive generations of young Asians return from Western universities.[170] Asia is today torn between two conflicting tendencies, tradition and revolt, eternal essence and modern materialism,[171] and every new day brings added vitality to the new tendency. If European hegemony is at last being challenged, it is with ideas and methods borrowed from Europe.[172] And so to those Europeans, led by Henri Massis, who argue that the spiritual tradition of the West is being threatened by Oriental mysticism Guénon retorts that, on the contrary, it is the West, in the shape of its Asian neophytes, which is today undermining the sacred principles of Oriental wisdom.[173]

Guénon's reference to the liquidation of sacred principles by returning generations of Westernized youth is the subject of Henri Maspéro's article in 'Les Appels'. Maspéro sums up the situation as follows:

S'il y a une liquidation commencée, c'est celle de l'Orient et non celle de l'Occident; dans tous les domaines, politique, social, artistique et intellectuel, les idées antiques reculent au profit des 'idées nouvelles' toutes occidentales.

One has, he continues, only to compare the Chinese student of today with his counterpart of twenty years ago to see that an enormous gulf separates the two generations.[174] Malraux will himself deal with this gulf between the old China and the new in the persons of the old Confucian Wang-Loh and Ling (*La*

100

Tentation de l'Occident) and, in more dramatic form, in the persons of Tcheng-Daï and Hong (*Les Conquérants*).

Like Maspéro, René Gillouin in an article alluded to in 'Les Appels' sees the 'generation gap' as the result of the disintegration of the Chinese world-view.[175] Before its destruction through the importation of Western ideals, Chinese philosophy, 'par la grandiose représentation qu'[elle] offre à ses fidèles de *la succession des existences* aboutissant pour tous à la délivrance finale a puissamment contribué à éteindre chez eux l'esprit de révolte dont notre monde occidental est agité.' He quotes the example of the Asian peasant content in the knowledge that all his present suffering 'n'est que pour une vie'. In Malraux's *Les Conquérants* the disintegration of the ancient belief in the transmigration of souls—which had induced passive acceptance of one's 'human condition'—inspires a whole section of Chinese youth, of which Hong is the chief representative, with burning hatred for those who would have them spend their 'single life' in poverty and oppression.

J. P. Palewski informs the reader—in terms similar to those in Malraux's *La Tentation de l'Occident*—that the traditional wisdom of the East places its faith in the primacy of Being, in the 'Tout Universel', as opposed to the Western belief in the supremacy of the individual and in the ability of 'intelligence' to conceptualize Being. And so, for the Oriental: 'illusion ce sens des perspectives dont l'esprit européen est si fier, illusion ces pays ordonnés, cette construction de l'avenir, cette mathématique du temps, cette chronologie du passé'.[176] The Oriental, stifling will and personality, loses himself to the world, whereas the European affirms his existence within it:[177] 'à l'encontre de l'Oriental, l'homme de l'Occident est perdu dès qu'il renonce à poser à l'origine de ses activités cette affirmation peut-être la plus orgueilleuse qui soit . . . nous sommes au monde'.[178] Edmond Jaloux, using *L'Évangile bouddhique* as a point of reference, sees in the European's proud affirmation of self the cause of the world's suffering.[179] Jaloux then offers the 'solution' which Malraux will himself consider and reject:[180] 'si l'on se persuade que le malheur de l'homme moderne vient d'un attachement exagéré à son Moi, ne suppose-t-on pas qu'il y ait dans la philosophie asiatique un antidote naturel'.[181]

It is evident from what has already been seen of 'Les Appels' that the opposition between East and West was not the concern of specialists only in Oriental philosophy, art forms and traditions.

The fact that it was a widely and hotly debated issue amongst some of the most eminent 'littérateurs' of the day, including Henri Massis, Romain Rolland, Henri Barbusse and the Surrealists, could not have gone unnoticed by the young Malraux, especially since he had been interested in the East as such since adolescence. Many of the ideas with which he will toy are already clearly present in this publication and their very *actualité* doubtless explains something of the startling success he was to achieve with *La Tentation de l'Occident* and *Les Conquérants*. It is also highly probable that Malraux was familiar with developments in the cultural crisis and Oriental movements in Germany especially since these were subjects of interest and concern in France. An article which explores this area of German thought, and of which mention is made in 'Les Appels',[182] is Régina Zabloudovsky's 'La Crise de la culture intellectuelle en Allemagne', published in *Mercure de France* on 15 July 1924. It is difficult to believe that Malraux was not familiar with this article or even, through his German wife Clara, with one of the books reviewed by Mme Zabloudovsky, *Die Zeit ohne mythos (L'Époque sans mythe)*.

War and its disturbed aftermath have, Mme Zabloudovsky writes, brought into the open a movement which is defined as 'le refoulement de la culture du dix-neuvième siècle'.[183] European thought has reached a decisive turning point in its history. Never has there been demonstrated such widespread anxiety concerning the structure and function of our culture. Rarely, if ever, has there been displayed a more pressing need to establish entirely new intellectual supports: 'de fonder la vie entière sur une autre base, de changer quelque chose d'essentiel dans l'existence intellectuelle qui ensuite puisse irradier sur tous les domaines'.[184] Europe is showing the symptoms of a growing 'malaise', a sense of the inadequacy of the existing ideal to satisfy the deepest aspirations of the modern soul.

Mme Zabloudovsky asks the reader to remember the great faith placed in scientific progress in the second half of the nineteenth century if he is to understand Europe's present disarray. Humanity had turned to 'les sciences exactes et leur réclamait une réponse nette'.[185] Its hope was quickly disappointed and there ensued—as Malraux himself was to note—an enormous depreciation of the value of scientific progress in particular and of Western civilization in general.[186] It is this state of mind which today explains the startling success of Spengler's *The Decline of the West*. European man is at last weary of the cult of materialism and all the trappings of utilitarianism which, for decades, have held sway in the West. There has been enough of rigorous logic and systematization. Never has German interest in philosophy, especially in that of Asia, been higher. This interest is neither wholly literary nor is it inspired by idle curiosity. It is born of 'la nostalgie d'un nouvel idéal', and Asia would appear to satisfy Europe's newest aspiration.

Mme Zabloudovsky now turns to what she considers to be one of the most important analyses of the modern crisis: Rudolf Kayser's *Die Zeit ohne mythos*, whose title alone is redolent of Malraux. In the universalism of the Middle Ages Kayser sees a single 'volonté dominatrice' governing all the diverse branches of human endeavour: religion, philosophy, art and science. The Renaissance marked the end of this universal spirit and must be regarded as the most radical cultural revolution ever known. Every revolutionary movement creates a concept of liberty, and that introduced by the Renaissance was called *individualism*. With the Renaissance the idea was born that 'toute existence est créée et dirigée par le Moi'.[187]

Man had taken freedom into his own hands but had omitted to create a new ideal to replace that which had disappeared. Henceforward 'psychological props' were required to shore up the void left by the disappearance of the Myth. The notion of authority, in society as in education, was one such prop. However, notes Kayser:

> L'heure devait fatalement venir où ces possibilités se trouveraient enfin taries et où la conception toute formelle de l'individualisme révélerait son insuffisance en face du monde démoniaque qui est en nous et du monde cosmique et métaphysique qui est en dehors de nous.[188]

Kayser claims that the notion of crisis first appeared around 1880 but that its 'manifestation empirique' (war, revolt, social, moral and intellectual chaos) is a more recent phenomenon. We have had to wait until today for 'la fin de l'époque individualiste et psychologique'.[189] The crisis arose at the very moment we began to analyse the age in which we live. It was then that our confidence in it was shaken. We suddenly discovered that we had

103

become the victims of a 'mécanique de l'esprit' and the dupes of our own systems of categorization. And yet these had been our only means of supporting 'l'absence de mythe' and of maintaining 'la fiction individualiste'.[190] Once we became aware of the great illusion we had no alternative but to remove it. Europe is 'privée de mythe' and the present crisis is the consequence of this deprivation.

It is the opinion of Kayser that an age which has no myth or governing ideal, where substance has been lost to form, cannot provide its youth with a doctrine or faith. It can furnish them certain opinions and 'techniques' but cannot create a god to whom they will entrust their souls, for its activity is wholly external, and, as such, valueless and empty.

That Kayser's analysis bore relation to a certain mood prevalent not only in Germany but also in France may be gathered from the following observations made, respectively, by Marcel Arland in February 1924 and by André Malraux in 1926:

> Aucune doctrine ne nous peut satisfaire, mais l'absence de doctrine nous est un tourment.[191]

> Il n'est pas d'idéal auquel nous puissions nous sacrifier, car de tous nous connaissons les mensonges, nous qui ne savons pas ce qu'est la vérité.[192]

Is all lost, asks Kayser? Is European culture doomed, its creative force now spent? Does Asia offer a remedy? Kayser answers his own questions by asserting that European culture can survive only by remaining truly European. We cannot import Oriental values as we would a cargo of rice. We cannot undo our European consciousness. Kayser sees the West's future task as 'la gigantesque œuvre de créer un mythe, d'enfanter un nouveau Dieu européen'.[193]

The death of individualism and the call for the creation of a new myth are reiterated in Malraux's writings of 1926 and 1927. In the *Nouvelle Revue Française*, in a critique of Massis's defence of the Graeco-Latin and Christian tradition, Malraux writes:

> La pensée européenne, dans le domaine de l'esprit, s'est toujours exprimée par la création de mythes cohérents. Elle travaille aujourd'hui à en construire un nouveau, et les plaidoyers sont sans force contre une recherche de cet ordre qui dérive d'une nécessité.[194]

And, in *Les Nouvelles Littéraires*:

> Le premier présent de notre génération, j'ai la conviction que c'est la proclamation de la faillite de l'individualisme, de toutes les doctrines qui se justifient par l'exaltation du Moi. L'objet de la recherche de la jeunesse occidentale est *une notion nouvelle de l'homme*.[195]

The search for a 'new man' and a 'new myth' (the former being the necessary condition of the creation of the latter) will be the focus of Malraux's attentions in his novels *Les Conquérants* and *La Voie royale*. The political itinerary of Drieu La Rochelle will also be marked by such a search.

A very general summary of the ideas to be found in 'Les Appels' is that the Oriental world-view, which might have aided a beleagured Europe, is in the process of disintegration as Western beliefs and values percolate the Oriental consciousness. Spiritual values have given way to a 'culte de la matière' and to the principles of self-affirmation through action and violence. A Europeanized East, encouraged by the Soviet Union, is now turning in hate-filled vengeance upon a divided and ailing West: 'pour l'Orient, l'Occident est la terre promise, la guerre, le point final du temps, l'Oméga'.[196]

To those in 'Les Appels' who regretted that the 'spirit of the West' had provoked the 'spiritual bankruptcy' of the East, *Clarté* responded with an assessment of the cost in human misery which the Oriental had had to pay for Europe's so-called 'triumph of the mind':

> L'Orient
> terre sur laquelle
> des esclaves nus meurent de faim;
> propriété collective de tous,
> sauf de l'Oriental;
> pays que la famine extermine;
> grange qui déborde de froment;
> grange de l'Europe.
> Asie . . .[197]

In June 1925 *Clarté* published two replies, by Jean Montrevel and Marcel Eugène, to 'Les Appels'.[198]

For the honourable contributors to 'Les Appels', writes Montrevel, Civilization, born and nourished in the Mediterranean basin, reserves the epithet 'barbarian' for all those who have not drunk at its sacred font.[199] And yet the mood of these enlightened souls is dark with despair, for they sense that their precious culture is doomed. Anxieties of this order are, of course, lost on their imperturbable overlords, the captains of industry and finance for whom, writes Montrevel, 'intellectual' pursuits are the perfection of means of production, the conquest of power and the manipulation of government, and for whom the fruits of life—raw materials and the labour of others—are gathered wheresoever they grow.

Marcel Eugène's article strikes a similar note. He is not interested in determining to what extent Europe has hellenized the East or created Graeco-Latin Asians, whether Mediterranean values are in decline or still capable of uplifting souls. Indeed, he regards such questions as a narcissistic obscenity, an imposture whose abstract assumption of Graeco-Latin 'principles' and 'values' serves as a screen for the most realistic of practices—the political and economic enslavement of four-fifths of humanity:

> Dénonçons hautement ce procédé bourgeois et social-démocrate qui consiste à *déplacer le problème* avec des apparences de raison et à parler de péril jaune ou de civilisations adverses, ou de spiritualités non équivalentes. Ce ne sont là que spéculations destinées à égarer les intellectuels. Les faits, dans leur réalité, sont là . . . pour tous les opprimés: L'IMPÉRIALISME CAPITA-LISTE EST L'ENNEMI DE L'HUMANITÉ. Le problème d'Orient et d'Extrême Orient ne se résoudra qu'avec le problème prolétarien. C'est un fait dont chaque jour accentuera l'importance. C'est un ·fait contre lequel vos discours [mes beaux Messieurs] ne pourront rien.

And to Henri Massis, for whom the conflict of the modern world is a struggle between a Christian West dominated by the beneficent authority of the Catholic Church and a faithless and corrupting East supported by Germanic and Slav heresies, Eugène addresses the words of the Roman Catholic Léon Bloy:

> Le bon jeune homme élevé par les bons Pères et rempli de saintes intentions, embrasse pieusement sa mère et ses jeunes sœurs avant

106

d'aller aux contrées lointaines, où il lui sera permis de souiller et de torturer les plus pauvres images de Dieu.

Eugène's point is that religious fervour will sanction any excess. It is in the name of the 'spirit' that Europe has justified her encroachments, excused her crimes and legitimized the slavery in which she holds almost the whole of humanity. She is never done talking of Man yet everywhere buries him in an avalanche of murders. But on this side of death and despair the Oriental has found his humanity. Through revolution, bloody and uncompromising, he has begun to 'humanize' himself and to re-humanize the world:

> Regardez!
> Déjà sont limités les jours,
> qui nous séparent de la délivrance.
> La révolution agite
> son mouchoir sanglant.
> Sur le vent de l'impérialisme
> nos chevaux rouges piaffent.[200]

It is this message, in articles like 'Confucianisme et Communisme',[201] 'L'Islam et la révolution mondiale',[202] and 'Le Paupérisme rural au Tonkin',[203] that *Clarté* delivers to those who, whether mourning the death of the old Asia or fearing the birth of the new, whether attacking 'Asiaticism' or defending the 'European tradition', obscure the true nature of the modern conflict, which is:

> La révolte de l'homme contre la colonisation sournoisement implacable de l'impérialisme de fait mais inavoué, des états soi-disant démocratiques, dont la phraséologie humanitaire et creuse, ne correspond à aucune réalité, mais favorise de son apparence généreuse, toute de façade, les pires excès de la concentration économique et financière.[204]

Romain Rolland's contribution to 'Les Appels' runs to one line: 'où est Henri Massis, Romain Rolland ne peut pas être'.[205] In a letter to Kalidas Nag in May 1925 he indicated the probable reason for this uncharacteristic brevity: 'ce même Henri Massis, qui me dénonce aujourd'hui comme livrant l'Europe à l'Asie, me dénonçait, pendant la guerre, comme livrant la France à l'Allemagne'.[206] Rolland's claim was well founded, as Massis's opening remarks in 'Les Appels' clearly demonstrate. Referring specifically to Rolland, Massis issues the following imperative:

> C'est en Occident qu'il faut d'abord chercher et dénoncer les idéologues qui, sous le prétexte de nous ouvrir aux idées de l'Orient, trahissent la civilisation d'Occident et leur vocation propre.[207]

Massis's article is one sustained assertion: 'Asiaticism', reinforcing as it does, existing European heresies, threatens the very fabric of Western civilization. After quoting Sylvain Lévi on Buddhism—'l'existence n'est qu'un accident éphémère dans une série de longueur incommensurable'—Massis catalogues those European heresies which draw strength from such a conception of life: agnostic relativism, evolutionism, pantheism and determinism. From the evolutionary monism of Haeckel and Spencer (akin to the cosmogony of Taoism) to the systematic nihilism of Stirner (which resembles the arguments of Mâdhyamikas), from fideism (whose Oriental counterpart is Yogacâras) to the idealism of Kant (announced in Dignana) every Western heresy, Massis claims, has the opportunity to renew its powers of seduction and error by transposing into its own language the sacred texts of Asia.[208] Massis then passes to Germany and to a still more sweeping arraignment. He claims that 'Asiaticism' would not have enjoyed such widespread recognition had it not been for its propagation by, and affinity with, Germanic thought. It is in, and through, Germanic thought—from Kant to Fichte, from Schopenhauer to Hartmann, from Nietzsche to Keyserling —that the West has become acquainted with Oriental metaphysics. Tagore is quoted as having proclaimed that a 'grande transformation s'est accomplie dans la pensée européenne sous l'influence de la philosophie de l'Inde qui a remué l'âme de l'Allemagne et s'est imposée fortement à l'attention des autres peuples de l'Occident'.[209]

If the 'dissatisfied children of the spirit of the West', like Romain Rolland, are seeking in the land of 'eternal thought' a new viaticum for exhausted Europe, they are, suggests Massis, wasting their time, for the Orientals whose wisdom they worship are in fact modernists: they have, as Drieu La Rochelle has written,[210] been Westernized. Gandhi, for example, is an admirer of Tolstoy and Ruskin, Tagore invokes Shelley, Wordsworth and the English lyric poets, and Coomaraswamy (introduced to the French public by Rolland) elucidates his writings by referring to Kant, Boehme and William Blake, compares the teachings of Chuang-Tseu with those of Walt Whitman and is fully acquainted with the Nietzschean doctrine of the Superman, in which he sees the influence of the Hindu Maha Purusha, the Boddhisatra and the Jîvan Muka. However, writes Massis, the real intention of Rolland and his Oriental allies—who include Japanese intellectuals[211]—is not to develop a new wisdom or to create new reasons to hope and to live but to inspire 'une vision catastrophique de l'univers'[212] in order to sap resistance and so make survival impossible: 'l'orientalisme n'est qu'un masque'.[213] Theirs is a *political* effort,[214] allied in ambition to the attempt by nation-states like Japan, Russia, China and Germany, to subvert and destroy the West.[215] Massis's final thought is for the saving grace of Christian doctrine in whose name he urges the European conscience to turn away from the Oriental temptation and its corrupting agents.

To add up the teeming millions of China and India, to multiply them by the military power of Japan, the revolutionary fervour of Russia and the philosophical nihilism of Germany might appear to be the arithmetic of Bedlam but it was, in part or in whole, a mathematical formula whose validity Massis never doubted. He had already applied it in an article appropriately entitled 'L'Offensive germano-asiatique contre la culture occidentale'[216] and was to employ it again, in more fluent and detailed form, in his *Défense de l'Occident* (1927). In his efforts to defend the European heritage against the encroachments of a mystic and revolutionary East, he was, as we have already seen, assisted by *La Revue universelle*, of which he was the editor.[217]

The very first sentence of Massis's *Défense de l'Occident* sets the tone of the whole work: 'le destin de la civilisation d'Occident, le destin de l'homme tout court, sont aujourd'hui menacés'. In this perilous condition Europe's first task is to denounce the propaganda of the 'merchants of doom'. The purpose of such propaganda, which is aimed far more at the overthrow of the order of the world than at its determination, can only be, argues Massis, to make uneasiness universal and renunciation possible, to sap resistance and to darken counsel, to cause Europe to lose sight of the rules of preservation and to neglect the measures vital to her recovery. There is, he feels sure, no sober-minded person heedful of the future who does not feel both the tragic greatness of the danger and the stern need to serve in order to survive. He is, he insists, making no vague conjectures: the facts, as an outcome of which Western civilization runs the risk of being engulfed, are 'clairs', 'impitoyables' and are in the newspapers. The revolt of a Berber chieftain, he writes (referring to the Riff uprising), has stirred the public conscience in France and given it a glimmering of the profound significance of an event that is less important for what it is than for what it presages: Asia and Africa, united by Bolshevism, are preparing to take possession of Europe, body and soul.[218]

During the war, writes Massis, European nations were not satisfied with defending their native soil and political independence; they found it necessary to bring into conflict spiritual and moral values, philosophies and dogmas, traditions and beliefs, Law and Justice, and a whole host of divine personages. Massis, who as much as anyone had contributed to this form of intellectual warfare, now declares that the ideals mobilized under the adverse banners are themselves laid waste, even more than the battlefields:

> C'est la *civilisation*, l'idée même de civilisation dont l'Europe se proclamait détentrice, qui se trouve la plus profondément atteinte. Aux yeux de cette partie du monde qui vivait sur l'illusion de notre homogénéité, la civilisation fait figure de vaincue.[219]

The very words we used to enrol our mercenaries, to rally them to the defence of 'Civilization and Right', are taken up and turned against us by the mercenaries. We may have laid aside our arms, Massis notes, but the 'battle of ideas' continues. From Calcutta to Shanghai, from the Mongolian steppes to the plains of Anatolia, the whole of Asia is stirred by an inexorable desire for 'freedom'. The supremacy to which Europe has been accustomed since the day when John Sobieski finally checked the onrush of the Turks and Tartars beneath the walls of Vienna, is no longer recognized by the Asiatic peoples, who have begun to unite against the 'white man', whose overthrow they proclaim. Overjoyed to see Europeans vilified and beaten down by themselves, Asia is today taking advantage of the state of reduced resistance in which it has surprised Europe to deaden her will and to destroy the last germs of unity that survive in her. For Asia, Massis stresses, is not merely arousing its native peoples to revolt in order to deprive 'notre continent appauvri des immenses ressources qu'elle détient';[220] it is attacking the very *soul of the West*, that soul, divided, uncertain of its principles, confusedly eager for spiritual liberation and all the more ready to destroy itself in that it has departed from its history, its civilizing order and its tradition. In this their hour of uncertainty, the 'idées-mères' of the West—personality, unity, stability, authority and continuity—are succumbing to an ascetic idealism, a 'certain Asiaticism' in which personality is dissolved and a return to nothingness advocated. This assault on the very 'lineaments of Man'—on the Graeco-Latin and Christian heritage—is, Massis claims, being supported by those newly formed nations who have not kept step with the others in the march of human civilization, notably Germany and Russia.

Germany, writes Massis, has made the 'Latin idea' responsible for her own demise and is now looking with a sort of messianic expectation to an East which has always shown remarkable affinities with her thought. She has at last turned away from the civilization whose ideal she had adopted only in so far as it once seemed to offer a clear path to spiritual hegemony. Her anticipation fell back upon her, and in defeat she concluded 'non point à son propre écroulement, mais à l'écroulement de la science, de la méthode, de la raison, à la faillite de la civilisation et de tous ses concepts'.[221] In a dream of dragging the rest of the world with her in her fall, Germany began to prophesy, in dark apocalyptic tones, the final bankruptcy of a world, the mastery of which had escaped her. Unconcerned by what disorders such a 'subversion' may let loose on the world the 'German thaumaturges' have devoted their energies to filling the world with their own disillusionment and to cultivating—like Keyserling and Romain Rolland[222]—the germs of a destructive Asiaticism. At the centre of this seditious enterprise Massis finds Spengler, whose *Decline of the West* has sold 50,000 copies and, even more disturbingly, adds Massis, given rise to numerous commentaries both in Germany and France.[223] At the heart of Spengler's catastrophic theory of history Massis discovers the affirmation that no Culture, no Civilization, can lay claim to an absolute precellence, for the universal value on which the justification for this claim is

111

based—the classical idea of man—is nothing but a false entity contradicted by nature and by history. The underlying purpose of this 'historical organicism' wherein life is deprived of finality, humanity of transcendent aim and civilization of content, is, Massis asserts, to liberate German thought from Humanist and Latin culture and so make any madness possible.[224]

What Spengler had attempted, in order to seduce the German individual from the standards of the Latin mind, Keyserling, Massis argues, meant to accomplish by appealing to his soul, by promising him that spiritual elevation the secret of which Asiatic wisdom possesses. However, adds Massis, far from being a new and higher form of consciousness, Keyserling's 'system' is an unconditional surrender to 'instinctive forces':

> Un affreux mélange d'idéalisme kantien, de bergsonisme, de freudisme, qui cherche à vider l'esprit de tout contenu objectif, exalte la primauté du psychique et de l'individuel, réduit la vérité à l'efficience affective, consacre l'extase de la chair et déchaîne les forces vitales sous prétexte de les spiritualiser.[225]

To the uneasy spirituality of a part of the young German generation, this appeal to 'nameless forces' offered new possibilities of escape. It flattered it, writes Massis, in its taste for the turbid, the unfinished, the thing that is not, the chaos whence anything may come, where the imagination may dream anything and where nothing possesses either form or limit; and no doubt it found in this 'spiritualism', 'rajeuni aux sources de la pensée hindoue et chinoise, cette philosophie contradictoire, aux plans infinis, ce panthéisme idéaliste qui dort au fond de son être'.[226] Better still than the texts of the Gospels and the Bible, from which the descendants of Luther had drawn their 'heretical exegeses', the ancient Oriental cosmogonies lent themselves to supplying with unexpected images the confused mysticity of a Germany whose faith no longer has any transcendent object. Out of this spiritual miasma the 'new Germany', Massis claims, has dreamed of fashioning a new spirit and a new ideal, a 'New Man' to lead other men. Quoting a witness of Germany's 'wounded generation', Massis declares: 'cet homme amènera avec lui, non pas seulement l'Allemagne nouvelle, mais la terre *des hommes nouveaux*'.[227] The call for the creation of a New Man—which Malraux in his own way will answer—has, Massis continues, found favour with Thomas Mann, who has written: 'the question of man himself, his condition and his state, rises up like an imperious case of conscience before all our eyes, and our clearly perceived duty is to pour a new content into the concept of humanity'.[228]

An ideal which would appear to have satisfied Germany's latest aspiration is, Massis informs us, that of Dostoyevsky's Karamazovs.[229] There are others, he adds, but whatever the doctrine or new interest all postulate at the outset the failure of Western culture, 'la définitive décadence de la latinité, son irrémédiable échec. Échapper à l'antique discipline romaine, voilà la pensée fixe de tous ces novateurs'.[230] Under the cover of an idealism that proclaims the downfall of technical and material civilization, repudiates the idolatory of organization and exalts the inner contemplation of the East, it is her own intellectual revenge, Massis insists, that the Germany of a Spengler is seeking to prepare, and her first care is to overthrow the values which assure to France too evident a supremacy. The cults of Keyserling and Dostoyevsky, of Confucius, Lao-Tseu and Tagore are all directed to this end.[231]

The same sedition against the order of the world—in a more acute form in so far as her connection with the West has been still more fortuitous and savage—may be observed, Massis claims, in that Russia which, after two centuries of forced Europeanization, is returning to her Asiatic origins and rousing herself and all the peoples of the East against a civilization that she endured only under compulsion and in a spirit of bitter resistance:

> Au lieu de se dire, comme au temps des Romanoff, l'avant-garde de l'Europe en Asie, la Russie bolchevique redevient, comme à l'époque des grands khans mongols et tartares, l'avant-garde de l'Asie en Europe.[232]

Accustomed to regard her as a European nation, Western politicians did not foresee that Russia, thrust out from the councils of 'civilized nations', would place herself at the head of that movement of 'independence' and 'liberation' which is exciting the whole of Asia. Even those who understood this did not go much farther, and did not perceive the disastrous consequences that may result for the future of the whole human race:

113

Ils ont pris pour une simple rupture de rapports politiques, ce qui se présente en fait, comme une véritable *brisure historique*, la plus grave que notre civilisation ait connue depuis qu'elle existe . . . Un retour des barbares, c'est-à-dire un nouveau triomphe des parties moins conscientes et moins civilisées de l'humanité sur les parties les plus conscientes et les plus civilisées, ne nous paraît plus impossible.[233]

Believing herself to be the annunciatrix of the regeneration of the world, the Soviet Union has taken upon herself the task of bringing face to face, in a decisive fashion, *the principles on which East and West have founded their ideal of life, their metaphysic and their belief.* At once 'the corpse and the murderer', 'the sickness and the prosector' of the old world, she is turning against what now appears to her only to have been the cause of her humiliations and her shortcomings:

Le tsar Nicolas II n'est pas tombé victime d'une doctrine européenne du progrès. C'est Pierre Ier qu'on a tué dans sa personne; et sa chute a ouvert devant l'âme populaire russe, non pas, comme on a pu le croire le chemin de l'Europe, mais celui du retour à l'Asie.[234]

Of all Civilization's enemies Russia is, claims Massis, the most dangerous, because—in politics as in thought—she is the very apotheosis of the 'anti-Western', 'anti-human principle':

La culture hellénique, le monde latin, la civilisation chrétienne n'ont jamais rencontré d'ennemi plus lucide, plus implacable que celui qui s'appuie aux contre forts de l'Oural.[235]

Turning to history for a judgement on the 'enemy from behind the Urals', Massis declares that the general laws of humanity are a closed book to it. None better than Chaadaev, he claims, has expressed the unhappy fate of his race, placed as it were outside time and unreached by the universal education of the human race:

Venus au monde, comme des enfants illégitimes, sans héritage, sans lien avec les hommes qui nous ont précédés sur la terre, nous n'avons rien dans nos cœurs des enseignements antérieurs à nos propres existences . . . Il n'y a pas chez nous de développement intime, de progrès naturel; les nouvelles idées balaient les anciennes, parce qu'elles ne viennent pas de celles-là et qu'elles tombent on ne sait d'où ... *Nous grandissons, mais nous ne mûrissons pas.*[236]

Deprived for centuries of a truly vivifying doctrinal enlightenment, left without any firm moral and religious direction, except for the more or less strict observance of the external part of religion, the Russian people have remained the prey of superstitions that hid the 'true faith' from them, and laid bare their soul to the 'morbid terrors' and irrational anxieties that tormented it. There is no tradition, writes Massis, either of criticism, of experience or of foresight; nothing but a sort of 'mystical naturism', which predisposed the Russians to submit to the influence of the most elementary negations. From the *Contrat social* and the antinomies of Kant to the absolute Ego of Stirner and the historical materialism of Karl Marx, there has been no chimæra that they have not welcomed with a sort of dark, logistic eagerness:

> Dès qu'une idée est entrée dans la pensée d'un Russe, elle cesse, en effet, d'être une abstraction; elle devient une vérité concrète; il juge toutes choses d'après elle; aucune difficulté d'interprétation, aucune obscurité ne l'arrête.[237]

There is, claims Massis, the example of the Soviet schoolteacher who, after an injection of Darwinian principle, drew up a plan for the suppression of the old and feeble, the upkeep of whom entailed unnecessary expense.[238] Of a populace without ideas, principles or feelings, the Soviet government has made a 'fearful automaton', a 'corpse' which, galvanized into action and striking at random, can still kill.[239]

In revolt against the West, its ideals and its institutions, the Soviet government has been quick to see the formidable advantage to be gained from stretching out its hand to the religious peoples of Asia. That is why, claims Massis, the Bolsheviks pose as 'idealists', 'mystics' and 'liberators'. In secret, however, they dream of giving an overlord to these Asiatic peoples in whom they detect an inarticulate desire for unity. Massis finds evidence for his claim in the 'Moscow Orientalist Review', *Novyi Vostok*:

> Recently, Russia has taken the name of Eurasia, and this new Russia is above all the master and guide of the East, which is

115

groaning in the chains of moral and economic slavery, and which is struggling for a better future. Moscow is the Mecca and the Medina for all these subject peoples.[240]

By the paths followed in the past by the soldiers and *chinovniki* of the Tsar, pioneers and organizers of another kind are, writes Massis, penetrating today into Persia, India, China, Japan, Korea and the Near East, fertilizing on their way that state of expectation, of prophetic, messianic and millennial exaltation which is the precursor of great migratory movements. So it is, claims Massis, that the period foretold by Renan is at hand, when 'le Slave, comme le Dragon de l'Apocalypse, dont la queue balaie la troisième partie des étoiles, traînera après lui le troupeau de l'Asie centrale, l'ancienne clientèle des Genghiskhan et des Tamerlan'.[241]

If a spiritual kinship today exists between Bolshevism and Oriental religiosity it is, writes Massis, because Bolshevism takes its inspiration from a sort of 'mystical syncretism' bequeathed to it by its 'Slav' forbears:

> Ce n'est pas seulement par son caractère violemment hostile à la civilisation occidentale que [la propagande russe] est propre à séduire [les Asiatiques], c'est surtout par la *mystérieuse consonance* qu'ils y aperçoivent avec leurs propres pensées.[242]

In support of his claim of a 'mysterious harmony' of Slav and Oriental forms, Massis refers to philological and literary resemblances—old Slavonic, Sanskrit and 'primitive Russian literature'.[243]

More expressive still of Russia's Oriental affinities are, claims Massis, the heresies into which the belief in an 'inner revelation' and 'free inspiration' has led Russian asceticism. Numerous are the sects in Russia that understand the dogmas of the Church in a symbolic manner. 'Ignorant muzhiks', writes Massis, interpret the Christian mysteries in a manner analogous with that in which the Buddhists understand their own precepts. For them, he adds, the Incarnation is reproduced in the life of each of the faithful, and, if they admit 'a primitive stain', they trace it back to before the creation of the world; for in their semi-gnostic cosmogony, they believe in the pre-existence of the soul. Some of them have carried their speculations to the point of denying to God any other than a 'subjective existence', and of identifying Him with

116

man: '"Dieu, disent-ils, est esprit: il est en nous, nous sommes Dieu"—ce qui constitue l'essence même de la théosophie orientale'.[244] The 'Scythianism' of the revolutionaries of today feeds on these ideas. There is to be found, in the service of violence, the same desire for universal regeneration, founded on the conviction that the Russian people are the body of God, the God-bearing people.[245]

Tolstoy, whom the messengers of the East rightly salute as one of their prophets, also wanted to destroy this 'accursed society' and, adds Massis, to renew the face of the earth, by setting up here below the Kingdom of God, which is nothing but 'peace among men'. Believing that Russia was called upon to play the part of mediator between East and West, he spent his last years in eager correspondence with Mussulmans, Chinese and Hindus. He entertained great hopes of these peoples who, according to him, had not been depraved by military, political and industrial life, and who had not lost faith in 'the divine law'. It is well known, continues Massis, to what bloody adventures and to what murderous xenophobia this 'idyllic vision' has already led the China of Sun Yat-Sen and his successors. From Tolstoy's teachings has also come the India of the Swaraj; from them have sprung those age-old passions which, reawakened under the pretext of preparing the ways for a reconciliation between Asia and Europe, are today poised to accomplish what Romain Rolland has imagined to be 'l'œuvre commune: la plus grande civilisation, le total génie humain'.[246]

How comes it, asks Massis, that on the plea of promoting 'the fusion of the minds' of East and West, the Tagores, the Coomaraswamys, the Okakuras, Gandhi himself, find themselves in agreement with all the most destructive elements in European doctrines? It must be obvious, writes Massis, that they know where the breaches are, and are seeking for the lines of least spiritual resistance, in order to find their way into the disunited body of the West. 'German philosophy', 'Russian mysticism', '[Leninist] idealism', these are the roads chosen, reconnoitred in advance, the 'mask' under which these Asiatics hide their 'devouring glance' in order the better to seduce us, the better to make themselves understood. Sustained and aided in enterprises hostile to the human race by refugees from all the European nations, by apostates from all the creeds, by the sectarians of all

117

the religious aberrations that form with them 'le concile
œcuménique des hérésies coalisées', they are working with our
worst ideas in order to turn them against us:

> Nous sommes ici au lieu géométrique où les diverses contrefaçons
> de communion spirituelle se relient, se pénètrent, rassemblent
> leurs forces diviseuses contre 'la grande école d'énergie' qui a fait
> la civilisation d'Occident.[247]

A 'shameful nationalism', Eastern thought disguises itself as love,
affects to live in the eternal, 'on the summit of the centuries'.
When it is exported, it is transformed into an 'humanitarian
pacifism', an 'idealistic syncretism' for the use of a world which,
claims Massis, it seeks to stupefy and to confound, for it sows
confusion only to reap rewards for itself:

> A ces ruses de vaincus, le poète Tagore dépense l'ingéniosité d'un
> charmeur de serpents et module ses chants de Kabir d'un bout à
> l'autre de l'univers; Gandhi, lui, s'attaque sur son propre sol au
> serpent qui l'entoure et ne lui oppose que la 'non-résistance', plus
> redoutable qu'aucune arme.[248]

For both, however, 'the snake', writes Massis, is the civilization
of the West, 'satanic and perverse', and exclusively dominated by
the 'worship of Mammon'. To the materialistic West, which is all
Machine, they compare, with frantic insistency, the spirituality of
the East, which is all spirit. And while Tagore holds that the East,
with its ideals, in which are deposited 'centuries of sun and starry
silence', can wait patiently until Europe 'loses breath' and 'the
Giant of Flesh disappears into the abyss', Mahatma Gandhi, who
is defending his threatened house, does not harbour these
convenient illusions: '*Le seul effort requis*, dit-il, *c'est de chasser
la civilisation d'Occident.*'[249] That is the final word, writes Massis,
of that 'spiritual system', 'où s'incarnent des forces élémentaires
qui visent, en fait, à notre anéantissement'.[250]

Returning to the subject which he had raised in 'Les Appels',
Massis claims that the prophets of the renaissance of Asia are
commanded by the very ideas which they pretend to oppose.
With liberal vocabulary and democratic concepts borrowed from
the West they are laying claim to things which are, he believes,
fundamentally foreign to them:

> Et ces grands mots de Justice, de Liberté, de Progrès, comme un

virus tout nouveau qu'aucune inoculation préalable ne saurait atténuer, sont ainsi rendus les véhicules de l'anarchie, dans un monde qu'ils contaminent irrémédiablement, qu'ils détournent de son destin et dont nous entendons déjà gronder la formidable émeute.[251]

By modernizing the Asian masses, by bringing to them her ideas, her codes and her technology, Europe has resuscitated forces that seemed to have died out:

> La conquête eut pour [les Orientaux] 'la valeur d'un risorgimento'; elle leur a rendu la conscience d'eux-mêmes. De la Chine des Mandchous . . . elle a fait la Chine de Sun-Yat-Sen et des révoltes cantonnaises . . . 'de l'européanisation de l'Asie est sortie la révolte de l'Asie contre l'Europe' . . . 'On salue et on aime les Soviets moins pour ce qu'ils apportent que pour ce qu'ils détruisent. On voit en eux le libérateur qui humiliera, qui écrasera les maîtres dont l'oppression a si longtemps fait souffrir.'[252]

From these observations with which *Clarté* (Drieu and, indeed, Malraux) would doubtless have agreed, Massis draws conclusions which *Clarté* had already pronounced as reactionary and diversionary. When, writes Massis, a Tagore or a Gandhi urge the West to listen to the spirit of India, when they labour to rehabilitate Asian culture and thought, and to denounce the destructive spirit of Western civilization, they are furthering plans of a political coalition, composed of China, Japan, Russia and Germany, that seeks to cast Western civilization into the abyss.[253]

Nowhere is the duel between Civilization and its enemies more in evidence, writes Massis, than in the Chinese crisis—a crisis, we will recall, which is the setting for André Malraux's *Les Conquérants*. Where the great Western powers delay, Borodin and his acolytes are prepared to act. Paul Morand was surely right, claims Massis, when he wrote:

> Canton, c'est le premier coup droit porté à Londres par Moscou. Nous réjouir d'une discrimination serait folie. Pour l'Asie, tous les blancs se ressemblent, ne font qu'un peuple. D'autres suivront et nous aurons notre tour. A l'Europe ignorante, isolée, divisée, sceptique, les yeux mal ouverts à l'évidente simplicité du conflit actuel s'oppose une doctrine ardente, cohérente, méthodique, parfaitement informée, tendue de toute la force de ses dirigeants

vers la destruction d'une vieille société qui ne se défend qu'avec des armes de paix contre qui l'attaque avec des armes de guerre.[254]

Such is the fact, such is the reality, claims Massis, that is hidden beneath the rhapsody of a Tagore and the Tolstoyan gospel of a Gandhi. It is doubtless some such anticipation, he continues, that intoxicates Romain Rolland when he writes of that 'great tide of spirit', rising in the depths of the East, that will not recede until it has overflowed the banks of Europe.[255] On the plea of welcoming the 'ample and calm metaphysics of India', its conception of the universe, its 'wisdom of life', the breach through which anarchy, no less barbarous than invasions, has always surged, dissolving our institutions and our customs, is being enlarged. The word, *so far in idealistic language*, is only a sort of 'spiritual invasion', ready to roll in upon us from the high plateaux of Asia to 'regenerate' the races of the West, 'abandoned in the night of their evil destiny'. We must not wait until the 'avalanches' longed for by certain 'European deserters' have destroyed our world before denouncing those who have become the accomplices of this 'Asiaticism': 'ceux-là sont les véritables fauteurs de la crise de l'esprit occidental et de l'esprit tout court'.[256]

Anti-Western propaganda may be recognized, writes Massis, by the fact that it takes advantage of the disorder in Europe to maintain in her the catastrophic feeling of deterioration and decline. The object is to disarm men's minds so that events may the easier overwhelm their whole being. Europe, who has now hardly any other education than the ruin of her memory is only too ready to yield to 'la plainte funeste de ce fatalisme historique'.[257] In a statement which goes to the very heart of the anxieties voiced by Malraux, Massis claims that the West feels only as a burden on its will and soul all those former civilizations that the immense work of erudition of the nineteenth century evoked from the past of humanity, and cannot harmonize in its mind. Hence the thirst for novelty that torments it. It adores change only because it feels bowed down beneath the weight of the weariness of the universe. Europe's learned men meditate in melancholy on the rise and fall of vanished communities and can find nothing better to do than to leave 'le poids des années déçues' to other misled generations, who will bear it onwards to sepulchres yet to come. Does not history, Massis asks, teach us other things besides scepticism? Does it not show us that the only societies to perish are those which neglect 'les conditions de toute vie et de toute liberté, les règles permanentes du salut et les moyens de la défense'? Does it not also bring into evidence what has rightly been called 'la loi du rempart'?[258] If we desire to defend the West against its detractors, we should not aim to apologize for its defects or its surrenders. The wretched state of the modern world, the 'cadavre du monde chrétien', goads us on with a special urgency to restore the true principles and traditions of our civilization, those indeed that may save it and the human race with it.

If, as an aid to this necessary recovery, we expect nothing from Asia, it is, writes Massis, because the 'pseudo-Orientalism' of her recent prophets is more often than not only an exotic variant of a Rousseauist 'return to nature', a thoughtless appeal to unsubdued instincts. Moreover, one has only to look at what 'faith' has done in the East to doubt whether it is quite the thing to present as a remedy for the evils from which the West suffers. Buddhism is nothing less than 'un chaos intellectuel et moral' and of India it has to be said that 'en politique comme en religion, c'est le pays de l'anarchie'.[259] The only feeling which Asia satisfies is, claims Massis, a craving for self-defeat, self-destruction and the annihilation of personality. Everywhere appears the identity of the subject and the object, of man and of God. Perfection is defined as the suppression of action and the acceptance of internal and cosmic vertigo, whereas for Christians it must be action, an active love for God and the acceptance of Judaeo-Christian monotheism with its emphasis on the unity, the personality and the finality of being: one sole God, one sole Truth and one sole Humanity, and at the same time one Law, one Right, one Reason and one universal and common morality.[260]

All the Asiatic ideas that are coming to the surface of the body of thought that covers them would be inoperative, writes Massis, if they were not, so to speak, galvanized by contact with the heresies of anti-Christian Western thought. There is no need to go to Tolstoy or Gandhi for them to teach us that 'Christ forbids his disciples all jurisdiction, all human justice, all coercive authority'. In the Middle Ages, at the very moment when St Thomas, taking up once more the ethics and politics of Aristotle, illuminated them with the truths of Revelation, Marsile of Padua

121

was already attacking the philosophy of natural order in these terms. It is not in the precepts of Lao-Tseu and Chan-Tung that the man of the West learned that 'everything that our understanding conceives, examines, resolves and contrives, is bad', but by listening to John Calvin. It is not the Sannyâsins of the Punjab, but the disciples of Luther who told him with their master that 'law is of demoniac origin', that everything in nature is nothing but matter, in man nothing but sin, and in intelligence nothing but pride and concupiscence of the spirit. Before anyone thought of looking for it in the maxims of the Boddhisatra, the idea that faith exempts from works had been preached by the Reformer. To the old moral and juridical order he had opposed, before Tagore, a false order of love, in which there is no longer either fixed measure or certain standard. From then onwards, Massis adds, the equilibrium was destroyed, nature attacked, the human person dissolved, society disunited, the Church rendered invisible, universality ruined and the spiritual world unbridled. And it is thus that, at the threshold of modern times, the West opened its heart to that 'metaphysic of identity' which, through 'German idealism', 'Slav mysticism' and 'Asiatic pantheism', seeks to settle once more among us. It is these Western heresies, Massis claims, that the 'Oriental parasites' of today foster and support.[261]

With atomism beaten, determinism wavering, mechanism in full flight and the scientific universe once more full of mystery, it is a propitious moment, writes Massis, for the equivocal enterprises of all the false mysticisms which mingle materialistic sensuality with spiritualistic confusions. Moreover, psychoanalysis, subconsciousness, dreams and inhibitions are the rage. The spirits are called, 'the divine' is mobilized, the 'invisible host' is introduced:

> Toutes les vieilles mystagogies resurgissent, et c'est du laboratoire que s'échappent les talismans et les charmes, les entités psychiques, les éons et les phantasmes occultes qui revivent d'une vie folle, désordonnée.[262]

'Mystery' envelops everything and is installed in the sombre regions of the ego it ravages, at the centre of the reason it drives away from its domain. Everybody is ready to reintroduce it everywhere except in the divine order in which it really resides. For, although the 'irrational mystics' have broken down all the

122

barriers, man has not for that reason opened himself to the 'commerce of God' and the revelations of faith.

The objective and the intellectual having been banished, theosophy can henceforward give itself free play; and, in so far as it still lives on the principles of 'idealistic individualism', the West has nothing to oppose to these 'ruinous dreamings'. Much more, it is logical that, being called upon to *remake a culture* and to *reconstruct a civilization* on these bases, it should listen to the voice of an Asia that invokes these metaphysical premises.[263] Is Christian asceticism so little known to Western minds, asks Massis, that they must needs seek the virtues of contemplation and sacrifice in the life of Mahatma Gandhi? Must we, continues Massis, call the *Summa* of St Thomas the *Baghavât Gita*, turn the Council of Trent into an assembly of Tibetan lamas, dress up St John of the Cross or St Francis of Assisi in a *bhiksu* or the Curé of Ars in a *cramana*—in short, disguise our own religion in 'Asiatic rags', for certain aesthetes, in their love of exotic wisdom, to undertake its discovery and to admire its profundities?[264]

Because it is no longer sure of its laws or its institutions, because it carries in a 'sick body' hostile and discordant souls, the West must defend itself against the false mysticisms which, under the cover of a 'second-hand Orientalism', exploit a dissatisfaction of mind and mask with the charm of exoticism, poetry and mystery, the 'savage appetites' of races in rivalry. Never in the course of history have these great controversies of civilization and culture taken on so tragic a character; for the differences that bring into play all the science of thought are of those that, some day or other, will bring into play all the science of war. For this reason, Massis insists, there is no more urgent need for the Western man than that he should *define himself* anew:

> La lutte qui ébranle la Cité, c'est d'abord en lui-même qu'elle fait rage. Et de quoi souffre-t-il? De ses pensées diverses, de ses fois différentes, de ses sciences inégales, de ses morales particulières, de ses éducations dissemblables. Il manque d'une vérité ordonnatrice où puiser l'âme de ses actes; ou plutôt il en a laissé corrompre la source, quand il ne l'a pas lui-même corrompue.[265]

Without a doctrine, without a common mind, without a philosophy which gives to the same things the same name and understands by the same signs the same idea, there is no remedy, writes Massis, for the evils that desolate States as well as individuals. The important thing, he stresses, is *to recreate the human person,* to re-establish the hierarchy of being, and to defend it against all the errors that weaken it and tend only to destroy it:

> Pour imposer à 'la matière amplifiée une âme vraiment vivante', pour donner aux progrès de la science moderne un esprit réellement humain, il ne faudra rien de moins qu'une restauration intégrale des principes de la civilisation gréco-latine et du catholicisme. Cette grande tradition de la sagesse antique et de la sagesse chrétienne peut encore sauver ce qu'il y a de viable dans le monde.[266]

If, as some have claimed, the East offers us a return to our lost spirituality, a well-balanced mind, writes Massis, would conclude that Europe and the world must be re-christianized. But this is not the path taken by the proselytes of Asiaticism. They dream only of exposing us to its strange cosmogony, and that at the very time when the East is sinking into the quicksand of nationalistic fanaticism, when it is succumbing to the 'fertile absurdity' of Western technology and materialism. For Asia, Massis claims, is as remote as Europe from its sources of spiritual integrity. Both here and there, disappointed souls are in search of spirituality. It is to be hoped, he writes, that the colloquy that is beginning between the East and the West, amid the disorders of our suffering planet, may serve to prepare the way of reconciliation in Christianity which alone can recreate human unity.[267]

Because it is the 'Church of Truth', and it connects 'natural law' with the 'eternal law' which is in God, the Catholic Church seems to Massis the sole power capable of restoring 'une civilisation véritable à caractère universel'. Though its integral unity springs from its spirituality, though its powers are ordained for the sanctification of souls and their salvation, the great principles of order and of stability of social life are indebted to it nevertheless for having defended them with constant energy and efficacy wherever its magistracy extends:

> Loin d'opposer ces intérêts, elle les harmonise, car cette compétence unique qu'elle manifeste dans l'organisation des choses humaines est en quelque sorte exigée par 'sa maternité universelle et sa mission illuminatrice'.[268]

In a century in which racial and cultural rivalries run riot, the Catholic Church is, Massis claims, the only institution which embodies a spiritual internationalism, establishes in the 'Love of the Living God' a universal kinship, and possesses an œcumenical jurisprudence founded on Law and Revelation. If Massis insists on its 'historical role' as the organizer of the West, it is, he asserts, because civilization has need of it to rediscover, with the integrity of its being, the secret of its apostolic force. He does not, however, restrict its message, which is addressed to the whole human race:

> Le Christ seul, placé au centre de tout, peut réconcilier l'Orient et l'Occident. *Ut sint unum* . . . S'il nous faut restaurer l'intégrité de notre Europe, et la défendre contre tout ce qui la menace, c'est pour que soit intacte la citadelle d'où partiront les missionnaires qui étendront le Royaume de Dieu jusqu'aux confins du monde.[269]

If Massis could find in Indian metaphysics and the Bolshevik ideal a sort of 'pre-established complicity', a 'secret connivance', an *'identical* fund of hostility' towards the principles of Romano-Christian civilization, Rolland and Barbusse, as their 'European representatives', seemed altogether incapable of honouring the 'unspoken agreement'. 'Spirit' and 'force', it seemed, still refused to recognize that 'mysterious reciprocity' with which Massis charged them. Barbusse, for example, in an article published in 1926 on the occasion of Rolland's sixtieth birthday,[270] took the opportunity of stressing once more the cosmic and impractical nature of Rollandist solutions:

> Il suffit d'un juste pour sauvegarder dans une société l'idée de justice. Mais pour construire l'œuvre d'équilibre pratique au milieu d'une civilisation et contre elle, il faut *toute une organisation* d'hommes prêts à rattacher sans cesse le ciel à terre.

Rolland, however, remained aloof and unconvinced, the more so because Barbusse's only prescription for social justice appeared to be brutal surgery. When, moreover, an Indian student of political economy, Lajpat Rai, suggested to Rolland that non-violence was not an absolute and universal principle and that recourse to armed force was, in certain circumstances, a political necessity, Rolland's response was unambiguous:

> Je ne suis point de son avis, même d'un point de vue strictement

politique et pratique; je crois qu'une lutte engagée dans de telles conditions mène à la ruine; et que la meilleure arme, la plus efficace, est la *résistance morale*, tenace d'un peuple *non-violent* et *non-acceptant*.[271]

As his reply to Lajpat Rai suggests, Rolland's opposition to violence was not determined by political or tactical considerations (even if they could be said to be a contributory factor) and not even by that fundamental attitude which, through contact with Gandhi, found potent expression in *ahimsa*, the doctrine of non-injury to any form of life. In the event Rolland was opposed to revolutionary violence not merely from the point of view of its effects but, more importantly perhaps, because of what he took to be the fundamental attitude governing its use: 'class hatred'. His view on this 'pernicious' and 'divisive' doctrine had already been expressed in his reply to Barbusse on 2 February 1922, as had his preference for that specific and active love—*amour amor caritas*—which he saw at work in Gandhi and in which, he believed, the salvation of mankind would be fired. His affinity with the Orient, especially with India and its thought, his refusal to admit two divisions of humanity based upon geographical factors and his rejection of what he described as the doctrine of 'neo-Marxist Communism'—acceptance of which implied acquiescence to force—were, therefore, linked. They derived from a fundamental belief in the essential unity of human thought and spiritual life. And so where Barbusse and his associates emphasized the irreconcilable division of humanity into warring classes, whether the protagonists were the industrial proletariat of Western Europe and the capitalist class, or the Asian masses and the imperialist bourgeoisie, Rolland stressed the universality of the human spirit and defended its implicit moral imperative, namely, that the 'homme de pensée' hold back his hand from the shedding of blood.

Rolland's biographies of Ramakrishna and Vivekananda, published in 1929, were to reveal that his attachment to the idea of progress in the spiritual sense had lost nothing of its appeal despite Barbusse's political objections. He continued to lay emphasis upon the unity of man's spiritual life. In his *Vie de Vivekananda*, for example, he claimed that a predisposition to Vedantism existed in the United States long before the arrival there of Vivekananda. This disposition, he further maintained, could not be attributed to a corpus of doctrines in any one country but was, rather, a universal tendency which, though its development was not uniform, was latent in the human soul at all times and in all places and especially strong in those who bore within them some spark of creation.[272]

Vivekananda's attempt to synthesize Hindu faith and modern science was of special interest to Rolland for it presaged (as he had already indicated in his preface to La Danse de Çiva) the imminent realization of man's 'total self'.[273] Here, at the very pinnacle of man's being, a new order of thought, freer and more universal, waited to illuminate the world and burn bright in eternal tribute to those in East and West who were struggling to give it life. The essential condition for this spiritual development was, Rolland insisted, 'Liberté'—that hotly disputed concept which had loomed large in the exchange between him and Clarté—and Vivekananda, Rolland was pleased to note, offered a concept of freedom similar to his own. He added that although Europe had been far more successful than India in bringing about this condition in the realm of politics she lagged behind in matters of the spirit.[274] Implicit, therefore, in Rolland's call for the fruitful cooperation of East and West was not only the desire to channel the finest expressions of the spirit and of social life, of Oriental intuition and Occidental action, into a new stream of human consciousness but the hope that Europe's spiritual life would, through contact with Oriental wisdom, be raised to the level of her social attainments.

Within the framework of Rolland's development, whose philosophical curve he regarded as similar to that plotted by Ramakrishna,[275] the period 1920 to 1930 was, despite its spiritual bent, one of political transition. During this period Rolland moved towards a more socially critical and politically oriented frame of mind which, in the following decade, would lend itself to that cause which Barbusse had long since urged him to espouse: that of the proletariat and of the Soviet Union. His uncritical support of the Soviet Union would be accompanied by his fight against Fascism which, in 1935, he defined in broad terms as a nationalist statism possessed of the delirious ideology of the supremacy of one race, people or nation over all others. In this respect, he wrote, it differed from the old imperialism whose conquests,

127

though pursued in the economic interests of the metropolitan State, did promote progress in that, incidentally or accidentally, they destroyed or undermined feudalism and absolutism, thereby paving the way for the democratic revolution and the demise of imperialism itself. Fascism, on the other hand, was an attempt to turn back the wheel of progress. It lived and thrived on war and on war alone.[276]

By 1926 Rolland began to appreciate the danger of the Fascist régime in Italy, and Tagore's flirtation with it did nothing to calm his fears. Tagore visited Italy in 1925 as the guest of the Orientalist, Formichi, who had presented the Hindu philosopher with a glowing report of, and gifts from, Mussolini.[277] To those Europeans like Rolland who looked upon Tagore as the incarnation of Justice and Freedom the visit came as a hammer blow. It was as if Tagore himself had chosen to drive another nail into the already martyred body of Matteotti.[278] Tagore's tacit support of the régime could be explained, suggested Rolland, only by the trust which he had placed in Italian intellectuals who, in the event, proved to have greater respect for *raison d'État* than for matters of the spirit.[279] Rolland was eager to take advantage of Tagore's visit to Villeneuve in June 1926 in order to address his guest, 'au nom de l'Italie bâillonnée, de l'Italie martyre'.[280] To this end he called upon the Italian exile Giusseppe Salvemini to meet with Tagore so as to expose the true face of Fascism to him who had been allowed to see only the deceptive mask.[281] Rolland was, however, totally unprepared for the shock he was to receive. In conversation with him, Tagore attempted to legitimize Fascism. In a statement that would, ironically, have done Massis proud, Tagore claimed that Fascism had brought order and prosperity to Italy, stimulated the economy and brought succour to the life of the spirit.[282] When, almost in the same breath, Tagore raised the question of British India and accused the European aggressor of having subjected the populace to untold misery, Rolland was able to restrain himself no longer. He retorted that if one is prepared to sanction the abuse of power and approve prescribed falsehood in Italy one has no right to defend the cause of India.[283] Rolland's strong remarks prompted Tagore to reply that he would give the matter urgent consideration and then present his conclusions in writing. When, furthermore, he expressed his willingness to be interviewed on

128

the subject of Italy, Rolland recommended Duhamel as the person best qualified to conduct such an interview. Duhamel promptly drew up a questionnaire for Tagore but the latter apparently chose to ignore it. Instead he submitted a Platonic critique of Fascism in which Mussolini was flatteringly described as a twentieth-century Alexander or Napoleon.[284] Duhamel was, understandably, stunned and, refusing to handle Tagore's statement, made the ironic suggestion that the venerable poet try his luck with the (right-wing) *Revue des deux mondes*. Rolland noted in his journal that 'Tagore parle de l'Italie et du fascisme, comme d'une plate-forme de sleeping, en touriste désintéressé, qui passe et qui s'en va . . . un tel article serait retenu en Europe comme l'apothéose du fascisme'.[285]

Only after considerable pressure from Rolland and Duhamel did Tagore agree not to make his views public at this stage. And yet a public statement, Rolland felt, was imperative. *L'Humanité* had already begun publishing remarks, allegedly made by Tagore in Italy, and J. R. Bloch and Jacques Mesnil were openly accusing the Hindu poet of complicity with Fascism.[286] And all the while Rolland was impressing upon Tagore that only the clearest denunciation of Fascism could recover the situation, to say nothing of its being the only morally acceptable solution. Responding to Rolland's constant appeals Tagore wrote to Professor Formichi that the idea of sanctioning a 'career of unscrupulous crime in any political body for the sake of the self-aggrandizement of a people' was extremely repugnant for him.[287] Rolland was, however, far from happy with the letter for in it Tagore had expressed regret at having had to break his 'neutralité silencieuse'.[288] Although his second letter to Formichi on 21 July 1926 was more forceful its criticisms remained vague and philosophical.[289] However, since a statement to the press had become an absolute necessity Rolland decided to send for publication those of Tagore's remarks which were the most critical of Fascism. They appeared in *Europe* on the 15 August, in *L'Humanité* on the 16th and in British and German newspapers shortly afterwards.[290] Public opinion, Rolland noted in his diary, had been reassured.

By 1927 Rolland had become so convinced of the prime necessity of combating Fascism that his dispute with Barbusse now seemed forgotten. Together they called for the creation of a

'Comité International contre le fascisme' and together accepted, along with Albert Einstein, the honorary chairmanship of the first great anti-Fascist rally at the Salle Bullier in Paris on 23 February 1927, under the chairmanship of Paul Langevin.[291] If Rolland still claimed, in principle, the right to criticize the errors and excesses of the Soviet Union, in practical terms he did no such thing, for the enemies of the Soviet Union were, he now recognized, the enemies of all humanity.[292] If the forward march of humanity was to be ensured the Soviet Union would have to be defended, international peace maintained, and the forces of progress uncompromising in their opposition to imperialism and Fascism. It was to this manifold task, with pamphlets, protests and signatures, that Rolland devoted his energies between 1928 and 1935.[293] After spending the spring and summer of 1932 busily preparing for the World Congress against War and Fascism, which met in Amsterdam in August and of which Barbusse was the principal organizer, Rolland was named honorary chairman of the 'Comité International Antifasciste' whose first meeting was held in June 1933 in the Salle Pleyel, Paris.[294]

While Barbusse and Rolland were informing world opinion of the horrors of Fascism and alerting it to the dangers of Fascist expansionism, Massis and his friends in the Action Française were extolling the regenerating effects of the 'Italian Revival'. When Italy revealed its intentions towards Abyssinia, and Britain, and then France, moved for sanctions, the Action Française, fearing for the Laval-Mussolini accords, launched the slogan: 'Les sanctions, c'est la guerre'.[295] On 4 October 1935, with the Abyssinian war barely twelve hours old, *Action Française* published Massis's 'Manifeste des intellectuels pour la défense de l'Occident et la paix en Europe'. The document interpreted Italian intervention in Abyssinia as a noble expression of the West's 'mission civilisatrice'. It dissociated itself from the 'juridical universalism' of Geneva, which, placing superior and inferior, civilized and barbarian, on the same pedestal, was prepared to sacrifice world peace and the supremacy of Western civilization to a people insensible to Christianity. Setting the West's historical vocation above egalitarian considerations, the Manifesto called for the continuation of the 'civilizing conquest'. Here then, it seemed, were those 'Christian missionaries'—of whom Massis had written in his *Défense de l'Occident*—whose 'spiritual internationalism', rising out of the Citadel which had nourished it, was destined to extend 'the Kingdom of God to the confines of the world'.[296] The 'reign of the spirit', to which Salazar and Franco would also bring their contribution,[297] had begun to settle on the face of the earth.

Rolland, no less than Massis, also believed that internationalism was of the order of the day, that all parties were international now. It was merely a question, Rolland felt, of which internationalism one served, that of Capital or that of Labour: Reaction or Revolution. Having made his choice he launched the following appeal, in which, clearly revealing his belief in the fact and necessity of class-struggle, he looked forward to the day when the victorious proletariat would lay the foundations of a new social order, classless and worldwide:

> Appel à la vie contre la mort, contre ce qui tue, contre les ravageurs de l'humanité, les puissances d'or: les impérialismes, les dictatures des grandes compagnies et des fascismes! Prolétariat, voici nos mains. Nous sommes tiens . . . Le vrai combat, le seul qui soit fécond et nécessaire, c'est sur le plan international qu'il doit se livrer. Je participe à tous les efforts, à tous les espoirs, à toutes les souffrances de ceux qui travaillent à renverser le vieux monde capitaliste et impérialiste . . . pour édifier un ordre nouveau. Et puisque la *Révolution prolétarienne* est l'avant-garde de l'armée en marche, qui livre la grande bataille internationale, dont la victoire doit assurer l'établissement de la communauté humaine sans frontières et sans classes, *je lui donne la main*.[298]

In France the party that was leading the way was the Communist Party to which, in a letter published in *L'Humanité* on 27 January 1936, Rolland expressed his joy at having discovered after a lifetime's search the broad highway leading to victory over the ruins of the past. In other letters to *L'Humanité*, notably on 25 January and 25 December 1937, he declared that because of its clear understanding of the historical line of march, the conditions and the ultimate general results of the proletarian movement, the Communist Party was the strongest and most logical representative of the French people and of social justice.

In considering how the 'historically more progressive class' assumes State power, establishes and consolidates its authority, Rolland was once more obliged to raise the question of violence.

His earlier objections were now forgotten; he dismissed them as 'out of season'.[299] If Reaction was to be defeated all methods had to be used, violent and non-violent, Leninist as well as Gandhist.[300] In a letter to Subhas Chandras Bose in April 1935 he wrote that he had come to the conclusion that non-violence could not be the pivot of all social action. It was only one of many possible forms of action and one still in its experimental stage. There was one duty to be done, one end to achieve: to *impose* the new order by *every* means in one's power, to win the concession of a charter of humanity from oligarchs and exploiters whose criminal régime, economic and military, enslaved nine-tenths of humanity and did not hesitate to attack its enemies by any and all means:[301]

> Si on n'y met une fin, ce sera la fin de toute société humaine. Il faut donc agir contre lui par toutes les armes de non-violence et de violence, qui peuvent le plus promptement, le plus sûrement, atteindre au but. Je ne répudie aucune arme . . . J'ai pris parti. Je suis pour le monde du Travail organisé par ses propres mains . . . *Je me refuse à condamner ceux qui recourent à la violence pour leur défense.*[302]

The death of the old world was, for Rolland, not only the decay and death of European capitalist society, but also the destruction of its 'commonwealth' of colonial and Fascist crimes. And yet it was much else besides, for out of this death, which heralded the imminent birth of a socialized, proletarian society, the future children of a horrible present would seize their humanity and, for the first time, proceed to make their own history, deliberately and responsibly:

> Qui de nous peut douter désormais, après que nos yeux se sont dégagés du bandeau, que les libres forces, pour lesquelles nous avons si longtemps lutté à tort et à travers, comme des aveugles, ne trouvent enfin leur naturel emploi dans la réalisation pleine et saine d'une société socialiste? . . . Ce sont nos rêves de toute notre vie . . . qui ont vaincu . . . Ils ont passé dans l'ordre nouveau. Et nous qui fûmes, qui restons leurs fidèles, nous les suivons; pour les servir, nous servons l'ordre qu'ils animent. C'est par leur feu dans ma poitrine que, sur une route sombre et semée d'obstacles, souvent meurtri, parfois tombant ou m'égarant, me relevant et reprenant, obstinément ma marche, je suis arrivé au monde nouveau. Qu'en lui ce feu devienne brasier! Que l'esprit

libre soit le ferment des peuples libres, des Républiques socialistes universelles, dont l'union imposera la paix au monde, et, dans la joie, ouvrira au Travail humain un champ de progrès illimité![303]

NOTES

[1] See *L'Art libre* (April 1922) for contributions from Kasimir Edschmid, René Schickele, Fritz von Unruh, and Stefan Zweig.

[2] Léon Trotski, 'Le Drame du prolétariat français', *Clarté* (1 October, 1922), pp. 507–11, and 'Une pièce qui est une date', *L'Humanité* (7 October, 1922), p. 1.

[3] e.g. Jean Maxe, 'L'Idole, ''l'Européen'' Romain Rolland', *Les Cahiers de l'Anti-France*, Vol. I (Bossard, 1922), pp. 10, 13, 67, 90, 91.

[4] Henri Massis, *Défense de l'Occident* (Plon, 1927), p. 19.

[5] André Malraux, 'Défense de l'Occident', *N.R.F.* (June 1927), p. 818.

[6] Henri Massis, 'L'Offensive germano-asiatique contre la culture occidentale', *Le Journal littéraire* (19 July, 1924), p. 2.

[7] Henri Ghéon, 'Réflexions sur le rôle actuel de l'intelligence française', *N.R.F.* (November 1919), p. 962.

[8] Jacques Rivière, 'Le Parti de l'intelligence française', *N.R.F.* (1919), pp. 614–15. See also Massis's reference to Rivière in 'L'Offensive germano-asiatique contre la culture occidentale', *Le Journal littéraire* (19 July, 1924), p. 2.

[9] Adrien Mithouard, 'Paris, capitale de l'Occident' (conférence du 22 mars, 1918), *La Revue hebdomadaire* (13 April, 1919), p. 162.

[10] Henri Massis, 'Pour un parti de l'intelligence', *Le Figaro, supplément littéraire* (19 July, 1919), p. 1A. See also his 'L'Offensive germano-asiatique contre la culture occidentale', p. 2.

[11] A. Vidal, *Henri Barbusse, soldat de la paix*, p. 91.

[12] See F. Vandérem, *Miroir des lettres* (Flammarion, 1921), pp. 111–16.

[13] A. Vidal, *op. cit.*, p. 92.

[14] R. Lefebvre, 'Pour que l'Internationale soit vivante', *Le Populaire de Paris* (22 March, 1919), p. 1.

[15] See 'A nos lecteurs', *Clarté* (15 January, 1921), p. 4; 'Les Conférences de Clarté', *Clarté* (29 January, 1921), p. 1. For Barbusse's support for the growing Communist tendency in the Socialist Party see 'A propos de Jaurès', *Clarté* (31 July, 1920), p. 1, and 'Le Devoir socialiste', *L'Humanité* (24 October, 1920), pp. 1–2.

[16] *Clarté* (12 February, 1921), p. 1. See also 'Clarté et les partis', *Clarté* (19 June, 1920): 'un parti est un pouvoir exécutif, c'est un organisme d'action directe; il se prépare à se saisir un jour du pouvoir, à établir de ses mains, dans les choses, l'ordre nouveau. *Clarté* a pour but de préparer l'esprit nouveau'. Quoted in Marcel Fourrier 'De ''Clarté'' à ''La Guerre Civile'' ', *Clarté* (December 1925/January 1926), p. 6.

[17] See 'Protestation', *Clarté* (5 February, 1921), p. 1, and 'Une Lettre du groupe Clarté de Nancy', *Clarté* (12 February, 1921), p. 2.

[18] See 'Un Appel d'Henri Barbusse', *L'Humanité* (22 February, 1921), p. 1;

'Une Protestation d'Henri Barbusse en faveur de Marius Hanot', *L'Humanité* (7 March, 1921), p. 1; and 'Anatole France et Romain Rolland dénoncent le scandale et l'injustice de ce procès', *L'Humanité* (9 March, 1921), p. 1.

[19] See 'Régime ignominieux', *L'Humanité* (16 June, 1921), p. 1.

[20] See Henri Barbusse, 'Les Étapes de Clarté', *Clarté* (8 July, 1921), p. 1.

[21] Paul Vaillant-Couturier, 'Le Mensonge des élections', *Clarté* (13 December, 1919), p. 2.

[22] See the following articles in *Clarté*:
P. Vaillant-Couturier, 'Comment le capitalisme fait la guerre, comment le bolchevisme fait la paix' (14 August, 1920); Francis Treat, 'La Russie combat la famine' (23 September, 1920); Wilhelm Herzog, 'Introduction à mon voyage en Russie' (16 October, 1920); M. Gorki, 'La Russie et la littérature mondiale' (6 November, 1920); Bohumi Smeral, 'Une Visite à Lounatcharski' (20 and 27 November, and 4 December, 1920); A. Lounatcharski, 'Littérature et Révolution' (25 December, 1920 and 8 January, 1921); M. Gorki, 'Le Chemin du bonheur' (29 April, 1921); Francis Treat, 'Le Prolétariat russe et le théâtre' (15 February, 1922); P. Vaillant-Couturier, 'A-t-on abandonné toute idée d'intervention en Russie?' (1 March, 1922); Jacques Sadoul, 'Les Socialistes révolutionnaires russes en face de la Révolution' (1 September, 1922); A. Lounatcharski, 'La Révolution et la culture en Russie' (1 February, 1923).

[23] Henri Barbusse, 'Aux anciens combattants', *Clarté* (4 February, 1920), p. 1. See also Henri Barbusse, 'Sauvons notre vraie patrie', *L'Humanité* (27 August, 1921), p. 1.

[24] The special issue appeared on the 20 December, 1922.

[25] Henri Barbusse, 'La Révolution russe retournera le monde', *L'Humanité* (6 November, 1922), p. 1.

[26] Romain Rolland, *Journal des années de guerre*, (Albin Michel, 1952), p. 1209 (entry dated 29 May, 1917).

[27] See Romain Rolland, 'Devant la Révolution Russe', *Le Populaire de Paris* (16 November, 1918), p. 1.

[28] See Romain Rolland, *Journal des années de guerre*, p. 1228, pp. 1426–7, p. 1700.

[29] Romain Rolland, *Quinze ans de combat* (Rieder, 1935), p. XIII (where Rolland is referring to an article he wrote in *L'Humanité* on the 26 October, 1919).

[30] Romain Rolland, *Journal des années de guerre*, p. 119.

[31] See Romain Rolland, *op. cit.*, p. 1622.

[32] For Rolland's support of the left-opposition in the Socialist Party see *Journal des années de guerre*, pp. 1208, pp. 1614–15.

[33] Romain Rolland, *op. cit.*, pp. 1000–1 (entry dated December 1916).

[34] Romain Rolland, 'Janvier sanglant à Berlin', *L'Humanité* (16, 17 and 18 February, 1919). See also Romain Rolland, *Quinze ans de combat*, p. LXIV note 2.

[35] See Romain Rolland, *Journal des années de guerre*, pp. 1071–2; and the appeal by the Groupe des Étudiants Socialistes Révolutionnaires Français, 'Aux étudiants socialistes du monde entier', *Le Populaire de Paris* (9 February, 1919), p. 3 (where Rolland's role is acknowledged).

[36] See Romain Rolland, *Journal des années de guerre*, pp. 1769–71, pp. 1824–32.

[37] See Romain Rolland, *op. cit.*, pp. 1071–2 (entry dated February 1917).

[38] Romain Rolland, *Quinze ans de combat*, pp. VI–VII (our italics).

[39] Romain Rolland, 'Devant la Révolution Russe', *Le Populaire de Paris* (16 November, 1918), p. 1.

[40] Romain Rolland, *Quinze ans de combat*, pp. X–XI.

[41] Romain Rolland, *op. cit.*, p. XVII.

[42] Romain Rolland, *op. cit.*, pp. X–XI.

[43] Romain Rolland, *op. cit.*, p. XIV.

[44] 'Pour un parti de l'Intelligence', *Le Figaro, supplément littéraire* (19 July, 1919).

[45] Dimitri Merejkowski, 'Choses vues pendant la Révolution russe', *La Revue universelle* (15 October, 1921), p. 181.

[46] Dimitri Merejkowski, p. 184.

[47] Paul Bourget, 'Psychologie des révolutions', *La Revue universelle* (1 February, 1923), p. 323.

[48] Paul Bourget, p. 330, and Dimitri Merejkowski, p. 185.

[49] Dimitri Merejkowski, p. 183.

[50] E. Gascoin, 'La Psychologie d'un révolutionnaire: Lénine', *La Revue universelle* (15 October, 1924), pp. 227–31.

[51] 'La Confession d'un bolchevik', *La Revue universelle* (15 May, 1922), p. 472.

[52] e.g. Jean Maxe, 'Les Conseils d'usine, levier du bolchevisme international', *La Revue universelle* (1 June, 1921), p. 567: 'le style hébraïque de Lénine . . . Le bolchevisme russe, plus ou moins aidé par le judaïsme, a dressé un plan mondial de subversion et de *domination*'; Georges Batault, 'Judaïsme et Puritanisme', *La Revue universelle* (1 April, 1921), p. 23: 'il y a aujourd'hui une judaïsation des sociétés contemporaines et de la culture moderne. Nous sommes dominés par les principes éthico-économiques issus du judaïsme, et l'esprit de révolte qui travaille le monde l'incline encore à s'enfoncer plus avant dans cette voie. Car, c'est au nom d'un idéal éthico-économique renforcé, que le socialisme et la révolution mènent leurs batailles'; Albert Mousset, 'L'Inconnue Slave et la Russie de demain', *La Revue universelle* (1 September, 1921), p. 546: 'le régime judéo-asiatique de Lénine'; Montjoye, 'Le Plan de conquête germano-russe' (1 March, 1924), p. 588.

[53] 'La Confession d'un bolchevik', *La Revue universelle* (15 May, 1922), pp. 470–80.

[54] 'La Confession d'un bolchevik', p. 470.

[55] René Johannet, 'La Menace de l'Asie', *La Revue universelle* (1 January, 1921), pp. 82–6.

[56] Berthe-Georges Gaulis, 'Le Mouvement asiatique et l'Europe', *La Revue universelle* (1 March, 1921), pp. 615–18.

[57] Roger Labonne, 'Le Nationalisme asiatique', *La Revue universelle* (1 May, 1923), pp. 301–27.

[58] René Johannet, 'Les Révolutions contre l'Europe', *La Revue universelle* (1 January, 1926), pp. 98–102.

[59] Saint-Brice, 'Les Soviets et l'Orient', *La Revue universelle* (1 December, 1926), pp. 607–12.

[60] Jean Maxe, 'Les Conseils d'usine, levier du bolchevisme international', *La Revue universelle* (1 June, 1921), p. 582. See also René Johannet, 'Un Avatar nouveau de l'impérialisme ouvrier', *La Revue universelle* (15 February, 1924), pp. 495–500 (The title of Johannet's article refers to Ramsay MacDonald).

[61] Jacques Bainville, 'L'Avenir de la civilisation', (1 March, 1922), p. 595: 'le divin capital. Sans lui, pas de science ni d'art. Sans lui, pas de ces études désintéressées grâce auxquelles se réalisent toutes les améliorations'. For René Johannet's views on capitalism see 'L'Europe et le mirage socialiste', *La Revue universelle* (15 October, 1921), pp. 216–24; 'La Victoire du capitalisme en Allemagne", *La Revue universelle* (1 January, 1922), pp. 93–8; 'Comment les bourgeois restaurent un pays ruiné par le socialisme', *La Revue universelle* (1 June, 1923); 'Défense du bourgeois français', *La Revue universelle* (15 November, 1923), pp. 433–53.

[62] René Johannet, 'La Consolidation du fascisme', *La Revue universelle* (1 August, 1923), p. 354: 'les bourgeois exaspérés d'être tondus ont mis la main à l'épée. Tout s'est évanoui à leur approche. Serait-il donc vrai que le jour où les bourgeois le *voudront*, ils n'auront qu'à faire un signe pour se débarrasser des simagrées révolutionnaires encore appesanties sur l'Europe.' See also René Johannet, 'Symptômes et pronostics pour 1925', *La Revue universelle* (15 January, 1925), p. 247: '[Mussolini] a rétabli les crucifix dans les écoles'.

[63] René Johannet, 'Causes et origines du coup d'état espagnol', *La Revue universelle* (1 October, 1923), p. 114 and p. 119.

[64] René Johannet, 'La Politique constructive du fascisme vainqueur', *La Revue universelle* (15 June, 1924), p. 767.

[65] René Johannet, 'La Situation du fascisme', *La Revue universelle* (1 August, 1925), p. 360. See also René Johannet, 'Le Coup d'état fasciste', *La Revue universelle* (15 November, 1922), pp. 467–73; Pierre Gorgolini, 'La Conquête du pouvoir par le fascisme et la marche sur Rome', *La Revue universelle* (1 December, 1923), pp. 570–87.

[66] See Pol Vandromme, *Robert Brasillach* (Plon, 1956), pp. 218–20.

[67] René Johannet, 'Les Révolutions contre l'Europe', *La Revue universelle* (1 January, 1926), p. 102.

[68] Renée Dunan, 'Les Livres', *Le Populaire de Paris* (21 September, 1920), p. 2.

[69] Romàin Rolland, *Quinze ans de combat*, p. XVII.

[70] Jean Bernier, 'Chronique de la vie intellectuelle', *Clarté* (11, 18, 25 December, 1920, and 1 January, 1921).

[71] Jean Bernier, 'Chronique de la vie intellectuelle', *Clarté* (25 December, 1920), p. 2.

[72] Jean Bernier, p. 2.

[73] Jean Bernier, 'Chronique de la vie intellectuelle', *Clarté* (1 January, 1921), p. 2.

[74] Henri Barbusse, 'L'autre moitié du devoir. A propos du Rollandisme', *Clarté* (3 December, 1921), pp. 25–8.

[75] Barbusse's faith in Reason and his refusal to accept violent action as an absolute principle of socialist advance were to be vigorously attacked by the

new leadership of *Clarté*; e.g. Marcel Fourrier, 'De "Clarté" à "La Guerre Civile"', *Clarté* (December 1925/January 1926), p. 6: 'Le corps de doctrine échafaudé par Barbusse pour *Clarté* repose essentiellement sur la Raison. Sans vouloir entreprendre une critique de cette conception, il va sans dire que son acceptation présuppose l'abandon de la doctrine marxiste. L'essence de toute la doctrine de Marx, c'est qu'il faut préparer systématiquement les masses à la conception de la révolution violente, du renversement de l'état bourgeois par le prolétariat . . . en effet, si la Raison suffit en elle-même à convaincre tous les hommes de la nécessité d'un changement social, que signifie le principe de la lutte des classes? . . . Barbusse a du devenir humain une conception métaphysique qui nie le matérialisme historique. Sa conception de la Révolution qui n'est en rien marxiste, peut en revanche être acceptée par n'importe quel républicain libéral'.

[76] *Clarté* (1 February, 1922), pp. 126–7. Rolland's reply is also to be found in *Quinze ans de combat*, pp. 33–9.

[77] With hindsight Rolland could write—*Quinze ans de combat*, p. XX—'Barbusse aurait pu me répondre . . . que la violence est, à certaines heures de l'histoire, une douloureuse nécessité, et que, dans l'action nécessaire, les moyens ne sont pas un luxe de l'esprit, qui fait son choix entre eux confortablement, mais qu'ils sont un couteau sur la gorge, qu'on est contraint, même si le cœur le déplore, d'empoigner d'une main ferme et de retourner contre l'assassin, si l'on ne veut pas qu'il vous assassine'.

[78] Henri Barbusse, 'A propos du Rollandisme', *Clarté* (1 February, 1922), pp. 127–8.

[79] Henri Barbusse, p. 128: 'Évidemment il serait souhaitable que tout s'arrangeât avec des paroles: que peu à peu l'humanité se mît à se transformer et à s'épanouir selon l'harmonie et la sagesse, par coups de baguette magique. Mais en attendant des transformations qui seraient peut-être plus longues que ce qu'il reste de vitalité à l'espèce humaine, il faut agir, et remplacer des lois par des lois. C'est dans cette voie de raison et de justice contructive que nous entendons orienter les prolétariats'.

[80] Romain Rolland, *Quinze ans de combat*, pp. 40–50.

[81] Romain Rolland, *op. cit.*, p. 42.

[82] Romain Rolland, *op. cit.*, p. 43: 'dans les masses profondes, je vois, au milieu de l'énorme égoïsme apathique du plus grand nombre, des forces violentes et tourmentées qui sont faites pour détruire et pour être détruites, beaucoup plus que pour édifier'.

[83] Romain Rolland, *op. cit.*, p. 46.

[84] Romain Rolland, *op. cit.*, p. 48.

[85] Romain Rolland, *op. cit.*, p. 49.

[86] See Romain Rolland, *op. cit.*, pp. XXIII–XXV.

[87] Romain Rolland, 'Lettre aux amis communistes', *Quinze ans de combat*, pp. 51–8.

[88] Romain Rolland, *op. cit.*, p. 55.

[89] Amédée Dunois, 'A propos du Manifeste Communiste', *L'Humanité* (10 March, 1922), p. 1.

[90] Romain Rolland, *Quinze ans de combat*, p. LXIX.

[91] Romain Rolland, *op. cit.*, p. XVII.

92 Romain Rolland, *Journal des années de guerre*, p. 353 (Entry dated May 1915).
93 Romain Rolland, *op. cit.*, p. 354 (May 1915).
94 Romain Rolland, *op. cit.*, p. 1481.
95 Romain Rolland, *Inde, Journal* (1915–1943) (Bâle-Lausanne; Éditions Vineta, 1951), p. 11. See also *Rabindranath Tagore et Romain Rolland*, p. 91.
96 'Que pensez-vous de la guerre du Maroc?', *Clarté* (15 July, 1925), p. 1.
97 Romain Rolland, *Inde, Journal* (1915–1943), p. 13.
98 *Rabindranath Tagore et Romain Rolland*, p. 91.
99 Tagore's letter to Kalidas Nag is to be found in *Inde, Journal* (1915–1943), p. 28 and in *Rabindranath Tagore et Romain Rolland*, p. 199.
100 Romain Rolland, *Journal des années de guerre*, p. 370. See also Rolland's letter to Tagore, *Rabindranath Tagore et Romain Rolland*, p. 22: 'je voudrais que désormais l'intelligence de l'Asie prît une part de plus en plus régulière dans les manifestations de la pensée d'Europe. Mon rêve serait que l'on vît, un jour, l'union de ces deux hémisphères de l'Esprit; et je vous admire d'y avoir contribué plus que quiconque'.
101 Romain Rolland, *Inde*, p. 11 (Entry dated February 1915).
102 *Rabindranath Tagore et Romain Rolland*, p. 50 (letter to Tagore dated 11 June, 1923): 'j'ai tant à apprendre de vous! Et je crois que j'aurais là une mission à remplir,—un devoir prédestiné, pour la fin de ma vie. L'union de l'Europe et de l'Asie doit être, dans les siècles qui viennent, la plus haute tâche de l'humanité.'
103 Rolland's letter to Tagore is to be found in *Inde*, p. 14 and *Rabindranath Tagore et Romain Rolland*, pp. 27–8. See also Rolland's letter to Amia Ch. Chakravarty (March 1917), *Inde*, p. 14: 'je sens, depuis quelques années, le besoin urgent de rapprocher l'esprit de l'Europe de celui de l'Asie. Ni l'un ni l'autre ne se suffit à soi seul'.
104 *Rabindranath Tagore et Romain Rolland*, p. 37: 'une revue française d'esprit largement international, *sans aucune tendance politique*, où non seulement fraternise la pensée des divers peuples d'Europe, mais où une vaste place est faite à la pensée d'Asie' (Letter dated 7 May, 1922). See also letter to Tagore in *Rabindranath Tagore et Romain Rolland*, p. 28 (26 August, 1919).
105 René Arcos, 'Patrie européenne', *Europe* (15 February, 1923), p. 108.
106 Ananda Coomaraswamy *La Danse de Çiva* (Abbeville: Paillart, 1922).
107 Romain Rolland, *La Danse de Çiva* (preface), p. 13.
108 Romain Rolland, *op. cit.*, p. 8.
109 Romain Rolland, *Journal des années de guerre*, p. 1481: 'j'ai été frappé de voir, dans ces dernières années, d'une part le puissant mouvement de réveil et d'union de l'Inde, de la Chine et du Japon; de l'autre l'effort que l'Allemagne a fait en pleine guerre pour pénétrer leur pensée' (Entry dated 2 May, 1918).
110 *Rabindranath Tagore et Romain Rolland*, pp. 34–5.
111 Quoted in Henri Massis, *Défense de l'Occident*, pp. 22–3.
112 See Henri Massis, *op. cit.*, pp. 269 ff.
113 Henri Massis, 'L'Offensive germano-asiatique contre la culture occidentale', *Le Journal littéraire* (19 July, 1924), p. 1.

114 Jacques Benoist-Méchin, *Le Journal littéraire* (2 August, 1924), p. 4.

115 Maurice Betz, *Le Journal littéraire* (2 August, 1924), p. 4.

116 Jean Caves, 'Le Nihilisme européen et les appels de l'Orient', *Philosophies* (March/April 1924), pp. 51–65; pp. 185–96.

117 Jean Caves, p. 59.

118 Jean Caves, p. 191.

119 Jean Caves, pp. 193–4.

120 Jean Caves, p. 57.

121 Jean Caves, p. 195.

122 N. I. Bukharin, 'La Crise de la culture bourgeoise', *Clarté* (1 March, 1923), pp. 177–9. Lenin had already written, *Selected Works* (Lawrence and Wishart, 1971), pp. 668–9: 'The old bourgeois and imperialist Europe, which was accustomed to look upon itself as the centre of the universe, rotted and burst like a putrid ulcer in the first imperialist holocaust. No matter how the Spenglers and all the enlightened philistines, who are capable of admiring (or even studying) Spengler, may lament it, this decline of the old Europe is but an episode in the history of the downfall of the world bourgeoisie, oversatiated by imperialist rapine and the oppression of the majority of the world's population. The majority has now awakened and has begun a movement which even the "mightiest" powers cannot stem'.

123 Maurice Muret, 'La Pensée allemande et l'Orient', *La Revue universelle* (15 August, 1921), pp. 415–28.

124 Maurice Muret, p. 416.

125 Maurice Muret, p. 418: 'on sait que le bolchevisme assigne à la Russie une mission surtout orientale. Les penseurs bolchevisants d'Allemagne—et ils sont nombreux—ont éprouvé pour le bolchevisme une tendresse accrue quand l'essence, plus orientale encore qu'occidentale, de la grande pensée de Lénine leur est clairement apparue'.

126 Maurice Muret, p. 428.

127 Fernand Baldensperger, 'Où l'Orient et l'Occident s'affrontent', *Revue de littérature comparée* (March 1922), pp. 5–29.

128 Fernand Baldensperger, p. 14.

129 Fernand Baldensperger, pp. 25–6.

130 Baldensperger (pp. 18–19) quotes the Hellenist, Williamowitz-Moellendorf who maintains that the spirit of the West 'consista à prendre la mesure des choses au nom de l'esprit, à instituer, face au déroulement de l'histoire ou au développement des forces, une norme qui ne procédât point d'elles et leur fût cependant applicable, une autonomie régulatrice qui dominât la simple chronologie familière aux mondes préhellènes, la passivité arithmétique des annalistes ou des calculateurs de l'Asie. Où ceux-ci se contentaient d'admettre la succession, l'esprit grec prétendît insérer l'enchaînement, la série logique, les corollaires découlant des théorèmes et les événements dérivant des causes'. Compare this statement with André Malraux, *La Tentation de l'Occident* (Grasset, 1951), pp. 67–8.

131 Fernand Baldensperger, p. 29.

132 Romain Rolland, *Quinze ans de combat,* p. XXXIV. See also, p. XXI, p. XXVIII, p. XXX, pp. LXVII-LXIX.

139

[133] See Rolland's preface to Gandhi's *La Jeune Inde*, translated by Hélène Hart (Stock, 1924), p. X.

[134] Ram-Prassad-Dubé, 'Les Aspects sociaux du mouvement Gandhi dans l'Inde', *Clarté* (1 March, 1922), pp. 188–91.

[135] Henri Barbusse, 'A propos du Rollandisme', *Clarté* (1 April, 1922), pp. 223–25.

[136] Romain Rolland, *Europe* (15 March, 1923), pp. 129–63; (15 April, 1923), pp. 267–310; (15 May, 1923), pp. 427–54.

[137] Mahatma Gandhi, *La Jeune Inde* (Stock, 1924), pp. V–XXI.

[138] Mahatma Gandhi, *op. cit.*, p. X.

[139] Henri Barbusse, 'Révolutionnaires d'Orient et d'Occident. A propos de Gandhi', *Clarté* (13 July, 1923), pp. 314–20.

[140] Mahatma Gandhi, *La Jeune Inde*, p. XX.

[141] See Romain Rolland, *Inde, Journal* (1915–1943), p. 69, p. 84.

[142] Evelyn Roy, 'Mahatma Gandhi, révolutionnaire ou contre-révolutionnaire', *Clarté* (1 November, 1923), pp. 437–9.

[143] 'Les Appels de l'Orient', *Les Cahiers du Mois* (February/March, 1925). The enquiry—hereafter referred to as 'Les Appels'—sought answers to the following questions:
   a) Pensez-vous que l'Occident et l'Orient soient complètement impénétrables l'un à l'autre ou tout au moins, selon le mot de Maeterlinck, il y ait dans le cerveau humain un lobe occidental et un lobe oriental qui ont toujours mutuellement paralysé leurs efforts?
   b) Si nous sommes pénétrables à l'influence orientale, quels sont les truchements—germaniques, slaves, asiatiques—par lesquels cette action vous semble devoir s'exercer le plus profondément sur la France?
   c) Êtes-vous d'avis avec Henri Massis que cette influence de l'Orient puisse constituer pour la pensée et les arts français un péril grave et qu'il serait urgent de combattre, ou pensez-vous que la liquidation des influences méditerranéennes soit commencée et que nous puissions à l'exemple de l'Allemagne demander à la 'connaissance de l'Est' un enrichissement de notre culture générale et un renouvellement de notre sensibilité?
   d) Quel est le domaine—art, lettres, philosophie—dans lequel cette influence vous semble devoir donner des résultats particulièrement féconds?
   e) Quelles sont, à votre sentiment, les valeurs occidentales qui font la supériorité de l'Occident sur l'Orient, ou, quelles sont les fausses valeurs qui, à votre avis, rabaissent notre civilisation occidentale?

[144] François Berge 'Les Appels', p. 336.

[145] François Berge, ibid.

[146] Alice Louis-Barthou, 'Les Appels', p. 246.

[147] André Siegfried, 'Les Appels', p. 327.

[148] Abel Bonnard, 'Les Appels', pp. 48–50.

[149] *Candide* (9 December, 1937; 6 January, 1938).

[150] *Je suis partout* (19, 26 May, 1941).

[151] Victor Barrucand, 'Les Appels', p. 245.

[152] Marcel E. Cahen, 'Les Appels', p. 259.

[153] Jean Schlumberger, 'Les Appels', p. 42. See also Edmond Jaloux, p. 23: 'la

confiance que nous avons donnée aux machines est en train de se retourner contre nous: l'homme intérieur cède à l'homme extérieur, l'homme extérieur lui-même délègue tous ses pouvoirs à un ensemble inerte de roues et de moteurs'.

154 See also René Jouglet, 'Les Appels', p. 284: 'la forme utilitaire de la civilisation européenne du XXᵉ siècle gagne rapidement l'Asie'.
155 Sylvain Lévi, 'Les Appels', pp. 11–13.
156 Marcel E. Cahen, 'Les Appels', p. 262.
157 Paul Masson-Oursel, 'Les Appels', p. 300.
158 André Malraux, 'Défense de l'Occident', *Nouvelle Revue Française* (June 1927), p. 815.
159 Paul Valéry, 'Les Appels', p. 16: 'il faut penser à ce qu'il adviendra de l'Europe une fois l'Asie organisée et équipée industriellement'.
     André Gide, p. 18: 'l'Orient peut apprendre de l'Occident à s'organiser, à s'armer, à se défendre, peut-être même à attaquer'.
160 Jean Bacot, 'Les Appels', pp. 115–17.
161 Azouaou Mammeri, 'Les Appels', p. 193. Alexandre Embiricos, pp. 272–4, makes a similar observation: 'Déjà aux yeux des races qu'il domine, l'Occident a perdu son prestige. Les barbares se sont réveillés et demandent leur part de vie. Pourtant, si l'Asie a secoué sa torpeur, c'est avec un esprit qu'elle lui emprunte . . . les plus européanisés des Orientaux sont ses ennemis les plus redoutables'.
162 Jean Schlumberger, 'Les Appels', p. 42.
163 For the European, writes Guénon, 'intelligence' is 'un moyen d'agir sur la matière et de la plier à des fins pratiques': *Orient et Occident* (Payot, 1924), p. 19.
164 René Guénon, *Orient et Occident*, pp. 45–53.
165 René Guénon, *op. cit.*, pp. 59–60: 'il n'y a qu'une chose qui puisse expliquer l'admiration sans bornes et le respect superstitieux dont cette science est l'objet: c'est qu'elle est en parfaite harmonie avec les besoins d'une civilisation purement matérielle'; p. 20: 'la science vaut surtout dans la mesure où elle est susceptible d'aboutir à des applications industrielles'; p. 78: 'religion de la science'; p. 78: 'quand on ne connaît rien au delà de cette science et de cette raison, on peut bien avoir l'illusion de leur suprématie absolue'.
166 René Guénon, *La Crise du monde moderne* (Bossard, 1927), p. 83. See also *Orient et Occident*, p. 82: '[l'Européen] apparaît comme essentiellement changeant et inconstant, comme voué au mouvement sans arrêt et à l'agitation incessante, et n'aspirant d'ailleurs point à en sortir'.
167 René Guénon, *La Crise du monde moderne*, p. 119: 'la réduction de la civilisation dans tous les domaines aux seuls éléments purement humains, c'est ce qui a été désigné à l'époque de la Renaissance sous le nom d'humanisme'.
168 René Guénon, *La Crise du monde moderne*, p. 120.
169 René Guénon, *Orient et Occident*, p. 80; *La Crise du monde moderne*, pp. 200–5.
170 René Guénon, *La Crise du monde moderne*, pp. 204–5.
171 René Guénon, *op. cit.*, p. 206.

[172] René Guénon, *op. cit.*, p. 205: 'si [les Orientaux] veulent combattre la domination étrangère, c'est par les méthodes mêmes de l'Occident, de la même façon que les divers peuples occidentaux luttent entre eux'.

[173] René Guénon, *La Crise du monde moderne*, pp. 208–25.

[174] Henri Maspéro, 'Les Appels', p. 296.

[175] The article appears in *La Semaine littéraire* (Geneva: 25 October, 1924).

[176] J. P. Palewski, 'Les Appels', p. 173. See A. Malraux, *La Tentation de l'Occident*, p. 28, pp. 33–4, p. 55.

[177] J. P. Palewski, 'Les Appels', pp. 173–4.

[178] J. Benoist-Méchin, 'Les Appels', p. 246. See also Théodore Lessing, 'L'Europe et l'Asie', *La Révolution surréaliste* (15 April, 1925), pp. 20–1.

[179] Edmond Jaloux, 'Les Appels', p. 29: 'toutes les catastrophes, toutes les douleurs, tous les périls du monde, viennent de l'attachement au Moi'.

[180] A. Malraux, *La Tentation de l'Occident*, pp. 165–6.

[181] Edmond Jaloux, 'Les Appels', p. 29.

[182] Charles Wolff, 'Les Appels', pp. 377–9.

[183] Régina Zabloudovsky, 'La Crise de la culture intellectuelle en Allemagne', *Mercure de France* (15 July, 1924), p. 289.

[184] Régina Zabloudovsky, p. 290.

[185] Régina Zabloudovsky, p. 291.

[186] See André Malraux, 'D'une jeunesse européenne', *Écrits* (Grasset, 1927), p. 145: 'notre civilisation, depuis qu'elle a perdu l'espoir de trouver dans les sciences le sens du monde, est privée de tout but spirituel'.

[187] Régina Zabloudovsky, '*La Crise de la culture . . .*', p. 296.

[188] Régina Zabloudovsky, p. 297.

[189] Régina Zabloudovsky, p. 298.

[190] Régina Zabloudovsky, ibid.

[191] Marcel Arland, 'Sur un nouveau mal du siècle', *Nouvelle Revue Française* (February 1924), p. 156.

[192] André Malraux, *La Tentation de l'Occident*, p. 216.

[193] Quoted by Charles Wolff, 'Les Appels', p. 379.

[194] André Malraux, 'La Défense de l'Occident', *N.R.F.*, (June 1927), pp. 817–18.

[195] André Malraux, 'André Malraux et l'Orient', *Les Nouvelles littéraires* (31 July, 1926), p. 2.

[196] Lugné Poë, 'Les Appels', p. 294. See also André Breton, pp. 250–1: 'je n'attends pas que l'Est nous enrichisse, ou nous renouvelle en quoi que ce soit, mais bien qu'il nous conquière'.

[197] Nazim Hikmet, 'Occident-Orient', *Clarté* (June 1925), p. 16.

[198] Jean Montrevel, 'Sur l'enquête des Cahiers du Mois: Les Appels de l'Orient', *Clarté* (June 1925), pp. 11–12; Marcel Eugène, 'Orient contre Occident ou la révolution de l'Humanité contre l'impérialisme du Capital', *Clarté* (June 1925), pp. 12–15.

[199] Jean Montrevel, 'Sur l'enquête des Cahiers du Mois', p. 11: 'il convient de connaître à fond la fleur intellectuelle de deux civilisations mortes. Grecque: pensée, humanisme. Latine: droit et langue, rigidité d'un système social et gymnastique mentale incomparable. Tous ceux qui n'ont pu puiser à ces sources de connaissances sont des barbares, des primaires ou encore, selon

les plus charitables, des personnalités très superficielles'.

200 Nazim Hikmet, 'Occident-Orient', p. 16.
201 Henri Rudyes, 'Confucianisme et Communisme', *Clarté* (15 November, 1922), pp. 18–19.
202 Charles Dassy, 'L'Islam et la révolution mondiale', *Clarté* (1 January, 1923), pp. 95–8.
203 N'Guyen-Doc, 'Le Paupérisme rural au Tonkin', *Clarté* (February 1923), pp. 149–50.
204 Marcel Eugène, 'Orient contre Occident', p. 13.
205 Romain Rolland, 'Les Appels', p. 322.
206 Romain Rolland, *Rabindranath Tagore et Romain Rolland*, p. 133.
207 Henri Massis, 'Les Appels', p. 31.
208 Henri Massis, 'Les Appels', p. 35.
209 Henri Massis, 'Les Appels', p. 36.
210 See Henri Massis, 'Les Appels', pp. 38–9.
211 Henri Massis, 'Les Appels', p. 37. Viscount Torio, writes Massis, has been quoted by Coomaraswamy as saying 'l'égalité dans la paix ne pourra jamais être atteinte tant qu'elle ne sera pas édifiée sur les ruines des États occidentaux anéantis et parmi les cendres des peuples occidentaux disparus'. Massis also quotes the words of Ikuta Choko, a Nietzschean commentator and founder of the 'Oriental League of Tokyo': 'la civilisation occidentale, enfoncée dans le matérialisme, paralysée, étouffée sous le poids de l'organisation capitaliste est à la veille de sombrer. La ligue orientale n'aura une raison d'être que si elle entreprend de renouveler la vie de l'humanité. *Ce qui s'impose, c'est d'orientaliser encore une fois le monde*' (pp. 37–8). Another leader of the League is reported as saying: 'la paix et le bonheur ne seront assurés que le jour où l'Asie vaincra les Blancs, non pas poussée par la haine mais seulement par la pensée de les ramener à la justice, à la véritable civilisation qui est spirituelle et non matérielle' (p. 38).
212 Henri Massis, 'Les Appels', p. 33.
213 Henri Massis, 'Les Appels', p. 32.
214 Henri Massi, 'Les Appels', p. 31: 'propagande politique qui vise à notre anéantissement'.
215 Henri Massis, 'Les Appels', pp. 37–8.
216 Henri Massis, 'L'Offensive germano-asiatique contre la culture occidentale', *Le Journal littéraire* (19 July, 1924), pp. 1–2.
217 Massis's *Défense de l'Occident* had already been serialised in part in *La Revue universelle,* e.g. 'Defense de l'Occident', *La Revue universelle* (15 October, 1925), pp. 145–58; 'La Russie contre l'Occident', *La Revue universelle* (1 November, 1926), pp. 257–74.
218 Henri Massis, *Défense de l'Occident* (Plon, 1927), pp. 1–4.
219 Henri Massis, *op. cit.*, p. 8.
220 Henri Massis, *op. cit.*, p. 14.
221 Henri Massis, *op. cit.*, p. 25.
222 Henri Massis, ibid.
223 Henri Massis, *op. cit.*, pp. 28–9 (Note 2).
224 Henri Massis, *op. cit.*, pp. 30–1.
225 Henri Massis, *op. cit.*, p. 42.

[226] Henri Massis, *op. cit.*, pp. 44–5.
[227] Henri Massis, *op. cit.*, pp. 47–8.
[228] Henri Massis, *op. cit.*, p. 48.
[229] Dostoyevsky's influence was also being felt in France. In his 'Sur un nouveau mal du siècle', *N.R.F.*, (February 1924), p. 158, Marcel Arland notes: 'L'actualité de Dostoïevsky est un signe fort net; jamais l'on ne s'était en France senti plus près de certains des héros des *Possédés* ou des *Karamazov*'.
[230] Henri Massis, *op. cit.*, p. 55.
[231] See Henri Massis, *op. cit.*, pp. 51–68.
[232] Henri Massis, *op. cit.*, pp. 72–3.
[233] Henri Massis, *op. cit.*, pp. 70–1.
[234] Henri Massis, *op. cit.*, p. 75.
[235] Henri Massis, *op. cit.*, p. 73.
[236] Henri Massis, *op. cit.*, pp. 85–6.
[237] Henri Massis, *op. cit.*, p. 104.
[238] See Henri Massis, *op. cit.*, p. 104 (Note I).
[239] Henri Massis, *op. cit.*, p. 106.
[240] Henri Massis, *op. cit.*, p. 110.
[241] Henri Massis, *op. cit.*, p. 112.
[242] Henri Massis, *op. cit.*, p. 122.
[243] Henri Massis, *op. cit.*, pp. 122–4.
[244] Henri Massis, *op. cit.*, p. 126.
[245] See Henri Massis, *op. cit.*, pp. 107–10.
[246] Henri Massis, *op. cit.*, p. 129.
[247] Henri Massis, *op. cit.*, p. 132.
[248] Henri Massis, *op. cit.*, p. 148.
[249] Henri Massis, *op. cit.*, p. 153.
[250] Henri Massis, ibid.
[251] Henri Massis, *op. cit.*, pp. 154–5.
[252] Henri Massis, *op. cit.*, p. 157 and p. 163 (Note I).
[253] See Henri Massis, *op. cit.*, pp. 168–9; pp. 174–5.
[254] Henri Massis, *op. cit.*, pp. 172–3.
[255] Henri Massis, *op. cit.*, p. 174.
[256] Henri Massis, *op. cit.*, p. 175.
[257] Henri Massis, *op. cit.*, p. 177.
[258] Henri Massis, *op. cit.*, p. 179.
[259] See Henri Massis, *op. cit.*, pp. 134–7.
[260] See Henri Massis, *op. cit.*, pp. 203–25.
[261] See Henri Massis, *op. cit.*, pp. 233–43.
[262] Henri Massis, *op. cit.*, pp. 244–5.
[263] Henri Massis, *op. cit.*, p. 246.
[264] Henri Massis, *op. cit.*, pp. 186–7.
[265] Henri Massis, *op. cit.*, p. 249.
[266] Henri Massis, *op. cit.*, p. 250.
[267] Henri Massis, *op. cit.*, p. 254.
[268] Henri Massis, *op. cit.*, p. 263.
[269] Henri Massis, *op. cit.*, pp. 269–70.
[270] Henri Barbusse, 'Romain Rolland', *Europe* (16 February, 1926), pp. 135–7.

271 Romain Rolland, *Inde*, p. 64.
272 Romain Rolland, *Vie de Vivekananda*, Vol. I, pp. 70–5.
273 Romain Rolland, *op. cit.*, pp. 24–5.
274 Romain Rolland, *Vie de Vivekananda*, Vol. II, p. 18.
275 Romain Rolland, *Vie de Ramakrishna*, p. 50.
276 See *L'Humanité* (25 July, 1935), p. 1; *L'Humanité* (11 September, 1936), p. 1; 'The Brussels Peace Conference', *Labour Monthly* (October 1936), pp. 625–8.
277 See Rolland's letter to Kalidas Nag (14 December, 1925), *Rabindranath Tagore et Romain Rolland*, p. 141.
278 Letter to Kalidas Nag (6–7 July, 1926), *Rabindranath Tagore et Romain Rolland*, p. 149.
279 *Rabindranath Tagore et Romain Rolland*, pp. 149–50.
280 Romain Rolland, *Inde*, p. 91.
281 *Rabindranath Tagore et Romain Rolland*, p. 147.
282 Romain Rolland, *Inde*, p. 96.
283 Romain Rolland, *op. cit.*, p. 114.
284 Romain Rolland, *op. cit.*, p. 115; *Rabindranath Tagore et Romain Rolland*, p. 151.
285 Romain Rolland, *Inde*, p. 116.
286 *Rabindranath Tagore et Romain Rolland*, p. 150, pp. 155–9.
287 Romain Rolland, *Inde*, p. 132.
288 Romain Rolland, *op. cit.*, p. 133: 'oui ou non, représente-t-il dans le monde un principe de liberté spirituelle, opposé à tous les abus de la force? Si oui, il ne lui est pas permis de détourner les yeux et de se taire devant le triomphe de la brutalité et de la dictature sans frein'.
289 Romain Rolland, *op. cit.*, p. 133. See also p. 135: 'Tagore a trouvé quelques phrases énergiques pour condamner en principe le fascisme. Mais il évite toute application précise aux crimes italiens. Et partout il noie ces blâmes dans une masse incolore et anodine, où il s'efforce de semer des compliments à Mussolini et au peuple d'Italie'.
290 Romain Rolland, *op. cit.*, p. 135, and *Rabindranath Tagore et Romain Rolland*, p. 163.
291 Romain Rolland, *Quinze ans de combat*, p. XLII.
292 Romain Rolland, *op. cit.*, p. XLIV: 'je rappelais à tous les hommes libres d'Europe que la Russie était en danger, et que si jamais elle était écrasée, ce ne serait pas seulement le prolétariat du monde qui serait asservi, mais toute liberté sociale ou individuelle. Le monde serait rejeté de plusieurs étapes, en arrière . . . Trêve aux discussions fratricides! La Révolution russe représente le plus grand effort social, le plus puissant, le plus fécond de l'Europe moderne. A son secours! L'ennemi est à nos portes. La guerre d'empires. Veillons au salut des libertés d'Europe!'
293 Romain Rolland, *op. cit.*, pp. XLVI–LI.
294 Romain Rolland, *op. cit.*, pp. LIII–LIV.
295 See *L'Aube* (29, 30 September, 1935); *Le Jour* (22 September, 1935); *Action Française* (7, 22, 26 September, 1935).
296 See Henri Massis, *Défense de l'Occident*, pp. 269–70.
297 See Henri Massis, *Maurras et notre temps* (Plon, 1961), pp. 419–20.

[298] Romain Rolland, *Quinze ans de combat*, pp. LVI–LVII.
[299] Romain Rolland, *op. cit.*, p. LII.
[300] Romain Rolland, *op. cit.*, pp. LII–LIII.
[301] Romain Rolland, *Inde*, p. 384.
[302] Romain Rolland, *op. cit.*, p. 384, pp. 450–3.
[303] Romain Rolland, *Quinze ans de combat*, pp. LXI–LXIII.

PART 2

CHAPTER V

Drieu and the Dream of Europe

Mon but politique a été, est et sera toujours la constitution des États-Unis d'Europe.

(*Genève ou Moscou*)

In previous chapters we saw that the Great War brought into conflict not only European nation-states but, within France itself, a whole host of spiritual and moral values, of philosophical and political principles, of dogmas and divine personages. Ideals and ideologies were shaken, and Valéry, refining and defining the doubt and anguish of an era, announced that Civilization was teetering on the edge of oblivion. Where the Surrealists sought to precipitate the fall, Morand to postpone it, and Massis to revive, uplift and sanctify, Rolland and Barbusse—each in his different way—cast off the dark despair of a tormented West to greet the light of inspiration shining out of the East. A new battle of ideas was joined wherein, even as Massis and Rolland rose to defend rival spiritual worlds, Barbusse and *Clarté* mobilized the weapons of a nascent socialism against the cultural defence and ideological armoury of capitalist and imperialist society. In the conflict over East and West adversaries, looking to all corners of the globe, pledged allegiances, expressed political preferences and sought their freedom and future in a European ideal which they hoped would take a living form. Those ideals, for Massis as for Rolland, were now inscribed on political banners beneath which, in Rome and in Moscow, historical forces were gathering for war. War broke out, and, for the second time in twenty years, Europeans fought Europeans.

One man whose dream, he claimed, had been to make war between Europeans impossible was Pierre Drieu La Rochelle. In *Mesure de la France* (1922) not only did he claim that France was now an insignificant power, that her very triumph belonged to

147

those without whose intervention she would have succumbed to a stronger foe, but he actually concluded, as had Rolland five years before, that the era of national entities within Europe was dead. In a world which Drieu felt would soon be dominated by the Soviet Union and the United States of America, he saw an urgent need for the creation of a federated Europe. With hindsight one might reasonably claim that Drieu went to the very heart of the problem which has dominated world politics for the past sixty years. Yet if his vision is often clear, and at times even prophetic, his general approach to the study of politics is singularly lacking in objectivity. Politics and history are represented as something of a private drama and frequently serve him as the pretext for deep introspection. Indeed, in his political writings he devotes as much space to self-analysis as to the analysis of French and European problems. The danger in such an approach is apparent; it lies in the temptation to take one's own desires for reality. In Drieu's case this temptation was to have more than literary results.

The heavy personal tone to Drieu's political writings does not, however, exclude them from a certain kind of representativeness. Kléber Haedens and Ramon Fernandez are not the only writers to have seen in Drieu a 'cas-témoin'.[1] François Mauriac, whose testimony cannot lightly be dismissed, has himself stressed Drieu's representative value:

> Je dis homme de droite en parlant de Drieu. Je sais que l'expression n'est pas exacte. Drieu était plutôt au centre, non pas au centre politique mais au centre nerveux, au centre magnétique des attractions et des tentations d'une génération.[2]

One need not therefore be surprised that political personalities as different as Léon Blum and Jacques Benoist–Méchin, to say nothing of literary critics as differently motivated as Georges Bonneville and Pierre Andreu, should find support for their varying views in Drieu's works, and often in the very same works.[3] Drieu himself was keenly aware of his role as a witness and observer of the various tendencies of his day. His first novel after the Great War, *État Civil,* in which he traces the impact of his family's inheritance upon him as a child and adolescent, can thus be read at once as an autobiography and as the 'témoignage d'une génération'.[4]

148

The central theme of the work, supported by variations on fear and courage, love of France and an anxiety for her failing strength, nationalism and a decided anglomania, is the divorce between the vitality of aspiration and the dreariness of life. The young hero, 'le petit Cogle', is the victim of this disembodied thought. Trapped in a narrow world of inherited notions and prejudices he contrives imaginary compensations. His maternal grandmother—'l'être au monde que j'ai le plus aimé'[5]—contributes to the development of his day-dreaming. Beset with the ideal of the 'homme réussi' she patiently grooms him for the elevated position to which neither her father nor husband was able to rise. However, her enthusiasm for the masculine virtues of strength and courage[6] is purely rhetorical. No less than those she chides, she too is the victim of a divorce between thought and action: 'un instant qu'elle m'avait répété quelque sentence belliqueuse, elle me rappelait auprès d'elle pour que nous reprenions le rêve de mon avenir en toute tranquillité'.[7] Words and wild imaginings become the child's substitutes for physical activity.

From his grandmother, Cogle inherits a cult for Napoleon which is further compensation for the immobility of his body and the monotony of his everyday life.[8] The Napoleonic era about which he reads and dreams is cherished by him as a sovereign synthesis of 'rêve' and 'action', since young men given to ambitions of grandeur could *live* them in physical commitment to the collective cause. Drieu's childhood admiration for Napoleon and his contribution to the 'virilizing' of Europe has, like much in Drieu's work, strong Nietzschean associations. In the *Joyful Wisdom* Nietzsche assessed Napoleon's importance in the following terms:

> We owe it to Napoleon . . . that several warlike centuries which have not had their like in past history, may now follow one another—in short, that we have entered upon the classical age of war . . . to which all coming millenia will look back with envy and awe as a work of perfection. . . To him, one will one day be able to attribute the fact that *man* in Europe has again got the upper hand of the merchant and the Philistine: perhaps even of 'woman' also . . . Napoleon, who saw in modern ideas and accordingly in civilization something like a personal enemy, has by this hostility proved himself one of the greatest continuators of the Renaissance: he has brought to the surface a whole block of the ancient

149

character, the decisive block perhaps, the block of granite. And who knows but that this block of ancient character will in the end get the upper hand of the national movement, and will have to make itself in a *positive* sense the heir and continuator of Napoleon—who as one knows, wanted *one Europe*, which was to be mistress of the world.[9]

Every proposition contained within this statement receives extensive treatment from Drieu both in novel and essay form. It would be no exaggeration to claim that the 'Wisdom' of these lines is the basis of Drieu's European ideal.

At the age of seven, as though by way of nourishment for his military fantasies, our young hero is given his first books, Marbot, Coignet and Bourgogne.[10] His dreams of military glory are still further encouraged by Joseph the servant, one time 'cuisinier d'un colonel', who assumes the proportions of a Ulysses in the boy's eyes.[11] His grandfather's role is an opposite one to Joseph's. Far from indulging Cogle's imaginary adventures he sets about destroying them with an atrocious zeal. The child is forced deeper and deeper into himself. His mother intensifies his sense of solitude by neglecting him, and his father constantly mocks him.

Cogle is allowed out only when accompanied by his elders and then only when the boundaries of the walk have been clearly delineated beforehand. Far from having the recreation necessary for a growing child, he is left to languish in physical torpor: 'tout mon être se crispe misérablement quand je songe combien tôt la substance de mes muscles a été touchée par l'inertie'.[12] His fantasies assume greater importance and his mind races back to the more romantic elements of the family past. In more recent times, however, there is, he remarks, 'rien à attendre du côté de ma famille'.[13] This private observation is extended to include the entire French nation. What vitality France once had is now spent in a country drained of physical endeavour and deprived of the last vestige of international renown. Trafalgar, the Franco-Prussian War and the disaster and humiliation of Sedan, together with the general sense of defeatism in the older generation have destroyed France's world position. Cogle's awareness of the decline of French power is the cause of great sorrow to him: 'je souffrais d'un malaise que je sentais partout. J'étais malade, et c'était le mal de tout un peuple . . . je connaissais toutes les défaites de la France, et j'étais sensible à toutes'.[14]

Here we are given a clear illustration of how Drieu makes an intellectual generalization of a basically individual and altogether emotional response to history. In his later works, he will take his private obsession even further until the whole planet is seen to participate in his own despair. *État Civil* is also, in its very conception, a telling illustration of what will remain one of the basic needs of our author: the desire to restructure the past in such a way as to justify his outlook in the present. This temptation to transform the world into a coherent pattern of his own creation—very much after the fashion of an artistic whole in its own right—would one day lead him to extract from his earlier works only those elements which appeared to prefigure a particular aspect of political movement in the present. Blind to this selective procedure he would then conclude that he had been a good prophet, would apologize for any doubts he might once have betrayed and then commit himself to that movement as if he never doubted its success or his own fidelity to it. His revival, during the Occupation, of the theme of European unity is perhaps the most striking example of his selective approach to the past.

Cogle's only reward for the love he lavishes on his country is the pained knowledge of its failing strength. The young man sulks at his youth and considers all effort useless. He does not want to disturb the process of death which he even solemnly desires at this time.[15] Whilst in England he visits Oxford and has the revelation of a harmonious civilization founded on the reconciliation of body and spirit: '[Oxford] honorait l'esprit et le corps comme des biens suffisants'.[16] It represents everything which he, France in microcosm, is not. The renaissance of sport in France had promised to restore the physical vitality of his nation, but he feels that the opportunity to participate was lost.[17] His enthusiasm for sport, as for all things physical, remains purely cerebral, and he lingers on as a prisoner of 'la pensée sans corps'.

Here we are given a further illustration of how Drieu takes his own desires for reality: desires which, moreover, betray a politically conservative temperament. To regard Oxford as a citadel of social harmony clearly reflects a traditionalist view of a holistically-conceived integrated society whose élite honourably expresses and coheres with its 'national integrity'. To this class-limited view Drieu attaches a symbolical value which he then

151

employs to expose French deficiency. France, like Drieu—and unlike England—has neglected her physical life and must accept the shameful consequences. Nowhere is her weakness more ruthlessly exposed than on the international rugby field, where she has no answer for 'l'énergie musculaire de la race anglo-saxonne'.[18] As Cogle's personal humiliation is also that of his country he no longer feels comfortable in dreams of individual glory: 'ce subtil isolement de chacun qui est la loi de la France'.[19] What he craves is some form of collective redemption for a whole generation lost in cerebral activity.

État Civil reveals the young Drieu as a Jeremiah, militant through his tears. Brought up on a diet of vicarious heroism, he could not fail to have answered the call of war. To one whose body had ached from the enervating effects of immobility it offered the thrill of direct action, and for one who had experienced personally the wounded pride of his country it brought the promise of national redemption. It is noteworthy that in many of his war poems Drieu feels qualified to speak for an entire generation of young men whose voracious appetite for life and action could be satisfied only in a great collective action such as war.[20] Patriotism—indeed any group of men bound inseparably by the ties of blood—seems to the author of *État Civil* one of the basic laws of humanity.

> Une patrie est . . . la clef de tous les prétextes de vivre. Quand on quitte les patries pour un parti qui veut en même temps les embrasser et les nier, on adhère encore à ce qui dans le patriotisme est la complaisance essentielle: être avec certains hommes. Or, quand on est avec certains hommes on est contre d'autres. Quand un homme fait un mouvement d'amitié vers un autre homme, ou bien il s'engage jusqu'à ce dernier, ce suprême geste, qui est seul patent, seul concluant: *la preuve par le sang*, se faire tuer ou tuer; ou bien cet homme s'arrête à mi-chemin, s'en tient à une réticence mentale, et alors il se dérobe dans le néant, n'existe pas. La mort violente est le fondement de la civilisation, du contrat social, de n'importe quel pacte. *C'est la seule certitude*. Il n'y a de certitude entre des hommes que si au bout de l'action qu'ils concertent ils sont sûrs de savoir mourir pour ce qu'ils ont mis en commun: gloire, lucre, amour, désespoir—et les uns pour les autres.[21]

The outbreak of war had the effect of adrenalin on Drieu.

Craving escape from the *caserne* of bourgeois mediocrity he was anxious to win his baptism of fire; man, as he then ardently believed, being born to give battle.[22] The 'evil' of war had at least the merit of revelation, returning man to man in his entirety, reinstating action—'expérience corporelle'—as a necessary constituent of wholeness:

> Et le rêve et l'action
> La totale puissance de l'homme, il me la faut.
> Je ne puis me situer parmi les faibles. Je dois mesurer
> ma force.
> Si je renonce mon cerveau meurt. Je tuerai ou je serai tué.[23]

Dreams—the substance of his former life—can no longer satisfy him, he informs us, for he has known the 'restauration du corps' and the ineffable revelation reserved for those who dare think and act, live and die in one movement.[24] Like his mentor, Nietzsche, whom he joins in arraigning the 'despisers of the body', he now has to experience life with his whole body, taste it in his very 'entrails':[25]

> Behind your thoughts and feelings, my brother, there stands a mighty ruler, an unknown sage—whose name is self. In your body he dwells, he is your body . . . your self laughs at your ego and at its bold leaps. 'What are these leaps and flights of thought to me?' it says to itself. 'A detour to my end. I am the leading strings of the ego and the prompter of its concepts'.[26]

Throughout Drieu's war poems, despite an element of questioning anxiety from which *Interrogation* takes its name, the thrill of war prevades. His wartime experience left him with the deep-rooted sense of belonging to a virile fraternity, of which the title of one of the poems of *Interrogation,* 'Plainte des soldats européens', is in itself an accurate description. Drieu's patriotism does not therefore preclude an admiration for the physical virtues of the enemy:

> A vous Allemands . . . Je parle. Je vous ai combattus avec le vouloir roidement dégainé, de vous tuer . . . Mais vous êtes forts. Je n'ai pu haïr en vous la force, mère des choses.[27]

In the present war, which is less a current conflict than a glorious expression of man's 'éternel esprit de guerre', courage alone is of importance. Ally and enemy is thus for Drieu a meaningless distinction. If one has to be made it is that between combatants and non-combatants. This essential distinction between 'Man in Europe' and the 'merchant'—to use Nietzschean terminology —will never be far beneath the surface of Drieu's European politics.

After some years, when Drieu returned to the theme of war, his attitude is seen to have changed considerably.[28] War as a spiritual congregation of those devoted to the most rigorous discipline of body and soul, a monastic order open to an aristocratic élite has been destroyed by conscription and mechanization.[29] Verdun signals the end of the classical age of war and the emergence of the 'guerre de fer et non des muscles, de science et non d'art'.[30] What Drieu regrets is not that war kills but that the killing is no longer ritualized in the form of hand-to-hand combat.

Drieu's first political essay after the war was *Mesure de la France*[31] where, in an unremitting battery of statistics and *pleurnicheries*, he draws up specific charges against his country and prescribes remedies for her ailments. France's crime—the intended title of this essay—is that she has not produced enough children.[32] The battlefields of the Great War were swarming with British, American and colonial troops where countless unborn Frenchmen should have stood and moved. One hundred years before, France, with 20 millions, had been the most populous and powerful nation in Europe. Today, she has surrendered that lead to Germany, Britain and Italy, and, Drieu adds, 'au delà de l'Europe comme nous nous rapétissons entre les 150 millions de Russes et les 120 millions d'Américains.'[33] France, like all individual European nations, stands dwarfed between these two powerhouses, whose growing influence gives relevance to the idea of a united Europe.[34] Whilst expressing strong nationalist reluctance to join a Europe in which France will necessarily lose something of her identity, Drieu feels that there is no alternative, especially in view of 'les formidables périls qui s'accumulent en Orient'.[35]

Having broached the subject of the 'Asian menace', Drieu then examines the nature of the renaissance with which, we will recall, Barbusse and Rolland were preoccupied at this time, and about which François and André Berge were to launch an enquiry in 1925. He writes:

154

On doit constater que l'Inde ou la Chine semblent bien taries et que les renaissances actuelles sont illusoires et commandées par les idées européennes mêmes auxquelles elles s'opposent. Tagore est-il plus qu'un habile et heureux écrivain régionaliste? Certes je crois à l'importance tragique de ce réveil de l'Orient qui fascine Allemands et Russes. Mais sera-ce autre chose que la formidable émeute d'une humanité qui a perdu le sens de sa destinée, qui est déviée irrémédiablement par l'exemple européen, et qui veut se débarrasser de ses oppresseurs pour ne rien faire d'autre que d'accomplir soi-même dans les pires conditions ce compromis entre l'idéal de l'Orient et celui de l'Occident qu'elle reproche à l'Europe de manigancer hypocritement ou d'imposer par violence égoïste? Un Gandhi lance contre notre cauchemar mécanique, un anathème que ça et là sur la terre des hommes réfléchis méditent déjà depuis quelque temps. Mais sera-t-il écouté par les siens qui ne veulent se débarrasser des Anglais que pour se mieux donner à la vanité de l'imitation? Et lui-même ne se relâche-t-il pas déjà, n'est-il pas forcé, par la fatalité d'un engrenage où il faudra bien que passe toute l'humanité, à tempérer le refus absolu qu'il oppose à la tentation européenne? Cette émouvante revendication de l'Orient, contre les excès de la concupiscence occidentale, on en a rêvé en Allemagne.[36]

Drieu, like Massis—who was sufficiently impressed by Drieu's observations here to quote them at length in his contribution to 'Les Appels'[37]—accuses Germany of having inaugurated a conspiracy on behalf of the East against a war-weakened West. Like Massis, also, he accuses the Asian prophets of a renascent East of being crypto-Europeans. Drieu's remarks upon the Eastern question are, as Mauriac advanced in a more general context, a clear index to his representative value, for they were echoed not only by Massis and his many supporters, but also by an impressive cross-section of the contributors to 'Les Appels'. However, where most of the comment in 'Les Appels' remains within the realm of cultural and philosophical speculation, Drieu focuses on political options. If, 'le salut de l'Occident'[38] has a meaning for Drieu, it would appear to be in the direction of European federation.

Drieu urges European nation-states to forget their differences, which are, he claims, only superficial, and become one united force. Thus can Europe constitute a third world-force and, at the same time, put an end to internal strife born of differing national interests and culminating in internecine war. He urges his countrymen to consider European federation not as 'une rêverie cosmopolite, une imagination de luxe', but as 'une nécessité pressante, une misérable question de vie ou de mort'.[39] Not only do the selfish ambitions of individual States divide Europe against itself but, within the national scheme of things, there is division and dissent in the form of petty party-politics. Drieu finds this division disconcerting because fallacious: all he can see is growing uniformity.[40] And the direction the world is taking is that of life's negation. Not the faintest glimmer of 'lueur spirituelle' is perceptible.[41] No matter where one looks, from Shanghai to Philadelphia it is, writes Drieu, the same depressing picture: 'seule la machine se dresse, seules ces mâchoires sont solides, qui dévorent tout le reste.'[42]

Drieu now considers the example of Russia to which, he notes, many Europeans had turned in 1918 as though to greet the coming of a new spiritual order.[43] He reflects sadly that the liberating note which reverberated in challenging tones around the world has been muted by the very forces it was designed to combat.[44] The spiritual revival has not come about and far from opposing the base materialistic concerns of the U.S.A. the Soviet Union is now avidly pursuing the very same goal. In Russia, as in America, 'le matériel se substitue au spirituel.'[45] For this reason, Drieu concludes, 'notre salut, hélas! ne dépend pas de la Russie.'[46]

In Drieu's estimation the only 'groupement de forces efficaces à l'heure présente' is capitalism.[47] In *Genève ou Moscou* he will once again underline the need to establish Europe on capitalist foundations.[48] This recommendation is, to say the least, surprising. How can Drieu's apologia for capitalism be convincing when he himself avows that capitalism, like Communism, is antispiritual and indeed pursues a similar aim.[49] His call for what in fact amounts to a modification of the capitalist system represents the attempt to revive those spiritual values which, he feels, have been lost in the modern world. What he has in mind is some sort of half-way house between capitalism and socialism with a strong 'spiritual' content.[50] It is for this reason that he asks the reader to consider the example of Fascism.[51] That Drieu is concerned more for the 'spirit' of Fascism than for its programme or politics may be gathered from the final declaration of *Mesure de la France*: 'il

156

ne s'agit pas de révolutions, de restaurations, de superficiels mouvements politiques et sociaux mais de quelque chose de plus profond, d'une *Renaissance*'.[52]

As early as 1922 we find Drieu 'measuring' the extent of Europe's weakness, revealing the relative unimportance of France in the overall world-picture, discussing the 'Asian question', and outlining the emergence of the two super-powers: all considerations of which lead him to the conclusion that a European federation is an urgent necessity. Opposing political camps within nations and national entities themselves must be transcended if Europe is to survive and prosper in the recovery of its lost spirituality.

If the prospect of a united Europe gives Drieu a reason to hope, his analysis itself is far from optimistic. The predominant mood is one of pessimism: the pessimism of an era, if one is to believe Valéry. Indeed, Drieu is in many respects the incarnation of Valéry's European intellectual brooding, like some latter-day Hamlet, on the broken battlements of an Elsinore stretching from the North Sea to the Alps. His gaze meets only desolation and beyond, in Asia, he knows that European supremacy has been broken. Drieu would rebuild his Elsinore and have it reassert its supremacy over Asia. His 'new Europe' would thus, in this respect at least, be the very image of the old. Another feature which his new Europe would inherit from the old is its capitalist infrastructure—all the more surprising given Drieu's attack on modern materialism and the 'associated vices' of alcoholism, inversion and onanism. His willingness to salvage 'fallen idols' lends a good deal of authority to *Clarté*'s assessment of the Drieu of *Mesure de la France* as the 'jeune représentant d'une bourgeoisie dirigeante qui prend soudain conscience de l'abîme où elle roule et qui ne recherche de salut possible qu'à l'intérieur même de sa classe.'[53] *Clarté*'s point is that Drieu is unable to 'think new thoughts', to envisage solutions other than capitalist ones. This assessment helps to explain a central contradiction in Drieu's outlook. All things in Elsinore have been laid waste—political parties, class divisions and national entities—but capitalism survives and must continue to do so since it alone can command those spiritual resources which its very practice, Drieu has just said, serves to smother. It is this wilful acceptance of capitalism's inherent spirituality—affirmed but not demonstrated

157

—that Drieu brings to bear on the Russian situation. His condemnation is not formulated after a reasoned consideration of the ideology or economic programme of the Soviet Union, or the appalling social conditions there before and after the Revolution. In fact, showing no interest at all in such matters, he willingly admits his 'ignorance de la réalité russe'.[54] It would appear that his rejection of the 'Soviet example' is founded quite simply on a private yet class-based preconception of what, in his eyes, constitutes fulfilment. Spiritual sustenance—provided by capitalism—can thus take pride of place over the pressing necessities of life since Drieu, presumably, had never wanted for the latter. On a more general level one or two further points could be made regarding contradictory or at least ambivalent elements of Drieu's analysis. Firstly, we find the disenchanted yet fervent nationalist side by side with the European: a tension which, as an abiding feature of Drieu's work, has allowed critics to stress one or other side of the ambivalence. Secondly, and contained within this ambivalence, how do we reconcile Drieu's 'éternel esprit de guerre' (as expressed in *État Civil* and his war poems) with his pacifism as implied in the idea of a united Europe? Emotionally, Drieu was never fully able to resolve this tension despite frequent attempts to convince himself that peace alone could satisfy modern needs. If the author of *Mesure de la France* accepts the need for peace, he does so grudgingly. His reasons for so doing may be gathered from a declaration he was to make in 1925 on the subject of Fritz von Unruh's *Nouvel Empire*.[55] Vituperating 'l'absurde gouvernement de la Machine',[56] Drieu announces that 'le génie infernal du moderne a pourri la guerre. Aujourd'hui les hommes de tête en Europe ne peuvent que déclarer la paix, du moins aux autres Européens'.[57]

At this stage Drieu's Europeanism would thus appear to be less a commitment to Europe as such than a kind of *pis-aller* made necessary to a large extent by the unacceptable conditions of modern war. If *Mesure de la France* reveals any commitment at all, it is to a form of spiritual and moral strength, the sense of which he feels to be lacking in Europe. It was fidelity to the notion of a spiritual renaissance which led him, three years later, to break with his closest friend Louis Aragon, whose new-found political persuasion and vociferous pronouncements

158

he contemptuously dismissed as 'des incartades facétieuses du côté de la tribune aux harangues'.[58] It was this vision of a rebirth which, above and beyond all economic and political considerations, would remain at the heart of Drieu's Europeanism.

In 1926 Drieu once again takes up the theme of European unity, this time in the form of a 'science fiction' short story entitled 'Défense de sortir'. Here Drieu looks into the future to tell us that 'la première fusée quitta la terre le 25 avril 1963'. The space travellers do not return, not because of any intergalactic catastrophe but simply because they have found more congenial surroundings 'elsewhere'. Drieu tries to imagine the reaction if, instead of party, national or even continental loyalties being put to the test, our terrestrial loyalties were challenged. He concludes that the nations of the earth would not hesitate to rally to Mother Earth. 'Ailleurs' would be vigorously condemned: 'sur tous les champs d'aviation furent apposées de vastes affiches qui se reflétaient la nuit sur les cieux des villes: DÉFENSE DE SORTIR.'[59] Drieu's message is that we are all children of the earth and that, looked upon from space, national boundaries must seem the height of absurdity. If the nations of the world could, for one moment, view things in this cosmic light, world unity, to say nothing of European solidarity, would be assured.

If this short story cannot be considered a piece of serious political analysis it nonetheless appears to demonstrate that Drieu was moving away from the national scheme of things towards a wider consideration of European and world problems. His next political essay will confirm this move.

In *Genève ou Moscou* (1928) Drieu informs us that his earlier nationalism has been completely lost and that he is now writing as a committed European: 'j'ai écrit en 1920: "La France n'a pas dit son dernier mot"; j'élargis ma pensée: l'Europe, dont la France fait partie, n'a pas dit son dernier mot.'[60] He reiterates the view that the ideal of *patrie*, bound inextricably to that of war, is today obsolete, given the inhuman nature of modern warfare.[61] Mussolini, for whom every technological innovation or educational discipline is a preparation for war, is therefore condemned. Drieu, who in *Mesure de la France* had urged the reader to consider the example of the 'Fascio', now praises

instead 'l'effort admirable et fécond d'Aristide Briand'. Paradoxically he also expresses his admiration for the Action Française
whose sympathies at this time were with Mussolini not Briand.[62]
This apart, Drieu's main argument remains consistent and firmly
directed. Restating his capitalist thesis and his abhorrence of
socialism,[63] he insists that the pooling and exploitation of resources on a European scale more properly translates the demands of
the modern world than do the parochial interests of twenty or so
individual nations vying for supremacy over one another.[64] Using
the same type of procedure as in 'Défense de sortir', Drieu asks
his compatriots to consider the absurdity of national divisions
when looked at from outside:

> Aux yeux d'un Chinois, quelle différence y a-t-il entre un Écossais
> et un Espagnol: même religion, même façon de manger, de se
> gouverner, même teint? Et le Chinois a raison. Si vous le niez,
> c'est que vous jouez sur les mots, c'est que vous êtes byzantins, ou
> que vous profitez abusivement d'une différence de développement
> historique qui sera abolie demain matin par le tunnel sous la
> Manche. Si le Chinois vous parle d'un certain sentiment de la vie
> et de la mort, qui vaut pour quatre cents millions d'humains,
> répondrez-vous par des distinctions sur le Christ écossais et le
> Christ catalan?[65]

If the Western democracies, England and France, do not acquire
one will, Europe, claims Drieu, will be united in spite of itself, by
Moscow. The choice is clear: 'allons à Genève pour ne pas aller à
Moscou'.[66]

Drieu's next political essay on Europe was *L'Europe contre les
patries*, published in 1931. He opens with a 'Discours aux
Allemands', in which, consistent with his earlier calls for a
peacefully united and democratically based European federation,
he tries to convince Germany of the futility of expansionist
ambitions:

> Jamais vous n'aurez l'hégémonie sur l'Europe. Personne n'a
> jamais pu l'avoir . . . L'Europe est formée de peuples courageux.
> Toute tentative d'hégémonie, le jour où elle se déclare, provoque
> aussitôt une coalition. . . On ne peut pas tuer les nationalismes par
> le triomphe de l'un d'entre eux.[67]

L'Europe contre les patries also deals at length with the States

160

created or revived by the Versailles treaties and offers specific suggestions to integrate them into a new European complex.[68] Finally, in the form of a dialogue with himself, Drieu declares that in the event of a European war he would refuse the mobilization call since as a man he considered modern warfare a betrayal of the species and as a European he saw Europe's only hope of survival in peaceful unity:

Moi: Je joue ma vie sur le pari que l'Europe peut vivre encore, c'est-à-dire par la paix. Je ne répondrai pas à aucune mobilisation, ni à celle des patries, ni à celle des partis. Je me ferai fusiller par n'importe quel gendarme—celui de Hindenburg ou de Tardieu, ou celui de Staline.

L'autre: Ce n'est pas vrai, je t'ai connu à la guerre, tu l'aimais. Tu répondras à l'appel aux armes, et tu te battras avec moi ou contre moi, pour Staline ou pour Mussolini, ou pour un troisième.

Moi: Non, il faut que quelques-uns résistent à toutes ces tentations et demeurent seuls, humains portant la paix dans leur cœur et l'unité de l'Europe.[69]

It is noteworthy that although Drieu's 'Moi' triumphs over his 'darker self', he nonetheless feels obliged, after a decade of peace, to give expression to both. Indeed his other self still feels remorse at having taken the side of non-Europeans against 'ceux qui étaient les plus forts en Europe':

Derniers mitrailleurs allemands, c'est avec un serrement de cœur que, perdu dans les rangs étranges de l'armée américaine, je vous voyais mourir à un nouveau Waterloo, sous les coups d'un ennemi de trop.[70]

To be fair to Drieu it could of course be argued that the dialogue has at least the merit of sincerity. To be prepared, moreover, to suppress a powerful instinctive drive in the interests of saner principles was, for Drieu, not an easy decision. If he was prepared to make that decision, it was because he, as the 'témoin d'une génération', believed it to be not unlike that which his compatriots and fellow Europeans were required to make in the interests of survival. His was a lead which he hoped others would follow.

In *Genève ou Moscou* Drieu had written of the role he assigned to himself in his generation. He was, he 'confessed', a 'man of letters', but he was also, he wrote, a man who was obliged, like everybody else, to muddle his way through this world seeking out its direction in order the better to orient himself.[71] The direction he found and the mission he assumed were recorded in that same essay: 'mon but politique essentiel a été, est et sera toujours la constitution des États-Unis d'Europe.'[72]

Some weeks before his death Drieu attempted to explain his reasons for collaborating with the Germans. He claimed that his decision was based entirely on the desire to see Europe united along socialist lines. Unlike Britain—a continental nation with extra-European interests—Germany, wrote Drieu, was a continental power with a thorough-going socialist programme. Commitment to her was, he insisted, the only attitude possible for one who placed Europeanism above nationalism and preferred socialism to capitalism: 'cela ne comportait donc aucun élément affectif. Je n'ai jamais été germanophile, je l'ai hautement dit'.[73] The final apologia for his commitment (and suicide) was recorded in the following terms: 'je ne suis pas qu'un Français, je suis un Européen. Vous aussi, vous l'êtes sans le savoir, ou le sachant. Mais nous avons joué, j'ai perdu. Je réclame la mort.'[74]

Drieu's last, passionate declaration of his Europeanism —taken in conjunction with earlier declarations—has convinced some critics that it was a commitment to socialism (as the corner-stone of a united Europe) that led Drieu to Fascism and collaboration.[75] An examination of Drieu's Fascism will reveal, however, that such an interpretation is unsatisfactory. There is, however, a further reason for examining Drieu's Fascism. As a leading spokesman of the largest Fascist party in France in the 'thirties, Drieu was not only familiar with Fascist ideology but in a position to effect its development.[76] To understand Drieu's Fascism is thus to shed light on the nature of French Fascism in general: a subject on which there has been some disagreement among historians.[77] All too often French Fascism has been defined as a form of socialism[78]—a view which Drieu's final words would appear to support. And yet, as we have claimed, the key to Drieu's Fascism (and collaboration) lies neither in adherence to socialism nor in a commitment as such to Europe.

In *État Civil* Drieu describes patriotism as 'la clef de tous les

162

prétextes de vivre'. In *Genève ou Moscou* he describes himself as a European. In *Gilles* (1939), a largely autobiographical novel, he returns to his earlier nationalist position. Gilles/Drieu stresses that a Fascist is above all a nationalist. He suggests that France should resist Germany even to the extent of forming alliances with nations hostile to Fascism. If Fascists of different nationalities can fight together in Spain under the banner of a common cause, they would nonetheless, he claims, have no alternative but to fight one another in the event of a conflict between their respective countries. To his two Fascist companions he insists that the triumph of Fascism in Europe can wait: 'mais vous ne pouvez sacrifier aux puissances qui se servent du fascisme le corps de vos patries'.[79] He even goes so far as to express his contempt for the ideal to which he had rallied some years before, and whose symbol was Geneva: 'Genève avait été une sale petite abstraction qui humiliait toutes les puissantes vies diverses.'[80] Gilles' Fascism in French colours is occasionally blurred, though never fully obscured, by declarations which appear to smack of political nihilism, as when he submits the following plan to a political leader:

> Ouvre un bureau immédiatement pour recruter des sections de combat. Pas de manifeste, pas de programme, pas de nouveau parti. Seulement des sections de combat, qui s'appelleront n'importe quoi. Attaque Daladier ou défend-le, mais par des actes qui soient tout à fait concrets. Envahis coup sur coup un journal de droite et un journal de gauche. Fais bâtonner à domicile celui-ci ou celui-là. Sors à tout prix de la routine des vieux partis, des manifestes, des meetings, des articles et des discours.[81]

In spite of this declaration it would be wrong to conclude that Gilles is a rebel without a cause, an individual drained of constructive purpose, a political nihilist. His call for action derives, as it does for Drieu, from a sense of frustration over the failure of both Right and Left to bring about radical change in French society. If it is true, nonetheless, that Gilles/Drieu has a natural disposition towards action for action's sake, it could be said that this tendency reinforces rather than contradicts his desire for change. For Gilles/Drieu the simple fact is that actions speak louder than words, far louder than the ideological squabbles that divide his countrymen and paralyse the nation. His

163

violent words are not the product of political nihilism, but the expression of a desperate need: to rescue France from intellectual and moral stagnation in order to lead her, through action, to a new order of strength and unity.

The heavy nationalist tone of *Gilles* was not a temporary aberration on the part of Drieu. As a member of Doriot's Parti Populaire Français, he had for some time been engaged in propagating the view that nationalism was a fundamental human passion, as vital to man as a mother to her child. In view of the German threat he suggested, as he was later to do in *Gilles*, that France would be better served by strengthening her ties with London rather than with Berlin. Ideology was of no consequence, he wrote, where national survival was at stake. His first loyalty, he insisted, was to France, not to Europe, to his compatriots and not to foreign Fascists: 'les systèmes changent mais les pays demeurent.'[82] The rallying call of the P.P.F. was 'Ni Moscou ni Berlin'—sentiments with which Drieu heartily agreed:

> C'est très joli de crier 'Vive les Soviets' ou 'Bravo Hitler', quand on est bien tranquille chez soi, entre Français, bien étanché. C'est beaucoup moins joli quand il y a des milliers de mercenaires staliniens ou hitlériens qui promènent leurs bottes sur votre sol, qui chantent leurs chansons, qui jurent dans leur langue, et regardent vos femmes. Comment voulez-vous que des Russes ou des Allemands, dressés par la dictature, se conduisent mieux que des Français qui s'étaient pourtant crus attendris par les discours utopiques des débuts de la Révolution? Ils ne peuvent pas ne pas être humiliants.[83]

Shortly after making these declarations Drieu was urging his compatriots to welcome the Nazis as architects of a united Europe. Hegemony, which he had previously rejected as incompatible with the idea of federation,[84] was now regarded as indispensable.[85] In view of the ease with which his Europeanism accommodated hegemony and made room for 'socialism' (where previously only capitalism seemed to satisfy) and given the facility with which he had abandoned his Europeanism in the years leading up to war, it is not unreasonable to assume that its importance was not as great as he now suggested. Moreover, to present Hitler as the Messiah of a socialist Europe was not merely curious in itself but in flagrant contradiction with many of his

164

earlier pronouncements on the subject of the Führer. In *Socia-lisme Fasciste* (1934) not only did he describe Hitler as a nationalist fanatic who would not hesitate to sacrifice the interests of Europe to those of Germany, but he dismissed his claims to socialism as pure hypocrisy. He claimed that the economic policy of the Third Reich was essentially conservative and in evidence he pointed to the fact that German capitalists were still making substantial profits.[86] By 1939 his impressions of German socialism were even less favourable than they had been five years before: 'c'est l'esprit de ruée, sans but, qui ne trouvera de but qu'au bout du monde ou dans les fossés de la ligne Maginot'.[87] One year later, having completed a seemingly impossible mental somersault, Drieu was hailing Hitler as the great hope of European socialism.

The socialism to which Fascists aspired had little, if anything, in common with the socialism of Marxists unless, for example, fundamental differences in economic theory and practice are overlooked in favour of facile assertions of the kind that 'dictatorship equals dictatorship' or that the political spectrum is more properly described as a circle rather than a straight line. The revolutionary, anti-capitalist, anti-bourgeois programme of Fascism was simply a recruiting slogan. Those who responded to slogans of this type or to appeals for national unity and solidarity between classes remained firmly ensconced in capitalist economic structures, controlled but not changed. Social-Fascists, unlike Marxists, saw no need to socialize the means of production. For them, profit remained the motor of production. However, our purpose in what follows is not to demonstrate that socialism and social-Fascism are spheres apart, but to show that Drieu's socialism was not only not socialist but largely a-economic in outlook. To this extent, and in so far as Drieu was a representative of French Fascism, historians' claims that French Fascism was in essence a form of socialism are unfounded.

The socialism of which Drieu dreamed had nothing to do with the satisfaction of material needs, the economic well-being of the working class or the socialization of the means of production. Indeed he found such questions a diversion from the real issue. Believing that all men had been corrupted by the idol of production, Drieu could see no good reason for distinguishing between them. The worker living on a pittance and the business-man living off a private income were, he claimed, not only indistinguishable the one from the other, but positively interchangeable. Since both were materialists all other considerations were unimportant.[88] The same was true of a Lenin and a Stinnes, of the Soviet Union and the United States, of Marxist socialism and modern capitalism.[89] If Drieu's rejection of capitalism proved to be more rhetorical than real,[90] there was no denying his contempt for the socialism of those 'qui veulent bien manger ou bien boire, et qui veulent, l'été, s'étendre sur les plages et, l'hiver, contempler au-dessus du feu et de la peluche cramoisie une pendule de zinc'.[91] It was on this basis that the Popular Front government of Léon Blum came under attack. Drieu accused it of being more interested in satisfying the hungry aspirations of the masses than in rescuing human dignity from physical and moral degeneration.[92] To 'socialism of the stomach' Drieu opposed the 'virile socialism' of the P.P.F., an organization which looked upon the peasantry and the petty bourgeoisie (and not the proletariat) as the vanguard of its hopes, and whose economic philosophy was one which far from being socialist regarded profit and private ownership as inalienable rights. In view of these observations it is difficult to believe that commitment to socialism—at least in any meaningful economic sense—was as crucial a factor in Drieu's conversion to Hitlerism as his final declaration suggests.

In 1937 Drieu declared 'le fascisme dépasse le socialisme (marxiste) par son sens de l'homme'.[93] If Drieu defended this view, as he was later to do in respect of Hitlerian socialism, it was because he regarded moral regeneration as more important than economic reform. In so far as the choice, for Drieu, lay between the 'material objectives' of socialism and the 'spiritual ambitions' of Fascism and Nazism, he opted for the latter. Thus, although his visit to Germany in 1934 left him disappointed over Hitler's failure to contain capitalism, the austerity, indeed the poverty, that he found there convinced him of the nobility of German intentions: 'au fond ils vont vers une conception spirituelle, esthétique, de la société'.[94]

In Fascism Drieu glimpsed a spiritual and corporal harmony, a mystic ecstacy the like of which he himself had experienced when, in war, he beheld the 'resurrection of the body'.[95] As a partisan of 'sword-intelligence', Drieu had hoped that war would

166

involve men in epic contests which would be famous for the courage, skill and strength of the participants. If these qualities were not altogether absent, his overall impression was that war could no longer satisfy man's aggressive needs. A substitute was sought and Drieu found it in sport: 'à cause de la déviation démoniaque qu'a subie la guerre moderne, nous nous contenterons de l'exercice transposé de la guerre: du sport.'[96] Sport revealed the importance of the body and became for Drieu the modern preserve of the 'Révolution corporelle'. It was in this domain, he believed, that Fascism proved its superiority over rival ideologies, especially over Marxism whose supporters, he claimed, had abandoned this vital need to an exclusive concern for economic and political reform:

> Ils n'ont pas compris que la réforme physique de l'homme devait être entreprise immédiatement comme une besogne urgente, concurremment avec la réforme de l'économie; et que la réforme de l'économie devait être modelée sur les nécessités de la réforme physique (ce qui est la démarche essentielle de la révolution fasciste).[97]

It was according to such criteria and not on 'socialist' merit that Drieu judged the Fascist movements of Italy and Germany. In 1937, for example, he wrote:

> Il se peut que les ouvriers italiens ou allemands mangent moins que les ouvriers français, mais ils ont eux et surtout leurs enfants, plus de grand air, plus de sport, plus de voyage, plus de fêtes collectives: splendides et enivrantes solennités physiques.[98]

In the same year, and with the French situation in mind, Drieu wrote:

> Je trouve que le meilleur jugement politique, c'est le plus simple jugement humain. Il est oiseux de juger un parti politique sur sa doctrine, sur son programme. Combien y a-t-il de militants socialistes qui ont lu plus de trois lignes de Marx? Et combien de députés socialistes avaient réfléchi au programme économique de MM. Auriol et Blum, avec toutes ses fabrioles? Non, il faut seulement demander: quelle est votre valeur humaine? Quel est votre potentiel de jeunesse et d'énergie? Quelle est votre force de création?[99]

What Drieu wanted was 'whole politics' (neither left-wing nor right-wing, but a full unity). 'Petty' ideological squabbles, Drieu believed, only served to retard the recovery of that 'integrity' and sense of life which had been France's honour and strength in the Middle Ages.[100]

It seems clear that Drieu's commitment to Fascism, like his later conversion to Hitlerism, was determined neither by economic preference nor by strong political conviction. And attachment to the idea of a united Europe cannot, as we have seen, be regarded as a decisive factor. In the final analysis he was drawn by what he regarded as Fascism's essential principle: the 'Révolution corporelle'. Consider his following definition:

> La définition la plus profonde du fascisme c'est celle-ci: c'est le mouvement politique qui va le plus franchement, le plus radicalement dans le sens de la grande révolution des mœurs, dans le sens de *la restauration du corps*—santé, dignité, plénitude, héroïsme—dans le sens de la défense de l'homme contre la machine.[101]

One event above all others launched Drieu on the Fascist course: the anti-parliamentary riots of February 1934. In *Gilles* Drieu later described the impact of this event upon Gilles Gambier. That they were Drieu's own feelings is attested to by the articles from 'La Lutte des jeunes' collected in *Socialisme Fasciste:* 'en un instant il fut transfiguré. Regardant à sa droite et à sa gauche, il se vit entouré par le couple divin revenu, la Peur et le Courage, qui préside à la guerre.'[102]

Drieu's interpretation of this event reveals that his commitment was not to Fascism as such but to Fascism such as he *imagined and desired it.* Drieu himself provides the evidence. Looking back on the life he had known in the trenches he declared: 'sous mon premier veston, portant les idées passionnées d'*Interrogation* j'étais tout à fait fasciste sans le savoir.'[103] Fascism was thus, for Drieu, a movement which reminded him of the 'mystical bond'—the pact of blood—established between the leader and the group, which he had experienced at Charleroi. It was, he sensed, a movement which restored to man his self-identity by accepting the darker side of his nature, while at the same time assuring him of a collective identity in a spontaneous and heroic community. It was the supreme expression of all he craved—the 'restauration du corps' and the reconciliation of 'rêve' and 'action'. In addition it seemed in no way to contradict either his nationalism or his Europeanism. Drieu would continue, except towards the very end, to see in Fascism only those elements which complemented his own vision. Unfortunately for him these same elements were themselves but part of the very different vision of a German demagogue— backed by very real economic and political forces—who would prove to have very little sympathy for the personal reminiscences and ardent athleticism of a French infantryman of the First World War.

It seems almost inevitable, given Drieu's lifelong insistence upon the value of virile virtue, that he should have interpreted the German victory as the just rewards of the strong. Having proved itself to be the most powerful nation in the West, Germany, Drieu believed, had shown itself to be not only capable of uniting Europe, but, more importantly, worthy of bringing forth a New Man:

> Un nouvel homme . . . restituant dans l'âme et dans le corps les valeurs de force, de courage, d'affirmation, avide d'embrasser l'expérience et l'épreuve, de s'établir sur un rapport direct et constant entre ce qui est senti, ce qui est pensé et ce qui est accompli.[104]

In this noble ambition Drieu was reminded of the Middle Ages,[105] and looked forward to a new dawn in Europe, a new 'Saint Empire' wrought of social and political stability, of cultural endeavour and, above all, of spiritual and physical harmony.[106] Convinced that his myth of the 'âge d'or' was the reality he now glimpsed, he could not believe that the Germans were capable of less nobility than he:

> L'Allemagne ne peut pas songer à l'écrasement de vingt peuples et à vivre solitaire sur le néant qu'ils feraient au-dessous d'elle. L'Allemagne ne peut pas songer à vivre comme ont fait les Turcs sur des ruines et des populations saignées à blanc, spirituellement et matériellement pulvérisées.[107]

This idealism Drieu invested in collaboration, believing that through it France would be metamorphosed. He urged his countrymen to respond and so demonstrate their worthiness to be transformed.[108] Important to that transformation was, Drieu now believed, the acceptance of Nazi (and Vichy) racialist doctrine. However, it would be wrong to assume, as does Alexander Macleod, that Drieu was 'un penseur raciste'.[109] Robert Soucy, on the other hand, is certainly correct in his claim that only after the French defeat did Drieu begin writing of 'lois très simples qui fondent la vie des peuples sur la fécondité du sol et du sang' and that even then he felt obliged to justify his claim by equating racialism with Aryanism and Aryanism with Europeanism: 'de ce point de vue', wrote Drieu, 'le germanisme n'est que la pointe de l'européanisme'.[110] Racialist ideas were not only late in appearing in Drieu's Fascism but they actually contradicted his fundamental conception of human nature. Drieu had long insisted on the fact that men, like nations, were capable of shaping their own destinies by force of will.[111] Superiority was not (as his novels of the 'twenties and 'thirties clearly show) a question of race, but of firm resolve. There seems little reason to believe that racialism was in any way responsible for Drieu's decision to collaborate.

Apart from adopting racialist formulae Drieu also expressed the conviction, dear to fellow spirits in Paris and Vichy, that Germany was the only country capable of saving Europe from Communism: 'Les Russes à Berlin, ce serait aussitôt le communisme dans tout l'Occident, instantané, irrésistible'.[112] Denouncing Bolshevism as non-European, as 'russe et juif russe', he urged solidarity with the German cause.[113] However, as the war wore on, Drieu became racked with disillusion in the face of Nazi realities. He finally came to doubt the existence, in the Germans, of those physical and spiritual resources which were necessary for the birth of the New Man.[114] As soon as he ceased to believe in the 'New Order' as the harbinger of a New Man, he announced his 'supreme evolution'. Communism alone now seemed to command those virile virtues needed for the resurrection of European man. Fascism was after all, he noted, what Marxists had always claimed it to be: a desperate bourgeois defence.[115] He now welcomed a Russian victory and the triumph of 'totalitarian man'.[116]

Drieu's change of attitude towards the Soviet Union demonstrates conclusively that his 'Europeanism' was neither political nor economic (since he was not a Marxist) nor indeed 'European' (since he himself denied that the Soviet Union was a European nation). And yet he urgently requested his friend Lucien Combelle to become a Communist: 'j'espère que vous vivrez et que vous défendrez ce que nous aimons; un socialisme fier, viril.'[117] We have already seen that socialism, in an economic sense, was far less important for Drieu than the adjectives he here uses to describe it. If he was 'converted' to Communism it was for no other reason than that it promised, indeed threatened, to establish a virile community throughout the West.

The power which the Russians had displayed in crushing the German invasion of their country and in launching their own offensive in Europe convinced Drieu that his earlier attacks on 'socialism of the stomach' were ill-founded. The Soviet Union was now the most powerful nation in 'Europe'—the 'homme stalinien' had superseded the 'homme hitlérien' as the agent of regeneration:

> je crois que si les Russes venaient en France la seule différence de leur tonalité vitale soufflerait littéralement les Français. Il n'y aurait même pas besoin de communisme et de massacres: la seule présence de quelques centaines de milliers de Russes éteindrait nos gens.[118]

In much the same way as Malraux's Garine contemplates joining his erstwhile enemies, Drieu here discovers his *raison d'être* in the might of his adversaries. In the final analysis his commitment to Fascism, as to collaboration, like his 'conversion' to Communism, was based neither on political persuasion nor on some 'esprit européen' but on the principle that might makes right.

The political itinerary of Drieu La Rochelle is that of a man who wanted desperately to participate in the great events of his time. Contrary to what he and many critics have maintained, Drieu was less a genuine visionary and 'good European' betrayed by the world, by History or by Hitler, than a victim of his own mythology. If he was betrayed by anything at all, it was by his own eagerness to see political events and historical forces as little more than instruments of his own private needs.

NOTES

[1] 'Un entretien avec Kléber Haedens', *Défense de l'Occident—numéro spécial* (February–March 1958), p. 33: 'devant chaque événement on se demandait

171

ce qu'en pensait Drieu, comment il réagissait, non pour l'imiter, mais parce que son attitude était un test exemplaire'. See also Ramon Fernandez, 'Plainte contre inconnu', *N.R.F.* (January 1925).

2 François Mauriac, 'Présence de Drieu La Rochelle', *Défense de l'Occident*, p. 20.

3 See for example Pierre Andreu's nationalist inclined thesis: *Drieu, témoin et visionnaire* (Grasset, 1952), pp. 137–203, and George Bonneville's analysis of Drieu's 'esprit européen': *Prophètes et témoins de l'Europe* (Sythoff: Leyde, 1961), pp. 92–106.

4 Marcel Arland, 'État Civil', *N.R.F.* (April 1922), pp. 491–5.

5 Drieu La Rochelle, *État Civil* (Gallimard, 1921), p. 51.

6 Drieu La Rochelle, *op. cit.*, p. 57: 'elle ne me parlait que de vigueur et d'audace, m'avertissant de la bassesse qui m'attendait si mon corps n'était pas redoutable. Le moindre de mes efforts pouvait me servir à vaincre les hommes.'

7 Drieu La Rochelle, *op. cit.*, p. 57.

8 Drieu La Rochelle, *op. cit.*, pp. 44–5.

9 'The Joyful Wisdom', p. 320, *Nietzsche,* translated by Oscar Levy (Edinburgh: Foulis, 1909–1914).

10 Drieu La Rochelle, *État Civil*, p. 45.

11 Drieu La Rochelle, *op. cit.*, p. 58.

12 Drieu La Rochelle, *op. cit.*, p. 75.

13 Drieu La Rochelle, *op. cit.*, p. 164.

14 Drieu La Rochelle, *op. cit.*, pp. 161–2.

15 Drieu La Rochelle, *op. cit.*, p. 165: 'je restais . . . boudant à ma jeunesse, me vouant rageusement à la stérilité, jurant de ne plus troubler par aucun effort inutile la mort de la France que je souhaitais alors d'une solennité sourde'.

16 Drieu La Rochelle, *op. cit.*, p. 173.

17 Drieu La Rochelle, *op. cit.*, p. 158.

18 Drieu La Rochelle, *op. cit.*, p. 165.

19 Drieu La Rochelle, *op. cit.*, p. 174.

20 e.g. 'La Guerre et la paix', *Écrits de jeunesse* (Gallimard, 1941), p. 56: 'La guerre pour nous, nés dans un temps de longue paix, parut une nouveauté merveilleuse; l'accomplissement qui n'était pas espéré de notre jeunesse. Je doute que la paix nous eût assouvis aussi magnifiquement.'

21 Drieu La Rochelle, *État Civil,* pp. 21–2.

22 Drieu La Rochelle, 'Le Jeune Européen', *Écrits de jeunesse,* p. 181: 'les hommes ne sont nés que pour la guerre, comme les femmes ne sont faites que pour les enfants.'

23 Drieu La Rochelle, *Interrogation* (Gallimard, 1917), p. 9.

24 Drieu La Rochelle, 'La Restauration du corps', *op. cit.*, p. 49.

25 Drieu La Rochelle, 'Paroles au départ', *op. cit.,* pp. 9–10.

26 Walter Kaufmann (ed.) *The Portable Nietzsche* (The Viking Press: New York, 1969), pp. 146–7.

27 Drieu La Rochelle, 'Plainte des soldats européens', *Écrits de jeunesse,* p. 13.

28 e.g. '*Nouvel Empire* par Fritz von Unruh', *N.R.F.* (December 1925), pp. 627–30; 'Le Jeune Européen', *Écrits de jeunesse,* p. 187.

172

[29] Drieu La Rochelle, *La Comédie de Charleroi* (Livre de poche, 1970), pp. 31–2, p. 47.
[30] Drieu La Rochelle, *op. cit.*, p. 75.
[31] Drieu La Rochelle, *Mesure de la France* (Grasset, 1964), Édition originale 1922.
[32] Drieu La Rochelle, *op. cit.*, p. 42: 'La France n'a plus fait d'enfants, ce crime d'où découlent les insultes, les malheurs qu'elle a essuyés depuis 50 ans elle l'a mûri à la fin du XIXe siècle et consommé au début du XXe siècle'.
[33] Drieu La Rochelle, *op. cit.*, p. 39.
[34] Drieu La Rochelle, *op. cit.*, p. 65 and p. 74.
[35] Drieu La Rochelle, *op. cit.*, p. 55.
[36] Drieu La Rochelle, *op. cit.*, pp. 67–8.
[37] Henri Massis, 'Les Appels de l'Orient', pp. 38–9.
[38] Drieu La Rochelle, *Mesure de la France*, p. 71.
[39] Drieu La Rochelle, *op. cit.*, p. 76.
[40] Drieu La Rochelle, *op. cit.*, p. 93.
[41] Drieu La Rochelle, *op. cit.*, pp. 95–6.
[42] Drieu La Rochelle, *op. cit.*, p. 97.
[43] Drieu La Rochelle, *op. cit.*, p. 98: 'en 1918 on a pu croire que la Russie était l'appellée. Ne se dressait-elle pas dans sa steppe, dont le mystère semblait plein de promesses pour jeter à l'Europe désorientée, affolée, un Évangile.'
[44] Drieu La Rochelle, *op. cit.*, p. 99.
[45] Drieu La Rochelle, *op. cit.*, p. 101.
[46] Drieu La Rochelle, *op. cit.*, p. 103.
[47] Drieu La Rochelle, *op. cit.*, p. 106.
[48] Drieu La Rochelle, *Genève ou Moscou* (Gallimard, 1928), p. 29.
[49] Drieu La Rochelle, *op. cit.*, p. 266: [le capitalisme et le communisme] travaillent à l'achèvement d'un certain monde moderne, merveilleuse mécanique sévère et dénuée de tout secours à l'esprit.'
[50] Drieu La Rochelle, *Mesure de la France*, pp. 110–11.
[51] Drieu La Rochelle, *op. cit.*, p. 111: 'l'exemple du Fascio mérite d'être médité.'
[52] Drieu La Rochelle, *op. cit.*, p. 115.
[53] Jean Bernier, 'Les Angoisses d'un jeune bourgeois', *Clarté* (15 April, 1923), p. 236.
[54] Drieu La Rochelle, *Mesure de la France*, p. 101.
[55] Drieu La Rochelle, 'Nouvel Empire par Fritz von Unruh', *N.R.F.* (December 1925), pp. 627–30.
[56] Drieu La Rochelle, 'Nouvel Empire par Fritz von Unruh', p. 629.
[57] Drieu La Rochelle, 'Nouvel Empire par Fritz von Unruh', p. 627.
[58] Drieu La Rochelle, 'La Véritable erreur des surréalistes', *N.R.F.* (1 August, 1925), p. 171.
[59] Drieu La Rochelle, 'Defense de sortir', *Écrits de jeunesse* (Gallimard, 1941), p. 284.
[60] Drieu La Rochelle, *Genève ou Moscou* (Gallimard, 1928), p. 113.
[61] Drieu La Rochelle, *op. cit.*, p. 83: 'l'idée de patrie est liée à l'idée de

guerre. Étant donné ce qu'est devenue la guerre, dans le monde actuel, elle fait de la patrie la force la plus immédiatement dangereuse qui circule au milieu de nous'.

[62] Drieu La Rochelle, *op. cit.*, p. 24.

[63] Drieu La Rochelle, *op. cit.*, p. 29: 'je me raccroche au capitalisme à cause du peu de confiance que je mets dans le pouvoir créateur qui pourra jaillir du désespoir et du désordre. Le prolétariat n'est qu'un mythe chaque jour plus affaibli; ce n'est que l'ombre de la Bourgeoisie.'

[64] Drieu La Rochelle, *op. cit.*, p. 113.

[65] Drieu La Rochelle, *op. cit.*, pp. 113–14.

[66] Drieu La Rochelle, *op. cit.*, p. 110.

[67] Drieu La Rochelle, *L'Europe contre les patries* (Gallimard, 1931), p. 17.

[68] Drieu La Rochelle, *op. cit.*, pp. 91–139.

[69] Drieu La Rochelle, *op. cit.*, pp. 150–1.

[70] Drieu La Rochelle, *op. cit.*, p. 36.

[71] Drieu La Rochelle, *Genève ou Moscou*, p. 208.

[72] Drieu La Rochelle, *op. cit.*, pp. 27–8.

[73] Drieu La Rochelle, *Récit Secret* (Chez A. M. G., 1951), p. 95.

[74] Drieu La Rochelle, *op. cit.*, p. 99.

[75] e.g. Pol Vandromme, *Drieu La Rochelle* (Éditions Universitaires, 1958); and Pierre Andreu, *Drieu, témoin et visionnaire* (Grasset, 1952).

[76] See Drieu La Rochelle, *Avec Doriot* (Gallimard, 1937), p. 7.

[77] Important Studies of French Fascism include the following: M. Cotta, *La Collaboration* (Armand Colin, 1964); Ernst Nolte, *Three Faces of Fascism* (New York: Holt, Rinehart and Winston, 1966); Jean Plumyène and Raymond Lasierra, *Les Fascismes français* (Éditions du Seuil, 1963); René Rémond, *La Droite en France de 1815 à nos jours* (Aubier, 1954); Paul Sérant, *Le Romantisme fasciste* (Fasquelle, 1959); Eugen Weber, *Varieties of Fascism* (New York: D. Van Nostrand, 1964); see also, Raoul Girardet, 'Notes sur l'esprit d'un fascisme français' (1934–1939), *Revue Française de science politique*, V, (January–March 1955), pp. 529–46; Victor Leduc, 'Quelques problèmes d'une sociologie du fascisme', *Cahiers Internationaux de Sociologie* (1952), pp. 115–30; René Rémond, 'Y a-t-il un fascisme français', *Terre Humaine* No. 7–8 (July–August 1952), pp. 37–47.

[78] For an excellent critique of this (and other) 'authoritative' opinion of the nature of French Fascism see Robert Soucy, 'The Nature of Fascism in France', *Journal of Contemporary History*, I, no 1 (January 1966), pp. 27–55.

[79] Drieu La Rochelle, *Gilles* (Gallimard, 1939), p. 474.

[80] Drieu La Rochelle, *op. cit.*, p. 479.

[81] Drieu La Rochelle, *op. cit.*, pp. 420–1.

[82] Drieu La Rochelle, *Chronique politique 1934–1942* (Gallimard, 1943), p. 79.

[83] Drieu La Rochelle, *Avec Doriot*, pp. 121–3.

[84] See Drieu La Rochelle, *Mesure de la France*, pp. 79–80: 'L'Europe est un continent où la vie n'est possible qu'à condition d'admettre et de pratiquer l'égalité'; *Genève ou Moscou*, p. 102: 'le mirage de l'hégémonie, à deux ou à trois, voilà la grande pierre d'achoppement des États-Unis d'Europe'. See also *L'Europe contre les patries*, p. 17.

[85] Drieu La Rochelle, *Chronique politique*, p. 267: 'point de fédération sans

hégémonie. L'égalité n'existe pas. Une hégémonie déclarée vaut mieux qu'une hégémonie dissimulée'.

86 Drieu La Rochelle, *Socialisme Fasciste*, (Gallimard, 1934), p. 210.
87 Drieu La Rochelle, *Chronique politique*, p. 206.
88 Drieu La Rochelle, *Mesure de la France*, p. 93.
89 Drieu La Rochelle, *Mesure de la France*, pp. 98–103.
90 Drieu's rejection of capitalism was more rhetorical than real in that he saw no reason to eliminate it in order to achieve the 'spiritual' revolution after which he hankered. Unlike 'socialism of the stomach', capitalism did not represent an obstacle to the fulfilment of his (or, indeed, of Fascism's) ambitions. Indeed— and despite the fact that Drieu's own brand of socialism was more 'ascetic' than economic—Fascist socialism was not only not hostile to capitalism but was positively devoted to it. See Robert Soucy's examination of the economic programme of Fascist socialism in 'The Nature of Fascism in France', pp. 36–41.
91 Drieu La Rochelle, *Écrits de jeunesse* (Gallimard, 1941) p. 170.
92 See Drieu La Rochelle, *Avec Doriot* (Gallimard, 1937).
93 Drieu La Rochelle, *Chronique politique*, p. 50.
94 Drieu La Rochelle, *Socialisme Fasciste*, p. 211.
95 e.g. 'Le Jeune Européen', *Écrits de jeunesse*, p. 181: 'de cette fureur de sang sortit un élan mystique qui, nourri de l'essentiel de la chair, rompit toutes les attaches de cette chair et me jeta, pure palpitation, pur esprit, dans l'extrême de l'exil jusqu'à Dieu'. See also *Socialisme Fasciste*, p. 102.
96 Drieu La Rochelle, *Socialisme Fasciste*, p. 153. See also *Chronique politique*, pp. 49–53.
97 Drieu La Rochelle, *Chronique politique*, p. 53.
98 Drieu La Rochelle, *op. cit.*, pp. 50–1.
99 Drieu La Rochelle, *op. cit.*, p. 42.
100 Drieu La Rochelle, *op. cit.*, pp. 237–8.
101 Drieu La Rochelle, *Chronique politique*, p. 50.
102 Drieu La Rochelle, *Gilles*, p. 418.
103 Drieu La Rochelle, *Socialisme Fasciste*, p. 220.
104 Drieu La Rochelle, *Notes pour comprendre le siècle* (Gallimard, 1941), pp. 149–50.
105 See Drieu La Rochelle, 'La France et le fait germanique', *Chronique politique*, pp. 237–8.
106 See Drieu La Rochelle, *Notes pour comprendre le siècle*, p. 9 and p. 28.
107 Drieu La Rochelle, *Chronique politique*, p. 381.
108 Drieu La Rochelle, *op. cit.*, p. 279.
109 Alexander Macleod, *La Pensée politique de Pierre Drieu La Rochelle* (Éditions Cujas, 1966) pp. 73–9.
110 Robert Soucy, 'The Nature of Fascism in France', p. 43. See Drieu La Rochelle, *Notes pour comprendre le siècle*, p. 164.
111 See, for example, Drieu La Rochelle, *L'Europe contre les patries*, p. 12.
112 Drieu La Rochelle, *Chronique politique*, p. 340.
113 Drieu La Rochelle, *op. cit.*, p. 335.
114 See, for example, Drieu La Rochelle, *Les Chiens de paille* (Gallimard, 1964), p. 109: 'je me suis aperçu depuis deux ans que les Allemands sont *très*

faibles eux-mêmes. L'hitlérisme n'a été que le sursaut de quelques-uns d'entre eux, qu'ils ont pu imposer à la masse parce que celle-ci était aux abois. Les Allemands n'etaient pas assez jeunes pour se jeter dans le communisme et y faire peau neuve. Au fond l'hitlérisme, en dépit de son côté héroïque n'a été pour eux que le juste milieu entre le capitalisme et le communisme, entre le nationalisme et l'internationalisme'. See also Pierre Andreu, *Drieu, témoin et visionnaire,* p. 199: 'je me suis complètement trompé sur l'hitlérisme, au fond je jugeais l'Allemagne beaucoup plus sainement, en 1933 et 1934; quand je suis devenu partisan, ma vue ensuite s'est brouillée. L'Allemagne participe aussi profondément que les autres nations à la décadence européenne'.

[115] See Frédéric Grover, *Drieu La Rochelle* (Gallimard, 1962) p. 55.
[116] Drieu La Rochelle, *Le Français d'Europe* (Éditions Balzac, 1944), pp. 340–9.
[117] Quoted by Pol Vandromme, *Drieu La Rochelle* (Éditions Universitaires, 1958), p. 114.
[118] Drieu La Rochelle, *Le Français d'Europe,* p. 349.

CHAPTER VI

Malraux and the 'Death of Europe'

Le drame actuel de l'Europe, c'est la mort de l'homme.

(A. Malraux)

The climate of doubt inspired by the political, social and psychological shock of four years of war and intensified by new and disturbing discoveries about the nature of man and the universe appears to have affected Drieu and Malraux quite differently. Drieu saw the problem largely in social terms and his response was, as we have seen, a 'political' one. A solution to Europe's problems did exist and it lay in the physical and moral recovery of European man. If Drieu's work thus offers a solution, Malraux's, positing as it does the irremediable bankruptcy of all the values to which European man has been attached, represents the metaphysical impossibility of any solution. In *La Tentation de l'Occident*, A.D., speaking also for Ling, draws the following anguished conclusion from his observations:

> Les mondes de faits, de pensées et de gestes dans lesquels nous vivons tous deux, sont peu propices aux convictions; et nos cœurs attardés ne me semblent points adroits à jouir, comme il conviendrait, de la désagrégation d'un Univers et d'un Homme à la construction de quoi tant de bons esprits se sont attachés[1]

In this conclusion Malraux is clearly representative of that climate of doubt and despair for which the fatalistic formulae of Spengler and Valéry had already provided a would-be rational justification. The immediate effect of this *crise de l'esprit* on Malraux seems to have been to make him ask basic questions and to answer them in a tone of discouragement. When the gods die, does the civilization that created them die also, only to reappear in another form, another place, another time? 'Le Grec croit

177

l'homme distinct du monde comme le chrétien croit l'homme lié à Dieu, comme l'Oriental croit l'homme lié au monde.'[2] The Greek, the Christian and the Oriental are all men, but are they the *same man*? Malraux's own answer to this question would appear to be that there is not one system of values applicable to all men at all times, but several systems with no apparent common basis. It seems impossible to speak of a 'human history' developing through time. All one can see are a number of 'mondes clos', each impenetrable to the others and all equally perishable. And if history has no direction, if it is metaphysically impossible, then Man is Absurd. Malraux's obsession with history is thus less a morbid fascination with contingency than the desperate search for some permanent element of a 'humanité fondamentale' to rescue history from discontinuity. For if history becomes intelligible, Man too is rescued. As Jeanne Delhomme, writing of Malraux, has observed:

> Ordre, progrès et conscience; processus totalitaire et englobant [l'histoire] exigerait de l'homme activité totale, travail et engagement; en contrepartie elle deviendrait sa justification et sa raison d'être, car faire l'histoire ce serait refaire la vie et refaire l'homme.[3]

For A.D./Malraux, God is dead and Man is dead. European man's idols and ideals have deserted him and in an empty world, beneath senseless stars, he stands alone, and for his solitude there is no palliative. And yet this solitude, as we have indicated, calls forth a tragic necessity: to forge a new and adequate idea of man. This aim is announced by Malraux from the outset: 'L'objet de la recherche de la jeunesse occidentale est une notion nouvelle de l'homme'.[4]

There is now ample evidence to suggest that the sense of disarray and disillusion of the post-war years, coupled with the will to have done with the past and the desire to reconstruct upon new foundations, deeply affected the young Malraux. He frequented various *avant-garde* circles and came away with a keener palate for new values and a sharper eye for the 'market' in which to purchase them: 'Entre dix-huit et vingt ans, la vie est comme un marché où l'on achète des valeurs; non avec de l'argent, mais avec des actes. La plupart des hommes n'achètent rien'.[5] Unlike Drieu, Malraux is particularly reticent about his early years.

What we know we owe largely to the testimony of Clara Malraux and the effort of André Vandegans.[6] Their accounts, taken in conjunction with such other information as emerges from interviews and stray remarks by Malraux himself, leave one with the impression that his predilection for a mythic projection of himself both in the form of tall stories, and as a man of action, sprang from the compulsion to compensate for the disappointments of his personal life.[7] The air of mystery which he exuded about his person, along with other very real qualities of course, proved sufficiently appealing to win the attentions of Clara Goldschmidt, who became his wife in 1920 when he was just 19. Free from family dependence and, thanks to Clara, financially secure, Malraux was now in a position to live out a sort of rationalized mythomania through travel and speculation on the stock-exchange. The latter venture left Clara and himself ruined.[8]

Malraux's early literary undertakings, mostly reviews, had very little impact upon public or critics.[9] Even his more ambitious works like *Lunes en papier* and 'Écrit pour une Idole à Trompe' inspired no great response, being in effect little more than expressions of the contemporary idiom. Jacques Rivière went so far as to decline to publish some of Malraux's works on the grounds that the future writer would one day regret having submitted for public scrutiny 'ce qui n'était que fantaisie sans importance'.[10] In any event, and if only because Malraux has said that he himself attaches no importance to them, it might seem that Vandegans lends too much importance to these early writings in his attempt to establish his particular view of the 'artist as a young man'.

At this time Malraux was above all interested in discovering the world through travel and books,[11] and interested in ideas, particularly perhaps the idea of adventure, which was very much in the air at this time: 'ce mot [aventure] connut vers 1920 un grand prestige dans les milieux littéraires'.[12] Again, of course, his long-standing interest in T. E. Lawrence was not so much an individual obsession as the expression of the malaise of a generation convinced of the failure of traditional values and driven by a determination to discover new values and forms outside accepted frames of reference. T. E. Lawrence was not the only adventurer to have left Europe's shores. Ernest Psichari had

179

preceded him, and Paul Nizan, Antoine de Saint-Exupéry and Malraux himself would soon follow his example.

There were other motives strengthening Malraux's resolve to leave Europe. One of them, after his unfortunate 'adventure' on the stock exchange, was a financial one:

> Eh bien, nous allons dans quelque petit temple de Cambodge, nous enlevons quelques statues, nous les vendons en Amérique; ce qui nous permettra de vivre ensuite tranquilles pendant deux ou trois ans.[13]

This is not to say that this was the only reason for his going East. At this time there was, as we saw in earlier chapters, a growing interest in the Far-East stimulated by articles upon Asian philosophy and culture. Malraux's awakened interest in the East doubtless had something to do with his decision to undertake an archaeological expedition to Cambodia. In his first essay on art he had indicated the purpose of just such an undertaking:

> Nous ne pouvons sentir que par comparaison. Le génie grec sera mieux compris par l'opposition d'une statue grecque à une statue égyptienne ou asiatique, que par la connaissance de cent statues grecques.[14]

It is important to note that here Malraux is concerned less with an elucidation of non-European cultures than with a deeper understanding of his own. Similarly, *La Tentation de l'Occident*—to which we shall come shortly—if overtly a comparison of Asian and European cultures, is, in essence, the diagnosis of the situation in Europe.

The 'Cambodian Affair', culminating in Malraux's appearance in the colonial law courts for misappropriation of art treasures, would continue to haunt him and finds expression in *Les Conquérants*.[15] If Malraux was for long considered a Communist sympathizer, the myth surely has its origins in his reaction to this humiliating public trial, which left him in the same camp as the Vietnamese nationalists by virtue of the fact that even if they had not the same goals they had at least 'des ennemis communs'.[16] It is of significance that Garine, the hero of *Les Conquérants*, makes very much the same statement. Although his problem is metaphysical, not political, he and the revolutionaries at whose side he is fighting are, to some extent, engaged in a common struggle. Both he and they hate the existing social order. He thus at least shares their hatred.

Although Malraux's second trip to Indo-China, in 1925, may have derived in part from a desire for vengeance against the colonial authorities, it is stubbornly unfair of Boak to reduce his stay there to mention of 'unscrupulous political journalism' and of a challenge he issued an adversary.[17] Malraux had escaped imprisonment by virtue of a legal nicety—a ruling in which the 'string-pulling' of a few influential friends at home and Malraux's own French citizenship had doubtless played a part. He was aware that a legal system which took account of such things was not likely to be as lenient with those less fortunate than himself. In view of this observation, the help which he furnished a local nationalist movement, 'Jeune Annam', becomes understandable. Malraux and Paul Monin used their newspaper, *L'Indochine*, to try and awaken the colonial authorities to the need for reform. In addition they sought to inspire Annamites with a sense of cultural identity with other Asian countries.[18] If not a 'deeply committed social reformer' when he returned home, as Langlois would have us believe, Malraux could not fail to have sympathized with the Annamite cause.[19] He did not, however, consider his mission that of a social reformer, and we should be wary of confusing artistic projection, in his novels, with political conviction.

In July 1926 Malraux published a short essay on the subject of the East, which he entitled 'André Malraux et l'Orient'. Here his view of East and West is a conventional one. Like the majority of contributors to 'Les Appels', and unlike the members of *Clarté*, he situates the problem in terms of antithesis:

> [Notre civilisation] n'a d'autre but que son développement matériel; elle ne nous propose que les raisons d'être les plus basses . . . elle est sans but spirituel; elle nous contraint à l'action. Ses valeurs sont établies sur le monde qui dépend du fait. Le point commun à toutes les civilisations de l'Asie est, au contraire, la passivité de leurs plus hautes expressions humaines.[20]

Like many other investigators of this subject Malraux proclaims the bankruptcy of individualism and of the entire value system based upon it,[21] and like many others he reveals that the European conquest of the East has brought forth bitter fruits[22]—a point he was to make more forcefully one year later when reviewing Massis's *Défense de l'Occident*:

> La substitution des valeurs d'énergie persévérante est la marque même des temps modernes. En détruisant ces valeurs spirituelles, nous avons préparé, chez nous et au loin, le règne de la force, et en particulier, de la plus grande, celle qui dure.[23]

The originality of Malraux's short essay of 1926 arises less from the ideas themselves, which, as we have seen, were very much in the air at the time, than from the general tone and manner of their fusion; above all, from the necessity to which they give rise. As a result, the problem of action—with which the novels are concerned—is clearly stated:

> On a dit que nul ne peut agir sans foi. Je crois que l'absence de toute conviction, comme la conviction même, incite certains hommes à la passivité, et d'autres à l'action extrême.[24]

Malraux's *La Tentation de l'Occident* brings forth the same conclusion. *La Tentation de l'Occident* takes the form of an exchange of letters between A.D., a Frenchman travelling in Asia, and Ling, a Chinese travelling in Europe, upon the contrasting notions of man, life and the universe prevalent in East and West. A thorough scrutiny of their differing philosophies culminates in the realization of the arbitrariness of both.[25] Its companion essay, 'D'une jeunesse européenne' is a *bilan* of an arbitrary and 'dead' Europe, much as Drieu's *Mesure de la France* is the 'balance-sheet' of the losses incurred by France in the Great War.

Ling considers the notion of love (and of eroticism) prevalent in Western civilization where, he claims, it is based upon a predominantly cerebral interpretation of that emotion. Love in the European divorces him from reality, for it exists independently of the person loved or desired, and any pleasure derived springs less from a physical gratification than from his own tortured imaginings—from imagining himself at once himself and the *other*.[26] Such a notion is totally alien to the Oriental, for whom sexuality, free of the tainting influence of the ego-passions is physical pleasure pure and simple. Indeed, the absence of 'ego-play' lies at the very basis of Oriental society, which considers its supreme achievement the 'attentive inculture du moi'.[27] This difference is, in fact, the distinguishing factor between the two civilizations. And so whereas the Oriental recognizes the primacy of Being and identifies with the world, the European, fashioned by the spirit of Greece, recognizes that of the *individual* and is distinct from it.[28] In the course of the exchange of letters, Ling analyses the values which constitute this 'différence de direction'.[29]

Ling accuses Europeans of confusing the idea of civilization with that of social order. For him civilization is not a social but a psychological thing; it is the expression of a total state of soul, not an attitude of mind.[30] Europeans live mainly through mental constructions, going so far as to impose geometrical necessity upon an incomprehensible universe.[31] The totality of the universe, Ling suggests, is beyond the comprehension of mind, and 'knowledge' of it accessible only to those, Taoists, who, by suppressing their rational faculties, are drawn mysteriously into the heart of cosmic rhythms.[32] The Westerner, on the other hand, moving from obvious to more obscure analogy, aspires to a total comprehension of the universe through the rational application of mind: 'en face d'un monde dispersé, quel est le premier besoin de l'esprit? Le saisir'.[33] The aim of the European, who is a geometer, even of divinity,[34] is to 'dresser un plan de l'univers, en donner une image intelligible'.[35] Europe is the very image of this attitude; it is 'un pays dévoré par la géométrie. Les cornes des maisons tombaient. Les rues étaient droites, les vêtements rigides, les meubles rectangulaires. Les jardins des palais démontraient—non sans beauté—des théorèmes'.[36]

For the Oriental, the universe, of which man is but a 'fragment' is in constant flux, and men's souls, in accordance with its essential movement, are gathered up and dispersed in its ebb and flow.[37] Death, regarded as tragic finality in the West, is thus considered by the Oriental to be but one stage in continuity.[38] Movement and flux being the very nature of the Oriental world-view, it is to be expected that this same notion will be expressed in its conception of the art form. For example, whereas the Westerner sees the cat in terms of 'une espèce [distinguée] des autres par sa ligne', that is, distinctive by its *form*, which is static and which, Ling claims, 'ne s'appuie que sur la mort', the Oriental perceives 'certains *mouvements* souples et silencieux spéciaux au chat', that is, the microcosmic counterpart of a great cosmic tide.[39]

Ling continues his comparison of East and West and we are informed that the Oriental, through meditation, aspires *to be*.[40] The European thirsts after action—'la création sans cesse renouvelée par l'action d'un monde destiné à l'action'[41]—and wants *to do*. 'Sagesse' and 'grandeur', which inspire the admiration of their fellows, are the apices of their respective aspirations.[42] In the Western concept of action Ling detects an ethic based on the exercise of force, the savage embodiment of which he finds in the ruins of ancient Rome:

> Je comprends bien . . . ce que disent ces fragments: Celui qui se sacrifie participe à la grandeur de la cause à laquelle il s'est sacrifié. Mais cette cause, je ne lui vois de grandeur que celle qu'elle doit au sacrifice. Elle est sans intelligence . . . Pour être puissante, la barbarie est-elle moins barbare?[43]

In the paintings and sculptures of the West, Ling discovers the same savage power; images stained with blood and tears in a great, harmonious suffering:

> J'ai parcouru les salles de vos musées; votre génie m'y a rempli d'angoisse. Vos dieux même, et leur grandeur tachée, comme leur image, de larmes et de sang, une puissance sauvage les anime.[44]

A.D., agreeing with Ling, replies with a striking definition of the European as a man committed to the test of the act and hence pledged to the bloodiest fate.[45] This fate, however, A.D. notes, is held in abeyance, for the European is at present nothing but an excess of dreams and formless desires. Swarming images invade his soul and solicit his thought:

> La lecture, les spectacles . . . sont des sources de vies imaginaires . . . Cette lutte des ambitions victorieuses ou vaincues d'un jour: un journal, quel monde, n'agite-t-elle pas derrière les prunelles au regard absent![46]

In this commotion of dreams breeding dreams incessantly the European lives his heroism vicariously; he dreams of 'a golden chain of victories':[47] 'Songez, mon cher Ami, que, chez nous, il n'est pas d'homme qui n'ait conquis l'Europe'.[48] The cinema is particularly suited to stimulate heroic fantasies,[49] but any book, any conversation has the power to summon up these images

184

which, reinvigorated by each new passion, change in accordance with recent pleasures or latest pains:[50]

> Acteurs misérables qui ne veulent plus quitter des rôles glorieux, nous sommes pour nous-mêmes des êtres en qui dort, mêlé, le cortège ingénu des possibilités de nos actions et de nos rêves.[51]

In the European Malraux would thus appear to have detected, as surely as had Drieu, a divorce between 'rêve' and 'action', that is, a conflict between the thinker and his thought. However, where Drieu, personally and in his fiction of the 'twenties, was unable to make the transition from 'thinking to acting', Malraux, breaking with the 'pestilence of desire', entered the world of action.

The more Ling moves about Europe, the more convinced he becomes that European culture rests upon a base of confusions. The European seems unable to distinguish being from acting or order from civilization. This confusion, however, is finally engulfed in a contradiction which Ling locates at the very heart of European civilization. He discovers that the European is in fundamental disharmony with the culture he himself has forged. He summarizes this view in a phrase which echoes through the remainder of the book: '*au centre de l'homme européen, dominant les grands mouvements de sa vie, est une absurdité essentielle*'.[52] A.D. agrees that European man is the creature of the Absurd and the rest of the text, like Malraux's other essay, 'D'une jeunesse européenne', investigates the origins of this Absurdity and explores the possible consequences. In this it lays the essential basis for the novels.

The Occidental world-vision has its origins in the 'miracle grec', which was the discovery of the individual. Man was conceived as a being distinct from the world. Into the Greek notion of the separateness of the *moi* and the world, Christianity incorporated the conception of man as a being distinct from his neighbour and personally responsible for making the choice between good and evil. Christianity had a personal Redeemer whose grace was accorded to each man individually. This was the driving force behind the Christian religion. Dignity and value were bestowed upon the *moi* by a religion 'qui ne cesse de vous faire croire à votre existence particulière'.[53]

The Renaissance was the supreme expression of individualism but also the beginning of a movement destined to deprive the individual of all that had sustained and given meaning to his existence. Hitherto human problems had been referred to a higher order. Henceforward an attempt would be made to resolve them at the human level. The Absolute was now lost: 'la Valeur ordonnatrice se brise en valeurs'.[54] These new values—*humanist* ones—found their most potent expression in the nineteenth century where the individual, despite the loss of God, still retained the possibility of giving meaning to the world and to his existence. Indeed he was sure that science could provide him with all the answers he required. He would never again have recourse to an extra-human system of explanation. It is of this epoch that Malraux can thus write:

> L'Homme prend en lui-même la place qu'il donnait à Dieu . . .
> Un élan dirige tout le XIXe siècle, que ne peut être comparé, pour la puissance et l'importance, qu'à une religion.[55]

However, in Malraux's estimation *'l'homme est mort* après Dieu'[56] since those very values to which the individual had turned after God's death are themselves now dead.

Here, Malraux would appear to be restating in dramatic formulae what were taken by many to be the philosophical implications of the scientific discoveries of the late nineteenth and early twentieth centuries. Brunetière had in 1896 announced 'la faillite de la science' and Jules de Gaultier, writing in 1911, had declared:

> Ce n'est pas parce que nous n'avons pas encore su inventer de chaîne causale assez longue que nous ne pouvons, en jetant l'ancre, toucher le fond de l'existence et y amarrer dans l'immobilité conquise la connaissance du tout, *c'est parce qu'il n'y avait pas de fond*, et que l'existence, qui est mouvement, échappe par sa nature à la possibilité d'un arrêt, aux prises du calcul et aux déterminations totales.[57]

The impression—'confirmed' by Einstein[58]—was that the European had been the victim of a great deception, the dupe of centuries of measurement, of painstaking calculation, of rational system. He had tried to explain the world, to give to it, and therefore to himself, a meaning, even as his former God had done. It now seemed, however, that he had not *described* reality but imposed a rational pattern on it; its order was nothing less than the projection of a human need for intelligibility. As Malraux puts it in 'D'une jeunesse européenne':

> Je tiens pour essentiellement mensongère la volonté d'édifier cette représentation [monde qui est ma représentation]. Quelle vanité, celle d'une allégorie du monde que je dois à de patientes constructions! . . . Et le monde se réduit à un immense jeu de rapports que nulle intelligence ne s'applique plus à fixer, puisqu'il est dans la nature même de changer, de se renouveler sans cesse. Il semble que notre civilisation tende à se créer une métaphysique d'où tout point fixe est exclus, du même ordre que sa conception de la matière.[59]

For the 'Young European' the corroding awareness that nothing is permanent is an admission of life's essential meaninglessness.

With science's failure to establish any meaningful world-picture the individual is deprived of all spiritual goal and suffers a total loss of specificity. Europe has no direction. The 'Young European' recognizes that his thought, woven of allegory, has no access to truth, is nihilistic and fundamentally negative.[60] He now realizes that the external world is a baffling complex of mysterious signs and symbols which cannot be deciphered. It cannot be humanized by any scientific reduction; it *is*. Ling speaks of this presence as:

> La sensation de l'existence d'une force plus grande que celle des hommes. Je ne parle pas d'une force divine. C'est au contraire *le caractère inhumain, incompréhensible, végétal de cette force qui nous saisit lorsque nous en prenons connaissance.*[61]

If science, from a rational investigation of the external world, cannot provide a basis for humanism, perhaps a meaningful direction to human existence can be found within man himself, in the recesses of his own inner world. Beginning with the premise: 'L'Homme est le seul objet digne de notre passion: Je suis le seul objet digne de me passionner',[62] Malraux enquires into just such a possibility. The first thing he notes, however, is that the 'notion of man' is no longer based on the concept of a human nature, but on *each* individual's awareness of himself.[63] It is the nature of this

187

awareness that Malraux attempts to analyse in 'D'une jeunesse européenne' and *La Tentation de l'Occident.*

Malraux begins with the claim that it is today impossible to establish a concept of self according to one's actions despite the temptation to do so.[64] The conviction that a man can judge himself by his actions has no more basis in fact than an idle profession of faith, for all we do is '[prêter] à la conscience se considérant elle-même, des traits qui ne sont que les siens que lorsqu'elle considère autrui'.[65] In short, it is mere illusion to claim to define self in objective terms, for even if we accept the possibility of judging others by their actions we can scarcely apply the same criterion to the self, which, being unconscious desire as much as waking thought, cannot be seized in its essence by any rational designs:

> Notre vie profonde, intensité, ne peut appartenir à l'esprit; il le sait et tourne à vide, belle machine que tachent quelques gouttes de sang. Car cette vie profonde est aussi la plus rudimentaire: et sa puissance, qui montre l'arbitraire de l'esprit, ne saurait nous délivrer de lui. Elle lui dit: 'tu es mensonge et moyen de mensonge, créateur de réalités'.[66]

We discover that our inner world is a chaotic network of 'vains désirs, d'espoirs et de rêves', a veritable 'palais du silence où chacun pénètre seul'.[67] We are at a loss to define self since there is within us 'rien de défini', and 'puissance latente' is by its very nature boundless and consequently beyond definition. The *moi* is essentially a world of wish-fulfilment. We would thus appear to be not only what we do but also and primarily what we feel ourselves capable of; in a word, we are the sum of our reveries. Our musings constitute a 'vie involontaire' whose discovery represents a threat to our freedom, for we see that this 'involuntary life', which is as much a part of ourselves as our 'voluntary life', 'dominerait l'autre sans un effort constant'.[68] Here Malraux would appear to be thinking of the revelations of Freud, whose *Introduction to psychoanalysis* was translated into French in 1921. In Malraux's estimation the door was now open to the Absurd:

> En acceptant la notion d'inconscient, en lui portant un intérêt extrême, l'Europe s'est privée de ses meilleures armes. L'absurde . . . nous le voyons préparer ses jeux les plus séduisants avec le concours fidèle de notre volonté.[69]

188

The *moi* can no longer be considered pure consciousness, that is, total lucidity, and the notion of a permanent and integral *moi* is untenable.[70] Confronted with evidence of the dissolution of the self yet at the same time craving an inner unity based upon this same self, the European, as the effort to understand advances is left face to face with the incomprehensible, the Absurd:

> Nous voici au point où l'individualisme triomphant veut prendre de lui-même une conscience plus nette. Mais si nul ne peut se saisir soi-même, qu'importe une notion du moi.[71]

Thus far, Malraux's analysis is the attempt to reveal the tragedy of 'modern man'. Rejected by history and caught between the arbitrariness of the external world and the inner chaos of the *moi*, the 'Young European' finds no point of anchorage. His itinerary is an aimless path under an empty heaven. Finding no doctrine to satisfy him, nothing with which to fill his inner void, which is oppressive 'like a cancer', he desperately casts about for a 'new object of love'. As Marcel Arland, analysing youth's 'nouveau mal du siècle', wrote: 'aucune doctrine ne nous peut satisfaire, mais l'absence de doctrine nous est un tourment'.[72] Having 'killed' God and now 'dead' himself the European encounters only a void. And yet, here, in the death of Christianity and the rejection of humanism we have the germ of Malraux's first 'anti-destin'.[73] A fundamental and death-dominated individualism based on will and action, even if it should result in a deeper perception of the Absurd—due to the pure contingency of the individual personality—has to replace the now empty humanism which itself had replaced religious belief. Nietzsche had already prophesied the birth of a New Man, and his re-emergence in the 'twenties demonstrates the persistence, for Drieu as for Malraux, of a profoundly felt problem. Malraux writes: 'Si Nietzsche trouve tant d'échos dans les cœurs désespérés, c'est qu'il n'est lui-même que l'expression de leur désespoir et de leur violence'.[74]

Malraux and Nietzsche have often been compared, and clearly Nietzsche's thought had a profound impact upon Malraux. However, there is an essential difference between these two thinkers which has to be stressed if we are to appreciate the depth of the metaphysical problem which Malraux sets himself. For Nietzsche 'God is dead' is a cry of triumph which heralds the birth of man.

Indeed man's birth is the effect of God's death. For Malraux this is clearly not the case since *'l'homme est mort* après Dieu'. For Malraux, therefore, the problem is how to re-create man in the face of 'destiny'.[75] Whereas for Nietzsche Christianity is the condition of man's servitude and has therefore to be eliminated, for Malraux the vital question is to determine whether Christianity—which has, after all, left a profound mark upon European man[76]—is a valid response to the problem of man's 'condition'. Here 'l'accent pascalien', of which Malraux himself has spoken with reference to his work, is clearly present.[77] Pascal's apologia attempted to demonstrate that man's condition ('misère de l'homme'), a consequence of the Fall, is redeemed by his Creator's love ('grandeur de l'homme'). This would appear to be the meaning of Malraux's statement, in 'D'une jeunesse européenne': 'avec le péché [le christianisme] fonde sa force sur la conscience aiguë de notre désaccord'.[78] One might even say that Pascal's antithesis has its 'ontological' equivalent in Malraux: the Absurd and its transcendence. Indeed, some, laying claim to Malraux's profound sympathy for Christanity, have tried to establish his 'esprit religieux'.[79]

In 'D'une jeunesse européenne' Malraux writes:

> Il semble que l'Église ait été préoccupée de détacher l'homme de lui-même. Elle s'appliqua à lui épargner, à la fois, la douleur et le droit de se juger. Pendant des siècles, soumettant toutes les velléités, toutes les singularités, toutes les craintes des cœurs chrétiens, elle construisit, comme une cathédrale, l'image du monde qui nous domine encore.[80]

In short 'le catholicisme romain a créé une civilisation *soumise*'.[81] If Christianity offers man a refuge from the forces of destiny, it obliges him to accept a subordinate position that makes for weakness and exhaustion:

> Certes, il est une foi plus haute . . . Elle est amour, et l'apaisement est en elle. Je ne l'accepterai jamais, je ne m'abaisserai pas à lui demander l'apaisement auquel ma faiblesse m'appelle.[82]

The 'temptation' of Christianity is resisted and the 'Young European' has to look elsewhere in his search for the basis of 'une notion nouvelle de l'homme'. The East, having a wholly different notion of man, constitutes, at the outset at least, a further 'temptation' for the despairing European.

As we saw in earlier chapters a host of writers were at this time concerned with the opposition between East and West, and with interpreting the wisdom and tranquillity which the former was supposed to bring to tormented souls. Others, like Drieu, were concerned more directly with the problems confronting Western civilization. Still others, like the Surrealists, while suggesting that Asia could give a regenerative boost to mummified Western minds, also looked upon the Orient as the homeland of the great destroyer, the very negation of all that granted supremacy in the West. This impatient section of the 'jeunesse violente' called upon the East to destroy their 'cardboard world'. If anything were calculated to inspire unfavourable criticism from traditionalists—like Henri Massis—it was this kind of vituperative repudiation of the European heritage, and the denunciation—more effective perhaps, for being less violent—of the cultural and political tradition of the West implicit in the writings of those soberer minds, like Rolland, who were now turning to the East.

The 'temptation' which the East holds out to the West consists in its having been able to merge man into the world and into communion with the deepest impulses of Being, instead of setting him apart from it and making of him an active, isolated and suffering individual. The East, considering man as but a fragment of the all important 'Whole', lifts from him the burden of personal suffering which Christianity has implanted, like a thorn, in the European's sensibility. Cultivate the doctrine of self-effacement, the Orient tells the European, and serenity will be yours, solitude, death and time will be relegated to the realm of appearance. Since self-awareness—consciousness of one's condition—would appear to be the source of the European's suffering, a doctrine which refuses to accord 'une valeur à l'homme en lui-même'[83] would seem to be the natural antidote. Malraux, this particular 'Young European', resists the temptation:

> Hélas! Tout cela me semble arbitraire, aussi arbitraire que le pire système, que la plus fausse de nos philosophies. A l'origine de votre recherche je trouve un acte de foi. Non dans l'existence du principe: dans la valeur que vous lui prêtez. Dans l'extase le penseur ne s'identifie pas à l'absolu comme l'enseignent vos sages; il appelle absolu le point extrême de sa sensibilité.[84]

The Oriental does not break through to another reality; he merely reaches the outer edge of his own circle of consciousness. The Absolute is his own representation. As such he is the dupe of his own flights of thought. Moreover, the European who seeks an answer here is required to abjure precisely that which constitutes his very being: intense self-awareness. And A.D. would choose rather the anguish that comes of this awareness than a repose born of spiritual suicide.[85] He rejects the wisdom of the East. He cannot undo his European consciousness.

In any event the Oriental world-view is itself in the process of disintegration as the 'temptation of the West' gains the East. The figure who incarnates China in her death-agony is Wang-Loh, whom A.D. visits during his stay in China. He describes to A.D. the collapse of the system which, for centuries, has sustained the Orient:

> Le confucianisme en miettes, tout ce pays sera détruit. Tous ces hommes sont appuyés sur lui. Il a fait leur sensibilité, leur pensée et leur volonté. Il leur a donné le sens de leur race. Il a fait le visage de leur bonheur . . . Qu'ont-ils cherché pendant deux mille cinq cents ans? Une parfaite assimilation du monde par l'homme; car leur vie fut une lente capture du monde, dont ils voulaient être la conscience fragmentaire . . . C'est ce qui s'oppose à ce que vous nommez l'individualisme.[86]

Today, the youth of China, penetrated to the core by the influx of Western values, retains of them only a furious desire for destruction.[87]

In this, as in what follows, Malraux's conclusions are remarkably similar to those expressed in Berge's enquiry into 'Les Appels de l'Orient'. *Les Conquérants* will *dramatize* these conclusions. As a result *Les Conquérants* is neither the description nor the dramatization of political revolution in China but the *mythic projection* of an Orient that existed in philosophical and literary journals of the 'twenties. If Malraux 'distorts' the Chinese Revolution—as Trotsky and the Communist George Altmann complained[88]—the distortion appears only if one interprets *Les Conquérants* as the dramatized account of a *real event*: the Canton uprising. This it is not.

In his reply to A.D.'s letter concerning the visit to Wang-Loh, Ling agrees with the old man. China, whose subjugation has been

192

hitherto restricted to the political and economic spheres, is today surrendering its very soul to the West as the educated élite boldly espouse European doctrines. The Western notion of man as an *active individual* is being born in China.[89] Wars, bloodshed and violence are the new climate of a Europeanized East conscious only of the injustice done it by its European oppressors.[90] Motivated by hatred the actions of those now desperately resisting European control can but be bloody and unpredictable.[91] This attitude prefigures the hate-filled vengeance of one of the characters of *Les Conquérants*: the terrorist Hong. And the new China in which Hong will reap his terrible harvest is now raising its fearsome head: 'Une Chine nouvelle se crée, qui nous échappe à nous-mêmes . . . la voix basse de la destruction s'entend déjà aux plus lointains échos d'Asie'.[92] Thus Asia, with its European legacy of violence and suffering, can offer no solution to the ills which afflict the 'Young European': 'l'Asie peut-elle nous apporter quelque enseignement? Je ne le crois pas. *Plutôt une découverte particulière de ce que nous sommes*'.[93]

What then *is* the European, caught between inner chaos and external absurdity, unable to know others and incapable of knowing himself objectively? He is real only as a sort of brute *intensity*, to which A.D. and Ling each once refer.[94] Intensity, swelling into violent self-affirmation, can be man's only frame of reference in the absence of a doctrine: 'la volonté lucide de montrer ses combats à défaut d'une doctrine'.[95] Such will be the driving force of the New Man Malraux will portray in the novels.

La Tentation de l'Occident and 'D'une jeunesse européenne' thus provide the essential basis for the novels. Indeed, from a reading of these two works we get a very clear indication of the metaphysical type we are likely to meet. In the first place we see that all that might diminish the climate of struggle necessary for the birth of the New Man must be rejected, for this struggle is the manifestation of life. Since life is expressed by 'intensité', reason is an escape from life. Like the Christian perspective through which we view reality, it drains life of its tragic essence by imposing a more perfect order upon the chaos of appearance. Man needs this faculty of illusion to make life bearable; the New Man does not. He must reject the luxury of a coherent world-view created by the mind and choose for himself another 'reality' and another point of departure. As Thierry Maulnier, referring to Nietzsche, has conveniently written:

> Le trésor pathétique du destin de l'homme n'est plus cherché dans l'univers de la connaissance, mais dans l'univers de l'action, il n'est plus la contemplation de l'existence la plus terrible mais l'épreuve de l'existence la plus terrible, ce n'est plus dans les maigres victoires de l'analyse, mais dans des créations, des ferveurs et des catastrophes où nous nous risquerons tout entiers, que nous trouverons des raisons nouvelles, des raisons enivrantes de vivre et de mourir.[96]

Action—whereby intensity gains projection—must replace the empty designs of reason, for if it brings man into contact with the tragedy of his condition, it alone provides a defence against it, not so much from the point of view of its results as from the fundamental attitude governing its use. Action is the expression of freedom, and freedom is the possibility to use action for action's sake. Indeed this action cannot be otherwise conceived. As Jeanne Delhomme has written:

> Seules l'action qui commence et la puissance qui s'exerce, sans espoir et sans but, sont créatrices d'univers et de temps; l'action terminée, la puissance possédée, tombent dans le monde empirique dont elles ne sont plus qu'un des aspects . . . c'est la passion de la passion beaucoup plus que la passion de quelque chose, et la puissance de la puissance beaucoup plus que la puissance sur quelqu'un qui sont recherchées, *parce qu'ainsi détachées et séparées elles sont libérées de leurs contenus sensibles ou affectifs et par ce fait détachées du monde et du temps, autre monde et autre temps.*[97]

In other words if the world is without meaning then man's free acts against it are not. Or, as Malraux puts it in 'D'une jeunesse européenne': 'des gestes vains qui luisent parfois comme des éclats d'armures'.[98] In each of these 'flashes' man becomes master of his destiny. The New Man need now only choose a place of action to put his metaphysical gamble to the test. This he will do in *Les Conquérants* and *La Voie royale*.

In view of the bankruptcy of values, humanist and transcendental, the New Man must necessarily gamble with his own

194

limitations and with the most demanding limitation of all—his own mortality.[99] As Malraux notes in *La Tentation de l'Occident*: 'Pour détruire Dieu, et après l'avoir détruit, l'esprit européen a anéanti tout ce qui pouvait s'opposer à l'homme: parvenu au terme de ses efforts . . . il ne trouve que la mort'.[100] Man's freedom demands that he face his ultimate metaphysical situation: an attitude which astonishingly, if fortuitously, mirrors Martin Heidegger's *Freiheit-zum-Töde* (Freedom-to-death). *Les Conquérants* and *La Voie royale* are the expression of this desperate undertaking.

It has to be said that Malraux's analysis of Western civilization is one of generalized abstraction. His preoccupation with thoughts as with independent entities inevitably involves a method which depends more on a free association of ideas or on a single comparison of terms than on a historical critique. It is a method based on certain presuppositions which are always tacitly active in it. One presupposition is analytic: it holds that a 'system of thought' (Western thought) is *reducible to its elements* (individualism, rationalism, science), a precondition that enables him to think any element of this system *on its own* and to compare it with *another* element from *another* system (Oriental thought). As a result Malraux ignores completely the historical question of the production of systems of thought and, concentrating instead on ideas *in their own right*, he proclaims that history has no continuity, that it is composed, in no meaningful pattern, of a number of 'mondes clos', each with its own ideas and myths. A gulf separates East and West just as, in the loss of the Absolute, a gulf separates Europe of the Middle Ages from modern Europe.

If Malraux finds no continuity in history it is surely because he fails to see that *between* real history and men there always comes an *ideological* explanation of history. Every society creates an ideology to explain, to justify and indeed to defend what is for its theoreticians the only conceivable society. Thus in the *feudal* society of the Middle Ages the Church offered all its flock—including, or perhaps especially, the most benighted serf—a very simple and clear explanation of history. History is made by God and obeys the laws or follows the ends of Providence; he who respects God's laws—and those of feudalism—shares in His glory. In eighteenth-century France the situation was different. The revolutionary bourgeoisie offered an 'enlightened' explanation of history. History is moved by Reason and obeys the laws or follows the ends of Reason; he who respects the laws of Reason respects also those of bourgeois rule, of 'free' capitalist society. History can therefore be seen not, as Malraux maintains, as a number of 'mondes clos' but as the record of the unceasing overthrow of the objective *economic and social* forms that shape men's lives and ideals. Clearly these forms, no less than the ideals they sustain, have no finality—something which Malraux in his preoccupation with myths notes with concern—and will be altered, improved or abandoned for a better scheme of things as new advances are made in, for example, industry and science.

Of science Malraux complains that it cannot provide the individual with a certainty. However, such an opinion depends for its meaning on the role one assigns to science. Clearly if one expects science to 'dominate' the universe, to freeze its movement in a sort of permanent, coherent and reassuring present—as God might have done—then one is likely to be disappointed. If, however, instead of seeking *metaphysical* certainty we apply science to the *real world*, the world in which we live, we *can* derive a certainty. We can say that our knowledge of the world around us is not a phantasmagoria of mental images but is known relative to conditions, to *present* knowledge, to our interests and values. We can say that 'Man' does know the world by active manipulation and utilization of his environment, that his knowledge of it is related to the level of his scientific and technological achievements and the successive forms of human association and organization which he has devised to make the best use of his means of controlling nature. In other words we can not only claim that history is a process, a series of social and economic forms, but we can assert that 'Man', (philosophy's ethical abstraction of the *homo œconomicus*), far from having 'died', has been and still is the prime mover in the process of constructing and reconstructing the world. If it is to be objected that Malraux does not refer to social and economic forms, only to the 'death' of ideals, we can reply that this omission does not prevent these same forms from appearing, symptomatically, in his analysis, in the very ideals he declares to be 'dead'.

In his analysis of Western civilization in the modern period, that is the period beginning with the Renaissance, Malraux identifies a number of features: individualism (which Christianity has reinforced)[101], science, rationalism (and materialism [102])—all of which he declares to be bankrupt. That these aspects of European civilization occur in almost every critique of the West submitted to the East/West debate of the 'twenties demonstrates, at the very least, that they are not the personal invention of Malraux. Yet no satisfactory explanation is provided, by Malraux or by others, of that 'species of individual' (as Hegel used to say) to which Malraux refers, unless one assumes that the individual achieves definition in association with science, rationalism and materialism. If this is so—and it would indeed appear to be the case—then a *historical* interpretation of Malraux's critique is possible.

In *Religion and the Rise of Capitalism* R. H. Tawney contrasts the 'medieval pattern' in whose social philosophy labour was declared to be necessary and honourable, trade necessary but perilous to the soul and finance sordid and disreputable[103] with the new commercial, capitalist spirit that found expression in the Protestant ethic, which, spurning antiquated morality and its corporate mood, invested in economic forces the belief that by a kind of happy, 'pre-established harmony', the self-interest of the *individual* would automatically secure the welfare of society. The acquisitive individual had Reason for his guide and Reason, as Tawney demonstrates, was as much a principle of social and economic life as it was of scientific optimism. Nowhere is the vigorous individualism and scientific rationalism of nascent capitalism more powerfully expressed than in Adam Smith's *Wealth of Nations* (1776). Smith taught that if free reign were given to the economic interests of capitalists the 'maximum freedom of competitive individuals' would produce as a resultant of the 'free play of forces' the greatest social good. This economic and social outlook, supporting and supported by rationalism, individualism and scientific optimism, remained coherent and, in real terms, unchallenged in Europe until the twentieth century.

It has to be remembered that Malraux's *La Tentation de l'Occident* and 'D'une jeunesse européenne', like Valéry's 'La Crise de l'esprit' and other post-mortems on civilization, were written in a Europe still reeling from the shock of war and the impact of the Russian Revolution; an era of political and economic crisis, of revolutionary uprisings in the West, of nationalist rebellions in the colonies. In such circumstances despair and pessimism might be construed not so much as the philosophical

197

fruits of an enquiry into the past but—as Barbusse and *Clarté* claimed—as the rationalization of social and political disintegration in the present. When Massis and his associates attempted to revive and defend civilization they did so in a manner that demonstrated that, for them at least, civilization was inseparable from a form of social and economic organization known as capitalism. In the context of these observations it seems not unreasonable to assume that Malraux's analysis, denying as it does all essential value to *present reality*, is less the vision of a 'dead civilization' than the reflected intelligence of a society no longer able to sustain a *myth*[104]—that of the 'individual'[105]—to serve the *objectives of the bourgeoisie*. Without trying to solve what are doubtless insoluble problems as to a possible relationship between artistic and human integrity, we can at least note that when Garine abandons Europe for the East he does so in the knowledge that he is not only fleeing a sinking ship, but renouncing his bourgeois past for a revolutionary movement sworn to the destruction of European power in China.

The diagnoses of the European situation offered by Drieu and Malraux at first sight appear to present no real basis for comparison. After all, Drieu situates the problem and its solution at the geopolitical level while Malraux, whose diagnosis is supported implicitly by the myth of the death of man, naturally regards any 'practical' solution as *inconceivable*. However, a very real parallel does exist and has to do with the heavy insistence both place upon the necessity for a tragic philosophy of action. As early as 1917 Drieu remarked that war made him believe not in progress but in the 'noble effort libre sans espoir'.[106] In 'Nietzsche contre Marx', published in 1934, he reaffirmed this view, which he now characterized as the Fascist vision of the world: 'L'homme est un accident dans un monde d'accidents. Le monde n'a pas de sens général. Il n'a de sens que celui que nous lui donnons, un moment, pour le développement de notre passion, de notre action.'[107] Such an outlook, with which the author of 'D'une jeunesse européenne' and *La Tentation de l'Occident* would have had no quarrel, and by which Garine (*Les Conquérants*) and Perken (*La Voie royale*) are in fact both driven, effectively defines Drieu's philosophical objections to Marxism. For Drieu, since the world has no general meaning it cannot become the world of the Marxists: it cannot be progressing inexorably towards the triumph of the proletariat. And here we are led back to Malraux's work. Garine, whatever his private or obsessional reasons for joining the revolutionary cause, has certainly not enlisted to realize the Marxist dream. He is not interested in transforming society in accordance with an ideal, least of all one based on socio-economic factors. His 'commitment', born of 'une passion parfaitement désespérée',[108] is a fierce metaphysical gamble upon 'une grande action quelconque', which in this case happens to be revolution. For Drieu, as for Garine, man's action like his being is autonomous, and invalidates itself as soon as it becomes allied to a cause based in a historical process which can itself but be illusory since the world has no meaning. Garine is less interested in the cause he has joined than in the action and the 'puissance' it permits him. For Drieu and Garine, therefore, action is espoused for its intrinsic 'value' rather than for its historical results. In Drieu's case this fundamentally non-partisan concept of action had much to do with his commitment to Fascism. By stressing the autonomy of man's action, Drieu indicated that the motor force of the human spirit and of social progress was the élite individual, the individual redeemed by action and through whom life's harmony was restored. Thus he posed implicitly the dual *social* element on which, for him, Fascism rested: the leader and the group around the leader, the 'fulgurating revelation' of which he had experienced during the charge at Charleroi.

The decisive experience in Drieu's life was, of course, World War I. It was his 'grande action' and the discovery of his 'puissance': 'Tout d'un coup, je me connaissais, je connaissais ma vie. C'était donc ma vie, cet ébat qui n'allait plus s'arrêter jamais.'[109] He was no longer, he discovered, an 'animal who dreams'—the vicarious hero denounced by the author of *La Tentation de l'Occident*—but a man for whom all thought was action and all action thought.[110] If he had written, it was, he believed, primarily because he was a soldier involved in a 'great action' and because action was the stuff of literature: 'je voulais faire l'écrivain comme j'avais voulu faire le soldat.'[111] In war thought and action had sustained each other and seemed to Drieu the proper ingredients of authentic literature, even if he considered his own particular brew somewhat sloppily prepared.[112] When in peace he cast about in search of 'authentic literature' he could find none:

Poètes lyriques qui n'aviez que vos journées étroites, analystes qui vous contentiez d'une si mince tranche de cœur sur votre pain sec de vieux enfants, vous n'alliez pas loin dans ce pays dangereux qu'était votre moi: pas plus loin que ne va le chien au bout de sa chaîne. Vos vies ne sont pas pour moi exemplaires.[113]

Drieu cannot forgive these writers the fact that their lives can be separated from their writings. The tragic sense of life which he had discovered in the trenches and of which his war poems had been the attempted expression seemed hard to find in the comfortable lives and writings of bourgeois France. Drieu felt that he had lived his writings, and here were writers talking of the life of the spirit as if that alone existed, 'diluting so little blood in so much ink'.[114]

Drieu's conception of life thus commanded his idea of literature. It is hardly surprising, therefore, that he should have hailed Malraux as 'l'homme nouveau', the first writer to his mind to have struck the perfect balance between life and art: 'entre cette action extérieure qu'on appelle tout court l'action, et cette action intérieure qu'on appelle la pensée'.[115] For both writers the particular 'volonté de vérité' of which Malraux writes in his preface to Andrée Viollis's *Indochine S.O.S.*[116] seemed more important than the creation of a wholly imaginary universe. For both, Drieu believed, literature had to express more than an intellectual assessment of life. To be *authentic* it had to be wrought of passionate emotional and physical involvement in a great event. It was this view of the literary act that led Drieu to write of *Les Conquérants*: 'premier né issu de l'union de la pensée et de l'action'.[117] We say 'Drieu's view of Malraux' because we now know from Clara Malraux that Malraux was never involved in the 'great action' which is the setting for *Les Conquérants*. Moreover, *Les Conquérants* is not, as Drieu seems to imply, a straightforward literary transposition of a great event. The context is a revolution but the adventure which it traces is a metaphysical drama. Even as early as 1930, therefore, there appears to have existed a 'legendary' view of Malraux as a man who had steeped his life and art in action. Nevertheless, the central truth remains. For Drieu, life and art found justification in action and he considered the same to be true of Malraux. Describing the author of *Les Conquérants* and *La Voie royale* as a 'frère en Nietzsche et Dostoïevski' he offered the following definition of 'adventure':

Je veux parler de l'aventure physique, du risque d'être blessé ou tué, d'être torturé par le supplice ou la maladie. Certes, il y a d'autres sortes d'aventures, il y a l'aventure intellectuelle, l'aventure morale. Mais toute aventure ne vaut que dans la mesure où elle est apte à se résoudre dans une aventure physique.[118]

Drieu would doubtless have seen in Perken's desire 'to leave a scar on the map' an aspiration which he and his comrades-in-arms had already realized: 'nous avons fait l'histoire, c'est autre chose que de l'écrire'.[119]

Drieu's insistence upon the virile virtues of strength and courage, upon the 'grande action' and the necessity to incorporate it in art naturally leads one to expect his literary world to illustrate this attitude, especially in view of his praise of Malraux and his condemnation of those who 'dilute so little blood in so much ink'. We shall, however, find a world very different from the one we would expect.

NOTES

[1] André Malraux, *La Tentation de l'Occident* (Grasset, 1951), p. 207.
[2] André Malraux, *op. cit.*, p. 67.
[3] Jeanne Delhomme, *Temps et Destin* (Gallimard, 1955), pp. 19–20.
[4] André Malraux, 'André Malraux et l'Orient', *Les Nouvelles littéraires* (31 July, 1926), p. 2.
[5] Quoted by Julien Green, *Journal*, I, (Plon, 1938), p. 23.
[6] Clara Malraux, *Nos vingt ans* (Grasset, 1966); André Vandegans, *La Jeunesse littéraire d'André Malraux* (J. J. Pauvert, 1964).
[7] I am largely discounting stories of the early Malraux's 'outlandish dress' and 'expensive tastes', since these are supported in the main by the (generally unfair) reports of his arrest in Indo-China in the Paris newspapers. His tall stories, on the other hand, are attested to by Clara Malraux in *Apprendre à vivre* (Grasset, 1963), p. 270 and p. 280 and *Nos vingt ans*, pp. 41–2.
[8] Clara Malraux, *Nos vingt ans*, p. 109.
[9] A very satisfactory account of these early works is to be found in André Vandegans, *La Jeunesse littéraire d'André Malraux*, pp. 22–9.
[10] Quoted by Clara Malraux, *Nos vingt ans*, p. 57.
[11] See André Malraux, *La Tentation de l'Occident*, pp. 15–23.
[12] Gaëtan Picon, *Malraux par lui-même* (Éditions du Seuil, 1953), p. 78, note 30.
[13] Quoted by Clara Malraux, *Nos vingt ans*, p. 112.
[14] André Malraux, Preface to an exhibition of Galanis: 3 au 8 mars, 1922, Galerie la licorne 1922, p. 4. Also in 'Galanis', *Dictionnaire biographique des artistes contemporains* 1919–1930, II, (Art et Édition, 1931), pp. 88–91.
[15] For a thorough investigation of Malraux's sojourn in the East see Walter

Langlois, *André Malraux: The Indo-China adventure* (New York: Praeger, 1966).

16 Clara Malraux, *Nos vingt ans*, p. 180.

17 Denis Boak, *André Malraux* (O.U.P., 1968), p. 11.

18 For a fuller account of Malraux's contribution to these movements see Walter Langlois, *André Malraux: The Indo-China adventure*, pp. 127–44.

19 Malraux defended the Annamite cause twice between 1926 and 1935: 'S.O.S.', *Marianne* (11 October, 1933) and the preface to Andrée Viollis, *Indochine S.O.S.* (Gallimard, 1935).

20 André Malraux, 'André Malraux et l'Orient', *Les Nouvelles littéraires* (31 July, 1926), p. 2.

21 André Malraux, 'André Malraux et l'Orient', p. 2: 'le premier présent de notre génération, j'ai la conviction que c'est la proclamation de la faillite de l'individualisme, de toutes les attitudes, de toutes les doctrines qui se justifient par l'exaltation du Moi'.

22 André Malraux, 'André Malraux et l'Orient', p. 2: 'chacune de nos victoires, de nos actions en appelle d'autres, et non le repos. Le cercle est fermé'.

23 André Malraux, 'Défense de l'Occident', *N.R.F.* (June 1927), p. 815.

24 André Malraux, 'André Malraux et l'Orient', p. 2.

25 André Malraux, *La Tentation de l'Occident*, p. 186: 'la suprême royauté de l'arbitraire'.

26 André Malraux, *op. cit.*, p. 102: 'tout le jeu érotique est là: être soi-même et l'autre; éprouver ses sensations propres et imaginer celles du partenaire'.

27 André Malraux, *op. cit.*, p. 112.

28 André Malraux, *op. cit.*, p. 67.

29 André Malraux, *op. cit.*, p. 154.

30 André Malraux, *op. cit.*, pp. 33–4.

31 André Malraux, *op. cit.*, p. 155.

32 André Malraux, *op. cit.*, pp. 161–2.

33 André Malraux, *op. cit.*, p. 158.

34 André Malraux, *op. cit.*, p. 50.

35 André Malraux, *op. cit.*, p. 155.

36 André Malraux, *op. cit.*, p. 28.

37 André Malraux, *op. cit.*, pp. 149–62.

38 André Malraux, *op. cit.*, pp. 47–9.

39 André Malraux, *op. cit.*, p. 121.

40 André Malraux, *op. cit.*, p. 108: 'rien ne l'incline à l'action. Même en rêve . . . il *est*'.

41 André Malraux, *op. cit.*, p. 28.

42 André Malraux, *op. cit.*, pp. 39–40.

43 André Malraux, *op. cit.*, p. 59.

44 André Malraux, *op. cit.*, p. 36. See also p. 35: 'je ne saurais imaginer sans trouble des méditations dans lesquelles toute l'intensité de l'amour se concentre sur un corps supplicié'.

45 André Malraux, *op. cit.*, p. 104.

46 André Malraux, *op. cit.*, p. 96.

47 André Malraux, *op. cit.*, p. 94: 'la rêverie hante [notre univers] avec son collier de victoires'.

[48] André Malraux, *op. cit.*, pp. 96–7.

[49] André Malraux, *op. cit.*, p. 97: 'regardez les gens qui sortent lorsque le spectacle est terminé: vous retrouverez sous leurs gestes ceux des personnages qu'ils viennent de suivre. Comme ils traversent héroïquement les avenues!'.

[50] André Malraux, *op. cit.*, pp. 99–100.

[51] André Malraux, *op. cit.*, p. 101.

[52] André Malraux, *op. cit.*, p. 78.

[53] André Malraux, *op. cit.*, p. 46.

[54] André Malraux, *Les Voix du silence* (Gallimard, 1951), p. 479.

[55] André Malraux, 'D'une jeunesse européenne', *Écrits* (Grasset, 1927), p. 138.

[56] André Malraux, *La Tentation de l'Occident*, p. 174.

[57] Jules de Gaultier, 'Scientisme et pragmatisme', *Revue Philosophique* (1911), pp. 672–3.

[58] See Paul Morand, *Bouddha Vivant* (Grasset, 1927), p. 174.

[59] André Malraux, 'D'une jeunesse européenne', p. 152.

[60] André Malraux, 'D'une jeunesse européenne', p. 148.

[61] André Malraux, *La Tentation de l'Occident*, p. 154 (our italics).

[62] André Malraux, 'D'une jeunesse européenne', p. 139.

[63] André Malraux, ibid.

[64] André Malraux, 'D'une jeunesse européenne', p. 140: 'les grandes doctrines occidentales ont toujours admis implicitement qu'un homme peut se juger lui-même, établir des rapports constants entre les principes qu'il a acceptés et ses actions'.

[65] André Malraux, 'D'une jeunesse européenne', p. 140.

[66] André Malraux, *La Tentation de l'Occident*, pp. 214–15.

[67] André Malraux, 'D'une jeunesse européenne', pp. 141–2.

[68] André Malraux, 'D'une jeunesse européenne', p. 142.

[69] André Malraux, *La Tentation de l'Occident*, p. 94.

[70] André Malraux, *La Tentation de l'Occident*, p. 102: 'avec quelque force que je veuille prendre conscience de moi-même, je me sens soumis à une série désordonnée de sensations sur lesquelles je n'ai point prise, et qui ne dépendent que de mon imagination et des réactions qu'elle appelle'.

[71] André Malraux, 'D'une jeunesse européenne', p. 145 and p. 147.

[72] Marcel Arland, 'Sur un nouveau mal du siècle', *N.R.F.* (February 1924), p. 156.

[73] Malraux later chose art as the 'anti-destin'.

[74] André Malraux, 'D'une jeunesse européenne', p. 140.

[75] André Malraux, *Les Voix du silence* (Gallimard, 1951), p. 628: 'le destin n'est pas la mort, il est fait de tout ce qui impose à l'homme la conscience de sa condition'.

[76] André Malraux, 'D'une jeunesse européenne', pp. 135–7.

[77] See André Malraux, 'Lignes de Force', *Preuves* (March 1955), p. 8.

[78] André Malraux, 'D'une jeunesse européenne', p. 135.

[79] e.g. Joseph Hoffman, *L'Humanisme de Malraux* (Klincksieck, 1963), pp. 92–7. Hoffman cites Mauriac in support of his claim.

[80] André Malraux, 'D'une jeunesse européenne', p. 136.

[81] André Malraux, 'D'une jeunesse européenne', p. 135.
[82] André Malraux, *La Tentation de l'Occident*, p. 217.
[83] André Malraux, *op. cit.*, p. 155.
[84] André Malraux, *op. cit.*, p. 165 and pp. 166–7.
[85] André Malraux, *op. cit.*, p. 208.
[86] André Malraux, *op. cit.*, pp. 182–3.
[87] André Malraux, *op. cit.*, pp. 187–8.
[88] See Léon Trotski, 'La Révolution étranglée', *N.R.F.* (April 1931), pp. 488–501; Georges Altmann, *L'Humanité* (22 October, 1928).
[89] André Malraux, *La Tentation de l'Occident*, p. 201.
[90] André Malraux, *op. cit.*, p. 202.
[91] André Malraux, *op. cit.*, p. 203.
[92] André Malraux, *ibid.*
[93] 'André Malraux et l'Orient', p. 2.
[94] André Malraux, *La Tentation de l'Occident*, p. 168: 'je ne puis plus concevoir l'Homme indépendant de son intensité' (A.D.); p. 174: 'l'intensité que les idées créent en vous me semble aujourd'hui expliquer votre vie mieux qu'elles-mêmes' (Ling).
[95] André Malraux, 'D'une jeunesse européenne', p. 148.
[96] Thierry Maulnier, *Nietzsche* (Gallimard, 1943), p. 103.
[97] Jeanne Delhomme *Temps et Destin* (Gallimard, 1955), p. 155.
[98] André Malraux, 'D'une jeunesse européenne', p. 148.
[99] See Lucien Goldmann, 'Introduction à une étude structurelle des romans de Malraux', *Revue de l'Institut de sociologie* (Brussels, 1962–1963), p. 300: 'si le comportement de l'individu ne peut . . . se fonder ni sur des valeurs transindividuelles (puisque l'individualisme les avait toutes supprimées), la pensée devait nécessairement se centrer sur les difficultés de ce fondement, sur les limites de l'être humain en tant qu'individu et sur la plus importante d'entre elles, sa disparition inévitable, la mort'.
[100] André Malraux, *La Tentation de l'Occident*, pp. 215–16.
[101] André Malraux, *op. cit.*, p. 46.
[102] See André Malraux, 'André Malraux et l'Orient', *Les Nouvelles littéraires* (31 July, 1926), p. 2.
[103] See Thomas Mann, *The Magic Mountain* (Penguin Modern Classics, 1967), pp. 403–4.
[104] See André Malraux, 'La Défense de l'Occident', *N.R.F.* (June 1927), pp. 817–18: 'la pensée européenne, dans le domaine de l'esprit, s'est toujours exprimée par la création de mythes cohérents. Elle travaille aujourd'hui à en construire un nouveau, et les plaidoyers sont sans force contre une recherche de cet ordre qui dérive d'une nécessité'.
[105] See André Malraux, 'André Malraux et l'Orient', p. 2: 'le premier présent de notre génération, j'ai la conviction que c'est la proclamation de la faillite de l'individualisme, de toutes les attitudes, de toutes les doctrines qui se justifient par l'exaltation du Moi'.
[106] Drieu La Rochelle, *Écrits de jeunesse* (Gallimard, 1941), p. 57.
[107] Drieu La Rochelle, 'Nietzsche contre Marx', *Socialisme Fasciste* (Gallimard, 1934), p. 70.
[108] André Malraux, *Les Conquérants* (Livre de poche, 1973), p. 75. Édition

originale, Grasset 1928.

[109] Drieu La Rochelle, *La Comédie de Charleroi* (Gallimard, 1934), p. 57.
[110] See Drieu La Rochelle, *Notes pour comprendre le siècle* (Gallimard, 1941), p. 155: 'point de pensée sans action'.
[111] Drieu La Rochelle, *Écrits de jeunesse,* p. 201.
[112] Drieu La Rochelle, *op. cit.*, p. 199.
[113] Drieu La Rochelle, *op. cit.*, p. 200.
[114] Drieu La Rochelle, *op. cit.*, pp. 191 ff.
[115] Drieu La Rochelle, 'Malraux, l'homme nouveau', *N.R.F.* (December 1930), p. 881.
[116] Andrée Viollis, *Indochine S.O.S.* (Gallimard, 1935), p. VII.
[117] Drieu La Rochelle, 'Malraux, l'homme nouveau', p. 882.
[118] Quoted by Frédéric Grover, *Drieu La Rochelle* (Gallimard, 1962), p. 80.
[119] Drieu La Rochelle, *Écrits de jeunesse,* p. 51.

CHAPTER VII

Drieu: The Decadent

*Je fus entièrement possédé par l'idée de décadence et
à jamais.*

(*État Civil*)

Far from projecting a heroic ideal in his writings of the 'twenties,
Drieu analyses the process of decomposition going on in civilization. He finds the task distressing for he still loves all the things
he despairs of.[1] Like Malraux he feels that Europe's myth-
making powers have been spent. Europe is moribund for it is no
longer able to create an ideal to which man might entrust his soul.
Only a vacuum remains: 'pas de mystique possible à notre
époque, mais aussi pas d'homme sans mystique. Donc il ne peut y
avoir d'homme à notre époque, donc notre époque va au néant'.[2]
Europe, like France, is decadent; its apparent life consists of the
last spasm of its agony and this agitation is self-destructive.
Drieu, like Malraux and many others, locates the origins of this
deep disorder in the Renaissance, where integral unity was
broken and transcendental value lost. Reason was cast adrift,
deprived of higher purpose. The Reformation consummated the
break and Reason, taking root in temporal affairs, brought forth
a flower: rationalism,[3] whose seeds of inspiration the Revolution
of 1789 scattered on the wind for all nations to enjoy. Today the
fruit is without sap; only a desiccated husk remains:

> Le rationalisme, c'est l'agonie de la raison. Oui il y avait eu une
> raison française mais si vive, si drue, si naïve et si large, embrass-
> ant tous les éléments de l'être. Pas seulement le raisonnement
> mais l'élan de la foi; pas seulement le ciel mais la terre, pas
> seulement la ville mais la campagne; pas seulement l'âme mais le
> corps—enfin tout. La France avait eu le sens de tout, elle l'avait
> perdu.[4]

Decadence being the product of life's 'de-mythification', Drieu's

206

fictional portrayal of the decadent is, in essence, the dramatic projection of the 'emptiness' left by the disappearance of a myth. In this consists the essential difference between Drieu and Malraux as novelists. Whereas Malraux attempts to project a new kind of man in the absence of a myth, Drieu makes this absence itself the 'subject' of his novels.

In our earlier chapter on Drieu we saw that the young Drieu grew up with the notion that France had entered a period of decadence. He finds support for this view in the example of his own family, which, despising the present in politics, art and religion, and fearful of the future, finds solace in the knowledge of France's past grandeur. Drieu takes a harsh view of this abrogation of the present in favour of a dead past. For him it represents the same flight from the real which the author of the *Will to Power* had identified in the Christian ethic: the 'world beyond' is our compensation for our present disorders and weaknesses. For those who 'remain faithful to the earth' there can be no recourse to the comfort of a metaphysical world. The real must be faced however difficult to endure. This attitude explains Drieu's uncompromising approach in *Mesure de la France*. France has not produced enough children and, as a result, is no longer able to affirm her beliefs by a show of strength. She is sterile and has lost her will to live and, therefore, her right to survive. For Drieu only what retains the will to live deserves to live. All the rest is decadence and should be destroyed. France is decadent and must die into Europe so that Europe may live. Indeed, Europe must die if Europe is to live.

Drieu's intentions, therefore, even as he portrays decadence are clear, as may be gathered from the quotation with which he prefaces *Le Jeune Européen*: 'nous sommes peut-être chargés seulement de liquider une succession spirituelle à laquelle il y irait de l'intérêt de chacun de renoncer'. This statement, which sets the mood of most of Drieu's fiction of the 'twenties, is taken from the 'Légitime Défense' of André Breton, to whom the book is dedicated. Between 1920 and 1925 Drieu, who was friendly with Louis Aragon, was very close to the Surrealists in their determination to 'liquidate' the European spiritual inheritance. 'La Suite dans les idées', which appeared in 1927, is written in this mood and reveals Drieu's desire to put his civilization to the test of battle: 'que cette civilisation soit morte ou vivante, il faut vouloir la tuer. Si elle est morte, ce sera vite fait; si elle est vivante, elle se défendra et alors on verra ce qu'on verra'.[5]

Like the Surrealists, Drieu was tempted by Communism. In it he detected a potential for destruction which, as he later wrote, he hoped would precipitate the end of everything, drive everybody against the wall, especially the working class.[6] *Une Femme à sa fenêtre,* published in 1930, reflects this attitude. The central figure of the piece is Michel Boutros, a Communist agent for whom destruction, stripped of purpose, is the *sine qua non* of the revolutionary process. Like Garine, Boutros is not interested in the doctrine, its objectives or 'pretentious details'.[7] If he is a revolutionary it is because, like Kyo in *La Condition humaine,* he regards the Communist movement as a great surge of life, a death-defying drive, because it happens to be, *at the time he lives,* the strongest force in the world.[8]

Boutros's involvement in revolutionary violence is not only a search for power; it is also, as he himself makes clear, an instrument of self-purification, a means of purging himself of all the sordid memories of his bourgeois past. His 'burden of suffering' is, however, more than family inheritance or personal disgust; it is (as it is for Malraux) the accumulated weight of dead ideals bequeathed to him, the European, by history. And so he flees history as he flees the police; he is afraid of remaining a prisoner of dead values as well as of their guardians.[9] Resisting the temptation to eat ashes he clings to the present in an effort to commune with what is alive in his day. This communion with the forces of life gives him an insight into the 'true function' of woman, who becomes for him the essential link between man and nature. This explains the atmosphere of spiritual elevation that presides over the sexual union of Boutros and Margot. They embrace, not for physical gratification, but because their 'souls' can no longer resist the 'longing for knowledge'.[10] The spiritual exercise climaxes in the fulgurating revelation of life's harmony, in the beatific reconciliation of body and mind, of mystic and material forms. This scene, rare if not unique in Drieu's fiction, is unconvincing if only because its optimism is not justified by the novel which contains it. Boutros, for whom life, to be meaningful, must be sustained by active defiance of death is, unlike Garine, not involved in a 'great action'. Forced into hiding he plays a wholly passive role. It is this period of forced inaction and

208

its effect on Boutros that the novel examines. As a result, we—like Boutros—are denied the world of events and confronted instead by a universe of subjectivities dominated by our hero's turgid exchanges with Margot, Count Rico and the arch-bourgeois Malfosse. The reasons for this approach are clear. For all his hatred of decadent bourgeois, Boutros, like Drieu, feels compelled to justify himself in their eyes. Despite the revolutionary veneer Boutros remains a prisoner of the past, unable or too afraid to sever the umbilical cord that binds him to the civilization, now a putrescent corpse, that gave him life. No less that Blaquans—the male protagonist of *Blèche* (1928)—he is a *bourgeois désaffecté*: a bourgeois ashamed of being one but unable to be anything else. Blaquans, too, had known a moment of revolt against the 'atrocious order' of the world but, like Boutros (and indeed like Drieu) he has not been prepared to face the consequences of his 'cri de colère'. He has drifted back to the ignoble miasma whence he came: 'je suis démasqué, je ne suis rien, je m'effondre'.[11] If Blaquans has come to accept the path of conformism, Boutros, after an initial outburst of splenetic 'self-purification', has proved to be no more defiant. Indeed he could, with justification, be described as the 'negative print' of the Malraux adventurer just as, in more general terms, we might characterize Drieu's literary world as that of the Decadent and Malraux's as that of the New Man.

The creatures who inhabit Drieu's novels and short stories are moral and emotional impotents seeking, in sensual gratification and frivolous activity, an opportunity to escape the sense of their own desolation. For this frustrated ambition and its weary impulse Drieu found the name 'the empty suitcase', a label which, though attached to only one of his heroes ('La Valise vide' in the four short stories of *Plainte contre inconnu*) applies equally to all the others, as they all reveal a yawning emptiness.

Plainte contre inconnu (1924) won Drieu instant acclaim. He was credited with having faithfully depicted youth's sense of absence, its misery and abandonment in a desolate world.[12] Even *Clarté* applauded him—not, however, with much sympathy.[13] He was 'congratulated' for having perceived and stated (not without a certain elegance and force) the obvious—that the bourgeoisie was festering:

Comment pourrait-il en être autrement dans un temps où l'artiste, à moins de s'enfoncer toujours plus en soi-même, jusque dans les abîmes de l'inconscient . . . est assailli, quand mû par le commun désir des hommes, il met le nez à la fenêtre ou le pied dehors, par une insupportable odeur de mort. La mort, la dissociation, la désagrégation, le détraquement . . . telle est la dominante de *Plainte contre inconnu*. Cela revient, comme un refrain, comme une obsession. . . . Décidément cela va mal, très mal dans la bourgeoisie.[14]

The 'empty suitcases' of *Plainte contre inconnu* create an infectious emptiness around them. The experience of war, frequently mentioned by the characters of these short stories, more easily explains the emptiness than does the emptiness itself. In war they had arisen from the dead to feel strong, free and heroic, but all too soon the note of exhilaration had been silenced:

> Dans un domaine étroit et profond, nous avons accompli des actes. Dans notre sang qui coulait, nous avons vu un amour prodigieux. Il n'était pas épuise. Nous aurions voulu faire quelque chose de plus. Si les hommes avaient osé, si les femmes avaient su.[15]

Their vital energy and thirst for action are now denied expression, and they drift aimlessly through a world with which they have no common measure.

Gonzague, the hero of 'La Valise vide'—the only story of the four which makes entertaining reading[16]—is intended (and was taken) to represent more than himself. He is, as it were, a 'case history' of that peculiar brand of alienation identified by Marcel Arland as a 'nouveau mal du siècle'. We should, however, emphasize the heavy personal tone of this work. Although the main character is taken from life—Jacques Rigaut[17]—Drieu uses this model as a platform for a kind of mythic self-projection, with the result that the finished article becomes, as Drieu himself wrote of Malraux's Garine: 'la figuration mythique de son moi'.[18] In other words Drieu selects those elements of the model which he feels to be aspects or tendencies of his own make-up and then develops them through the characters: 'ces personnages m'empruntaient ce qu'ils avaient de plus particulier. Tout en eux s'infléchissait selon les pentes habituelles de mon expérience'.[19] This approach to characterization, taken in conjunction with Drieu's self-confessed role as critic of the age, undoubtedly explains his ambivalence towards these creatures. For if reprobation is displayed, so too is complicity. Nor is a certain degree of exhibitionism absent. Indeed, Drieu seems to make a positive virtue of choosing the least flattering aspects of his own personality to embody in these characters. This tendency is even more pronounced when the model in question would appear to be Drieu himself rather than an acquaintance or friend—as, for example, in the novels where Gilles/Gille appears. The result is that if we can call Malraux a mythomaniac, Drieu, because of the spiritual and physical debility of his characters, would surely qualify as a 'mythomane à rebours'.[20]

The narrator of 'La Valise vide' meets Gonzague for the first time at the home of Gertrude who is, to a very large extent, a caricature of the 'emancipated' woman of the 'twenties. Her passion for *avant-garde* poetry is simulated and her liberal attitude in sexual matters is purely verbal. Her likes and dislikes are not so much her own as the result of what she feels she ought to like or dislike. If she admires Gonzague it is because he defies definition. When Gonzague leaves Gertrude's to go for a drink with the narrator, we learn that he feels 'empty', yet has no sense of anything precise which might make him full. If he craves affection, he nevertheless lacks the vitality, constancy and emotional depth which make friendship and love possible. Unable to attach himself to anyone or anything, he seeks only the sensation of passing quickly from one thing to another.[21]

When next we meet Gonzague he is in a bar, surrounded by a flock of admirers. He speaks only infrequently but when he does each proposition is greeted with enthusiastic approval. Of particular interest to the fascinated assembly are Gonzague's new 'pastimes', which include excessive drinking and gambling. Petty theft, including the removal of any bizarre object which takes his fancy, is the latest in his long line of fads, and the one to win greatest applause. With a pair of scissors in his possession he has become unstoppable. One deft snip in the underground and another button takes its place in his mounting collection of handkerchiefs, pens and matchboxes.[22] His reputation is further enhanced by the fact that he has never been known to read a book, attend a concert or visit an art gallery.[23] Nothing interests him, neither his job nor even his own game. He remains outside everything he does. The narrator welcomes the day when someone will oblige Gonzague to open his 'empty suitcase' to reveal the nothingness out of which his life is made.

We are given the first clue to the nature of Gonzague's strange malady when the narrator is informed that Gonzague has been seen in the company of a young man who has a reputation for homosexuality. The narrator, content to wait and observe, looks about him to see if Gonzague's suspected sexual 'disorder' can be traced to a more general sickness within society. What he sees appals him. His contemporaries inordinate concern for the sexual lives of others betrays a basic anxiety; people are frantically seeking in others the disorders which threaten everyone. He sees everywhere a perversion of human nature; normality has become the exception.[24] Gonzague, Drieu implies, is nothing less than the emanation of a rotting society, the personification of a spiritual void. He can make nothing of life because life offers nothing; he cannot rise above its conditions. He realizes that his 'experiments'—imagined and attempted—are so much wasted energy. He never really intends writing a pornographic novel or marrying an heiress. The effort required would be too much. If he mentions suicide it is in the same lethargic way he speaks of all matters: 'le matin, en me couchant, au lieu de tourner le bouton électrique, sans faire attention, je me trompe, j'appuie sur la gâchette'.[25]

The final episode of 'La Valise vide'—which takes place in a brothel—provides the key to the character of Gonzague, and it is characteristic of Drieu's ideas on decadence that it should concern his sexual life. The sexual aspect of decadence seemed to Drieu to be the evil where all the deficiencies, all the decadences were summed up and consummated.[26]

In his conversation with the narrator Gonzague reveals that as a young soldier he had adopted the worst habits of army life. His captain, who was a homosexual, had introduced him to cocaine, and Gonzague cannot be sure what happened while he was under the influence of the drug. A whole side of his personality, it is suggested, can thus be explained by drugs '[qui] favorisent dans les milieux où on en use une grande indifférence aux choses sexuelles'.[27] Mme Lemberg, with whom Gonzague was at the time having an affair, gradually faded into the background. He soon found himself, 'loin de Mme Lemberg, loin des femmes, loin de tout ce qui vivait'.[28] Of late his only sexual life has been with the few prostitutes who frequented his district and whom, through weakness of will, he could not refuse. Since moving to another district he has discovered that even masturbation is superfluous. His whole life is empty.

On 5 November 1929 Jacques Rigaut committed suicide. Drieu wrote an 'Adieu à Gonzague' and then began work on *Le Feu follet* where he would, as in 'La Valise vide', combine a portrait of Rigaut with one of himself.[29]

Like Gonzague, Alain of *Le Feu follet* is drifting along the path of life's negation, whose symbol is drugs. He knows that his habit is only a delayed suicide, and to remind himself of the fact he keeps the syringe and the pistol in the same place. His refusal of life involves an indifference to women, contempt for the law of 'forced labour' (work) and a decided unconcern for the attractions of the external world:

> Alain n'avait jamais regardé le ciel ni la façade des maisons, ni le pavé de bois, les choses palpitantes; il n'avait jamais regardé une rivière ni une forêt; il vivait dans les chambres vides de la morale: 'Le monde est imparfait, le monde est mauvais. Je réprouve; je condamne, j'anéantis le monde'.[30]

The only worldly consideration of this 'mystic of a materialistic age'[31] is how to obtain his next dose of heroin. Here the inherited prejudices of his bourgeois background (which he formally rejects) have proved to be of some use. They may have prevented him from working for a living but not from living by other means. He has turned to women for money—not, however, without a sense of guilt. He is a *bourgeois désaffecté*, able to see the vices germinated by his prejudices but unable, because of his prejudices, to enjoy his vices.[32] His influence over women is, however, failing. His marriage to Dorothy, which had taken place while he was temporarily off drugs, is being dissolved and he is unable to make Lydia, the American divorcee with whom he is having an affair, stay in France. Before returning to the United States she does, however, leave him 10,000 francs with which he intends purchasing more drugs.[33]

Shortly after marrying Dorothy, Alain suffered a relapse and found himself taking heroin in larger and more frequent doses.[34] In desperation he agreed to take a cure, but quickly discovered that what was left of life in him was impregnated by drugs and forced him back to them.[35] The cure failed and yet he knew that he no longer

213

derived any pleasure from his habit. Indeed he recognized that his life had assumed all the characteristics of the kind of life he hated—settled, sedentary, sedate. The sheer boredom of living a 'routine of old maids' convinced him to make one last effort to be rid of his addiction.[36] To this end he has entered the clinic of a Dr. de la Barbinais.

Dr. de la Barbinais's sanitorium is a picture of decadence, a dark canvas of weakened and depraved instincts. Mlle Cournot, galloping about like some bewildered monster, is the victim of a sexual urge which knows no bounds. The Marquis d'Averseau is another representative of sexual 'abnormality', the precise nature of which may be gathered from the title of his publication: *Histoire des princes français qui furent sodomites*. The other inmates include a pair of crazed metaphysicians, Brême and Moraire, Mme de la Barbinais who is a lunatic, and Mlle Farnoux, an animated but not very communicative corpse. As for the doctor whose task it is to help and encourage Alain, he is a hypocrite who tries to convince his new patient, without believing it himself, that life is good, that everything will be better tomorrow, that will-power can cure all. How, asks Alain, can a race worn out by civilization believe in will-power? Modern science has itself refuted this 'myth of another age'.[37] He takes refuge in his room and attempts to put a semblance of order in his feelings by writing. For a moment he feels relieved. The writer imposes order in the world. Perhaps literature can be his salvation. But he is discouraged by the memory of those who, in his youth, had taught him nothing but the futility of literature. He himself has seen nothing, felt nothing, loved nothing. He puts down the pen. Perhaps salvation lies elsewhere—with his friends. He decides to find out if their lives can offer him any reason to live and hope.

Urcel, writer and opium-smoker, claims that drugs permit their users to tread the narrow path between life and death and thus provide the risk element essential to man.[38] Alain is unconvinced. He argues that many opium-smokers live to a ripe old age. Lethargy, not risk, is involved. As for Urcel's desire to 'sauver le prestige poétique de la drogue',[39] Alain retorts, 'la drogue, c'est encore la vie; c'est embêtant, comme la vie'.[40] Urcel, it is implied, has merely rationalized his situation. The mystic reverence with which he explores other-worldly considerations is no more than a flight from the real, a sign of weakness, of decadence.

Alain's other friends are just as uninspiring. Dubourg's retreat into papyri is also an abdication of life; it, too, other-worldly. How can he, warm and secure in his little world of Egyptology, know anything of the solitude of the outsider. His words of encouragement are false, for they are not really spoken to Alain. They are uttered in abstraction to an object he barely recognizes. Alain's only consolation is the certainty of dying soon: 'l'attitude de Dubourg, entre autres prétextes, lui donnait toute raison de mourir: la vie à travers lui n'était point parvenue à se justifier'.[41] At the Lavaux's he finds no real warmth or example either, only 'ce vague de sollicitude'.[42] There he meets the adventurer Marc Brancion, recently back from Asia, and as despairing an advertisement for humanity as ever could be found: 'Brancion avait entendu, une fois pour toutes, la foule humaine et avait fermé ses oreilles à ce concert de mendiants, de charlatans de carrefours, de tire-laine sentimentaux'.[43] He is a brute, but no more indifferent than the rest. They are all alike, all equipped with blinkers. They see only what they have chosen to see, and ignore all the rest. Their artificial paradises—Egyptology, religion, literature, sex, money—prevent them from seeing the hell which they and others are living. They will never know anything but the reassuring aspects, never the solitude, the inhumanity. He takes his leave of them: 'mensonge, mensonge. Ils savent qu'aucune sincérité n'est possible et pourtant ils en parlent. Ils en parlent, les salauds'.[44]

Alain runs into Milou—'mon semblable, mon frère'[45]—a fellow sufferer of life's indifference. It is at this point that Alain realizes that his bohemian life-style is just as inauthentic as the comfortable lives he has condemned. If 'les autres' are the dupes of their 'professions', then he has been the dupe of his own outlandish ways. His role of 'dandy spleenetique' is merely the pretext for *his inability to love or to be loved.* When he wakes up the next morning to the cold prospect of going through the same soul-destroying routine once again he becomes desperate. He is dying too slowly, and decides to speed up the process. He takes out a revolver: 'un revolver, c'est solide, c'est en acier. C'est un objet. Se heurter enfin à l'objet'.[46]

Perken of *La Voie royale* makes the same gesture without, however, carrying it through. Here we are presented with a perfect

215

example of the differing outlooks of the decadent and the New Man. The former is a man whose awareness of the futility of life has rendered him incapable of action. Or rather, the only act of which he is capable is that of self-destruction: 'le suicide, c'est un acte, l'acte de ceux qui n'ont pu en accomplir d'autres'.[47] For Malraux's New Man, on the other hand, it is the awareness of life's meaninglessness which is the very inspiration to act.[48] Rejecting suicide as a gesture which acknowledges man's defeat, he is determined to act—as Mounier puts it—in order to try to 'ranimer la valeur dans une vie sans valeur, donner un sens au non-sens'.[49]

Alain had seen, towards the end, that his 'disorder' was largely the outcome of his own inability to love or to be loved. That Drieu is to a large extent writing about his own experience is confirmed not only by his approach to characterization—to which we have already referred—but by the most conclusive statement by him on this subject. In that section of *Le Jeune Européen* entitled 'Le Sang et l'encre' Drieu informs us of his inability to reach women despite his passion for them: '"je ne sais pas aimer les femmes", et cela tournait "les hommes ne savent pas aimer les femmes", et puis j'ajoutai pour un balancement: "Ni les femmes les hommes"'. He is aware that he has generalized his own despair, but decides nonetheless to take up his pen in order to 'démontrer pourquoi un homme et une femme d'aujourd'hui ne s'entendent pas'.[50]

Drieu's lovers—homosexuals excepted—all have the 'parfum d'herbe des femmes' in their nostrils, live on the charity of women and spend much of their time in the company of prostitutes. What they are seeking and what they cannot find in their relationships with women is the creature of their dreams. And yet they continue, hoping for the ideal they cherish, corrupted by the reality they embrace. From marriage they demand the miracle of communication between two souls, participation in the 'solemn mystery' of paternity; they are offered instead carnal contact, fruitless 'pederastic unions' consummated by an appetite for money, dissolved when the money runs out.[51] Unable to love or to be loved,—'sans femme, sans famille, sans situation, sans ami'—impotent to recover a grandeur absent from their lives, but of which they have had an intimation, trapped in an adulterous cycle of erotic dissipation yet all the time craving a 'pure love',

216

they are driven onwards as others (like Alain) are driven on by drugs: women have become for them a form of self-destruction.

Life for Gille—the hero of *L'Homme couvert de femmes* (1925)—is an endless succession of sordid affairs punctuated only by the need to eat and sleep:

> Il se déshabille pour la troisième fois de la journée avec patience et application, seul, car elle a disparu. Quand il est nu il est tout de même content, il s'allonge sur le lit. Il attend. Elle rentre. Il ne bouge pas. Elle sourit, elle dit des phrases de courtoisie, elle retire un voile. Elle s'agenouille devant lui. Où manger maintenant?[52]

Gille's dissatisfaction with himself and with his rather ordinary friends, together with a curiosity towards the outlandish and a desire to be liked, bring him into contact with a group of people in whom he detects a perversion of human nature. However, if disgust is felt, so too is a fascination with corrupted, corrupting and self destructive instincts: 'c'est que [Gille] préférait un vice virulent qui montrait la vivacité et la promptitude de la mort violente à une vertu faite de fatigue vitale'.[53]

Finette's brother Luc is a homosexual. His primary role, however, is that of a catalyst for Gille's rigorous self-analysis. Gille begins to wonder—not surprisingly—whether his defence of the sexual act as participation in God's enthusiasm for Creation is no more than a sham.[54] Is he, no less than Luc, haunted by physical shapes—feminine ones in his case—and is not his fitful passage from one woman to the next evidence of the meaningless prayer which every sophist bears on his lips as the next best thing to conviction? Luc at least is certain—Gille's 'divine quest' is at best a form of esthetic concupiscence, at worst self-justification. Gille objects: 'je cherche une âme, une seule, telle que Dieu l'a faite, de ce limon dans sa main de sculpteur pour Adam, l'homme occidental'.[55] What he is seeking, he stresses, is the path to the 'communication incroyable' between two of God's creatures.[56] He would like to escape Don Juan's 'law of numbers' and devote himself to the exploration of one soul. He yearns to experience paternity, which he calls the symbol of the physical union and tangible token of love's reality, and in which he sees man's one opportunity to participate in the 'divine mystery' of life. Love without issue, on the other hand,

217

he regards as a desiccated formula muttered in a senile way. All the guests at Finette's country retreat, including Gille, are guilty of this mortal sin:

> Luc, Bernard, les gitons, les gouines, Jacqueline, les yeux fermés, précipitée aux doigts noirs, moi et Finette tous pareils. Chant cassé, parce qu'ils ont perdu le goût de moduler, de donner forme à tous les gestes de la vie, parce que cela ne les intéresse plus de créer.[57]

Finette, in particular—with whom Gille has an attack of impotence—expects nothing of life and gives nothing in return. Woman's function as 'nœud profond entre la terre et le ciel'[59] means nothing to her. She will not allow children into her life. Her sin, therefore, like Gille's (indeed like that of France) is the sin of sterility. Gille leaves, intent on devoting himself to one woman who will be his wife and the mother of his children.

One year before the publication of *L'Homme couvert de femmes* Marcel Arland wrote an article entitled 'Sur un nouveau mal du siècle'.[60] It is a curious fact, or a measure of Arland's diagnostic skill, that *L'Homme couvert de femmes* displays many of the major symptoms of this 'new disease'. The absence of God—which Arland identifies as the central preoccupation and main source of anguish in his generation—is perhaps the major 'presence' in the novel, and the quest for an absolute, exemplified in the oscillation between the extremes of order and anarchy, is clearly active in Gille's desire, on the one hand, for one woman and, on the other, in his consuming passion for all women. One of the factors by which the twentieth-century *mal du siècle* is distinguished (by Arland) from that of the nineteenth century is in the former's insistence on the need for sincerity.[61] All the characters of *L'Homme couvert de femmes* want to be sincere. Contact with others brings them to a deeper understanding of themselves and they betray no inhibitions in revealing their findings to others. Indeed, as we have already noted with regard to Drieu himself, this sincerity verges on the exhibitionist. Gille in particular seems to take a masochistic delight in expressing to others his sense of his own inner degeneracy.

L'Homme couvert de femmes ended with Gille deciding to turn his back on brothel and boudoir in order to seek out and marry some innocent young girl. *Drôle de voyage,* published in 1933, shows how the intended project turns out. After a brief flirtation with Beatrix, an English heiress, Gille considers himself engaged. When she leaves for her home in Granada, Gille, driven by loneliness, begins an affair with a married woman in Paris. Unable to inspire or experience love in this 'illicit union', he decides to rejoin the ever hopeful Beatrix in Spain. No sooner arrived, however, than he recognizes his error. She possesses neither the sophistication nor exquisite beauty which his perfect dream requires. So he resumes his weary search for that ethereal female who will satisfy at once his senses and his heart, and appease his longing for God's finest creation.

Gille's search for the right woman (and his inability to find her) is only the apparent subject of the novel. Drieu's real concern is to indict the society that makes woman (and, therefore, weak and senile instincts) man's only possibility in the modern era. Images of senility abound, inscribed within a picture of decadence that encompasses art, religion and politics. Gille's mind gets quite used to racing back and forth from the ugliness of the present with its meagre and vain agitation to the beauty and creative youth of the past with its calm and full harmonies.[62] His thoughts are drawn, in particular, to the Middle Ages, which he worships as a period of great enterprises and adventures, an era of the cathedrals.[63] His nostalgic envy is made all the more acute by what he sees during his visit to the country estate of some rich Jews. The picture is highly symbolic. The setting is a medieval château but its inhabitants are Gille's contemporaries, degenerate 'successors' to whom the modern world has refused creative talent, fading shadows living on the last resources of a dwindling inheritance. Whether Gille is in France or in Spain, whether investigating politics or religion, art or marriage, his perception is the same: everything is rotten, but everything is still standing. He would destroy it all if he thought its raked ashes would yield one glowing ember with which to refire European civilization. But he knows that no warmth would be found. His whole life is a deception. He yearns for the possibilities of renewal but cannot locate them. He seeks a wife but cannot find her. He requires art to recompose the organic universe but sees only 'painters of ruins'.[64] He craves a young, virile, united Europe but feels incapable of being either a Fascist or a Communist.[65] In all things he aspires only to despair. Indeed, one gets the impression that

219

he aspires only the better to savour his despair; his hopes are already touched by the exquisite anguish of certain defeat. It is doubtful whether he (or Drieu) could live in any environment but a decadent one. He seems unable to live without his pain.

Drieu was now approaching the end of his studies of decadence. The prisoner of a cowardly society clinging insincerely to an obsolete order was about to break his chains. In this respect *Béloukia*, published in 1936, is at once characteristically autobiographical and strangely prophetic in tone. Hassib's destiny prefigures our author's own. Béloukia's last meeting with Hassib signals the rebirth of the man of action. She hands him the dagger, of which women have for years deprived him.[66] Drieu had already been stirred by the political events of February 1934 and was on the eve of joining Doriot's Parti Populaire Français. So began his flirtation with the forces that would destroy decadence and bring forth life. The nature of the life to which he looked forward may be gathered from the vision of depravity which he sought to escape:

> Je souffre pour le corps des hommes. Le corps des hommes est ignoble en France du moins. Horrible de se promener dans les rues et de rencontrer tant de déchéances, de laideurs ou d'inachèvements. Ces dos voûtés, ces épaules tombantes, ces ventres gonflés, ces petites cuisses, ces faces veules.[67]

Believing it impossible to separate body and mind, Drieu naturally felt that to neglect the body was to starve the spirit.[68] Conversely a 'restauration du corps' would have the effect of promoting a spiritual renaissance from which would be born a New Man in whom a courageous soul would be sustained by a strong and well-balanced body. The only organization which appeared to be working to such an end was the P.P.F., otherwise known as the 'Parti du corps vivant'. Its leader was Jacques Doriot whom Drieu saw as a living Dionysus—'notre champion contre la mort':

> Nous avons vu vivre, travailler Doriot. Nous avons vu le fils du forgeron, nous avons vu l'ancien métallurgiste dans la houle de ses épaules et de ses reins, dans le hérissement de sa toison, dans la vaste sueur de son front, continuer et épanouir devant nous le travail de quinze ans. Devant nous, il a pris à bras le corps toute la

220

destinée de la France, il l'a soulevée à bout de bras comme un grand frère herculéen.[69]

When the Nietzschean Prometheus turned out to be just another 'comfortable' bourgeois, Drieu resigned himself to the fact that France would remain an effete and decadent nation. It was this failure by the French to save their souls by serving their bodies that Drieu identified as the cause of the French defeat of 1940:

C'est cela en réalité, c'est que nous souffrons dans notre corps comme dans notre âme. Ces deux éléments si évidemment inséparables de l'être humain étaient disjoints, méconnus et maltraités séparément par le marxisme et par le libéralisme. Ils ont, dans toute la communauté et dans chacun de nous, périclité séparément. De là notre déchéance, notre inadaptation insensée aux conditions inexorables de la vie, notre sens perdu de la vraie pensée et de l'action complète. De là notre défaite, notre malheur, notre faim d'aujourd'hui. Faim de l'âme et faim du corps.[70]

We have already seen that Drieu was drawn to Fascism (and thereafter to Nazism) because of its virility and sense of life, because of its concept of the 'whole man'. The *point de départ* for his commitment was the dissolution of the modern world. Fascism was for him a reaction against decadence (the analysis and artistic projection of which we find in the novels):

Je suis fasciste parce que j'ai mesuré les progrès de la décadence en Europe. J'ai vu dans le fascisme le seul moyen de contenir et de réduire cette décadence, et par ailleurs, ne croyant plus guère dans les ressources politiques de l'Angleterre comme de la France, réprouvant l'intrusion d'Empires étrangers à notre continent comme ceux des États-Unis et de la Russie, je n'ai vu d'autres recours que dans le génie de Hitler et de l'hitlérisme.[71]

Drieu's claim to have 'measured' the progress of decadence in Europe is a little exaggerated to say the least. His characters—upper-middle class and Parisian almost to a man—hardly qualify as a representative sample of European society. Instead they illustrate the point which we have already made in connection with *État Civil,* that Drieu has an élitist conception of society. Whence the symbolic value he attaches to these creatures who are, we must remember, both fictional representations of social acquaintances and friends as well as the projection of personal anxieties. In other words they represent merely a *limited* sector of that social élite to which Drieu attaches symbolic value. As a result, if he offers a critique of decadence it is that of a world which is his own *literary* representation of a small group at whose centre he himself stands. The irony, of course, is that it was Drieu's reaction to decadence which led him to Fascism. It is not too difficult to see why. One cannot help feeling that given the autobiographical, self-critical and self-pitying tone of the work, Drieu is, in an antithetical kind of way, justifying his sense of his own decadence. The contradiction in all this—the denouncer of decadence is himself a decadent—created a sort of paralysis from which Drieu could not escape. It required a *deus ex machina* in the shape of Nazism to rescue him or at least to offer him the illusion of salvation.

NOTES

[1] Drieu La Rochelle, *Écrits de jeunesse* (Gallimard, 1941), p. 213: 'je souffre d'être l'homme d'aujourd'hui, l'homme qui va se noyer et se crispe. Je suis désespéré, moi l'Européen, j'aime encore tout ce qui fut et qui s'en va'.

[2] Drieu La Rochelle, *Notes pour comprendre le siècle* (Gallimard, 1941), p. 112.

[3] Drieu La Rochelle, *op. cit.,* p. 50: 'L' Église catholique à partir du XVIᵉ siècle perd le sens de la grande création spirituelle en Europe, et toute véritable initiative'.

[4] Drieu La Rochelle, *Gilles* (Livre de poche, 1962), p. 407. Édition originale, 1939.

[5] Drieu La Rochelle, 'La Suite dans les idées', *Écrits de jeunesse,* p. 168.

[6] Drieu La Rochelle, *Le Français d'Europe* (Éditions Balzac, 1944), p. 217.

[7] Drieu La Rochelle, *Une Femme à sa fenêtre* (Gallimard, 1930), p. 286.

[8] Drieu La Rochelle, *op. cit.,* p. 144.

[9] Drieu La Rochelle, *op. cit.,* p. 169.

[10] Drieu La Rochelle, *op. cit.,* p. 263.

[11] Drieu La Rochelle, *Blèche* (Gallimard, 1928), p. 22.

[12] See Ramon Fernandez, 'Plainte contre inconnu', *N.R.F.* (January 1925), pp. 104–6.

[13] See Jean Bernier, 'Les Livres', *Clarté* (1 November, 1924), pp. 455–7.

[14] Jean Bernier, pp. 455–6, p. 457.

[15] Drieu Rochelle, *Plainte contre inconnu* (Gallimard, 1924), p. 13.

[16] In his preface to *Écrits de jeunesse* (p. 7) Drieu, writing of 'La Valise vide', reported—and we would agree—that it was 'la seule qui y fut lue et qui y est peut-être encore lisible'.

[17] See Frédéric Grover, *Drieu La Rochelle and the fiction of testimony* (Berkeley: University of California Press, 1958), p. 89.

[18] Drieu La Rochelle, 'Malraux, l'homme nouveau', *N.R.F.* (December 1930), p. 884.

[19] Drieu La Rochelle, *Le Jeune Européen* (Gallimard, 1927), p. 80. See also *Socialisme Fasciste* (Gallimard, 1934), p. 244.

[20] The expression is Bernard Frank's: *La Panoplie littéraire* (Julliard, 1958).

[21] Drieu La Rochelle, *Plainte contre inconnu*, pp. 52–4.

[22] Drieu La Rochelle, *op. cit.*, pp. 56–7.

[23] Drieu La Rochelle, *op. cit.*, p. 58.

[24] Drieu La Rochelle, *op. cit.*, p. 67.

[25] Drieu La Rochelle, *op. cit.*, p. 92.

[26] See Drieu's preface (p. 37) to D. H. Lawrence, *L'Homme qui était mort* (Gallimard, 1933).

[27] Drieu La Rochelle, *Plainte contre inconnu*, p. 118.

[28] Drieu La Rochelle, *op. cit.*, p. 118.

[29] In a letter to Marcel Arland on 9 January 1932, Drieu wrote: 'j'ai écrit *Le Feu follet* tout d'une traite, pour me débarrasser d'un poids, en passant par le chemin où l'homme était passé avec son poids qui était aussi le mien. Aucune des péripéties n'est textuelle mais elle s'est présentée à moi dès l'abord avec toutes les autres comme typique d'une série de faits cruellement inscrits en moi'. Quoted in Frédéric Grover, *Drieu La Rochelle* (Gallimard, 1962), p. 38.

[30] Drieu La Rochelle, *Le Feu follet* (Gallimard, 1963), p. 126. Édition originale, 1931.

[31] Drieu La Rochelle, *op. cit.*, p. 102.

[32] Drieu La Rochelle, *op. cit.*, pp. 103–5.

[33] Drieu La Rochelle, *op. cit.*, p. 41.

[34] Drieu La Rochelle, *op. cit.*, p. 49.

[35] Drieu La Rochelle, *op. cit.*, p. 50.

[36] Drieu La Rochelle, *op. cit.*, pp. 51–2.

[37] Drieu La Rochelle, *op. cit.*, p. 57.

[38] Drieu La Rochelle, *op. cit.*, p. 137: 'nous avons le risque dans le sang'.

[39] Drieu La Rochelle, *op. cit.*, p. 138.

[40] Drieu La Rochelle, ibid.

[41] Drieu La Rochelle, *op. cit.*, p. 110.

[42] Drieu La Rochelle, *op. cit.*, p. 160.

[43] Drieu La Rochelle, *op. cit.*, p. 165.

[44] Drieu La Rochelle, *op. cit.*, p. 176.

[45] Drieu La Rochelle, *op. cit.*, p. 178.

[46] Drieu La Rochelle, *op. cit.*, p. 192.

[47] Drieu La Rochelle, *op. cit.*, p. 177.

[48] e.g. André Malraux, *Les Conquérants* (Livre de poche, 1973), p. 264: 'pas de force, même pas de *vraie vie* sans la certitude, sans la hantise de la vanité du monde'. *La Voie royale* (Livre de poche, 1973), p. 109: 'vous ne connaissez pas l'exaltation qui sort de l'absurdité de la vie, lorsqu'on est en face d'elle'.

[49] Emmanuel Mounier, 'Malraux ou l'impossible déchéance', *Esprit* (October 1948), p. 479.

[50] Drieu La Rochelle, *Écrits de jeunesse*, p. 204.

[51] Drieu himself was married and divorced twice, and in each case to a very rich woman. Frédéric Grover, in his *Drieu La Rochelle* (Gallimard, 1962) pp. 33–9, gives a brief but interesting account of the 'riche Drieu', his love affairs

and disappointments. Many of the experiences of this period of his life are reflected in the novels.

52 Drieu La Rochelle, *L'Homme couvert de femmes* (Gallimard, 1925), pp. 84–5.
53 Drieu La Rochelle, *op. cit.*, p. 63.
54 Drieu La Rochelle, *op. cit.*, p. 189.
55 Drieu La Rochelle, *op. cit.*, pp. 192–3.
56 Drieu La Rochelle, *op. cit.*, pp. 194–5.
57 Drieu La Rochelle, *op. cit.*, p. 209.
58 Drieu La Rochelle, *op. cit.*, p. 56: 'le lit, et cette reconnaissance du ventre qui dure quelques minutes tout de même, un peu de camaraderie encore. C'est tout ce qu'on peut souhaiter, et ça peut être très suffisant. Je crois bien que je n'ai besoin de rien d'autre. D'abord il n'y a rien d'autre' (Finette).
59 Drieu La Rochelle, *op. cit.*, p. 198.
60 Marcel Arland, 'Sur un nouveau mal du siècle', *N.R.F.* (February 1924), pp. 149–58.
61 Marcel Arland, p. 155: 'vers l'absolue sincérité, voilà de quel côté s'orienteront sans doute les quatre ou cinq individus, qui suffisent pour représenter, sinon exprimer une génération'.
62 Drieu La Rochelle, *Drôle de voyage* (Gallimard, 1933), p. 20.
63 Drieu's works abound in references to the strength and vitality of the Middle Ages: e.g. *Notes pour comprendre le siècle*, p. 28: 'l'Europe tient au Moyen Âge comme l'être mûr tient à sa jeunesse. Tout ce qu'elle a de dru vient de là'. See also Maurice Martin du Gard, *Les Mémorables,* Vol. II (Flammarion, 1960), p. 316: 'Drieu regrette notre jeunesse, le temps de l'armistice, lorsqu'il pensait comme moi que nous nous aimerions tous, que la France remporterait une nouvelle victoire, sur elle-même cette fois-ci. Il l'imaginait prise en charge par des gens de la Renaissance, du Moyen Âge, très intelligents, poètes, joueurs de rugby, pères de familles nombreuses et en plus constructeurs de cathédrales'.
64 Drieu La Rochelle, *Drôle de voyage,* p. 19 and p. 156.
65 Drieu La Rochelle, *op. cit.*, p. 309.
66 Drieu La Rochelle, *Béloukia* (Gallimard, 1936), p. 218.
67 Drieu La Rochelle, *Socialisme Fasciste* (Gallimard, 1934), p. 111.
68 e.g. *L'Émancipation nationale* (5 August, 1934): 'l'homme est fait d'un corps et d'une âme. Il ne peut rien que dans l'accord de ces deux éléments. Si le corps est négligé, l'âme s'étiole bientôt, si l'âme est négligé le corps n'est qu'un amas des esprits animaux voués à l'anarchie et à la dissolution rapide'.
69 *L'Émancipation nationale* (14 November, 1936). See also *L'Émancipation nationale* (27 August, 1937): 'Doriot le bon athlète, devant la France, ce n'est pas un gros intellectuel ventripotent de l'autre siècle qui regarde sa 'mère' malade en fumant sa bouffarde radicale, c'est un athlète qui étreint ce corps débilité et qui lui insuffle la santé dont il est plein'.
70 *Le Fait* (7 December, 1940).
71 Drieu La Rochelle, *Le Français d'Europe* (Éditions Balzac, 1944), p. 211.

CHAPTER VIII

Malraux: The New Man

Pour détruire Dieu, et après l'avoir détruit, l'esprit européen a anéanti tout ce qui pouvait s'opposer à l'homme: parvenu au terme de ses efforts ... il ne trouve que la mort.

(*La Tentation de l'Occident*)

Malraux's *La Tentation de l'Occident* and 'D'une jeunesse européenne' were the attempt to reveal the tragedy of modern man. Rejected by history and confronted with proof, through the discovery of dead civilizations, of the annihilation that awaits all his efforts, he stands alone and disarmed, trapped between the arbitrariness of the external world and the inner chaos of the self. Dead as Christian and dead as humanist this ghostly derivative of dead realities has nothing to which to relate himself except death itself.[1] He does, however, have a choice: to sit amid the ruins, being nothing, remaining nothing and quietly waiting for death, or, gambling his mortality on 'une grande action quelconque', to *actualize* his metaphysical situation in order, hopefully, to give some meaning to his existence. He chooses the latter for if it is a despairing gamble it is the only *authentic* possibility in a world where death is now the defining reality.

We recall that Ling and Wang-loh had prophesied the death of Old China (and the birth of a new and violent one) as a result of the destructive impact of Western values, especially that of individualism. A.D. had expounded the bankruptcy, in the West, of the same individualism now a prey to the Absurd. At the same time there was the suggestion of a New Man to come who would live fiercely and experimentally by relating to his one remaining value: his immediate awareness of himself as 'intensity'. *Les Conquérants*, in which abstract musings have given way to a concrete presentation in novel form of the same drama, confirms these prognostications and sets the scene for Malraux's New Man's first metaphysical adventure.

Although we do not meet Garine until well into the novel we are provided fairly early on with a portrait of him by the narrator. We learn that he is, above all, a creature in pursuit of the most efficient use of force.[2] As a young man he frequented anarchist circles looking for a 'temps de troubles' in which to release his energies.[3] It was at this time that the first truly decisive event in his life took place. He was convicted of financing a number of abortions. His trial impressed him as a grotesque, unreal farce in which 'les faits en cause et cette cérémonie'[4] seemed strangely unrelated and during which he was overcome by a 'sentiment d'impuissance navrante, de mépris et de dégoût'.[5] The effect of this monstrous ceremony, which was an affront to his will,[6] was to convince him not so much of the injustices as of the irremediable absurdity of the social order[7]—a view that was soon applied to all things human.[8] Revulsion at the very idea of participating, even externally, in a society from which he felt himself to be alienated drove him into the Foreign Legion which he deserted, however, after a year of enforced inaction.[9] After coming into contact with a group of Bolshevik émigrés in Zurich, he managed—despite his indifference to revolutionary discipline and doctrine—to get the International to send him to China, where he has now risen to the post of head of propaganda in Canton.[10]

Referring to the slogans of the Chinese Revolution as democratic gibberish Garine nonetheless immerses himself in revolutionary activity in an effort to determine the flow of power. Only a sense of power, he feels, can free him from the 'human condition' and make him the adversary of a world that would appear to have every chance of crushing him in the end.[11] He is aware of the risk but regards himself as a 'gambler' and like all gamblers he thinks only of gambling, stubbornly and passionately.[12]

The Chinese Revolution, then, is not so much the subject of the novel as the pretext and the setting for Garine's personal drama, while of course it also helps to unify the material as a whole. However, to the extent that it was an actual historical event, Malraux obviously had to provide political 'local colour'. This he does by politicizing his metaphysical creatures: Hong is thus at once death-dominated individual (the tortured consciousness of a 'dead' China) and an anarchist,[13] whilst Tcheng-Daï is both the incarnation of the meditative tradition of Old China

226

(Wang-loh transposed) and the leader of the right-wing of the Kuomintang. The illusion of political specificity is further encouraged by the inclusion of Michael Borodin who, like 'General' Galen, is a real historical figure: the Comintern's political adviser to the Canton government. His 'satellite' characters, Klein and Nicolaieff, constitute an allied force. Indeed, such is their plausibility as active associates or political symbol that none other than Trotsky was persuaded to describe them as typical representatives of Stalinist bureaucracy.[14]

Even the metaphysical Garine has his political side—not merely by virtue of his function as head of propaganda but also, to some extent, in his motives for joining the revolution. For if driven by metaphysical anguish and a will-to-power he is driven also by his disgust and hatred of the social class to which he belongs.[15] Whence, of course, the irony that whatever his subjective intentions this metaphysical pessimist is participating in history, in the very social organization he rejects. This contradiction, which is Malraux's own, has its origins not so much in *Les Conquérants* as in the intellectual and moral adventure which precedes it: in *La Tentation de l'Occident* and 'D'une jeunesse européenne'. There, writing in the immediate historical context of post-war Europe, Malraux has placed Europe (and the East) under the sign of Death. As a result, he has not only universalized a 'private experience of estrangement into the alienation of Man the Absurd'[16] but given a metaphysical twist to the disarray of a social system, which, having just demonstrated bloodily the bankruptcy of its humanist tradition, was now revealing its apparent inability to find alternative values. Through Garine, fleeing a 'dead Europe' *and* a bankrupt social order, Malraux has given this sense of disarray not only metaphysical projection but political definition as well. In a sense he could hardly fail to have done so since his metaphysical outlook is itself based on an intimate if unconscious association with a real historical impasse.[17] Whence the contradiction, or irony, attendant upon Garine's activity. Garine 'gets involved in history'[18] because his creator's anxieties still reside there; Garine's metaphysical pessimism is the *product* of historical despair (Malraux's) just as his political activism, which returns him to history, is the product of metaphysical pessimism. He cannot break the vicious circle because a 'metaphysical alibi' prevents him from committing

227

himself to history—the source of his anguish—and, through it, to a *future* which is already coming to birth in the movement he has joined but from which he feels alienated. Emmanuel Berl, writing in his *Mort de la pensée bourgeoise* (1929), has characterized the dilemma—metaphysics excluded—in the following terms:

> L'intellectuel tend vers le communisme parce qu'il sent sur la bourgeoisie l'odeur de la mort et que la tyrannie capitaliste l'exaspère ... Mais l'ouvrier ne nous demande pas la disqualification du capitalisme: il nous demande la qualification du communisme et c'est ce que nous ne pouvons pas lui donner. Il ne se contente pas d'une critique: il exige une espérance ... que nous ne pouvons partager. Nous savons trop que le communisme n'est pas autre chose qu'un capitalisme aggravé. Nous le voyons déjà pourri, déjà parlementaire, déjà militariste. Il réclame de nous ... un optimisme sur la valeur des machines qu'aucun esprit consciencieux ne peut actuellement garder.[19]

If one were not constantly reminded of Garine's metaphysical problem one might, with Berl's description in mind, be tempted to describe Garine (despite the narrator's protestations)[20] as little more than an anarchist. Garine's contradiction—between being at once metaphysical pessimist and political activist—is resolved, artistically at least, by his being inscribed within a revolutionary situation which is itself ordered in accordance with his own hopeless estrangement. Thus, if Garine is driven by a 'passion born of despair'[21] so too is the revolutionary movement of which he is the leading propagandist. Malraux has done more than give his metaphysical hero artistic projection, he has placed *historical* China in the grip of a death-dominated impulse—something which he had of course already done in *La Tentation de l'Occident*. Tcheng-Daï is thus, despite the political veneer and Gandhist associations,[22] the Moral Force of old China, Confucianism in its death-agony, while Hong is the tortured, mythless derivative of this dying authority.

If the dramatization of metaphysical disintegration seems a far cry from genuine historical movement, there is, nonetheless, a sense in which this disturbing image of a decaying China is perfectly valid, as may be gathered from the fact that one of the prime targets of Mao-tse-Tung's cultural revolution was the vestigial structure of Confucianism. (Mao pointed out at the time—as had Lenin before him—that ideas can linger on in a socialist society long after the objective social factors which gave rise to them cease to exist.) And so, however unlikely it might at first appear, Malraux has effectively dramatized a 'real' aspect of the Chinese situation. The precise nature of that 'reality', already apparent from Malraux's preoccupation—in *La Tentation de l'Occident* and 'D'une jeunesse européenne'—with the death of ideals, is the *disintegration* of an *ideological* form[23] (in this case Confucianism). Such a vision might well qualify Malraux as a 'myth-maker of some size and suggestiveness',[24] but it is equally true that in his morbid fascination with things dying and dead Malraux is effectively ignoring the vital character of what in *political* terms is *coming to birth*. In short, a social and political movement which produced Mao-tse-Tung and Chou En-lai (not to mention Chiang Kai-shek) seems wildly out of place under the banner of death-dominated individualism.

Garine's success in transforming the propaganda office, which was entrusted to him more or less by chance, into one of the main centres of revolutionary action is the result of a strategy based not on revolutionary politics but on a private intuition: the discovery that 'toute l'Asie moderne est dans le sentiment de la vie individuelle, dans la découverte de la mort'.[25] It is this new awareness, brought to fever pitch by Garine (and ignored by Borodine, the professional revolutionary),[26] which is seen as the very driving force of the revolution. The poor have begun to discover that they *exist*, simply that they exist.[27] This discovery, Garine explains, has brought them face to face with the hopelessness of their condition and convinced them that a 'new life' has nothing to offer them, since with this new life, purchased at the expense of Chinese belief, has been born the new idea of a death which involves nothing, neither compensation nor atonement.[28] At the same time, however, they have seized upon the desperate hope that each man has it in his power to overcome the collective life of suffering and to 'parvenir à cette vie particulière, individuelle, qu'ils tiennent confusément pour le bien le plus précieux des riches'.[29] By encouraging the masses to affirm their existence *qua* individual, Garine has sought not only to consummate their rupture with the old ideal of self-effacement, of deference to Being, but to harness their *new* lives to the revolution: 'ce qu'il faut, c'est que chaque homme sente que sa vie est liée à la Révolution, qu'elle perdra sa valeur si nous sommes battus, qu'elle redeviendra une loque'.[30]

Standing between Garine and the masses is Tcheng-Daï, the prestigious representative of Chinese tradition and dedicated opponent of violence. Preaching a universal principle that transcends life and individual authenticity, he denies not only the value of action but the very right of China *to exist in the world*.[31] His living antithesis is Hong, the moralist of violence and terrorist assassination.[32] Animated by an all-inclusive hatred, born of misery and hopelessness, he states his philosophy in fourteen staccato words: 'tout état social est une saloperie. Sa vie unique. Ne pas la perdre, voilà!'[33] The man whose teaching has produced Hong and many of his kind is Rebecci,[34] symbol of European influence, but symbol also of Europe's ultimate futility. Reduced to selling cheap junk in a Saigon shop where he idles his life away in empty talk, he embodies one of the principle dangers that permanently threaten the 'European conqueror'. Like Grabot in *La Voie royale*, he has become 'Nothing'.[35]

From Rebecci, his European mentor, Hong has learned that he has been granted one life and one only.[36] That this single, fleeting life should be vitiated by poverty and injustice enrages him. In torture and terrorist assassination he has discovered the only means of answering all those, like Tcheng-Daï, who would deny him his life and oblige him to *accept*:[37]

> 'Il n'y a que deux races, dit-il, les mi-sé-ra-bles et les autres' . . . 'Un pauvre, dit-il encore, ne peut pas s'estimer'. *Cela, il l'accepterait s'il pensait avec ses ancêtres que son existence n'est pas limitée au cours de sa vie particulière*. Mais, attaché au présent de toute la force que lui donne sa découverte de la mort, il n'accepte plus, ne cherche plus, ne discute plus; il hait.[38]

Like Garine, for whom the trans-individual and individual realities of God and Man are dead, Hong has been deprived, by his European conquerors, of the trans-individual reality of the transmigration of souls. Finding no individual reality with which to fill this void he is forced into the world with nothing to guide him except his own urgent and exclusive desire to possess mortality. He is, in effect, Garine's Asian homologue. And yet, unlike Garine, whose existence derives a meaning, however precarious or fleeting, from revolutionary efficiency, Hong cares nothing for the revolution. Neither does he recognize any value that supersedes him:

> Il ne veut point abandonner, au bénéfice d'un avenir incertain, sa haine présente. Il parle avec rage de ceux qui oublient que la vie est unique, et proposent aux hommes de se sacrifier pour leurs enfants.[39]

Because of his taste for murder Hong threatens the revolution and so become Garine's enemy.[40] And yet, despite their being enemies, both characters are marked by a common determination: to affirm themselves as individuals in opposition to death. Hong, like Garine—like the revolutionary situation itself—is governed, therefore, not by the *political* realities of China in the mid-twenties but by an idea (born of *La Tentation de l'Occident* and 'D'une jeunesse européenne') which Malraux has superimposed upon the world: his own very 'European' idea of Destiny, or, to adapt a term from Emmanuel Berl, an idea conditioned by the death of bourgeois *ideology*.

The European metaphysical drama which Malraux is concerned to project is brought out sharply in Garine's attitude to the aims of revolution. Unlike the orthodox revolutionary, who is seeking in revolutionary action the transformation of a social system, Garine retains of this ambition only the action it permits in the present. In other words, for Garine revolutionary action is not a means to the all-important end but the all-consuming, self-sufficient means itself. Attached to the revolution as a 'state of things',[41] he has nothing but contempt for considerations of doctrinal discipline. At one point he angrily declaims that he did not throw Europe into a corner like a pile of rags and take the risk of ending up like some Rebecci only to teach people obedience, or to learn it himself.[42] Of Borodine, 'dominé par l'insupportable mentalité bolchevique', he remarks disdainfully that his aim is to manufacture revolutionaries in the same way Ford manufactures cars.[43] As for the 'pauvres gens' in whose name the revolution is being fought Garine willingly admits that in his eyes they will become objects of contempt as soon as victory has been achieved.[44] His unorthodoxy makes him an expendable commodity. He knows that the cause which he has adopted whilst refusing to comply with its demands for observance of collective discipline must finally reject him. It can have no place for 'celui qui veut d'abord être lui-même, enfin, exister séparé des autres'.[45] As an individualist he is only temporarily useful, for individualism is a 'bourgeois malady'.[46] However, this was a risk he had accepted when gambling on action and 'puissance'.

Garine's sense of power is greatest when he has paralysed a city—the very symbol of social order—and made of it a 'clenched fist' for the whole world to see. At the very same moment, however, he has connived at his own defeat. For by paralysing Hong Kong he has made victory possible for the revolution, and with revolutionary success revolutionary action ceases and social order, in another form, is restored. For one convinced of the absurdity of social order *in any guise*, this restoration of order— to which he, above all others, will have contributed—is defeat in its most ironic form. Consequently, the nearer to victory the insurrectionists move, the greater becomes his sense of defeat.[47] His only possible escape from the absurdity he himself will have created will be to instigate a revolution against the revolution. The real irony of Garine's situation is that although he has abandoned Europe and, indeed, chosen a course of action directly opposed to its designs he has, by virtue of this choice, become part of a movement conducted in terms of that distinctively European Marxist outlook which he has rejected along with the rest of nineteenth-century 'rubbish'.

The more committed Garine is to the pursuit of will-in-action the more *authentic* his life becomes, so much so that the more he *exists* the less he *thinks*, of illness, failure and death. At the moment of action, he is all will, all consciousness moving onwards, all-conquering purpose, to the necessity to be achieved. However, if activity in the service of 'puissance' allows him to escape absurdity's hold, illness disarms him and brings him back to himself, to his trial and to death.[48] At such moments he doubts the value of his presence in Canton, of his whole life. One such moment—and the signal for his decline—comes with the discovery of the mutilated corpses of Klein and his companions. All Garine's hopes now avail him nothing and the meagre fruits of his labour lie in the shocking realization of the futility of all his efforts: 'qu'ai-je fait de ma vie, moi? Mais, bon Dieu, que peut-on en faire, à la fin'.[49] When, some time later, he shoots the

232

well-poisoner in an attempt to re-establish contact with the world of action, he knows that he is finished. Sick and delirious, with his trial returning to haunt him and death threatening to plunge him back into that same nothingness which action had enabled him to escape, he expresses his intention of going to England to join the cause of British imperialism—the very power he has been fighting: 'Maintenant je sais ce qu'est l'Empire. Une tenace, une constante violence. Diriger. Déterminer. Contraindre. La vie est là'.[50] Although it is clear that Garine is only trying to convince himself that his energies and abilities are still active forces, he would, of course, be just as much at home (or equally out of place) in the imperialist camp. For the simple fact is that *no cause* can satisfy the alienated Garine, for whom the will to power expressed in these three verbs can have no constructive principle, neither imperialist nor socialist.

Garine's quest for meaning through self-affirmation has resulted in personal defeat. The 'conqueror' who had temporarily detected a glimmer of hope in the bond of virile fraternity established in a common struggle and whose only value lay in not being conquered, stands alone and conquered. His consciousness of death, dominated until now by action and a sense of life, is reactivated, and his life and action now seem, retroactively, to lose all value.

Since Garine makes no secret of his personal reasons for joining the revolution it is only to be expected that some critics should have questioned his authenticity as a revolutionary. Trotsky was one of the most severe of these.[51] Interpreting *Les Conquérants* as a 'fictional chronicle' of the first period of the Chinese Revolution, he accuses Garine of being a 'révolutionnaire qui méprise la doctrine révolutionnaire', labels him a 'dilettante et vedette de passage', and suggests that a substantial inoculation of Marxism would have done his creator a great deal of good. He goes further and, ignoring (as we do) the properly literary structure of the work, accuses the International of pursuing a policy of class-collaboration in China.

Malraux's reply to Trotsky, published in April 1931,[52] operates on two different levels. In the first place he makes the point that Trotsky knows little of artistic creation. Stressing that novels, like revolutions, do not make themselves, he states that *Les Conquérants* is not a 'fictional chronicle' of the Chinese Revolution if only because the main emphasis has been placed on the relation between *individuals and a collective action*, not on collective action alone. In other words, *Les Conquérants* is not a fictionalized document but a novel dominated by a novelistic vision, by 'reality' as perceived by characters in the novel. In this way Malraux answers Trotsky's objections to Borodine who, though a bureaucrat from Trotsky's point of view, appears as a professional revolutionary to Garine and his followers. In short, to Trotsky, who is looking for a revolution (and its betrayal) and the author's personal affidavit, Malraux replies with a reference to the conditions of fiction and the viewpoint of the novel. However, doubtless aware that 'reality' as perceived by the characters of the novel is itself *ordered* by the novelist, Malraux offers his own assessment of *Les Conquérants*. He states that it is not intended as 'une apologie de la révolution' but as a portrayal of 'man's condition': 'ce livre est d'abord une accusation de la condition humaine'. He had already made this point when, in an article published in 1930, he wrote: 'les révolutionnaires ont cru que j'avais eu l'intention de peindre la Révolution chinoise. Ce n'est pas du tout ce que je voulais faire'.[53] And, one year earlier, in a debate inspired by the publication of *Les Conquérants*, he stated quite categorically that the fundamental question facing Garine was to know how to escape the Absurd not how to participate in a revolution.[54]

Escape from the Absurd is, as we have already seen, attempted through action, which is itself challenged by the ever-threatening intrusion of death. The real subject of *Les Conquérants* is, therefore, as Malraux has written, the 'fundamental solitude of Man in the face of death'.[55] The 'Man' in question is Garine, the mythless derivative of a 'dead Europe'. However, it could be argued that Garine's metaphysical adventure is Malraux's own *rationalization* of the disorder of a social and political order to which he can no longer relate himself—in which case Garine appears not as 'Man' (the twentieth-century version of Pascal's 'roseau pensant') but as the 'faithless' (anarchistic) derivative of a bankrupt society. His activity in Asia is not beyond such an interpretation, for as surely as it is *not* governed by a determination to establish a new social order, it is most certainly an expression of his rupture with the old.

The second part of Malraux's reply to Trotsky is, in effect, a defence of the International's policy in China. His central point is that the Chinese Communist Party's only alternative to fusion with the Kuomintang was disappearance. Since the Communists were beaten when they had their own army they would surely have been beaten, Malraux argues, when they were still without one. In other words, Malraux supports the (not unreasonable) view that an objective assessment of the balance of forces in China called for a *defensive* tactic of the kind carried out by the International at the time the events described by *Les Conquérants* took place. Trotsky was unhampered by such concerns. He advocated an *offensive* policy, not because it promised victory in itself, but because it held within it the *possibility* of sparking off the proletarian revolution in Europe, without which victory could not be permanent and socialism not possible at all.

The significant thing about Malraux's reply to the political problems posed by Trotsky was not that he defended the policy of the International but that this defence was punctuated with examples drawn from *Les Conquérants*. In other words Malraux was doing the very thing for which he had criticized Trotsky— presenting *Les Conquérants* as a kind of document of the Chinese Revolution. Malraux's ambivalence derives, as we have already suggested, from the fact that his metaphysical outlook is the (unconscious) product of historical despair, the rationalization of an ideological impasse. In *La Tentation de l'Occident* and 'D'une jeunesse européenne', history, as social and political movement, was present in Malraux's analysis only in repressed (ideological) form (the death of ideals); in *Les Conquérants*, based on a real historical event, history is forced back into consciousness, but now associated with death it is unable to win Garine for its *future*.

Malraux's ambivalence *vis-à-vis* his creation began to appear in 1929 with the publication of 'La Question des *Conquérants*'. Here, whilst stressing the metaphysical value of his New Man's rebellious spirit, he also tried to defend his hero's revolutionary sincerity.[56] In view of the very complexity of Garine's response Malraux's claims were not wholly untenable. Despite his unorthodoxy Garine clearly emerges in a better light than does Borodine, the professional revolutionary, who looks upon the proletariat less as human beings than as the means to an end.[57] Garine does at least realize that the struggle is conducted by men, with men, for men. If he is aware of having become an instrument of the 'machine' he is equally conscious of having served the people, of having created their hope.[58] Whilst freely admitting to Tcheng-Daï that he has no

235

particular love of those in whose name he is fighting, this does not prevent him from taking their side against an imperialist order which he clearly despises. At one stage he asks Tcheng-Daï to consider whether a child would prefer to have a nurse who loves him but lets him drown or one who does not love him but is able to swim.[59] Although an individualist with personal likes and dislikes he does, nonetheless—claims Malraux— '[mettre] ce qu'il possède d'individualisme au service d'un anti-individualisme . . . [mettre] en jeu sa vie pour une cause à laquelle il adhère plus ou moins parfaitement'.[60] The Marxist may regret Garine's antipathy for Marxism but can hardly deny that he is engaged on the right side.

Malraux's defence of 'Garine the revolutionary' left him in a somewhat curious position. He found himself not only defending a point of view which he had not intended Garine to represent in the first place, but discovered that in so doing he was undermining the real metaphysical significance of his character. Moreover, his defence only served to confirm the impression already left by Garine: that his essentially individual, metaphysical adventure had from the very outset been compromised by his involvement in a collective political movement.

That Malraux wished to avoid a repetition of the confusion left by the ambiguous Garine is evidenced by his choice, for *La Voie royale*, of a purely individual action itself created by the hero. However, before moving on to *La Voie royale*, one or two points have to be clarified. It is, today, a common practice for critics to consider *La Voie royale* before *Les Conquérants*, for a number of reasons. *La Voie royale* would seem logically to precede *Les Conquérants*, since it is the literary transposition of Malraux's first experience in the East—his archaeological expedition to Cambodia in 1923. In other words, to consider it first is to re-establish the correct chronology of events in Malraux's life, and at the same time to effect a smoother transition from *Les Conquérants* to *La Condition humaine*—Malraux's novels of revolution.

Our first objection to such arguments is to ask what right the critic has to re-establish chronology and impose logicality. To do so is to demand that Malraux should have written in the first place to accommodate the critic's passion for chronology. If there is a concern for logical development, let it be the writer's own and not the invention of the critic. Malraux *was* concerned with a certain pattern of development, and this pattern emerges from work to work rather than from his or our observance of a chronology of events in his personal life. If *La Voie royale* should, chronologically speaking, precede *Les Conquérants*, then *Les Conquérants*, logically speaking succeeds *La Tentation de l'Occident*, itself written in 1926. Secondly, a novel based—in external terms—upon a historical event is certain to inspire more public interest, and, consequently to have a greater sales potential if published as near to the actual event as possible. The importance of *actualité* was certainly not unknown to Malraux. *L'Espoir* and *Les Noyers de l'Altenburg*, based respectively on the Spanish Civil War and World War II, were both published whilst these wars were still going on. If nothing else, this observation does at least suggest that Malraux was more concerned with situating his metaphysical dramas in 'great actions' than in personal adventures. To invert the order of *Les Conquérants* and *La Voie royale* is to ignore this fact. Thirdly, as we have already suggested, *La Voie royale* is Malraux's attempt to clarify his position after the confusion left by his ambiguous 'aventurier-révolutionnaire'. Finally, although one could undoubtedly argue that had *La Voie royale* been written before *Les Conquérants*, the first three novels could be said to assume a more logical order, one would then be obliged to ignore the logical progression from *La Tentation de l'Occident* to *Les Conquérants*. In any case, since Malraux has himself written that '*La Voie royale* a été écrite après *Les Conquérants*',[61] we shall respect the traditional order.

LA VOIE ROYALE

The European's search for an identity continues in *La Voie royale*, where the revolutionary world of China finds its metaphysical equivalent in the jungle world of Cambodia and where the hero's obsession with absurdity here focuses on death. Claude and Perken are both obsessed with death.[62] No less than the hero of *Les Conquérants*, the two adventurers of *La Voie royale* are gamblers who stake their all on a willed confrontation with the forces that would destroy them. As Malraux commented in an interview with *Candide* in 1930:

> Disons que l'aventure est l'obsession de la mort . . . [l'aventurier]
> se fuit lui-même, c'est-à-dire qu'il fuit sa hantise de la mort en
> même temps qu'il court vers elle.[63]

Not so much Heidegger's 'beings-for-death', they are, in Malraux's estimation, beings 'contre la mort'.[64] Their adventure is thus far less the search for art treasures than the expression of a determination to overcome the nothingness of their condition: 'la vie de poussière des hommes'.[65] Perken has no illusions as to the ultimate effectiveness of his action, but realizes that if life is simply 'une matière' there are several ways of making nothing of it.[66] More positively, his willingness to 'jouer contre la mort' is the extreme form of his quest for 'authenticity', for in a world of appearance death stands as the only defining reality.

On a ship out of Djibouti, Claude meets Perken who is returning to Indo-China after his failure in the West to obtain funds for the guns with which he had hoped to arm the tribesmen of his private kingdom in the interior. Claude, who is hoping to unearth art treasures in the Cambodian forest, persuades Perken to join him in exchange for half the profits. With his share of the profits Perken will buy the guns he needs and so realize his ambition of leaving a 'scar on the map'[67]—an armed enclave opposed to the Kingdom of Siam and to the territory administered by the French. As in the case of Garine there is a more private and obsessional side to Perken's historical action: the attempt to overcome the threat of nothingness and death. He does not fear the prospect of disappearing suddenly and forever but he is haunted and terrified by the death that grows within him, slowly, like a cancer[68]—in short, by the process of ageing, which, of course, he is powerless to reverse:

> La vraie mort, c'est la déchéance . . . Vieillir . . . accepter son destin, sa fonction, la niche à chien élevée sur sa vie unique . . . Vous ne savez pas ce que c'est que le destin limité, irréfutable, qui tombe sur vous comme un règlement sur un prisonnier: la certitude que vous serez cela et pas autre chose, que vous *aurez été* cela et pas autre chose, que ce que vous n'avez pas eu, vous ne l'aurez jamais.[69]

The fullest expression of Perken's sense of solidarity is the keen hope that his companion die early, and so escape the corrosive power of ageing.[70] Since for Perken the one sin is acceptance he must resist every sign of age and elect the course which will let him show that his decline has not yet begun. The pursuit of the erotic, less for pleasure than as an integral part of the general ethic of will, is one such course. Eroticism brings him on a limited level what action brings him on a broader, more essential level: the consciousness of existing and the possibility, however precarious or fleeting, of escaping his sense of impotence and nothingness.[71] Passivity, on the other hand, whether sexual or historical, brings him back to himself, back to the nagging nothingness of that subconscious world of dream, memory and aspiration which the conscious application of will in action allows him to escape.[72] The impossible dimensions of this aspiration may be gathered from his own assessment of the forces that would constrain him:

> Exister contre tout cela (Perken montrait du regard la menaçante majesté de la nuit), vous comprenez ce que cela veut dire? Exister contre la mort, c'est la même chose.[73]

Defiance of the forces of negation begins with the adventurers' first steps into the Cambodian forest—a domain where the formless powers of the natural world attack even the mind:

> L'unité de la forêt, maintenant, s'imposait; depuis six jours Claude avait renoncé à séparer les êtres des formes, la vie qui bouge de la vie qui suinte; une puissance inconnue liait aux arbres les fongosités, faisait grouiller toutes ces choses provisoires sur un sol semblable à l'écume des marais, dans ces bois fumants de commencement du monde. Quel acte humain, ici, avait un sens? Quelle volonté conservait sa force? Tout se ramifiait, s'amollissait, s'efforçait de s'accorder à ce monde ignoble et attirant à la fois comme le regard des idiots, et qui attaquait les nerfs avec la même puissance abjecte que ces araignées suspendues entre les branches, dont il avait eu d'abord tant de peine à détourner les yeux.[74]

Claude is confronted by something alien, something which exists *in its own right* and which cannot be disposed of by any reduction. That consciousness which sets him apart from matter, gives pattern to the world and meaning to objects has no shaping powers here. Things resist. More than that they attack with all the destructive power they can muster:

> Le mur traversait la végétation comme un chemin, mais sous une mousse gluante. La chute, si Claude voulait marcher, était d'un

239

extrême danger: la gangrène est aussi maîtresse de la forêt que l'insecte.[75]

As he wriggles his way along the temple façade his every movement becomes a victory over crawling, stinging forms, a victory also over his own chattering nerves and quivering flesh.[76] Refusing to accept the dictates of the flesh he drives himself forward only to discover that the temple does not contain the prize he has been looking for.[77] When the stone is finally located it is alive with insects, which, even as they dart for cover, are ready to advance again once the stone has been removed. And yet, for a moment, the forest surrenders its grip and Perken tastes salvation:

> La forêt, la force des lianes et des feuilles spongieuses s'affaiblissaient pourtant: ces pierres conquises le défendaient contre elle. Sa pensée n'était plus là: elle était enchaînée au mouvement qui poussait en avant les charrettes alourdies. Elles s'éloignaient en grinçant, avec un son nouveau, né de leur charge, vers les montagnes prochaines. Il secoua sa manche sur laquelle étaient tombées des fourmis rouges, sauta à cheval et rejoignit le convoi.[78]

After testing the quality of his humanity against crawling things Perken couches his whole enterprise in the language of insect symbol: 'toutes ces saletés d'insectes vont vers notre photophore, soumis à la lumière. Ces termites vivent dans leur termitière, soumis à leur termitière. Je ne veux pas être soumis'.[79] And so, when confronted by a line of warriors ranged behind their chief, Perken no longer sees a wall of human flesh but a viscous mass of insects breeding insect-thoughts.[80]

In the Stieng village Perken finds Grabot, a former acquaintance and fellow adventurer whose philosophy of life has already been made known to us by Perken. In the early part of the novel Grabot is depicted as a sort of masochistic *Ubermensch* whose acts of inner strength include driving a resisting hand on to the sting of a scorpion and blinding himself in one eye with gonorrhoeal pus after being accused of malingering by an army doctor.[81] His relations with eroticism afford a point of contrast with those of Perken for whom the opposite sex, like any human personality, is an object to be dominated, a consciousness to be consciously denied.[82] For Grabot, on the other hand, sexual contact is an opportunity to succumb, and 'pleasure' the imposs-

240

ible desire to possess the wild imaginings that float about his naked, tethered body.[83] And so, whereas Perken's courage, like his eroticism, is allied to his will, Grabot's derives from the attempt to compensate for his acceptance of humiliation.[84] As such his courage is flawed, for surrender is its original source and ever its temptation. His status in the Stieng village reveals just how far he has regressed and stuns Perken, whose expectations were not allied to such a possibility. Grabot has become the slave of the natives and now lives his condition in a cruel parody of his former self: the man who, in a defiant act of will, had blinded himself in one eye has now been blinded in the other by his captors, and the sexual deviant who had allowed women to strap him naked to the bed has now been tethered to a mill wheel which he is forced to turn. When Grabot set out to build an empire of his own he was convinced, like Perken, that in the last resort—when action was spent and 'déchéance' inevitable—he could always commit suicide. Perken had already explained this to Claude:

> Toute ma vie dépend de ce que je pense du geste d'appuyer sur cette gâchette au moment où je suce ce canon. Il s'agit de savoir si je pense: je me détruis, ou: j'agis . . . Pour vivre *d'une certaine façon*, il faut en finir avec ses menaces, la déchéance et les autres: le revolver est alors une bonne garantie, car il est facile de se tuer lorsque la mort est un moyen. C'est là qu'est la force de Grabot.[85]

Grabot's imposture lies specifically in the fact that he had 'willed' to live and die as a conqueror, whereas at the 'moment of truth' he did not have the courage to kill himself. In response to the question—*What* are you?—this blinded derelict answers with an avowal of his revealed truth: 'Rien'.[86] In a paroxysm of revulsion Claude feels tempted to empty his revolver into this dead face, in order to 'chasser cette preuve de sa condition d'homme'.[87]

Claude and Perken free Grabot and take him to their hut. After several hours of extreme tension Perken decides to brave his fate by going out to face the tribesmen. As he stumbles across the compound with an image of his own slaughter and castration fixed in his mind,[88] he suddenly finds himself glued to the spot: 'vaincu par la chair, par les viscères, par tout ce qui peut se révolter contre l'homme. Ce n'était pas la peur, car il savait qu'il continuerait sa marche de taureau. Le destin pouvait donc faire

241

plus que détruire son courage: Grabot était sans doute un double cadavre'.[89] Then the memory of an ancient warrior-chief who had leaped to his death with a battle hymn upon his lips revives him and a sense of power surges through him. In a supreme act of will he throws himself 'sexuellement sur cette liberté à l'agonie'.[90] But at the very height of his power, in full possession of himself, he (like Garine) tastes defeat. He trips and falls upon a bamboo spike planted by the natives and sustains a gangrenous wound to the knee. He is now refused 'the death that consummates', and has instead to await 'the grinning death which creeps up like a thief and yet comes as the master'.[91]

Since for Perken death is something which is happening to his poisoned body he tries to resist it as he had resisted his own flesh when crossing the compound to the natives.[92] And so when both doctors tell him that there is absolutely nothing to be done he feels 'séparé de son corps, de ce corps irresponsable qui voulait l'entraîner dans la mort . . . Il était si étranger à cette mort aux aguets en lui qu'il se sentait de nouveau en face d'un combat: mais le regard de Claude le rejeta dans son corps'.[93] After this experience Perken reads his fate in the gaze of all those about him. Like Garine his rabid desire to deny his 'déchéance' is expressed in the most violent terms—by the murder of those who by their gaze would seal his fate.[94] His first act on learning of his fatal condition is to procure a woman for a last erotic experience only to realize, at the very moment of orgasm, that 'jamais, jamais, il ne connaîtrait les sensations de cette femme, jamais il ne trouverait dans cette frénésie qui le secouait autre chose que la pire des séparations. On ne possède que ce qu'on aime'.[95] Thrown back into himself and now tasting defeat, his final feeling is a desire to 'anéantir, à force de violence, ce visage anonyme qui le chassait vers la mort'.[96] The woman remains irrevocably *other* and just as unreachable as his historical goal of 'leaving a scar on the map'.

Perken's relations with women are analogous, therefore, to his relations with historical reality which, like the partner escaping at the end of the union, will also escape his domination in the end. In *La Condition humaine* Malraux will, through Kyo, modify these relations. Not only will Kyo go beyond Perken and 'give away' his death in a will-to-fraternity but he will also, in his moving relationship with May, recognize something which

Perken has recognized but has been unable *to live,* namely that 'one possesses only what one loves'. Of that will-to-fraternity (linked to the idea of death) which will form the corner-stone of *La Condition humaine* we already have a brief glimpse in Claude's profound sympathy for his dying friend: 'il y avait en ce regard une complicité intense où se heurtait la poignante fraternité du courage et la compassion, l'union animale des êtres devant la chair condamnée'.[97]

When Perken learns that the government of Siam is sending a punitive expedition against *his* tribesmen he rediscovers the world of action and sets out to organize the resistance. If he is to die he is determined to exert his will right up to the moment of death, to live every moment of his dying, to personalize it as his own in order to achieve the ultimate paradox of turning this imposed death into a free act. His 'project' now fills his being and he once again feels possessed of life: '"Mais d'ici-là, dit-il en français à Claude, je serai peut-être mort". Saisissant accent: de nouveau, il croyait à sa vie'.[98] For a time Perken's determined effort to reach his own territory excludes by its very presence any return into himself, any thoughts of illness and death.[99] However, as the poison spreads, his determination subsides and he yields to the solitary thought that he will never see his jungle fortress. With insects swarming about his bleeding wound and dogs barking at the loud presence of government troops Perken drifts into solitude.[100] He will die in the world of the Absurd with no possibility of changing the present and now eternal significance of his life.[101] With his hopes being driven into the grave with him[102] and having become alien to everything around him including Claude,[103] and his own body,[104] he is, at the last, estranged also from death itself. This 'being-against-death' who had desperately hoped to 'incorporate' death as the mainspring of being, to *recover* and possess it as his own, discovers at the last that it cannot be personalized: it is an external contingency.[105] One can only die: 'il n'y a pas . . . de mort . . . Il y a seulement . . . *moi* . . . qui vais mourir'.[106] Perken dies as he has lived—alone. The adventurer who had determined to have his 'revenge on the universe' and to leave a 'scar on the map' has been crushed, and disappears without trace.

In *La Voie royale* we see the adventurer-type hero in triple projection: Claude, Perken and finally Grabot, who, blind and tethered like an animal before the end of the novel and reduced to 'Nothing'—'[tournant] dans la case comme autour du cadavre de son courage'[107]—is the *reductio ad absurdum* of the New Man. Perken's situation, like Garine's, is also not without bitter irony. The adventurer who abandoned Europe has taken with him a distinctly European notion of sexuality:[108] the domination and denial of the personality of others, which, equated with action, has made of him the most brutal form of 'European conquistador'. If *Les Conquérants* contained the faintest hint that life may acquire meaning through the fraternity of revolutionary action, then *La Voie royale* is dark with the apprehension of death and the futility of all action. And there is no question whatsoever of a restoration of human dignity. Indeed, Perken's action is the very kind which makes it necessary to fight for human dignity.

Although presented as 'metaphysical' creatures having general validity, Garine and Perken are not wholly convincing in this role. In fact the New Man has much that seems *psychologically* suspect. At one stage Garine is considered in the context of damaged personalities who have been unable to accept 'la vie sociale' and Claude and Perken are described as sexually irregular. Might not Garine be said to be driven by a private obsession which has grown out of the inability to resolve a personal psychological defeat in a Swiss court? Is not Perken obsessed by the discovery of the 'uniqueness' of life; in a word, that he is finite? Is not this personal obsession the essence of his attempted 'revanche contre l'univers'? In other words, the New Man's estrangement might be seen as deriving from a private psychological necessity, and the Absurd as nothing more than the rationalization of his own alienation. As such the lucidity with which he accepts his estrangement becomes quite simply a function of that estrangement itself. And yet, in opting for this estrangement, he is attempting to be 'authentic' in the face of life's absurdity. Since death is there as irrefutable proof of life's absurdity he is called upon to challenge it. However, through its everyday idiom of time, death hardly allows him room for manoeuvre. He nonetheless gambles—on his youth and sexual vigour. As such he is doomed from the outset. Garine knows full well that the revolution will replace him and that time will force the brute intensity that he is into inertia. Perken realizes that an

244

enterprise based on eroticism must, with time, dwindle into impotence. With freedom, that element which sets him apart from the rest of creation, the New Man has attempted to face death, and escape the stupid slavery of life. But freedom is hardly a bargaining force since it is defined as 'freedom-towards-death'. Although Malraux has converted Heidegger's 'being-towards-death' into a 'being-against-death' this conversion is little more than a philosophical sleight of hand. Death is still master of the man who writes off his own life. If life has no meaning then life simply has no meaning. Freedom therefore is empty, action sterile, and consciousness self-regarding nihilism, for ultimately they are all gestures by which the New Man consents to end his life. Life is a delayed suicide whether he believes suicide to be inauthentic or not.[109]

Malraux's definition of life, and acceptance of 'authentic living', as the constant expectation of death strikingly parallels the terminology of Martin Heidegger, whose *Sein und Zeit* appeared in 1927. For Malraux as for Heidegger all that is left of History is an impoverished 'subject', the *Dasein* ('être-là'). Emptied of content the *Dasein* surfaces to two possibilities: 'authenticity' and 'inauthenticity'. The *Entschluss* ('décision') moves for 'authenticity' and the *Dasein* becomes 'resolute' and 'authentic'. But, one might ask, resolute and authentic in what? Could it not be argued that 'activism' in such circumstances runs the risk of acquiring *any content*? Here one need look no further, perhaps, than the example of Heidegger himself. In 1933 his speculative theory on the nature of 'authenticity' and 'resolute decision' (*Entschlossenheit*) found a convenient repository in Nazi Germany's decision to withdraw from the League of Nations —a decision, he claimed, which revealed the people's will-to-exist and existence's will to retain and safeguard its essence (*'dass es sein eigenes Wesen erhalte'*).[110] Heidegger may have had his mind on nobler things but it is difficult to believe that he was totally insensible to the fact that the Nazi régime was no abstraction. If he later resigned his university post—his view of 'authenticity' now soured—the fact remains that his esoteric formulae had lent themselves all too easily to active and, in the event, brutal 'subjects' in the historical world.

If we have touched upon Heidegger it is because the dangers to which he fell victim are inherent in Malraux's outlook—a fact to

245

which Italian Fascists were not insensible.[111] The central verity in Malraux's desperately sad universe is the estrangement, the total failure of the individual to communicate. Hong cannot communicate with Tcheng-Daï, and Perken and Garine can communicate with no-one. Their answer to this impasse is to dominate and, if needs be, to eliminate the *other*. They are not prepared to recognize any authority or truth outside their own will, for to do so is to make themselves into *en-soi* objects for the *other* and so deny their *pour-soi* attributes.

Now Malraux was not, in his creation of the New Man, seeking an opportunity for lyrical gestures. He was trying to be honest in the face of dead values. This led him not only to formulate a new moral distress—which inspired great interest at the time—but to explore the possibilities of an alternative value system. Consider the following remarks made by him in 'La Question des *Conquérants*' in 1929:

> Je crois que depuis que la chrétienté a disparu en tant qu'armature du monde, le romancier après le philosophe est devenu un homme qui propose—qu'il le veuille ou non—un certain nombre de modes de vie.

The particular 'life-style' which Malraux portrays in his first two novels is both a function of, and a reaction to, that climate of doubt and negation which Valéry has described as 'la crise de l'esprit' and Berl as 'la mort de la pensée bourgeoise'. If one were to look at Malraux's novels in terms of a purely philosophical crisis one might describe them as a demonstration of man's inescapable aloneness in a world without purpose and without values, direction or any valid standards of right and wrong, a world where the validity of man's value judgements rests on no more than his arbitrary but wilful and 'authentic' choice. Politically, however, these novels reflect not so much the 'death of bourgeois thought' as its desperate search for a political (as well as philosophical) solution to its own anguish. In this they bear the mark of incipient Fascism. Indeed, Garine and Perken seem to fit Manuel's description (in *L'Espoir*) of a Fascist: 'un homme actif et pessimiste à la fois, c'est ou ce sera un fasciste, sauf s'il y a une fidélité derrière lui'.[112] No such fidelity holds Perken back, whilst Garine's 'fidelity' hangs on the fragile conviction that whatever is not the revolution is worse than the revolution.

The 'defenders of civilization' were certainly not Marxists but they would have had no quarrel (as René Johannet's declarations make clear)[113] with Dimitrov's proposition that Fascism's accession to power was not an ordinary succession of one bourgeois government by another, but a substitution of one state form of class domination of the bourgeoisie—bourgeois democracy—by another form—open terrorist dictatorship.[114] For those dedicated to the preservation of capitalism Fascism represented—as the 'defenders of civilization' conclusively demonstrate—a very real temptation. This temptation, as we have already suggested, is present in Malraux's analysis of what appears to him as Civilization in dissolution. More particularly it is revealed in his concentration on what is, after all, an abiding feature of Western (capitalist) society: (competitive) individualism, which was not conceived as a philosophy before Hobbes and Locke in the seventeenth century, or as a system of economy before Adam Smith in the eighteenth century. Although Malraux proclaims individualism to be 'dead' (*La Tentation de l'Occident* and 'D'une jeunesse européenne') he does not abandon it. It 'survives' in the novels, now death-dominated and bereft of all humane standards of right and wrong. Despite Berl's claim, Malraux has not gone beyond 'bourgeois thought'; he remains a prisoner within its frontiers in much the same way as Garine is unable to break through the limits of 'bourgeois thought' to grasp the whole historical process that puts the past and the present in their place and proceeds to create the future. The 'life-style' which Malraux projects is *new* only in so far as it is an *old* life-style stripped of the rational determinants and idealist justifications of classical bourgeois thought (Progress, Reason, Civilization). In this it reveals affinities with aspects of Fascist ideology.

In *La Voie royale* the 'acquisitive society' and the innate possessiveness of the individual run riot. As one reviewer of *La Voie royale* wrote in 1930, 'l'aventure est née avec la première économie mercantile'.[115] Not only is Perken driven by a territorial imperative to grab as much land as he can hold and defend by force of arms but he is prepared to possess and dominate, even to eliminate, all human obstacles in his path. Unlike his European forbears, this European conquistador does not justify his enterprise as a civilizing mission; he defends it as if its viciousness and competitive strife for mastery were a necessary part of the 'human predicament'. If, as Freud has claimed, the basic human instinct of aggression and destruction is 'the greatest obstacle to civilization', Perken is the very apotheosis of that brutal instinct. In him human nature has been reduced to instinctive drives, conditioned reflexes, and mechanical reactions to uncontrollable external stimuli and pressures. He has lapsed into a sub-human world of thought and action in which others are seen as little more than vermin (insects to be precise). It was when humans regarded other humans as vermin that Buchenwald and Auschwitz became possible. The particular 'life-style' which Malraux portrays in *La Voie royale* would, if adherents were forthcoming, lead almost certainly to a world of concentration camps and to the extermination of one section of humanity by another. Whence the prophetic note of this work.

The creation of the New Man by Malraux coincides with the world economic slump of the late 'twenties and with the rise in Europe of new and terrifying historical forces in which there were to be many new and vulgarized versions of the New Man. The 'thirties would be an era in which the 'Supermen' of Germany would attempt, through the domination, economic enslavement and even the systematic annihilation of others, to exalt and deify themselves. Malraux, the 'Communist' writer, has established a notion of Fascist man before the 'thirties and, we hasten to add, even at this point in time rejected it. For Malraux, a vigorous opponent of the 'temps du mépris', the representation of the New Man's defeat was something of a moral achievement and clarification. One can understand why from a reading of his preface to William Faulkner's *Sanctuary*. Here Malraux makes the important point that the modern novelist expresses what 'fascinates' because in this way he can effectively dominate his own dangerous values and master certain obsessions.[116] The obsessions which Malraux mastered were not merely (Freudian) demons of his or of Civilization's inner depths, but *political* temptations latent in that Civilization whose 'death' he had analysed but which his abstract, mythological predication of 'Man's death' had concealed. It was only when Malraux took these obsessions (and temptations) to the limit in his novels, there to superimpose them on the *historical* world, that he recognized their dangerous possibilities.

With the failure of 'heroic individualism', as represented in *Les Conquérants* and *La Voie royale*, the Malraux hero is, as Cecil

248

Jenkins has noted, 'flung back upon the common fold',[117] there to struggle in the hope that the sharing of a social destiny might somehow mitigate his sense of solitude and, at the same time, give some larger historical and human significance to his 'being-towards-death'. His success, as *La Condition humaine* demonstrates, is only partial, for if Kyo and Katow can now *die for a cause*—and in the process relieve the agony of solitude—that cause and the sense of fraternity which it inspires would appear to have validity only in defeat and death. Indeed, death is master of the entire situation. Thus, if each of the main characters can be said to embody an aspect of the 'Chinese scene'—Tchen youth's angry confusion amid dead ideals, Gisors the contemplative tradition of the East, Ferral the Western grip on China, Kyo and Katow revolutionary action and Clappique the Absurd—it is also true that all betray a kind of negative sameness, for all are different modes of 'being-towards-death'. So it is that Ramon Fernandez can, justifiably, claim that 'la mort est le sens même de la condition humaine'.[118] Malraux's view of the world, therefore, remains fundamentally unchanged; his characters are still dominated by an *Angst* for which historical action has no remedy. Indeed, far from involving his revolutionaries in the hopeful enterprise of social transformation, Malraux reveals them to us as strangers to such hope, strangers also to themselves and others, irremediably alone in the midst of fellow solitaries who illustrate the variety of sad forms which 'Man's destiny' can take. It would appear that in trying to move beyond the narrowly individualist world of the early novels, without accepting intellectually all the implications of the failure of 'heroic individualism',[119] Malraux has succeeded in generalizing his own despair. He has also demonstrated that it is not enough to choose a revolutionary theme to create a revolutionary work of art.

It is in this light that Marxist critics have generally viewed Malraux's work.[120] They challenge his right to tear man out of his social and historical context, accuse him or his characters of 'activisme', and reject his metaphysical slant as an alibi, 'divertissement', the escape route of the privileged. For Malraux, the world has no meaning and the individual is alienated. The Marxist, on the other hand, claims to understand the world, is certain of the nature of man's alienation and knows the remedy. Alienation is the expression of the contradictions of a *social*

249

system. Transform that social system, destroy man's alienation in its historical roots, and man is delivered. Revolutionary action is, therefore, the expression of a hope arising out of intellectual certainty, and not of 'a passion born of despair' launched by the meaninglessness of life and by the impossibility of knowledge. Malraux would doubtless reply that man is not simply a social animal seeking political dignity and social justice but a creature who, tortured by the consciousness of his own mortality—the only animal who knows he must die—wants also to feel free and dignified in the face of an indifferent universe. The meditations of a Pascal, a Kierkegaard or a Nietzsche would therefore retain their resonance even if all racial, religious, social and political injustices were eliminated:

> Bien entendu il faut d'abord vaincre, mais il reste à savoir si, la victoire obtenue, l'homme ne se retrouvera pas en face de sa mort, et ce qui est peut-être plus grave, en face de la mort de ceux qu'il aime.[121]

We, in turn, might argue that a social and political order no longer humiliating for the mass of humanity is, if not everything, at least a very good start. Indeed it is all one can reasonably hope for, since it is at least within my 'possibilities', whereas death is beyond them. Indeed, death is the annihilation of all my possibilities, unless I am a Christian—and Malraux clearly is not.

NOTES

[1] André Malraux, *La Tentation de l'Occident* (Grasset, 1951), pp. 215–16.
[2] André Malraux, *Les Conquérants* (Livre de poche, 1973), p. 69: 'en l'occurrence, il n'y a qu'une raison qui ne soit pas une parodie: l'emploi le plus efficace de sa force'. Édition originale, 1928.
[3] André Malraux, *op. cit.*, p. 68.
[4] André Malraux, *op. cit.*, p. 73.
[5] André Malraux, ibid.
[6] André Malraux, *op. cit.*, p. 72: 'jouer sa vie sur cette carte sale, ridicule, qu'il n'avait pas choisie, lui était intolérable'.
[7] André Malraux, *op. cit.*, pp. 74–5: 'je ne tiens pas la société pour mauvaise, pour susceptible d'être améliorée; je la tiens pour absurde'.
[8] André Malraux, *op. cit.*, p. 196.
[9] André Malraux, *op. cit.*, pp. 75–6.
[10] André Malraux, *op. cit.*, pp. 79–90.
[11] André Malraux, *op. cit.*, pp. 83–4: 'ma vie ne m'intéresse pas. C'est clair, c'est net, c'est formel. Je veux—tu entends?—une certaine forme de

puissance; ou je l'obtiendrai, ou tant pis pour moi . . . Si c'est manqué, je recommencerai, là ou ailleurs. Et si je suis tué, la question sera résolue'.

12 André Malraux, *op. cit.*, p. 249.

13 Malraux himself describes Hong as an anarchist: 'Réponse à Trotski', *N.R.F.* (April 1931), pp. 501–9. The article is also to be found (in translation) in *Malraux: A collection of critical essays*, ed. R. W. B. Lewis (Englewood Cliffs, N.J.: Prentice-Hall, 1964), pp. 20–4.

14 Léon Trotski, 'La Révolution étranglée', *N.R.F.* (April 1931), pp. 488–500. The article is also to be found (in translation) in *Malraux: A collection of critical essays*, pp. 12–19.

15 André Malraux, *Les Conquérants*, p. 83: 'ce qui est bien certain, c'est que je n'ai qu'un dégoût haineux pour la bourgeoisie dont je sors'.

16 André Malraux, *La Condition humaine* ed. with introduction by Cecil Jenkins (University of London Press, 1968), p. 15.

17 See above, pp. 194–8.

18 Cecil Jenkins, p. 17.

19 Emmanuel Berl, *Mort de la pensée bourgeoise* (Grasset, 1929), p. 136 and p. 140.

20 André Malraux, *Les Conquérants*, p. 68.

21 André Malraux, *op. cit.*, p. 75.

22 André Malraux, *op. cit.*, p. 29, p. 110, p. 135.

23 See above, pp. 192–3, pp. 228–9.

24 Cecil Jenkins, p. 13.

25 André Malraux, *Les Conquérants*, p. 137.

26 André Malraux, *op. cit.*, pp. 20–1.

27 André Malraux, *op. cit.*, p. 20.

28 André Malraux, *op. cit.*, p. 137.

29 André Malraux, ibid.

30 André Malraux, *op. cit.*, p. 139.

31 André Malraux, *op. cit.*, pp. 135–6.

32 See André Malraux, 'Reply to Trotsky', in *Malraux: A collection of critical essays*, p. 22.

33 André Malraux, *Les Conquérants*, p. 183.

34 André Malraux, *op. cit.*, p. 34: 'l'accoucheur de Hong'; p. 32 'un des hommes qui ont formé les terroristes'. See also p. 43.

35 See André Malraux, *La Voie royale* (Livre de poche, 1973), p. 119. Édition originale, 1930.

36 André Malraux, *Les Conquérants*, p. 39: 'la seule chose que l'Occident eût enseignée [à Hong] avec assez de force pour qu'il fût impossible de s'en délivrer, c'était le caractère unique de la vie'. Rebecci states his philosophy in the following terms: 'quand on a une vie seulement, on ne cherche pas à changer l'état social' (p. 38).

37 André Malraux, *op. cit.*, p. 173: 'La torture—moi je pense—est, là, une chose juste. Parce que la vie d'un homme de la misère est une torture longue. Et ceux qui enseignent aux hommes de la misère à supporter cela doivent être punis, prêtres chrétiens ou autres hommes. Ils ne savent pas. Il faudrait—je pense—les obliger (il souligne le mot d'un geste, comme s'il frappait) à comprendre. Ne pas lâcher sur eux les soldats. Non. Les lépreux.

La bras d'un homme se transforme en boue, et coule; l'homme, il vient me parler de résignation, alors c'est bien. Mais cet homme-là, lui, il dit autre chose'.

[38] André Malraux, *op. cit.*, pp. 177–8 (our italics).

[39] André Malraux, *op. cit.*, p. 179.

[40] André Malraux, *op. cit.*, pp. 179–80.

[41] André Malraux, *op. cit.*, p. 78.

[42] André Malraux, *op. cit.*, p. 256.

[43] André Malraux, ibid.

[44] André Malraux, *op. cit.*, p. 83.

[45] André Malraux, *op. cit.*, p. 260.

[46] André Malraux, *op. cit.*, p. 261.

[47] See last pages of the novel, where the distant approach of the Red Army, borne in on the still night air, preludes the triumphant arrival of the forces of Absurdity.

[48] André Malraux, *op. cit.*, p. 195: 'je ne désire pas rester seul. Je n'aime plus penser à moi, et, quand je suis malade, j'y pense toujours'; p. 196: 'naturellement, on ne devrait pas tant parler quand la fièvre est trop forte. C'est idiot. Penser à soi toute la journée! Pourquoi est-ce que je pense à ce procès? Pourquoi? C'est si loin! C'est idiot, la fièvre, mais on voit des choses'.

[49] André Malraux, *op. cit.*, p. 239.

[50] André Malraux, *op. cit.*, p. 280.

[51] Léon Trotski, 'La Révolution étranglée, *N.R.F.* (April 1931), pp. 488–500.

[52] André Malraux, 'Réponse à Trotski', *N.R.F.* (April 1931), pp. 501–9.

[53] 'André Malraux nous parle de son œuvre', *Monde* (18 October, 1930), p. 4.

[54] 'La Question des *Conquérants*', *Variétés* (15 October, 1929), pp. 429–37.

[55] 'André Malraux nous parle de son œuvre', p. 4.

[56] See 'La Question des *Conquérants*', p. 435: 'le sentiment essentiel de Garine est la fraternité d'armes. Il n'est pas possible qu'un homme qui mène pendant quatre ans, avec d'autres hommes, un combat qu'il a choisi, soit indifférent à leur sort'. See also 'André Malraux nous parle de son œuvre', p. 4: 'c'est oublier un peu vite que Garine et les hommes qui combattent avec lui ont, à défaut d'autre chose, les mêmes haines'.

[57] See, for example, *Les Conquérants*, pp. 256–63.

[58] André Malraux, *op. cit.*, p. 196, p. 240.

[59] André Malraux, *op. cit.*, p. 168.

[60] 'La Question des *Conquérants*', p. 432.

[61] Quoted in Joseph Hoffman, *L'Humanisme de Malraux* (Klincksieck, 1963), p. 134 (footnote 4).

[62] André Malraux, *La Voie royale* (Livre de poche, 1973), p. 36: 'Et tout à coup, Claude découvrit ce qui le liait à cet homme qui l'avait accepté sans qu'il comprît bien pourquoi: l'obsession de la mort'.

[63] 'Un quart d'heure avec André Malraux', *Candide* (13 November, 1930), p. 3.

[64] Gaëtan Picon, *Malraux par lui-même* (Éditions du Seuil, 1953), p. 75 (note 29).

[65] André Malraux, *La Voie royale*, p. 38. See pp. 37–8.

[66] André Malraux, *op. cit.*, p. 108.

[67] André Malraux, *op. cit.*, p. 60.

[68] André Malraux, *op. cit.*, pp. 37–8: 'Être tué, disparaître, peu lui importait: il ne

tenait guère à lui-même, et il aurait ainsi trouvé son combat, à défaut de victoire. Mais accepter vivant la vanité de son existence, comme un cancer, vivre avec cette tiédeur de mort dans la main. (D'où montait, sinon d'elle, cette exigence de choses éternelles, si lourdement imprégnée de son odeur de chair?)'. See also p. 107.

[69] André Malraux, *op. cit.*, p. 36 and p. 59.

[70] André Malraux, *op. cit.*, p. 58.

[71] André Malraux, *op. cit.*, pp. 36–40.

[72] André Malraux, *op. cit.*, p. 27: 'Agir au lieu de rêver.' (The remark is Claude's but in this as in other aspects of his outlook he is very much like Perken).

[73] André Malraux, *op. cit.*, p. 108.

[74] André Malraux, *op. cit.*, pp. 66–7.

[75] André Malraux, *op. cit.*, p. 68.

[76] André Malraux, *op. cit.*, pp. 69–70: 'il ne voyait que la tache de lumière qui l'absorbait, mais ses nerfs ne voyaient que les insectes écrasés, n'obéissaient qu'à leur contact. Déjà relevé, crachant, il vit grouillantes d'insectes, une seconde, ces pierres du sol sur quoi pouvait s'écraser sa vie; dérivé du dégoût par le danger, il retomba sur le mur avec une brutalité de bête en fuite, avançant de nouveau, ses mains gluantes collées aux feuilles pourries, hébété de dégoût, n'existant plus que pour cette trouée qui le tirait par les yeux'.

[77] André Malraux, *op. cit.*, p. 70.

[78] André Malraux, *op. cit.*, pp. 87–8.

[79] André Malraux, *op. cit.*, p. 107.

[80] André Malraux, *op. cit.*, p. 137: 'Sa destinée, à lui, Perken, se jouait sur cette masse vivante. Sa vie aboutissait comme à un passage à ces jambes couvertes d'eczéma, à ce pagne ignoble et sanglant, à cette humanité capable seulement de pièges et de ruse, ainsi que les bêtes de la forêt. Il dépendait totalement de cet être, de ses pensées de larve. Quelque chose en cet instant vivait sourdement dans cette tête, comme s'ouvrent les œufs de mouches pondus dans le cerveau. Depuis une heure, il n'avait pas eu une aussi violente envie de tuer'.

[81] André Malraux, *op. cit.*, p. 97 and p. 64.

[82] André Malraux, *op. cit.*, p. 10.

[83] André Malraux, ibid.

[84] André Malraux, *op. cit.*, pp. 96–7.

[85] André Malraux, *op. cit.*, p. 108.

[86] André Malraux, *op. cit.*, pp. 118–19: "Qu'est-ce que vous etes?" ... "Rien" ... L'homme n'était pas fou. Il avait traîné ce mot, comme s'il cherchait encore; mais ce n'était pas un homme qui ne se souvenait pas, ni qui ne voulait pas répondre: c'était un homme qui disait *sa vérité*'.

[87] André Malraux, *op. cit.*, p. 126.

[88] André Malraux, *op. cit.*, pp. 131–2.

[89] André Malraux, *op. cit.*, p. 132.

[90] André Malraux, *op. cit.*, p. 134.

[91] *Nietzsche*, selected and translated by Walter Kaufmann (New York: Viking Press, 1969), pp. 183–4.

[92] André Malraux, *La Voie royale*, p. 153.
[93] André Malraux, *op. cit.*, p. 153.
[94] André Malraux, *op. cit.*, p. 174.
[95] André Malraux, *op. cit.*, pp. 157–8.
[96] André Malraux, *op. cit.*, p. 158.
[97] André Malraux, *op. cit.*, pp. 153–4.
[98] André Malraux, *op. cit.*, p. 171.
[99] André Malraux, *op. cit.*, p. 176.
[100] André Malraux, *op. cit.*, pp. 176–7.
[101] See Jeanne Delhomme, *Temps et Destin* (Gallimard, 1955), p. 43: 'Ce qu'il y a de terrible dans la mort c'est qu'elle transforme la vie en destin: par le fait que le trait est tiré et que les jeux sont faits, elle donne le visage de l'éternité et de l'immobilité à ce qui—caractère, action ou œuvre—était en sursis'.
[102] André Malraux, *La Voie royale*, pp. 177–8.
[103] André Malraux, *op. cit.*, p. 177 and p. 182.
[104] André Malraux, *op. cit.*, p. 178.
[105] André Malraux, *op. cit.*, pp. 179–81. See Jean-Paul Sartre's treatment of the 'interiorized death': *L'Être et le néant* (Gallimard, 1943), pp. 616–19.
[106] André Malraux, *La Voie royale*, p. 182.
[107] André Malraux, *op. cit.*, p. 130.
[108] One might dispute Malraux's 'claim' that eroticism is a purely European phenomenon. However, the significant point is that Malraux presents it as such (*La Tentation de l'Occident*). When Perken leaves Europe he takes with him this 'European malady'.
[109] André Malraux, *La Voie royale*, p. 13.
[110] See Jean-Pierre Cotten, 'Heidegger: sur une philosophie de la crise', *L'Humanité* (31 October, 1975), p. 8. See also, by the same author, *Heidegger* (Éditions du Seuil, 'Écrivains de toujours', 1974).
[111] See, for example, '*La Condition humaine* d'André Malraux, jugé par les fascistes italiens', *Lu* (9 March, 1935), p. 14.
[112] André Malraux, *Romans* (Grasset, 1947), p. 547.
[113] See above, pp. 65–8.
[114] G. Dimitrov, *The United Front* (Lawrence and Ward, 1938), p. 12.
[115] Brice Parain, 'La Fin de l'individualisme', *L'Humanité* (4 November, 1930).
[116] William Faulkner, *Sanctuaire*, avec une préface d'André Malraux (Gallimard, 1933), p. iii.
[117] Cecil Jenkins, p. 19.
[118] Ramon Fernandez, 'La Condition humaine', *Marianne* (24 May, 1933), p. 4.
[119] See Cecil Jenkins, pp. 18–19.
[120] See, for example, Roger Garaudy, *Une Littérature de fossoyeurs* (Éditions Sociales, 1947).
[121] 'André Malraux nous parle de son œuvre', *Monde* (18 October, 1930), p. 4.

Conclusion

In the course of this study we have seen something of the intellectual crisis of the inter-war period in France; a crisis born of the devastation of war and aggravated by fears of revolutionary change. An important feature of this crisis was intellectual warfare between Left and Right, and within the Left itself. The first shots were fired before the war. Rolland was accused by Massis and his associates of sacrificing the cultural and philosophical values of French civilization to the dark disorders of the Germanic soul. When, with war in Europe raging, Rolland declared 'peace', the nationalists did not hesitate to call him a traitor. When, moreover, he launched a frontal attack on the French cultural establishment and expressed sympathies with revolution in Russia, it was clear, the nationalists asserted, that he had been captured by the German and Bolshevik fiction which attributed the cause of the war to French imperialism. With the return of peace, some of Rolland's former sympathizers deserted him, claiming that he had surrendered the cause of 'independence of mind' to the mass politics of Communism. Such claims, occasionally drawing upon alarmist comparisons between Lenin and Genghis Khan[1], were more significant for the fears they betrayed than for their basis in truth. Indeed, at this time, not only had Rolland not surrendered his 'independence of mind' but he was actually defending it more vigorously than ever. In fact it was fidelity to this very principle that brought him into conflict with Barbusse.

The antinomies of the Rolland/Barbusse debate involved conflicting interpretations of and allegiances to principles. Not only did it appear to contrast freedom and equality, independence and duty, 'will and idea', but it revealed, on these issues as on the question of the relation of the means to the end, a fundamental opposition between the ideology of the 'one against all'[2] and the politics of organizational structures. This clash between the principles of personal transformations and the necessities of

255

class-struggle gave rise to the question of violence. Barbusse's challenging assertion that dictatorship and violence, though temporary, were necessary tactics with which to impose social progress, forced Rolland to advance a strategy that would confound the charge that the 'fire of individual conscience' was the impotent choice of men frightened of radical solutions to society's injustices. In seizing upon the weapon of Ghandhian non-violent resistance, Rolland was not only seeking to reaffirm his faith in the spiritual and moral resources of the individual and to integrate the processes of individual liberation and collective emancipation, but examining the possibility of Gandhism replacing Marxism as a viable international strategy and political philosophy on a mass scale. Although Rolland's outlook retained its ethical bias throughout the 'twenties, his clash with Barbusse was decisive, for it obliged him to face the problem of power relations, of how to advocate radical change yet refuse to adhere to existing organizations and parties presenting a political challenge to the old society. Rolland's agonizing consideration of this dilemma, which Barbusse had done so much to inspire, led him, in the following decade, to conclude that conditions in Western Europe were not only unfavourable but actually contrary to the effectiveness of an ideal which, he now believed, had failed even in a country of 300 million souls accustomed for centuries to the teaching of *ahimsa*. He now recognized that the 'free individual conscience', like political and philosophical Orientalism, were—unlike Marxism—powerless to inaugurate the 'liberating future'.

The problem of the intellectual's relationship to mass political organizations also affected Surrealism and, as in the Rolland/Barbusse debate, it found explosive ambiguity in 'Orientalism'. Surrealism's interest in the dream world, its experiments in simulated madness, its faith in automatic writing and its confidence in chance were all expressions of protest against organized reality and its rational network of cultural and political certainties. This refusal to be bound by the rational controls of a 'bankrupt civilization' was the basis of Surrealist interest in the East. The Orient was presented as the very antithesis of the Western over-valuation of external reality; it was the sublime instance of spiritual perfection. At the same time, however, it was, with its reservoir of 'barbarian hordes', the homeland of the great destroyer—the arch-enemy of civilized standards. This image was not mere poetic fancy; a modern 'Genghis Khan' did exist, and reactionaries were not alone in noting his influence. If Surrealists disowned Lenin and his programme of construction, they made no secret of their support for the destructive forces, massing in the dark depths of Asia, which he was said to command. The fact that Civilization's defenders, Massis and Maurras, lived in fear of these 'demons', made Surrealists all the more eager to provoke the apocalypse:

> Monde occidental, tu es condamné à mort. Que l'Orient, votre terreur, enfin à notre voix réponde. Juifs, sortez des ghettos. Bouge, Inde aux mille bras, grand Brahma légendaire. A toi Égypte! Soulève-toi, monde! Voyez comme cette terre est sèche et bonne pour tous les incendies.[3]

Angry dreams were, however, no substitute for political realities, especially since the latter, Surrealists soon discovered, lay at the very heart of Western fears. Marxism and Freudianism met, and life in its full unity could now launch an irresistible offensive against Civilization's repressive agencies. The synthesis proved to be untenable. Naville raised the question of priority: liberation of the mind and its concomitant of relative independence from mass political parties, or abolition of the bourgeois conditions of material life and its necessary correlative of revolutionary duty? Oriental nonsense and false antitheses, Naville insisted, would have to be jettisoned:

> Le salariat est une nécessité matérielle à laquelle les trois-quarts de la population mondiale sont contraints, indépendante des conceptions philosophiques des soi-disant Orientaux et Occiden-taux. Sous la férule du capital les uns et les autres sont des exploités. . . . Les querelles de l'intelligence sont absolument vaines devant cette unité de condition.[4]

The Surrealist movement as a whole was unable to accommodate Naville's demand, and each crisis betrayed, in a clash between the Freudian and Marxist forces, the ambivalence, if not the antinomy, of the Surrealist position. The cause of 'révolte de l'esprit', sustained by the principle of independence of mind, retained its devotees, while the Marxist apostles of 'révolution de

257

l'esprit' joined Barbusse and, later, Rolland in the cause of proletarian internationalism.

To the cause of proletarian internationalism the defenders of civilization opposed the cause of national and international reaction. Their commitment began in 1914 when they were driven into a temporary acceptance of the Republic that they opposed in principle. Thereafter they became guardians of the 'patriotic' conscience—a reactionary mélange of the virtues of le pays réel. Their enemies—apart from the Germans—were the 'artificial' Frenchmen of le pays légal: Republicans and revolutionaires, Jews and 'métèques'. As a 'Germanophile' and a 'Jew', a 'Romantic' and a Republican, Rolland could not fail to have been indicted. His crime was 'neutrality', tantamount, in Massis's estimation, to treason and blasphemy. When, in the 'twenties, he turned to India for inspiration, his 'conversion' and 'messianic' zeal were attributed to the devilish intent of a German-inspired Russo-Jewish crusade to 'Asiaticize' the West. This extraordinary equation, whose dominant factor was Bolshevism, remained intact throughout the 'twenties and for most of the 'thirties. By the late 'thirties, however, anti-Germanism became a luxury which many of the self-appointed guardians of civilized standards no longer felt able to indulge. Indeed, some concluded that in view of the 'Judeo–Bolshevik' menace reconciliation with Nazi Germany was not only a reasonable expectation but a vital necessity if Europe was to survive. Such hopes went unrealized, and war with Germany left France broken and divided. Some, like Bonnard and Brasillach, chose collaboration. Others, led by Maurras, rallied to Pétain, the 'symbol of salvation'. Step by step these once-incorruptible enemies of Germany became the servants of German will. What made them denounce their own resisting countrymen with vicious contempt was less a hierarchy of values than a hierarchy of fears, dominated by an obsession with the Red glare in the East. Quite apart from any judgements passed upon them by the courts they were guilty also from a 'metajuridical' point of view; verdicts simply expelled them from a French polity which they themselves had long rejected and denied. In the case of Massis there could, perhaps, be no more damning or ironic a verdict than 'neutrality' vis-à-vis the 'German monster', the very crime for which he had execrated Rolland.

It is within this context of intellectual crisis and political ferment that we have attempted to situate the diagnoses and literary expression of Drieu and Malraux. The first thing to note is that although both clearly reflect the 'objective' *crise de l'esprit* (represented among others by Valéry and Spengler) they also tend to mythify their own private estrangement. As a result we find a curious mixture of subjective projection and 'objective' representation.

Drieu, for example, discovered early that he was sick, but blamed his century for this. The whole planet was sick. His fundamental pessimism, which began in his childhood as an emotional response to France's declining world-role, was reinforced by the example of his own family and by his now-biased vision of the ambient society. It was then translated into political formulae; France like the characters of his fiction—like Drieu himself—is 'sans enfants'. If Drieu's vision of a united Europe of 400 million people was a legitimate response to the political necessities of the day, was it not equally the attempt to escape the conviction of national decadence, which was itself the rationalization of a personal disorder? However, Drieu was too attached to the notion of sincerity to spare his personal failings. He felt himself to be weak and was all the more keen to identify with what was strong and virile. Personal weakness and the aspiration to strength led him to see within himself the existence of two conflicting selves which are clearly illustrated in his work.[5] For example, how do we reconcile his 'éternel esprit de guerre' and his pacifism as expressed in the idea of a united Europe; his fervent nationalism and his belief that the age of nationalism is dead; his attachment to tradition and his obsession with the future; his intellectualism and his thirst for action; his solitary nature, his aristocratic misanthropy and his nostalgia for a mystique of collective life; his vital enthusiasm and his morbid fascination with suicide; his faith in the New Man and his despairing vision of decadence? Drieu's uncertainty made him all the more eager to choose. Historically, he made the wrong choice. Morally, his choice was that of the weakling who aspires to be strong.

Although Malraux's 'heroic' world-view could also be said to derive from a sense of personal inadequacy, his response goes far beyond the private obsessions and compensations of an individual. His central preoccupation, like Drieu's, is the plight of modern man—'an accident in a world of accidents'—for whom

God is dead and who, feeling his own turn coming, is desperately seeking humanist values in a world which has lost its human character. In this, both not only reflect the deeper anxieties of their day but, by the very nature of their response, anticipate the existentialist vision. Like Sartre they both accept the world as *other*, on which the self, defined in terms of will, asserts its individuality by acting. Will is also exercised in sex; woman is the *other* and must be dominated. Even as transcendental values are rejected, so too is any notion of psychological determinism, since individual choice would thereby be reduced.

However, although Drieu expressed the above views in his war poems, they do not appear in his fiction of the 'twenties. The return of peace and its accompanying despair were largely responsible for this change. If his heroes are alienated, they are, unlike Malraux's, weak-willed. Nowhere is this contrast more evident than in sexual matters. Whereas Drieu's characters are sensual creatures, sexual stimulation for Perken is of the cerebral kind. It is eroticism and not physical or emotional communion, for only thus can it be of service to the will. What Perken craves is domination, which he identifies with pure volition. Sex for Drieu's characters is the very reverse; it is a masochistic humiliation of the will. These antithetical attitudes are themselves simply a function of the very different approaches of Drieu and Malraux to the 'emptiness' of Europe in the 'twenties. Whereas Malraux attempts to project a new kind of heroic individual in the absence of a governing ideal, Drieu makes this absence itself the subject of his novels. In this consists not only the essential difference between Drieu and Malraux as novelists but the basis of Malraux's originality as a post-war novelist—something which Berl defines as Malraux's formulation of man's anguish and desperate strength in the modern world.[6] To Berl's observation the literary historian might add a more general definition of Malraux's originality as a novelist in the post-war period.

'Humanist' art was the expression—for reader as for writer—of the sensibility of a man who feels about him stable conditions of life. This is why Boileau, in a France grown rich on commerce, could define aesthetic norms, and why the years of peace and economic stability of the late nineteenth and early twentieth centuries favoured a particular form of artistic perspective. This humanist literature portrayed misfortune and suffering, but inscribed them within a certain literary felicity which was itself the artistic domination of this suffering. Thus art, by transposing 'evil', by describing it with measure, assurance, clarity and facility, seemed to overcome it. But when the universe loses its stability and the world erupts in war, when economic disaster strikes and established values crumble, art becomes less sure of human potential and of its own ability to dominate anguish by transposing it. It is within this scientific and political, socio-economic and philosophical complex that Malraux conceived the novel as a 'domaine de recherches' wherein a 'système d'affirmation' has given way to 'un art de Grands Navigateurs'.[7] The 'grid' which in humanist literature presented a coherent and reassuring picture (reassuring because no matter how violent it still revealed an anthropomorphic world), now looks out on to a nightmarish landscape of mysterious signs and symbols which human concepts can do nothing to interpret. The hero is cast into a world which surpasses him and which cannot be *humanized*. The reader is confronted by the same problem, for no moral co-ordinates or clear metaphysical images are given. He has no alternative but to accept the terms in which reality is now formulated—*through the eyes of the hero,* for it is he rather than the descriptive artist who imposes his presence.

This new perspective signifies a modification of the very aim of the novel. Whereas humanist literature 'explained' to the reader, this new novel, by giving only the brute existence of the hero and the inhuman world confronting him, aims to raise a question, to awaken the reader to a problem which it does not claim to be able to resolve. For the problem is that of 'man's destiny' in the godless, mythless world of the twentieth century:

> Dans un univers soudain privé d'illusions et de lumières, l'homme se sent un étranger . . . ce divorce entre l'homme et sa vie, entre l'acteur et son décor, c'est proprement le sentiment de l'absurdité.[8]

Between man and inhuman silence there is now only man's will and courage to live out a tragic adventure in the grim hope of discovering his own possibilities. Berl has expressed this drama in the following terms:

> Aller sans savoir où, première, seule noblesse de la pensée de la vie. Si, comme il est bien possible, l'existence humaine n'est

qu'une aventure dans un univers d'absurdités, l'homme ne vaut que comme aventurier et ne se légitime que par sa manière de provoquer l'inattendu.[9]

The metaphysical lesson given by Malraux's adventurer is the 'uniqueness', the meaninglessness and the irremediable loneliness of life and death. In political terms, however, he must be considered a disturbingly pre-Fascist phenomenon. For bourgeois social relations, veiled by religious, humanitarian and idealist justifications, Malraux has substituted—in his adventurer—naked, shameless, direct, brutal exploitation. This in itself reveals the artificiality of the Communist label attached to the Malraux of the 'thirties. For it is he and not the Fascist Drieu who has established a kind of ideal image of Fascist man. Indeed, while Malraux was portraying this troubling prototype of the New Man, Drieu was describing (bourgeois) man's weakness, his utter impossibility. And yet Drieu could never bring himself to dissociate his fate from that of his country or continent. If salvation were possible it had to come from within Europe. He could never forget the mystic experience of war or the dull emptiness which followed its end. In 1934 that essential self which had been buried in bourgeois comforts awakened suddenly and spoke again. It was all the proof that Drieu needed to proclaim the rebirth of European man. His Fascism was thus, contrary to what most critics maintain, inevitable, for it was pre-existing. It was the only possible response from one who was less the probing critic of his time than a symptom of its confusion and desperation—the dupe of a world-view which, for all its geopolitical spread, was a class-limited one. In the final instance he was the victim of an already existing set of attitudes to which Fascism gave substance and force. The cruel irony in all this is that nowhere in the 'twenties does he offer an image of that brutal strength—portrayed by Malraux—associated with Fascism. For the Drieu of the 'twenties there were no hidden depths, no latent strength in man, only spiritual and physical decadence. The supreme irony is that it was his attempt to overcome this decadence which led him to declare his Fascism when the 'Fascist' Malraux had already rejected Fascism. For the truth surely is that by taking the temptations of a troubled time to the limit in his *art*, by establishing artistically its horrifying possibilities, Malraux had

262

himself already recognized the danger of such a vision. While Drieu, in his portrayal of Fascism's New Man, was trying to save himself from the decadent, Malraux had already saved himself from Fascism by portraying the failure of the New Man.

NOTES

1   e.g. Paul Sieppel, 'Les Derniers livres de Romain Rolland', *Journal de Genève* (27 September, 1920), p. 1.
2   See W. T. Starr, *Romain Rolland: one against all* (The Hague: Mouton, 1971).
3   M. Nadeau, *Histoire du surréalisme* (Éditions du Seuil, 1964), p. 80.
4   M. Nadeau, *op. cit.*, p. 99.
5   e.g. the dialogue between 'moi' and 'l'autre' in *L'Europe contre les patries*.
6   E. Berl, *Mort de la pensée bourgeoise* (Grasset, 1929), p. 88.
7   A. Malraux, *Les Voix du silence* (Gallimard, 1951), p. 602.
8   A. Camus, *Le Mythe de Sisyphe* (Gallimard, 1942), p. 18.
9   E. Berl, *Mort de la pensée bourgeoise*, pp. 9–10.

Index

Action Française, 2, 17, 130
Aragon, Louis, 40, 45, 48, 51, 52, 158, 207
Arland, Marcel, 7, 104, 189, 210, 218

Bacot, Jean, 98–9
Baldensperger, Fernand, 87–8, 95
Barbusse, Henri, viii, 8, 13–19, 39, 50, 51, 53, 58, 60, 61, 62, 63, 65, 69–71, 72, 73, 74, 75, 77, 89–91, 92, 95, 102, 125, 126, 127, 129, 130, 147, 154, 198, 255, 256
Barrès, Maurice, 2, 10, 32
Benoist-Méchin, Jacques, 81, 148
Berge, François, 95–6, 154, 192
Bergson, Henri, 30, 36
Berl, Emmanuel, 228, 231, 246, 260, 261
Bernier, Jean, 45, 48, 68–9
Betz, Maurice, 81, 95
Bloch, Jean-Richard, 14, 129
Bonnard, Abel, 96–7, 258
Bonnet, Georges, 4–5
Borodin, Michael, 119, 227, 229, 231, 234
Brasillach, Robert, 67, 258
Breton, André, 39–41, 43, 46, 49, 50–1, 52, 58, 207
Brunetière, Ferdinand, 29, 186

Cachin, Marcel, 67, 68
Caves, Jean, 82–4
Cazin, Paul, 6
Clarté, viii, 13, 26, 45, 47, 48–9, 61–2, 63, 64, 65, 68, 69, 71, 72, 84–5, 88, 90, 91, 94, 105, 107, 119, 127, 147, 157, 181, 198, 209–10
Claudel, Paul, 46
Coomaraswamy, Ananda, 79, 109, 117

Dadaïsts, 8, 19, 39, 43
Desnos, Robert, 48
Dimitrov, Georgi, 247
Dispan de Floran, Henry, 5
Doriot, Jacques, 164, 220
Dostoyevsky, Fyodor, 32, 83, 113, 200
Drieu La Rochelle, Pierre, vii, ix–xii, 19, 26, 37, 38, 44, 48, 84, 99, 105, 108, 119, 147–71, 177, 178, 182, 185, 189, 191, 198–201, 206–22, 259–63
Béloukia, 220
Blèche, 209
'Défense de sortir', 159
Drôle de voyage, 218–19
État Civil, 148–52, 158, 162, 206, 221
Europe contre les patries, L', 160–1
Femme à sa fenêtre, Une, 208
Feu follet, Le, 213–15
Genève ou Moscou, 156, 159–60, 162, 163
Gilles, 163–4, 168
Homme couvert de femmes, L', 217–18
Interrogation, xi, 153, 168
Jeune Européen, Le, x, 207, 216
'Malraux, l'homme nouveau', x, 200
Mesure de la France, 147–8, 154–8, 159, 182, 207
Plainte contre inconnu, 209–10
Socialisme Fasciste, 165, 168
Valise vide, La, 209, 210–13
Duhamel, Georges, 6–7, 60, 129
Dunois, Amédée, 75–6

Einstein, Albert, 30–1, 36, 74, 79, 130, 186
Eugène, Marcel, 105, 106–7

France, Anatole, 32, 45, 48, 60, 61
Freud, Sigmund, 31, 40, 52, 53, 188, 248, 257
Fribourg, André, 3

Gandhi, Mahatma, 22, 58, 74, 76, 83, 88–94, 108, 117, 118, 119, 120, 121, 123, 126, 132, 155
Gaultier, Jules de, 186
Gide, André, 10, 32, 98
Guénon, René, 99–100

Heidegger, Martin, 195, 238, 245

Jaloux, Edmond, 101
Jaurès, Jean, 14
Johannet, René, 11, 18, 66–8, 247

Kayser, Rudolf, 103–4
Keyserling, Hermann, 35, 79, 81, 82, 108, 111, 112, 113

Lefebvre, Raymond, 60, 63
Lemercier, Eugène, 3
Lenin, V. I., 15, 16, 25, 62, 64, 66, 83, 92, 166, 229, 255, 257
Lévi, Sylvain, 97, 99, 108
Lintier, Paul, 6
Louis-Barthou, Alice, 96

Malherbe, Henry, 3–4
Malraux, André, vii, viii, ix–xii, 8, 19, 33, 37, 38, 59, 82, 95, 98, 99, 100, 101, 102, 104–5, 112, 119, 120, 171, 177–201, 206, 207, 208, 209, 210, 216, 225–50, 259–63; 'D'une jeunesse européenne', x, 182, 185, 187–90, 193, 197, 198, 225, 227, 229, 231, 235, 247
Condition humaine, La, 208, 236, 242–3, 249
Conquérants, Les, 98, 99, 101, 102, 105, 119, 180, 192, 193, 194, 195, 198, 200, 225–37, 244, 248
Espoir, L', 237, 246
Noyers de l'Altenburg, Les, 237
Tentation de l'Occident, La, 37, 98, 99, 101, 102, 177, 180, 182–93,
197, 198, 199, 225, 227, 228, 229, 231, 235, 247
Voie royale, La, 105, 194, 195, 198, 200, 215–16, 230, 236, 237–44, 247–8
Mann, Thomas, 80, 81, 113
Mao Tse-tung, 228, 229
Martinet, Marcel, 74–5, 76
Maspéro, Henri, 100, 101
Massis, Henri, vii–viii, ix, 10–11, 12, 18, 19, 26, 38, 39, 50, 59, 60, 65–6, 81, 82, 83, 84, 85, 95, 100, 102, 104, 106, 107–25, 128, 130–1, 147, 155, 182, 191, 198, 257, 258; Défense de l'Occident, 109–25, 130–1, 182; Manifesto (1919) 65; Manifesto (1935) 130
Mauriac, François, 148, 155
Maurras, Charles, 2, 11, 32, 45, 50, 66, 257, 258
Montrevel, Jean, 105, 106
Morand, Paul, 28, 34–8, 39, 81, 119–20, 147
Muret, Maurice, 85–6

Naville, Pierre, 49–50, 257
Nietzsche, Friedrich, x, xi, 32, 108, 149–50, 153, 189–90, 194, 200, 250
Nizan, Paul, viii, 180

Owen, Wilfred, 4

Palewski, J. P., 101
Pascal, Blaise, 190, 234, 250

Rai, Lajpat, 125, 126
Ram-Prassad-Dubé, 88–9
Revue universelle, La, 11, 12, 26, 66–8, 85, 87, 109
Rigaut, Jacques, 210, 213
Rivière, Jacques, 59, 179
Rolland, Romain, viii, ix, 2, 8, 9–12, 13, 18–19, 26, 33, 39, 53, 58, 60, 61, 62–4, 68, 69–71, 72, 73–4, 75, 76–80, 88, 89, 90–1, 92, 93, 94–5, 102, 107, 108, 109, 111, 117, 120, 125–33, 147, 154, 191, 255–6

Clérambault, 68, 88
Danse de Çiva, La, (preface), 79, 127
Jean-Christophe, 9–10
Quinze ans de combat, 63–4
Vie de Ramakrishna, La, 9
Vie de Vivekananda, La, 126–7
Roy, Evelyn, 91–4

Sartre, Jean-Paul, xi, 260
Schlumberger, Jean, 99
Siegfried, André, 96
Soupault, Philippe, 42–3
Spengler, Oswald, 33, 35, 81, 86, 103, 111, 112, 113, 177, 259

Surrealists, ix, 19, 30, 39–53, 102, 147, 191, 207, 256–7

Tagore, Rabindranath, 77–8, 79, 83, 87, 91, 94, 108, 113, 117, 118, 119, 120, 122, 128–9, 155
Tolstoy, Leo, 32, 83, 108, 117, 121
Trotsky, Leon, 58, 192, 227, 233–4, 235

Vaillant-Couturier, Paul, 60, 63
Valéry, Paul, 7–8, 28, 50, 147, 157, 177, 197, 246, 259

Zabloudovsky, Régina, 102–3